SHORT- AND LONG-TERM MEMORY IN INFANCY AND EARLY CHILDHOOD

SHORT- AND LONG-TERM MEMORY
IN INFANCY AND EARLY CHILDHOOD

Taking the First Steps Toward Remembering

Edited by
Lisa M. Oakes
Patricia J. Bauer

UNIVERSITY PRESS
2007

OXFORD
UNIVERSITY PRESS

Oxford University Press, Inc., publishes works that further
Oxford University's objective of excellence
in research, scholarship, and education.

Oxford New York
Auckland   Cape Town   Dar es Salaam   Hong Kong   Karachi
Kuala Lumpur   Madrid   Melbourne   Mexico City   Nairobi
New Delhi   Shanghai   Taipei   Toronto

With offices in
Argentina   Austria   Brazil   Chile   Czech Republic   France   Greece
Guatemala   Hungary   Italy   Japan   Poland   Portugal   Singapore
South Korea   Switzerland   Thailand   Turkey   Ukraine   Vietnam

Published by Oxford University Press, Inc.
198 Madison Avenue, New York, New York 10016

www.oup.com

Oxford is a registered trademark of Oxford University Press

Library of Congress Cataloging-in-Publication Data
   Short- and long-term memory in infancy and early childhood : taking the first steps toward
remembering / edited by Lisa M. Oakes, Patricia J. Bauer.
        p. cm.
   Includes bibliographical references.
   ISBN 978-0-19-518229-3
   1. Memory in infants.   2. Memory in children.   3. Short-term memory.   I. Oakes, Lisa M.,
1963–   II. Bauer, Patricia J.
   BF720.M45S56 2007
   155.4'1312—dc22   2006022111

9 8 7 6 5 4 3 2 1
Printed in the United States of America
on acid-free paper

Contents

Contributors   vii

Introduction   ix

**Part I   Short-Term or Working Memory in Infancy
and Early Childhood**

1 Working Memory in Infants and Toddlers   3
   J. Steven Reznick

2 Individual Differences in the Development of Working Memory
   During Infancy   27
   Martha Ann Bell and Katherine C. Morasch

3 Continuity of Format and Computation in Short-Term
   Memory Development   51
   Lisa Feigenson

4 The Development of Visual Short-Term Memory in Infancy   75
   *Lisa M. Oakes, Shannon Ross-Sheehy,
   and Steven J. Luck*

5 Things to Remember: Limits, Codes, and the Development
   of Object Working Memory in the First Year   103
   Alan M. Leslie and Zsuzsa Káldy

6 What Infants Can Tell Us About Working Memory
   Development 126
        Nelson Cowan

**Part II   Long-Term Memory in Infancy
             and Early Childhood**

7 Developmental Aspects of Visual Recognition Memory
   in Infancy 153
        *Susan A. Rose, Judith F. Feldman,
        and Jeffery J. Jankowski*

8 Neural Mechanisms of Attention and Memory in Preferential
   Looking Tasks 179
        Kelly A. Snyder

9 Infant Memory Development: New Questions, New Answers 209
        Harlene Hayne

10 In the Language of Multiple Memory Systems: Defining and
   Describing Developments in Long-Term Declarative Memory 240
        Patricia J. Bauer, Tracy DeBoer, and Angela F. Lukowski

11 How Do We Remember? Let Me Count the Ways 271
        Jean M. Mandler

12 To Have and Have Not: What Do We Mean When We Talk About
   Long-Term Memory Development? 291
        Nora S. Newcombe and Stacie L. Crawley

Author Index 315

Subject Index 329

Contributors

Patricia J. Bauer, Duke University

Martha Ann Bell, Virginia Polytechnic Institute and State University

Nelson Cowan, University of Missouri, Columbia

Stacie L. Crawley, Temple University

Tracy DeBoer, University of California, Davis

Lisa Feigenson, Johns Hopkins University

Judith F. Feldman, Albert Einstein College of Medicine/
    Children's Hospital at Montefiore

Harlene Hayne, University of Otago

Jeffery J. Jankowski, Queensborough Community College/
    CUNY and Albert Einstein College of Medicine

Zsuzsa Káldy, University of Massachusetts, Boston

Alan M. Leslie, Rutgers University

Steven J. Luck, University of California, Davis

Angela F. Lukowski, University of Minnesota

Jean M. Mandler, University of California, San Diego

Katherine C. Morasch, Virginia Polytechnic Institute and State University

Nora S. Newcombe, Temple University

Lisa M. Oakes, University of California, Davis

J. Steven Reznick, University of North Carolina, Chapel Hill

Susan A. Rose, Albert Einstein College of Medicine/Children's Hospital
at Montefiore

Shannon Ross-Sheehy, University of Maryland

Kelly A. Snyder, University of Denver

Introduction

Considering Memory and Its Development in Infancy

PATRICIA J. BAUER AND LISA M. OAKES

The ability to remember the people, objects, and events one encounters is critically important for effective functioning in the world. Remembering your mother's face, where you left your keys, and that it is your daughter's birthday tomorrow allow you to successfully manage your day as well as your relationships with others. Questions about the processes of memory and how they develop are age old. In developmental science, research on memory has been prominent since the writings of Jean Piaget became available to English-speaking audiences in the 1950s and 1960s. In the 1970s, a large body of research investigated whether young children used memory strategies such as rehearsal, and how their successes and failures in strategy use influenced their memory abilities (reviewed in Pressley & Hilden, 2006). Recently, a number of researchers have focused on children's autobiographical memory, both as an indicator of how memories are maintained and changed over time (Nelson & Fivush, 2004) and as insight into how children's memory for past events shapes their sense of self (Howe & Courage, 1997).

Common to all research on memory is focus on the question of how the organism takes information that is out in the environment right now and preserves that information beyond its physical duration. Some researchers focus on maintenance of information over the short term. For example, they ask how the infant or young child keeps information active in short-term or working memory. Others focus on understanding the development of long-term memory or the representation of information over longer periods of time.

Both of these memory systems are profoundly important for the young child. Consider a child who sees a cat go behind a couch and then reemerge a few seconds later from the other side, for instance. Recognizing that it is indeed the same cat requires that the infant maintain information in working memory. Similarly, developing a close relationship with a caregiver, for example, requires that the infant remember that caregiver from one day to the next. Thus, both working memory and long-term memory are critically important for infants' learning about the world around them, as well as their development and maintenance of social relationships. This volume is organized along this important temporal dimension—the first section focuses on short-term and working memory and the second section on long-term memory.

Whereas division of memory on the basis of temporal duration is relatively uncontroversial, other distinctions within the domain are less universally accepted. Indeed, some of the greatest challenges in the field of memory development have arisen from attempts to import into the developmental literature distinctions that have arisen in the adult cognitive science and neuroscience literatures. In particular, using experimentally induced and natural lesions as well as neuroimaging techniques (e.g., fMRI and PET), researchers have suggested that there are different systems of memory that are subserved by different neural substrates (e.g., Schacter, Wagner, & Buckner, 2000). As the field of developmental cognitive science has begun to move from description of age-related changes to explanation of them, we have started to investigate the implications of these distinctions for the development of memory. In the process, as described in the present volume, we have met with many successes. The attempts have not been without challenges and controversies, however. A major goal of this volume is to address some of the most significant issues with the aim of identifying areas of consensus and areas in which further theoretical and empirical work is necessary.

Why a Volume About Early Memory?

In October 2003, the Cognitive Development Society hosted its third biennial meeting, in Park City, Utah. This book is a product of that meeting, albeit an unofficial one. During this meeting, we (Bauer and Oakes) had a conversation with Oxford acquisitions editor Catharine Carlin about the need for an edited volume in memory in infancy. Specifically, we discussed the fact that the study of early memory has exploded in recent years. Using new methods, many of them adapted from adult cognitive neuroscience, and guided by enhanced understanding of the neuroanatomical structures that underlie different aspects of memory, researchers have developed new theoretical models of memory and its development. Although several previous volumes have explored various aspects of memory, none had as its focus early memory development and the mechanisms of developmental change. As a result of that casual conversation, we planned this volume.

The present volume is unique in another way. Its organization was inspired by a format used by Akira Miyake and Priti Shah in their 1999 edited volume *Models of Working Memory: Mechanisms of Active Maintenance and Executive Control,* published by Cambridge. In the volume, Miyake and Shah gathered 12 scholars who were studying working memory and asked them each to address the same set of specific questions. The resulting volume was influential in defining working memory and highlighting areas of consensus and disagreement in its conceptualization and measurement. We have adopted this general approach in the current volume. The specific questions we asked of our authors were different, but the goals were similar: to bring greater precision to definitions of memory in infancy, examine the benefits and limitations of its measurement, evaluate our progress in describing and explaining developmental changes in memory, and suggest some directions for future research. Eight labs took us up on our offer. Six other scholars (across four chapters) accepted our invitation to provide commentary on the contributions. The result is a volume that more than meets our goals.

Why Infancy?

The volume focuses on recent empirical and theoretical advances in the study of memory development in infancy and very early childhood. Extension of theories derived from the study of memory systems in adults and use of behavioral and neuroscience methods have led to new questions about the mechanisms that underlie those memory systems and how they develop. Importantly, as we learn more both about the neural substrates of different memory systems in adults and the development of those brain structures, new questions are being asked about how and why memory systems develop in infancy. That is, we are moving beyond describing developmental changes in memory systems to attempting to understand the mechanisms of those changes. Progress toward this goal has been made across the developmental literature. We think that nowhere has it been more pronounced than in the infancy literature. Moreover, we focused on infancy and very early childhood because we are not aware of any other volumes that have as their focus the study of memory development in this critical age range. More common are volumes such as that by Wolfgang Schneider and Michael Pressley (1997), *Memory Development Between Two and Twenty.* The editors and authors of the current volume are working to address developmental changes overlooked by such efforts.

The Temporal Dimension of Memory

This volume is divided in half along a temporal dimension. The first four chapters and two commentaries (chapters 5 and 6) concern memory over the short term; memory that lasts for seconds to minutes, but not hours or a life-time. Chapters 7 through 10 and two commentaries (chapters 11 and 12) focus on memory over the long term. By default, if memory over the short term extends only minutes, then memory over the long term is anything longer. In actuality, the chapters on long-term memory concern retention of information over minutes to months. Dividing memory along a temporal dimension is reasonable and informative for a number of reasons, not the least of which is that one of the editors (Oakes) studies short-term memory and the other (Bauer) studies long-term memory. More than that though, the temporal dimension is reasonable because both the mechanisms and the methods are different for short- and long-term memory. As is illustrated in the first part of this volume, retention over the short term is tested by tasks in which infants are asked to locate objects after short delays or determine whether two briefly presented displays are similar or different. In contrast, a typical method for measuring retention over the long term is to ask infants to imitate the actions of another after a delay of weeks to months.

More than methods differentiate the types of memory at the temporal extremes. Work with healthy adults and adults with lesions and disease, animal models, and neuroimaging studies are making it increasingly clear that the different types of memory rely on different neural substrates. As outlined in the first section, a number of neural structures and networks, including prefrontal and posterior parietal cortex, mediate memory over the short term. In contrast, for long-term memory, attention is focused on the hippocampus and surrounding cortices. These neural structures are impli-cated in the type of memory that most of us have in mind when we talk about memory or remembering something, such as a husband's date of birth or where we parked our car this morning. The fact that different neural structures and networks are involved in different types of memory means that adequate descriptions and explanations of the development of these memories need to be considered somewhat separately. (Though of course, short- and long-term memory work together and so an equally important issue is how they communicate and cooperate with one another.)

Finally, use of the temporal dimension as an organizational strategy is logical because many questions and issues are specific to one or the other temporal dimension of memory. In the domain of working memory, for example, there is the question of whether there is a single working memory system, or separate systems for remembering different types of information, such as information processed by the dorsal stream of the visual system (the *where* or *how* system) and information processed by the ventral stream of the visual system (the *what* system). Another major question is whether working memory is short-term memory or is the activation of longer-term memories. In the domain of long-term memory, the elephant in the room is the distinction between declarative (or explicit) and nondeclarative (or implicit, procedural) forms of memory. A major question is whether the dis-tinction is necessary to account for the data on developmental changes in long-term memory, or whether a better account would be provided by elaboration of a single system. These issues are central to the discussions of memory in cognitive science. They contribute to our understanding of how memory develops.

Five Framing Questions

When we talked about this volume and what we hoped it would accomplish, five questions came to mind virtually immediately. With some refinement, they were the questions we presented to our authors. The first questions are definitional and descriptive. We felt it was important for contributors to be explicit about what they are doing and how they are doing it. Other questions have broader theoretical and developmental implications. Our goal here was to ask the contributors to consider these broader issues, both to provide a deeper understanding of the particular questions they address in their research and to allow for comparisons of the chapters at conceptual and empirical levels. In the sections that follow, we describe these questions and preview some of the answers. The commentaries by Cowan, Leslie and Káldy, Mandler, and Newcome and Kovacs provide more elaborate discussions of how the different chapters addressed these questions.

Question 1: What Kind of Memory
Are You Studying?

Although on the face of it the question, what kind of memory are you studying? is easy, academics are notorious for making things complicated. Scholars of memory and its development are no exception. Infancy researchers have the added challenge of defining constructs in organisms that cannot be tested with the agreed-upon methods used with adults because so many of the methods depend on language (e.g., digit span, recall of word lists, narratives about past events). Yet clear positions on the fundamental question, what type of memory is it? are critical to progress in the area, to the mission of comparison of different programs of research, and to evaluation of the conclusions that can be drawn from the collection of chapters as a whole. For this reason, definitional issues figure prominently and merit the significant attention paid to them by the authors and commentators in this volume.

The similarities and differences in how authors answered the question of the type of memory they are studying are striking. For example, Reznick (chapter 1) argues for the term *working memory* over *short-term memory* on the basis that short-term memory is nested within working memory. He points out that in many tasks, infants must store information in memory, retain it over some interval, and use it in the service of some behavior (such as searching) after that interval. He argues that this is clearly working memory. Oakes, Ross-Sheehy, and Luck (chapter 4) make exactly the opposite argument, suggesting that although we can know that infants have remembered something over the short term, it is much more difficult to know whether the memory they have formed is "working" in the sense of Baddley's model of working memory.

In their discussion of one type of long-term memory, Rose, Feldman, and Jankowski (chapter 7) argue that infants' visual recognition memory (as assessed in the visual paired comparison task) is explicit. They cite adult lesion and animal data in support of this claim. Snyder (chapter 8) comes to the opposite conclusion based on exactly the same set of data. These two examples illustrate the importance of providing clear, explicit definitions of the type of memory one is discussing or studying. The chapters in this volume reveal that many disagreements about the development of memory systems stem from fundamental differences of interpretation about what kind of memory is being studied.

Question 2: How Do You Measure the Type of Memory You Are Studying?

Questions of measurement are of course intimately tied to the definition of memory. The bond is especially tight in the infancy literature. As will become apparent, in some cases authors rely on methods originally developed in the adult literature and then adapted for use with infants (e.g., change detection, chapter 4). In other cases, the methods were born in work with infants and have since been exported for use with adults (e.g., the visual paired comparison used by Rose et al., chapter 7, and Snyder, chapter 8, was used with adults by McKee & Squire, 1993; and the imitation task used by Hayne, chapter 9, and Bauer, DeBoer, and Lukowski, chapter 10, was used in adults by McDonough, Mandler, McKee, & Squire, 1995). In yet other cases, the methods are specific to infants (e.g., mobile conjugate reinforcement, chapter 9). In still others, methods are used across species (e.g., methods described by Bell and Morasch, chapter 2 and by Reznick, chapter 1, are similar to delayed nonmatching to sample, used with nonhuman primates: Bachevalier, 2001). In each case, scholars and researchers have conducted careful analyses of the tasks they use, to determine—as best they can—precisely what is demanded by the method and thus what processes might underlie performance on the task.

For the present volume, we asked the contributors to comment on the particular tasks and methods they use in studying memory development. The discussion of the methods in each chapter clearly articulates how memory is assessed in that program of research and also identifies some of the challenges faced in measuring that aspect of memory. This discussion is critically important for a full understanding of the findings that have been reported. As will become apparent, there is not universal agreement on the type of memory a given method tests. The case of the visual paired comparison method, discussed by Rose et al. (chapter 7) on the one hand and Snyder (chapter 8) on the other, is perhaps the clearest case in point. These authors recruit the same methods and the same supporting evidence yet come to dramatically different conclusions regarding the construct they are studying. These chapters are a vivid illustration of how far the field of infant memory development has come and also of the significant distance we have yet to travel.

The discussion of how to measure memory in infancy and early childhood also brings to the forefront consideration of what kind of evidence is needed to demonstrate a particular type of memory. Reznick (chapter 1) provides an elegant discussion of this with regard to working memory, and the chapters by Hayne (chapter 9) and Bauer et al. (chapter 10) provide contrasting discussions of the methods for assessing long-term declarative or explicit memory in prelinguistic children. These chapters illustrate the problem of measuring particular memory structures in infancy and how researchers can disagree about the best methods of measurement.

Question 3: What Do We Know About the Development of This Aspect of Memory?

Addressing the first two questions set the stage for contributors to deal with the core questions of how the specific type of memory under question changes with development (i.e., description of developmental change). This questions is of course phenomenally important: The first step toward explanation of change is description of it. In their descriptions of developmental change, the authors make clear the maturity of the field of infant memory development. Eight research programs provide eight tales of age-related changes in memory over the course of the first two years of life. The chapters in part II reveal developmental changes in exposure durations before children show evidence of remembering in both visual tasks (chapters 7 and 8) and imitation tasks (chapters 9 and 10). The chapters in part I show changes in the capacity of short-term memory (chapters 3 and 4) and increases in how long infants can hold information in working memory (chapter 2). In short, these chapters illustrate dramatic changes in several aspects of long- and short-term memory that occur over the first year of life.

Question 4: What Are the Mechanisms of Developmental Change?

Descriptions of developmental changes in memory naturally lead to the question of the reasons for the change: Why does this type of memory change and why does change take the form that it does? What are the mechanisms underlying the development of this type of memory? Are there differences in the encoding, storage, or retrieval of information? To address these questions, contributors must push the envelope. Recent years have been witness to significant advances in our understanding of how memories are formed, retained, and later retrieved. The question is answered at the levels of neural systems and at the level of molecules and cells. Though none of the scholars in this volume are working across the entire spectrum, many are making serious attempts to relate what they see in the eyes and the hands of infants to the processes carried out by neurons and neural systems. The goal is being furthered by considering all that we know, from multiple sources, to converge on likely explanations.

Researchers are aided in addressing these questions by the addition of psychophysiological techniques from neuroscience, such as electroencephalogram, event related potentials, and heart rate measures. Use of these measures, especially in conjunction with behavioral measures, has allowed deeper insight into how nervous system functioning relates to the changes we have observed in memory development. The efforts to understand the mechanisms of change bring into sharper focus areas of agreement in the literature and also some of the many disagreements. Examples include debates over whether infants have two long-term memory systems or one (chapters 9 and 10), whether visual recognition memory tasks tap declarative or nondeclarative memory (chapters 7 and 8), and what is necessary for a working memory system (chapters 1, 2, and 4). Contributors' descriptions of developmental changes in memory systems, and the mechanisms responsible for those developmental changes, reveal many of these controversies and provide the reader with a complete view of the literature.

Question 5: What Is on the Horizon for This Area of Memory Development?

The final question—what is on the horizon—is always challenging to address. None of us has a crystal ball, yet we asked authors to peer into one and make informed speculations regarding next steps in their areas. Their speculations are illuminating, and we hope they will guide future researchers to think about important problems. Bell and Morasch (chapter 2) and Reznick (chapter 1) call for the development of additional tasks to allow us to understand the development of working memory. Snyder (chapter 8) calls for continuing our exploration of explicit and implicit memory in infancy. Rose et al. (chapter 7) and Bauer et al. (chapter 10) point to furthering our understanding of the sources of developmental changes in memory behavior—in terms of both the processes of memory (e.g., encoding versus retrieval) and the underlying neuroanatomical structures. We engage in this exercise because science is a developmental process and it does not move forward if it does not stretch.

The Cast of Characters

One of the challenges facing editors of volumes of collected works is deciding on the cast of characters. In the field of infant memory research, the
decision is difficult indeed because this area has successfully attracted
clever and dedicated scholars. Many labs have achieved the critical body of
work that we desired for the volume. To select among them, we considered
several things. One of the things we hoped to accomplish was to provide
opportunities to examine the assumptions that guide research programs. For
that reason, we wanted to feature scholars whose work seems to be guided
by different assumptions. We succeeded. Within each section, readers will
be treated to different perspectives on seemingly the same phenomena.
Contributors to the volume differ in how they define the type of memory
they are studying; they draw different conclusions based on similar methods; and they implicate different sources of developmental change.
Importantly, their assumptions are clearly stated and thus open for examination. We thank the contributors for accepting our invitation to bare their
souls and hope the field will benefit from the exercise as much as the
editors have.

Another goal with this volume was to provide an opportunity to hear
some new voices. Each part features a chapter authored by a newcomer to the
field. We hope that Lisa Feigenson (Johns Hopkins University) and Kelly
Snyder (University of Denver) do not mind this very public debut. We think
their work is terrific and we will be very pleased if being featured in this
volume brings them a higher profile. We also welcome several more junior
coauthors of chapters, including Tracy DeBoer and Angela Lukowski (chapter 10), Katherine Morasch (chapter 2), and Shannon Ross-Sheehy (chapter 4).

Finally, with this volume we desired a forum for thoughtful reflection on
the perspectives and arguments made by the contributors. To ensure it, we
invited four noted scholars to read and consider the chapters and share their
thoughts on the issues that motivated them. Each of the discussants could
have contributed a chapter based on her or his own research program. We
were delighted that they agreed to play somewhat different roles for this
volume. We were also pleased that two of the discussants extended the
invitation to junior colleagues, Stacie Kovacs (chapter 12) and Zsuzsa
Káldy (chapter 5), thereby furthering our goal of featuring new voices.

The discussants were chosen because they have different areas of exper-
tise and represent a range of opinions on the critical issues that form the core
of this volume. As such, they have different perspectives on the major controversies and even on the areas of apparent agreement and disagreement
among the contributors. Moreover, each approached the role somewhat
differently. Nelson Cowan (chapter 6) and Alan Leslie and Zsuzsa Káldy
(chapter 5) provided thoughtful commentaries on the short-term or working
memory section. These scholars have studied this aspect of memory in their

own work. Leslie and Káldy put the current work in the context of recent discussions of object files (e.g., Scholl, 2001) and FINSTs (Pylyshyn, 1989), and therefore represent an important view in contemporary cognitive science. Cowan discusses the four content chapters in the context of his own model of working memory, in which the focus of attention plays a central role. Jean Mandler (chapter 11) and Nora Newcombe and Stacie Kovacs (chapter 12) provide thoughtful insights into the issues raised in the chapters in part II. Both commentaries describe at length the issue of explicit versus implicit memory systems in infancy. Mandler gives a thoughtful, detailed discussion of whether the visual paired comparison task does or does not tap explicit processes. Newcombe and Kovacs provide an insightful discussion of how we measure capacities and what it means to have an ability.

The commentators succeeded royally in their important role of placing the individual chapters in a broader theoretical and empirical context, as well as providing a balanced discussion of the issues raised in each chapter. The volume is all the richer for the diversity of approaches they took, as well as their perspectives.

Plan for the Volume

As should by now be clear, this edited volume is divided into two parts, the first concerning maintenance of information in memory over the short term and the second concerning maintenance of information over longer periods. Within each part, there are four chapters, each of which concerns the five framing questions we charged the authors to address. Each part also includes two commentaries.

The intended audience for this volume is students and scientists in the area of cognitive development and cognitive science. It is a unique volume in several respects. First, the focus of all of the chapters is early development. The first two years are a period of rapid developmental change, and therefore we can gain deep insight into both memory processes and how memory develops by focusing on this period. Moreover, because language skills during this period are limited, there are controversies about how to best measure memory, what types of memory those measurements reflect, and how the memory assessed in this period is related to the type of memory processes observed in adults. One goal of this book is to provide a full discussion of these controversies.

Second, the volume focuses on mechanisms of change, with a particular emphasis on the neural substrates involved in memory. As a result, the volume moves beyond documentation of early developmental change in memory abilities to provide insight into how those developmental changes come about. The volume is also unique in that each contributor addressed a common set of questions, and discussants provided commentaries on the collections of chapters as a whole. Certainly, each chapter stands alone.

Together, the volume provides a coherent set of chapters that address a common set of issues. As a result, the reader will gain a appreciation of the issues in the field. In addition, the common organization facilitates comparison of the individual chapters. The contributors' willingness to adopt this structure means that we are able to provide a coherent volume, rather than a collection of related chapters. We hope you enjoy it.

References

Bachevalier, J. (2001). Neural bases of memory development: Insights from neuropsychological studies in primates. In C. A. Nelson & M. Luciana (Eds)., *Handbook of developmental cognitive neuroscience* (pp. 365–379). Cambridge, MA: MIT Press.

Howe, M. L., & Courage, M. L. (1997). The emergence and early development of autobiographical memory. *Psychological Review, 104*, 499–523.

McDonough, L. M., Mandler, J. M., McKee, R. D., & Squire, L. R. (1995). The deferred imitation task as a nonverbal measure of declarative memory. *Proceedings of the National Academy of Science, 92*, 7580–7584.

McKee, R. D., & Squire, L. R. (1993). On the development of declarative memory. *Journal of Experimental Psychology: Learning, Memory, and Cognition, 19*, 397–404.

Miyake, A., & Shah, P. (Eds.). (1999). *Models of working memory: Mechanisms of active maintenance and executive control.* Cambridge, UK: Cambridge University Press.

Nelson, K., & Fivush, R. (2004). The emergence of autobiographical memory: A social cultural developmental theory. *Psychological Review, 111*, 486–511.

Pressley, M., & Hilden, K. (2006). Cognitive strategies. In W. Damon (Ed.-in-Chief) & D. Kuhn & R. Siegler (Vol. Eds.), *Handbook of child psychology: Cognition, perception, and language* (6th ed., pp. 511–556). New York: Wiley.

Pylyshyn, Z. W. (1989). The role of location indexes in spatial perception: A sketch of the FINST spatial-index model. *Cognition, 32*, 65–97.

Schacter, D. L., Wagner, A. D., & Buckner, R. L. (2000). Memory systems of 1999. In E. Tulving & F. I. M. Craik (Eds.), *The Oxford handbook of memory* (pp. 627–643). New York: Oxford University Press.

Schneider, W., & Pressley, M. (1997). *Memory development between two and twenty* (2nd ed.). Mahwah, NJ: Erlbaum.

Scholl, B. J. (2001). Objects and attention: The state of the art. *Cognition, 80*, 1–46.

PART I

SHORT-TERM OR WORKING MEMORY IN INFANCY AND EARLY CHILDHOOD

1

Working Memory in Infants and Toddlers

J. STEVEN REZNICK

Coming to Terms With Memory; Coming to Memory With Terms

The phenomena that we identify as referents for the term *memory* are varied, complex, and salient aspects of our personal experience and our interactions with others. Memory's prominence has produced a rich psychological tradition with descriptions of relevant phenomena, insights into mechanisms, and well-established dimensions of development and individual difference. Unfortunately, memory's overabundance of sense meaning has sometimes interfered with our commitment to rigorous measurement and definition, leading to a virtual Tower of Babel in which conversations about memory can occur with shared terms that do not have shared meanings. My main goal in this chapter is to advance the discussion of memory development by clarifying the theoretical and operational meaning of the term *working memory* as it applies to infants and toddlers.

Type of Memory

The aspect of memory that is the theme of this chapter has been investigated by psychologists for well over a century. William James (1890/1981) described primary memory (he also called it *elementary memory*) as the awareness of the just past, and he compared this directly intuited past with "properly recollected objects" that have been absent from consciousness altogether and then

3

revived anew, what we now call long-term memory. To quote from James's poetic description:

> [T]he practically cognized present is no knife-edge, but a saddle-back, with a certain breadth of its own on which we sit perched, and from which we look in two directions into time. The unit of composition of our perception of time is a duration, with a bow and a stern, as it were—a rearward- and a forward-looking end. (p. 574)

James is clearly talking about a memory system that is short term, affecting experience within parameters of seconds and minutes. Research on short-term memory emerged strongly during the 1960s, buoyed by the productive Brown-Peterson paradigm (Brown, 1958; Peterson & Peterson, 1959) in which participants attempted to retain letter sequences during a short interval while they performed some interfering task (e.g., counting backward). Short-term memory subsequently thrived as a prominent component in information processing models (e.g., Atkinson & Shiffrin, 1968, 1971), establishing a place (figuratively, a "black box") in which information could be stored temporarily pending either forgetting or transfer to long-term storage.

The more problematic definitional issue is to bridge the gap between short-term memory and the various phenomena that have been labeled working memory. Miller, Galanter, and Pribram (1960), in their seminal book on the conception and execution of plans, used the term *working memory* as a neural locus where "plans can be retained temporarily when they are being formed, or transformed, or executed" (p. 207), and they speculated presciently that this locus would reside in the forward portion of the primate frontal lobe. Anderson and Bower (1973), in their model of human associative memory, used the term *working memory* to describe a currently active partition of long-term memory in which structural modification affects associative linkages. Baddeley and Hitch (1974) used the term *working memory* to refer to processes that allow the maintenance of task-relevant information during the performance of a task, and they are often awarded pride of place for launching the prodigious flood of research on working memory that has inundated cognitive psychology and related fields for over two decades.[1]

What do these definitions of working memory have in common that distinguishes them from short-term memory per se? Short-term memory implies the availability of information for some relatively circumscribed period of time. This information might be considered to reside dynamically or passively in a temporary buffer or it might be an activated subset of a long-term store, but in either case, the focal construct refers to the fact that information is available temporarily. Working memory implies a broader system that nests the short-term store within executive processes that keep the information activated (e.g., rehearsal) or organized (e.g., semantic chunking) or that extract meaning or formulate plans. The expanded functionality of working memory is closer to James's original concept of short-term storage because it would enable the future-oriented processing that James described.

The dissociation between short-term memory and working memory can be demonstrated empirically. For example, Engle, Tuholski, Laughlin, and Conway (1999) tested adults and Kail and Hall (2001) tested 7- to 13-year-olds using a battery of tasks that measured simple storage (e.g., a span task in which participants attempted to remember digit strings of increasing length) or working memory (e.g., a reading span task in which participants read a set of sentences and attempted to remember the last word of each sentence in the set). The requirement that participants remember some words while reading other words supports the inference that working memory is involved. Short-term memory scores and working memory scores were correlated, but factor analysis identified a set of short-term memory tasks that were distinct from the working-memory tasks. Thus, within tightly constrained task contexts, short-term memory can be differentiated from working memory per se, even though from a theoretical perspective, short-term memory is a component of working memory.

From the present perspective, two questions emerge. First, can we distinguish short-term memory from working memory in infants and young children? I am confident that interesting theoretical opportunities would emerge if we could draw a distinction between short-term memory and working memory in this age range, but I argue here that we have not yet found measurement operations that will support the distinction and, given the operating characteristics of our research participants, we are unlikely ever to do so. Given that we cannot draw a distinction between short-term memory and working memory in infants, what is the most appropriate label for the short-term storage that researchers currently measure? I argue on various grounds that working memory is the appropriate term, although we cannot claim that working memory in infants and young children is the same process as working memory in adults.

Operational Definition

The path from theory to operation is difficult at best and notably arduous when infants are the focal population. The well-worn joke about the man looking for his keys under the lamppost rather than where he dropped them "because the light is better" is often relevant for researchers who must study infants doing what infants can do. The infant's labile states and limited skill and motivation often cause a considerable gap between the phenomenon as measured and the researcher's theoretical interest.

As a sine qua non for labeling a phenomenon as either short-term or working memory, the measurement context must require the participant to encode information and, after some brief duration of time, make a response that is based on this information per se rather than on information that had been acquired previously (e.g., long-term memory) or that is available at the time of testing (e.g., a specific cue). Various procedures have been used to explore short-term storage in infants, and these procedures can be described within three broad categories: hide-find procedures, observe-perform procedures, and familiarize-recognize procedures. A thorough description of these procedures contributes to the effort to characterize short-term storage in infants.

Hide-Find Procedures

The delayed-response task, introduced by Hunter (1913, 1917) to study symbolic behavior in humans and other animals, captures the essence of the short-term storage construct. This task has been used extensively with infants (see Pelphrey & Reznick, 2003, for a review), and many researchers consider it to be the canonical procedure for assessing short-term memory (Goldman-Rakic, 1987). The participant in a delayed-response task is given a cue that specifies which location among various alternatives is to be considered correct on that particular trial. In Hunter's original paradigm, the cue was a light that was illuminated above a location. In recent instantiations of the task, the cue is the hiding of an attractive object at a particular location, for example in a covered well (e.g., Diamond & Doar, 1989), an undifferentiated box of sand (Huttenlocher, Newcombe, & Sandberg, 1994), or in a naturalistic room (DeLoache & Brown, 1979). In the eye-gaze version of the task, the cue is a visual stimulus at a particular location in the peripheral visual field (Funahashi, Bruce, & Goldman-Rakic, 1989; Gilmore & Johnson, 1995). In a version of the delayed-response task designed for use with young infants, the cue is the examiner appearing in a window and communicating with the infant (Schwartz & Reznick, 1999).

The second phase of the delayed-response task is the imposition of a specific delay and some type of distraction. The circumscribed delay is important because the hallmark of short-term storage is the durability of a representation over a relatively short period of time. The distraction serves two purposes. First, it breaks the participant's attention to the cued location and thus ensures an active choice rather than the passive continuation of attention to the cued location. Further, the distraction causes the participant to engage in some degree of ongoing processing while retaining the representation of the target location. In the final phase of a delayed-response trial, the participant is allowed to make a choice. Participants in the hiding task usually select a location and, if correct, retrieve the desired contents. Participants in visual analogues of the delayed-response task choose by shifting gaze toward a particular location, and they often receive a reward for correct performance.

The syntax of the hide-find task seems straightforward, but some caveats are relevant. Recent uses of the procedure require a distinction between short-term and long-term memory. In contrast to short-term memory's dynamic, continuous, and transitory nature, long-term memory implies notable durability and a distinct gap in time between an initially active representation and the reemergence of that representation when it is recalled. Any particular instance of memory performance in a hide-find task could reflect short-term or long-term storage. For example, an infant who watches her father put her cherished pacifier in his desk drawer may retain a short-term representation that enables her to search in the drawer, and it is also possible that she retains a long-term representation that would allow her to search successfully when she encounters the same context hours or days later. For example, Moore and Meltzoff (2004) found that 14-month-old infants who saw a bell hidden in a container were highly likely to search for the bell in the container when they returned to the same locale 24 hours later. Because long-term storage must be posited to account for the infant's behavior in this hide-find task, the appropriate designation for a memory-based response at a shorter delay is ambiguous.

To support the claim that a hide-find procedure is tapping short-term storage, long-term storage must be ruled out as an alterative claim. If long-term storage can be demonstrated in the same context, a short-term storage interpretation seems less compelling. One way to rule out long-term storage is to test for memory across multiple trials in the same context with the focal representation varying across trials. That is, allow the infant to search for a hidden stimulus at a delay appropriate for challenging short-term storage across a series of trials in which the location of hiding varies randomly with replacement. This configuration does not preclude the possibility that the infant is encoding a long-term representation of each hiding location, but it makes a short-term memory interpretation more compelling.

A second concern emerges for hide-find procedures that link memory for location with violation of expectations. Infants are often uniquely attentive to an event that violates the bounds of the possible, and this response has been used to map infant expectations across a wide range of dimensions (see Baillargeon, 1995, for a summary). The infant's response to an impossible outcome is evoked in the hide-find procedure with a configuration in which the examiner retrieves a hidden object from a place where it was not hidden. Ten-week-old infants are particularly attentive when a toy is retrieved from an impossible location after 5 seconds (Wilcox, Nadel, & Rosser, 1996); 5-month-olds do so after 50 seconds (Newcomb, Huttenlocher, & Learmonth, 1999); and 8-month-olds after up to 70 seconds after the toy was hidden (Baillargeon, DeVos, & Graber, 1989; Baillargeon & Graber, 1988). These results could suggest an early and potent short-term storage capacity, but the use of a single trial is problematic because it could reflect either long-term or short-term memory. Given the unexpectedly long memory span shown by these young infants, a long-term memory interpretation seems more likely.

Observe-Perform Procedures

In an observe-perform procedure, a sequence of actions is presented, a delay is imposed, and the participant attempts to repeat the sequence of actions. For example, Knox (1913) developed a cube imitation test in which an examiner would tap a sequence of blocks and the participant attempted to repeat the sequence of taps immediately afterward. The better known

Corsi blocks test (Corsi, 1972) uses a similar strategy but a more complex stimulus configuration, with nine blocks arranged irregularly in two dimensions. Memory capacity is challenged with longer tap sequences defined by sampling with replacement among the set of blocks.

From a developmental perspective, infants who observe a multistep action sequence are likely to produce those very actions when given the opportunity at a later time (Kagan, 1981; Meltzoff, 1985; Piaget, 1962; see Bauer, 2002, for a recent review), suggesting long-term recall memory. This approach has potential as a measure of short-term memory if the steps in the action sequence are independent (like the sequential touches in the Corsi block procedure) and if sequence steps are sampled with replacement across successive trials. For example, Alp (1994) reported an imitation sorting task that revealed changes in short-term memory capacity in children from 12 to 36 months of age. An examiner sorted disparate objects into two containers, then retrieved the objects and gave them to the child, requesting, "Now you do it." Older children imitated the examiner's sort correctly for an increasingly large set of objects. This task holds promise as a measure of short-term memory capacity because it is compelling for children, and it would be amenable to interesting parametric manipulations such as increasing the delay between presentation and sort, varying the number of locations and items, altering the distinctiveness of locations and items, and requiring the child to engage in specific ongoing processing.

Infants and toddlers are adept at performing actions, which is a plus for observe-perform procedures, but performance is a double-edged sword. The observe-perform procedure requires that the participant have a general motivation and competence to imitate a modeled action and the motor ability to perform the target action. It is unclear exactly when infants become capable of imitating the actions of others (Ainsfeld, 1991; Meltzoff & Moore, 1983). This ability is certainly present for some actions from early in life, but it is difficult to distinguish between a failure of motivation or motor competence and a failure of memory.

Familiarize-Recognize Procedures

Saul Sternberg (1966) explored short-term memory by presenting participants with a set of digits that were to be remembered and then testing them with probes, some of which were from the original presentation. Participants indicated whether each probe had been presented previously, leading to the general conclusion that the number of items being held in short-term memory affected subsequent performance. This approach to memory assessment is relevant for research on infants because young infants are adept at differentiating familiar and unfamiliar stimuli, often showing a marked preference for the unfamiliar (Fantz, 1956). Research on infant attention has revealed some limits on when infants will show a preference for unfamiliar stimuli (Hunter & Ames, 1988) and how this preference is affected by the magnitude of discrepancy between familiar and novel (McCall & Kagan, 1967), but these considerations notwithstanding, preference for the unfamiliar has been the foundation for much of our knowledge about infant cognitive ability.

De Saint Victor, Smith, and Loboschefski (1997) extended Sternberg's procedure to 10-month-old infants. Infants were familiarized with a set of one, two, or three photographs of objects (e.g., a bike, a ball, a bunny) and then saw test trials pairing a familiar stimulus with a novel stimulus. Fixation to the familiar stimulus increased as a function of familiarization set size, suggesting that infants perform an item-by-item scan of the contents of short-term memory in order to determine that the stimulus was familiar. Rose, Feldman, and Jankowski (2001, 2003) reported similar results: Preference for the novel stimulus varied as a function of age, the number of objects in a familiarization set, and the serial position of the object within the set, suggesting an increase in memory capacity between 5 and 12 months of age and a recency effect.

The results of these studies are interesting, and the familiarize-recognize procedure is efficient and flexible, but three concerns emerge. First, as noted for hide-find procedures, it is important to discriminate between short-term and long-term processes because this is another context in which either process might be relevant. An infant who responds differentially to a familiar stimulus that is presented immediately might respond similarly to that stimulus when it is presented hours, days, or weeks later, which belies the claim that an active representation was sustained during the interval and questions the interpretation that short-term memory is being tapped. The inference that short-term memory is being assessed in the familiarize-recognize procedure would be more impressive if a limited set of familiar objects were used for the presentations and tests across blocks. In each test, the challenge would be to remember whether a particular stimulus was presented in the most recent familiarization set. This decision would be much more difficult than a judgment of whether a stimulus is generally familiar or novel, but the difficulty emerges precisely because the modification would require short-term memory per se rather than mere recognition of novelty.

Second, the ability to discriminate between a familiar and an unfamiliar stimulus implies some level of representation, but the articulation of this representation is not obvious. At one extreme, we can imagine an explicit representation of the familiarized stimulus being retained and used as the basis for recognition, which would support a short-term memory interpretation. Alternatively, we often encounter situations in which a stimulus seems familiar, but we have no idea where or when it was encountered, and we surely have not held a representation for the duration (e.g., when we recognize a former classmate whom we have not seen in decades or we recognize an object in an antique shop that once graced our childhood kitchen). This distinction is important in the present context because a key feature of short-term memory is the notion that an explicit representation is being sustained for some brief duration of time. A corollary of this concern is that it is often easier to recognize a stimulus than to recall it. For example, Logie and

Pearson (1997) tested 5- to 12-year-old children on memory for patterns and memory for sequences of movements with responses that required either recall or recognition of the original stimulus. Developmental patterns were similar across formats, but absolute measures of memory span were notably different, with greater memory span when the response was recognition.

An alternative approach to the familiarize-recognize format holds promise as an assessment of infant memory. Ross-Sheehy, Oakes, and Luck (2003; see chapter 4, this volume, for a detailed presentation) modified a sequential comparison procedure that had been used with adult participants (e.g., Luck & Vogel, 1997) and that could be considered a variant of the familiarize-recognize paradigm. In this procedure, infants see displays on two separate computer monitors, and the focal dependent variable is which of the two displays attracts the infant's gaze. To explore short-term memory capacity in infants, Ross-Sheehy and colleagues parsed the stimulus presentation into 500-millisecond bursts followed by 250-millisecond intervals. The stimulus (a small square) on one display remained constant over trials while the stimulus on the other display changed color on each trial. An infant who formed a representation of the color of the stimulus and kept that representation active for at least 250 milliseconds would be attracted to the changing display. There are various reasons why an infant might not prefer the changing display, but a lack of memory capacity is a salient interpretation. Oakes, Ross-Sheehy, and Luck (chapter 4, this volume) describe several experiments using this procedure to explore changes in the duration of short-term memory capacity and the nature of the stored representation.

What Shall We Call Short-Term Storage in Infants?

The term *short-term memory* is identified with a distinct research tradition that can be contrasted with research focused on working memory. There is a large degree of overlap between these approaches, but working memory is a broader construct that includes not only storage but also additional mechanisms including rehearsal strategies and manipulation of stored representations. What term, then, should we use to label the short-term storage that we are able to assess in infants? I suggest that the term *working memory* is appropriate for three reasons.

First, when short-term memory is contrasted with working memory, the research tasks that load more heavily on short-term memory always require extensive instructions and thus are not appropriate with infants. Indeed, from one perspective, short-term memory per se is a notably unnatural, theoretical fractionation of naturally occurring working memory that exists only as a by-product of artificially induced laboratory conditions. Thus, while there are reasons for attempting to distinguish between short-term memory and working memory in infants, that goal is not attainable at present, and it is unlikely to be attainable in the future. If short-term memory cannot be extracted, the appropriate label for the undifferentiated holistic process is working memory.

Second, hide-find procedures, and in particular the delayed-response task, have been our main source of data on this type of memory in infants, and these procedures are inextricably linked to working memory. Infants in a delayed-response task must store a representation, retain it during a distraction interval, and then use it to guide their search. On subsequent trials, target locations vary. We cannot identify the executive processes that infants use to retain visual representations in this context, but it is important to note that some models of working memory focus on cue salience rather than rehearsal as the primary influence on successful retrieval (Nairne, 2002). Executive processing would also be invoked to inhibit responses that had been correct on previous trials and to award greater salience to the present target. From a biological perspective, a vast research literature links delayed-response behavior to specific neural mechanisms involved in working memory (Goldman-Rakic, 1987) on the assumption that the delayed-response procedure and its variants are essentially marker tasks for working memory.

Finally, there is a reductio ad absurdum argument that would falsify a claim that 1-year-old infants have no working memory capacity. By their first birthday, infants can solve problems (Mosier & Rogoff, 1994; Willatts, 1984, 1999), which implies the ability to hold a goal in mind while formulating a plan, to hold the plan in mind while executing it, and to revise the plan if it fails (Zelazo, Carter, Reznick, & Frye, 1997). This feat would be impossible without working memory. For another example, 1-year-olds can communicate using words and gestures (Bates, Beninni, Bretherton, Camaioni, & Volterra, 1979; Bruner, 1975; Harding & Golinkoff, 1979). Working memory and language have been linked in many ways, described below, and it is hard to imagine that language acquisition could occur in an organism that has no working memory capacity. Finally, given that the research community has no qualms about positing working memory capacity in children as young as 4 to 7 years on the basis of their general abilities as well as their performance in working memory tasks (e.g., Cowan, Saults, & Elliott, 2002; Gathercole, 1998; Pickering, 2001), it seems unlikely that working memory could emerge, more or less fully formed, this late in development. A more plausible account would posit a gradual emergence of working memory capacity predating childhood and likely beginning in infancy or toddlerhood.

Moving beyond the claim that infants have working memory, it is important to note that infant working memory is likely to be quite different from adult working memory. As noted earlier, procedures for assessing working memory in adults almost always depend upon providing the participant with complex instructions, some degree of verbal fluency (either to understand instructions or to provide a response), and the stamina and motivation needed to endure a long series of trials. Obviously, infants fail to align on each of these dimensions, and it remains to be determined how infant working memory differs quantitatively and qualitatively from adult working memory.

Age-Related Phenotypic Changes

Dozens of studies have explored age-related changes in infant short-term storage. I will adopt the usual "more research is needed" stance later, but for now, I offer some general conclusions about age-related phenotypic changes.

Onset

Claims regarding the onset of psychological capacities in infancy are embargoed in an inductive limbo because some new procedure, conceptualization, or measurement strategy is likely to emerge and reset the ontogenetic timetable. Thus warned, we can posit a tentative onset for working memory by using a procedure that offers the least challenge to working memory capacity and that does so in a context engineered to evoke maximal performance. I offer our report of working memory in 5- to 6-month-old infants (Reznick, Morrow, Goldman, & Snyder, 2004) as setting a possible date for the onset of measurable working memory capacity.

An examiner appeared in one of two windows and interacted with the infant, who was seated comfortably on his or her mother's lap. The examiner then disappeared behind a curtain, imposed the briefest possible delay (1–2 seconds, during which she used her hand to draw the infant's attention to the center of the apparatus), and then the curtains were opened to reveal empty windows. The infant's first gaze toward a window was considered to be the infant's attempt to locate the examiner, and the percentage of correct gazes across the 12 trials, with correct location counterbalanced across trials, was our measure of working memory ability. Figure 1.1 is a plot of individual percentage correct scores as a function of age in months. On the basis of various statistical techniques for defining chance performance, we concluded that appreciable working memory for location emerges for many infants in the middle of their sixth month.

6–12 Months

Our review of the research in this domain (Pelphrey & Reznick, 2003) included an inventory of findings about working memory late in the first year, and the general conclusions in that report remain valid but unsatisfying. Working memory capacity as measured in hide-find tasks emerges at around 6 months and increases by seconds more or less linearly through 12 months at least, a finding first noted by Diamond and Doar (1989). Research by Rose et al. (2001) and Ross-Sheehy et al. (2003) using alternative methodologies converged on the same general conclusion. We have only vague hints about distinct aspects of working memory capacity that might underlie this general progress. One consideration is that estimates of working memory capacity will be affected by the valence and distinctiveness of the target. Bell (1970) demonstrated that infants are more likely to search for their mother than for

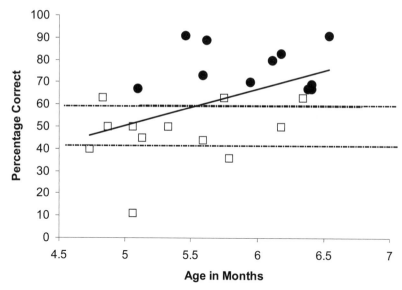

FIGURE 1.1. Individual percentage correct scores plotted as a function of age in months. The dashed lines at 42% and 58% represent chance performance plus or minus 2 standard errors of the mean. The large circles represent individual infants whose percentage correct has a binomial probability of less than .20.

a toy, and delayed-response procedures that use a person as the contents of the to-be-remembered location have consistently suggested greater memory capacity (e.g., Schwartz & Reznick, 1999). This consideration is particularly salient in the context of Nairne's suggestion that short-term memory performance is explained better by cue salience and distinctiveness than by general decay processes (Nairne, 2002).

A second consideration in interpreting the literature on infant working memory capacity is the strong effect of response modality on estimates of memory capacity. Specifically, Diamond (1985) and Hofstadter and Reznick (1996) reported better performance in a delayed-response task when infants are allowed to gaze toward a correct location rather than reach for that location. Various interpretations have been offered to explain this phenomenon (discussed in detail by Pelphrey & Reznick, 2003). From the present perspective, modality effects are a nuisance when we try to synthesize a general description of working memory development in infancy, but hopefully will be a leverage point as we continue to accrue knowledge about working memory development. For example, one perspective is that processing for perceptual purposes differs from processing for the control of actions. Goodale and Milner (1992; Milner & Goodale, 1995) applied this distinction to the well-established mapping of visual projections in the primate cerebral cortex into a ventral stream, which arises in area V1 and projects to the inferotemporal cortex, and a dorsal stream, which arises in V1 but projects to the posterior parietal cortex (Ungerleider & Mishkin, 1982). If Goodale and Milner are correct in their assertion that the ventral stream provides the infrastructure for perceptual representations and the dorsal stream mediates control of actions (see James, Culham, Humphrey, Milner, & Goodale, 2003, for supporting evidence), this perspective provides a theoretical distinction between gaze responses and reaching responses in the delayed-response procedure and points out a possible neural locus that underlies these differences.

Finally, alternative definitions of capacity may provide insights into the development and function of working memory. Baddeley and Hitch's model of working memory may rely too heavily on outmoded conceptualizations of decay and rehearsal but, to its credit, it draws a clear distinction between working memory for auditory and visual information. From an ontological perspective, working memory should be able to maintain information about what occurred, where it occurred, and when it occurred; and dimensions of capacity might include durability of a representation, the number of representations that can be held, the relative salience of previous and other competing representations, or the coherence of memory storage in the context of other ongoing processing. From this perspective, research to date on working memory development in infants and toddlers is narrow and thin, and few studies have compared aspects of capacity. A more differentiated approach to working memory is likely to be productive. For example, Pelphrey et al. (2004) explored working memory for location in infants ages 6–12 months using a cross-sectional design, with assessments based on gaze and on reach responses and with working memory capacity challenged across varying delays and across a varying number of locations. A general description of working memory development emerged that was consistent with the linear pattern described earlier, but there were also unique patterns of development across specific dimensions of working memory challenge.

1 to 3 Years

Working memory capacity should continue to improve across the toddler years, but we have few long-term comparisons. Kagan (1981) plotted scores on a memory-for-locations task administered in cross-sectional and longitudinal designs to children in the United States and abroad and found a steep improvement across the second year followed by a plateau that could reflect a response ceiling. Reznick, Corley, and Robinson (1997) reported comparable results for a large sample of identical and fraternal twins. Cowan and others (e.g., Cowan, 1997; Cowan et al., 2002; Gathercole, 1998; Pickering, 2001) described changes in working memory across childhood, with some articulation of relevant dimensions and processes. This level of sophistication is possible because older children can be given task instructions, because they can provide verbal responses or well-trained motor responses, and because comparable tasks can be used across ages with parametric manipulations that accommodate increasing working memory ability or that are insensitive to task difficulty. Unfortunately, the 1- to 3-year age range is more difficult to work with, and the procedures that are effective with younger and older children are not appropriate. This gap in our knowledge about working memory development is particularly noteworthy because the toddler years are a rich wellspring for intellectual and social development that is likely to be affected by underlying cognitive capacities such as changes in working memory.

Developmental Mechanisms

Neural Substrate

Working memory can be assessed in nonhuman primates and in tasks that can be administered during neural imaging. This confluence of rich data has allowed researchers to pinpoint a relatively specific neural substrate that is particularly relevant for working memory. Goldman-Rakic (1987) summarized a strong case for the role of prefrontal cortex in short-term working memory on the basis of data from surgical ablation and direct recording from relevant cells. Nelson et al. (2000) presented an elegant use of an n-back task and appropriate control conditions to explore spatial working memory in children aged 8–11 years, with functional magnetic resonance imaging revealing activity in dorsal prefrontal cortex and in posterior parietal and anterior cingulate cortex. Other reports using similar techniques converged on comparable conclusions regarding the neural locus of working memory (e.g., Smith, 2000) and extended the model to include contributions of the hippocampus and posterior perceptual and motor cortex (O'Reilly, Braver, & Cohen, 1999).

It seems reasonable to expect that the well-established neural descriptions of working memory within the primate brain would give us some purchase on a mechanism that drives development, but alas, our understanding of cortical development is still far too thin to support strong theory. Herschkowitz, Kagan, and Zilles (1997) described many structural and functional neural changes that occur during the first year that could be related to working memory. Huttenlocher's pioneering morphometric studies of cortical development (see Huttenlocher & Dabholkar, 1997, for a summary) and Chugani's research using positron emission tomography (e.g., Chugani, 1998) are often cited as evidence for a link between working memory and cortical development in infancy. Unfortunately, the neural development that has been linked to working memory is still much too general and persistent (i.e., continuing through adolescence) to circumscribe specific predictions about when working memory abilities will emerge, how working memory will be structured, and how or why working memory will change over time. Indeed, my personal opinion is that the direction of effect is likely to be the opposite: Sophisticated behavioral research will eventually provide guidance for neuroscientists, advising them to look for a specific underlying mechanism to explain why a particular aspect of working memory seems to be changing at a particular time in ontogenesis.

Social Context

It seems reasonable to expect that working memory development is facilitated by the opportunities to use working memory and, given the ecology of human development, these opportunities will emerge in the infant's immediate experience as well as in interactions with the social and nonsocial environment. We make use of these social interactions in many of our research procedures for assessing working memory (e.g., the windows and curtains delayed-response procedure is an instantiation of the game of peekaboo, and the delayed-response procedure itself is a variant of hide-and-seek). More broadly, infants who engage in goal-oriented activity, which requires working memory, are regarded by parents as behaving intentionally, and this evokes a degree of investment and interaction that would be less likely to occur and less easy to sustain with an infant who does not have these capacities (Reznick, 1999). Beyond these generalizations, we have no idea exactly how social interaction affects development of working memory and how the infant's use of working memory provides important exercise and modification of working memory capacity.

Functional Significance of Infant Working Memory

Working memory is so firmly ensconced in our cognitive architecture that it is difficult to imagine and describe mental life without it, although impairments of working memory occur in a wide range of circumstances. Working memory deterioration is adduced to explain the poorer performance of older adults on reasoning tasks (Phillips & Forshaw, 1998), and age-related declines in working memory have been described as reflecting less efficient updating (Hartman, Bolton, & Fehnel, 2001), reduced ability to overcome interference (Lustig, May, & Hasher, 2001), less efficient storage (Belleville, Rouleau, & Caza, 1998), or slower cognitive processing (Salthouse, 1996). Working memory and related processes are also affected to some degree in Down syndrome (Jarrold, Baddeley, & Phillips, 1999; Lanfranchi, Cornoldi, & Vianello, 2004), fragile X syndrome (Munir, Cornish, & Wilding, 2000), autism (Mottron, Belleville, & Menard, 1999), Turner's syndrome (Cornoldi, Marconi, & Vecchi, 2001), traumatic brain injury (Ewing-Cobbs, Prasad, Landry, Kramer, & DeLeon, 2004), and low birth weight (Vicari, Caravale, Carlesimo, Casadei, & Allemand, 2004). Working memory's contribution to these maladies is unclear. An early emerging defect in working memory could cause or contribute to a broad range of subsequent problems in cognitive or social-emotional domains (e.g., poor language or reasoning, poor social cognition). Alternatively, working memory deficits could reflect underlying deterioration of neural structures and processes concomitant with other malevolent effects. Thus, although it seems quite obvious that deficits in working memory have distinct functional significance, it is less clear exactly how working memory deficits are linked to specific effects.

From an ontogenetic perspective, it may be useful to describe phases of development during infancy as reflecting the availability of more or less sophisticated working memory. Measurable working memory capacity emerges in most normally developing infants at around 5 or 6 months of age (Reznick et al., 2004), and this capacity increases steadily in the months and years thereafter. Two sets of questions follow from this perspective. First, What cognitive and emotional processes become possible when working memory capacity reaches appreciable levels? Second, How does phenomenal experience change as working memory capacity increases? These questions are issues on the frontier of research, but for now, general answers can be offered.

The functional opportunities afforded by increasing working memory capacity are conjectural at present, pending specific research on this topic. One domain of interest is the relation between working memory and language. Working memory capacity and aspects of language are strongly linked in adults (Engle & Conway, 1998; Gathercole & Baddeley, 1993; Just, Carpenter, & Keller, 1996). The relation between working memory and language acquisition is less well established but equally compelling (Adams & Willis, 2001), with specific links between aspects of working memory and word learning, spoken language, and reading (e.g., Adams & Gathercole, 1996; Baddeley, Gathercole, & Papagno, 1998; Ellis & Sinclair, 1996; Gathercole, Hitch, Service, & Martin, 1997). It seems quite reasonable to expect that working memory would provide the opportunity for the language learner to detect the phonetic regularities that provide a basis for word segmentation and primitive syntax (Marcus, Vijayan, Rao, & Vishton, 1999; Saffran, Aslin, & Newport, 1996) and to notice and learn the sound-object correlations that supply the early lexicon (Bates, Bretherton, & Snyder, 1988; Fenson et al., 1994). More broadly, working memory would allow the infant to bind information across perceptual channels, recall information from long-term storage, project future states, and engage in goal-oriented activities and strategic problem solving.

Changes in phenomenal experience also seem likely, but this domain is even more conjectural. Theorists have posited a relation between working memory and consciousness because functions in working memory, such as the binding of information across sensory domains, reflecting on current information and comparing it with long-term storage, forming expectations, and formulating and executing plans are similar to the functions of consciousness (Baddeley, 1993). Furthermore, manipulations of working memory affect psychological processes that are associated with consciousness, such as the vividness of images (Andrade, 2001). The relation between working memory and consciousness is far from clear, but there could be some utility in describing infants from the perspective of a changing level of consciousness. For example, a young infant without significant working memory capacity could be viewed as living in a perpetual present. That is, sensations would replace sensations in an ongoing cascade, but no aspect of experience would linger in consciousness as an object of contemplation; ongoing sensations would not be melded with explicit expectations regarding upcoming states or events; and previous experiences would not be available for additional processing. We may never remember or rediscover what it is like to be an infant, but working memory provides interesting dimensions for projecting differences between infant and adult cognition.

Research Frontiers

Measurement Challenges and Limitations

One salient challenge is the need to expand working memory assessment to include additional paradigms. The delayed-response task has been a reliable workhorse, but constructs that rely too heavily on a single source of data are risky at best because theoretical considerations are too easily trumped by methodological constraints. Modifications of the delayed-response task that incorporate gaze responses and that make the context more gamelike are improvements, and additional development is needed.

The extensive literature on working memory in adults and in nonhuman primates draws important distinctions regarding the type of information that is stored (e.g., location versus identity versus order), the type of rehearsal that is possible, and the ways that stored information is used. One hopes that our description of infant working memory will eventually reflect empirical continuities and discontinuities across systematic methodological and theoretical parameters. At present, the database is too narrow and shallow to afford more than minimal conjecture on this perspective. Advances are likely to follow from good methodologies, which I would define as those that are not only valid for assessing infant working memory but also efficient and flexible. I am particularly impressed with several new procedures such as recognition of serially presented stimuli, sequential comparison, and memory for item clusters.

Finally, we must recognize that special effort is needed to assess individual differences in infant working memory ability. Age-related group differences emerge despite random errors of measurement. Individual difference effects (e.g., change and stability over time, comparisons among related abilities) are much more vulnerable to poor measurement and thus require procedural modifications such as multiple assessment and performance enhancement to minimize error. For example, Pelphrey et al. (2004) assessed infant working memory in multiple procedures administered in multiple sessions in order to obtain robust estimates of working memory capacity for each participant. Extensions of this approach are likely to be productive.

Comparisons Among Types of Memory and Other Cognitive Abilities

Various taxonomies have been introduced to distinguish among memory skills that emerge at different times and have different characteristics. For example, Nelson (1995) uses a cognitive neuroscience perspective to identify preexplicit, explicit, procedural learning, conditioning, and working memory. A general factor model of intelligence might predict strong association among different aspects of memory, but a neurological perspective would expect clear differentiation, particularly during early phases of development in which areas and functions of the brain mature at different rates. Theory leads to specific predictions regarding some aspects of memory. For example, if working memory is a necessary step toward long-term memory, there is likely to be a strong association between individual differences in these two domains. Research is needed that explores concurrent, predictive, and discriminative relations among different types of infant memory. More broadly, we need to position working memory within the broader context of cognitive abilities. Cognitive abilities such as language comprehension, imitation, selective attention, means-ends analysis, and categorization would seem to be intimately related to working memory. Other abilities like object segmentation seem less related to working memory, but few other candidates come to mind. If working memory has no discriminant validity among cognitive abilities, it veers dangerously close to the construct "intelligence."

Contrasting Typical and Atypical Development

Studies cited earlier indicate that working memory deficits are associated with various disorders such as fragile X syndrome and autism. It is possible that these deficits are merely outcomes of the disorders that can be linked to some underlying neural mechanism, but more interesting scenarios are possible. For example, if working memory is viewed as a formative problem, other symptoms such as defects of language or social cognition could emerge as outcomes of a defective working memory. From this perspective, it is interesting to ponder interventions, pharmacological or behavioral, that could affect working memory and thus ameliorate this suboptimal development.

Conclusion

Efforts to describe our cognitive capacity, and particularly our ability to store and use representations of experience, always include some form of short-term buffer that allows the present to linger and that provides a working space for analysis and planning. Researchers often differentiate short-term storage into components designated as short-term memory and working memory. We suggest that this differentiation is not relevant for infants and that research in this context is tapping working memory. The mapping of a well-established, top-down construct such as working memory on a set of ad hoc methodologies and their resultant data is a dialectic that requires flexibility and self-criticism, particularly when data from different procedures do not align. Attention to methodology and theoretical issues, with reference to higher order constructs but not predestined allegiance to those constructs, will move us beyond the current phase of description and hopefully, into a rich vein of sophisticated theoretical explanation and practical significance.

Acknowledgment

I thank Jerome Kagan, Kevin Pelphrey, Barbara Goldman, and Deb Childress for their comments on drafts of this manuscript. I also appreciate the graduate students in my spring 2005 seminar on memory development (Ilana Berman, Deb Childress, Jennie Grammer, Ned Norland, Priscilla San Souci, and Angela Wong) for teaching me so much about this topic.

Note

1. Ericsson and Kintsch (1995) used the concept *long-term working memory* to describe the mechanism that allows the maintenance of task-relevant information for a relatively long duration (e.g., for text comprehension or expert performance). From this perspective, the term *working memory* as used in this chapter is shorthand for *short-term working memory*.

References

Adams, A., & Gathercole, S. E. (1996). Phonological working memory and spoken language development in young children. *Quarterly Journal of Experimental Psychology, 49A*, 216–233.

Adams, A., & Willis, C. (2001). Language processing and working memory: A developmental perspective. In J. Andrade (Ed.), *Working memory in perspective* (pp. 79–100). Hove, UK: Psychology Press.

Ainsfeld, M. (1991). Neonatal imitation. *Developmental Review, 11*, 60–97.

Alp, E. (1994). Measuring the size of working memory in very young children: The imitation sorting task. *International Journal of Behavioral Development, 17*, 125–141.

Anderson, J. R., & Bower, G. H. (1973). *Human associative memory.* Washington, DC: Winston.

Andrade, J. (2001). The contribution of working memory to conscious experience. In J. Andrade (Ed.), *Working memory in perspective* (pp. 60–78). Hove, UK: Psychology Press.

Atkinson, R. C., & Shiffrin, R. M. (1968). Human memory: A proposed system and its control processes. In K. W. Spence & J. T. Spence (Eds.), *The psychology of learning and motivation* (Vol. 2, pp. 89–195). New York: Academic Press.

Atkinson, R. C., & Shiffrin, R. M. (1971). The control of short-term memory. *Scientific American, 225,* 82–90.

Baddeley, A. D. (1993). Working memory and conscious awareness. In A. F. Collins, S. E. Gathercole, M. A. Conwahy, & P. E. Morris (Eds.), *Theories of memory* (pp. 11–28). Hove, UK: Erlbaum.

Baddeley, A., Gathercole, S., & Papagno, C. (1998). The phonological loop as a language learning device. *Psychological Review, 105,* 158–173.

Baddeley, A. D., & Hitch, G. J. (1974). Working memory. In G. A. Bower (Ed.), *The psychology of learning and motivation* (pp. 47–89). New York: Academic Press.

Baillargeon, R. (1995). A model of physical reasoning in infancy. In C. Rovee-Collier & L. Lipsitt (Eds.), *Advances in infancy research* (Vol. 9, pp. 305–371). Norwood, NJ: Ablex.

Baillargeon, R., DeVos, J., & Graber, M. (1989). Location memory in 8-month-old infants in a non-search A-not-B task: Further evidence. *Cognitive Development, 4,* 345–367.

Baillargeon, R., & Graber, M. (1988). Evidence of location memory in 8-month-old infants in a non-search A-not-B task. *Developmental Psychology, 24,* 502–511.

Bates, E., Beninni, L., Bretherton, I., Camaioni, L., & Volterra, V. (1979). *The emergence of symbols.* New York: Academic Press.

Bates, E., Bretherton, I., & Snyder, L. (1988). *From first words to grammar.* Cambridge, UK: Cambridge University Press.

Bauer, P. J. (2002). Long-term recall memory: Behavioral and neurodevelopmental changes in the first 2 years of life. *Current Directions in Psychological Science, 11,* 137–141.

Bell, S. M. (1970). The development of the concept of the object as related to infant-mother attachment. *Child Development, 41,* 291–311.

Belleville, S., Rouleau, N., & Caza, N. (1998). Effect of normal aging on the manipulation of information in working memory. *Memory and Cognition, 26,* 572–583.

Brown, J. (1958). Some tests of the decay theory of immediate memory. *Quarterly Journal of Experimental Psychology, 10,* 12–21.

Bruner, J. S. (1975). The ontogenesis of speech acts. *Journal of Child Language, 2,* 1–19.

Chugani, H. T. (1998). A critical period of brain development: Studies of cerebral glucose utilization with PET. *Preventive Medicine, 27*(2), 184–188.

Cornoldi, C., Marconi, F., & Vecchi, T. (2001). Visuospatial working memory in Turner's syndrome. *Brain and Cognition, 46,* 90–94.

Corsi, P. M. (1972). *Human memory and the medial temporal region of the brain.* Unpublished doctoral dissertation, McGill University, Montreal.

Cowan, N. (1997). The development of working memory. In N. Cowan & C. Hulme (Eds.), *The development of memory in childhood* (pp. 163–199). Hove, UK: Psychology Press.

Cowan, N., Saults, J. S., & Elliott, E. M. (2002). The search for what is fundamental in the development of working memory. In R. Kail & H. W. Reese (Eds.), *Advances in child development and behavior* (Vol. 29, pp. 1–49). New York: Academic Press.

DeLoache, J. S., & Brown, A. L. (1979). Looking for Big Bird: Studies of memory in very young children. *Quarterly Newsletter of the Laboratory of Comparative Human Cognition, 1*, 53–57.

De Saint Victor, C., Smith, P. H., & Loboschefski, T. (1997). Ten-month-old infants' retrieval of familiar information from short-term memory. *Infant Behavior and Development, 20*, 111–122.

Diamond, A. (1985). Development of the ability to use recall to guide action, as indicated by infants' performance on A-not-B. *Child Development, 56*, 868–883.

Diamond, A., & Doar, B. (1989). The performance of human infants on a measure of frontal cortex function, the delayed-response task. *Developmental Psychobiology, 22*, 271–294.

Ellis, N. C., & Sinclair, S. G. (1996). Working memory in the acquisition of vocabulary and syntax: Putting language in good order. *Quarterly Journal of Experimental Psychology, 49A*, 234–250.

Engle, R. W., & Conway, A. R. A. (1998). Working memory and comprehension. In R. H. Logie & K. J. Gilhooly (Eds.), *Working memory and thinking* (pp. 67–91). Hove, UK: Psychology Press.

Engle, R. W., Tuholski, S. W., Laughlin, J. E., & Conway, A. R. A. (1999). Working memory, short-term memory, and general fluid intelligence: A latent-variable approach. *Journal of Experimental Psychology: General, 128*, 309–331.

Ericsson, K. A., & Kinstch, W. (1995). Long-term working memory. *Psychological Review, 102*, 211–245.

Ewing-Cobbs, L., Prasad, M. R., Landry, S. H., Kramer, L., & DeLeon, R. (2004). Executive functions following traumatic brain injury in young children: A preliminary analysis. *Developmental Neuropsychology, 26*, 487–512.

Fantz, R. L. (1956). A method for studying early visual development. *Perceptual and Motor Skills, 6*, 13–15.

Fenson, L., Dale, P., Reznick, J. S., Bates, E., Thal, D., & Pethick, S. J. (1994). Variability in early communicative development. *Monographs of the Society for Research in Child Development, 59*(5, Serial No. 242).

Funahashi, S., Bruce, C. J., & Goldman-Rakic, P. S. (1989). Mnemonic coding of visual space in the monkey's dorsolateral prefrontal cortex. *Journal of Neurophysiology, 61*(2), 331–349.

Gathercole, S. E. (1998). The development of memory. *Journal of Child and Adolescent Psychology and Psychiatry, 39*, 3–27.

Gathercole, S. E., & Baddeley, A. D. (1993). *Working memory and language*. Hove, UK: Erlbaum.

Gathercole, S. E., Hitch, G. J., Service, E., & Martin, A. J. (1997). Phonological short-term memory and new word learning in children. *Developmental Psychology, 33*, 966–979.

Gilmore, R. O., & Johnson, M. H. (1995). Working memory in infancy: Six-month-olds' performance on two versions of the oculomotor delayed response task. *Journal of Experimental Child Psychology, 59*, 397–418.

Goldman-Rakic, P. S. (1987). Circuitry of primate prefrontal cortex and regulation of behavior by representational memory. In F. Plum & V. Mountcastle (Eds.), *Handbook of physiology* (Vol. 5, pp. 373–417). Bethesda, MD: American Physiological Society.

Goodale, M. A., & Milner, A. D. (1992). Separate visual pathways for perception and actions. *Trends in Neuroscience, 15,* 20–25.

Harding, C. G., & Golinkoff, R. M. (1979). The origins of intentional vocalization in prelinguistic infants. *Child Development, 50,* 33–40.

Hartman, M., Bolton, E., & Fehnel, S. E. (2001). Accounting for age differences on the Wisconsin Card Sorting test: Decreased working memory, not inflexibility. *Psychology and Aging, 16,* 385–399.

Herschkowitz, N., Kagan, J., & Zilles, K. (1997). Neurobiological bases of behavioral development in the first year. *Neuropediatrics, 28,* 296–306.

Hofstadter, M., & Reznick, J. S. (1996). Response modality affects human infant delayed-response performance. *Child Development, 67,* 646–658.

Hunter, M. A., & Ames, E. W. (1988). A multifactor model of infant preferences for novel and familiar stimuli. In C. Rovee-Collier & L. P. Lipsitt (Eds.), *Advances in infancy research* (Vol. 5, pp. 69–95). Norwood, NJ: Ablex.

Hunter, W. S. (1913). The delayed reaction in animals and children. *Behavior Monographs, 2,* 1–86.

Hunter, W. S. (1917). The delayed reaction in a child. *Psychological Review, 24,* 74–87.

Huttenlocher, J., Newcombe, N., & Sandberg, E. (1994). The coding of spatial location in young children. *Cognitive Psychology, 27,* 115–147.

Huttenlocher, P. R., & Dabholkar, A. S. (1997). Developmental anatomy of prefrontal cortex. In N. A. Krasnegor, G. R. Lyon, & P. S. Goldman-Rakic (Eds.), *Development of the prefrontal cortex: Evolution, neurobiology, and behavior* (pp. 69–83). Baltimore: Paul H. Brookes.

James, T. W., Culham, J., Humphrey, G. K., Milner, A. D., & Goodale, M. A. (2003). Ventral occipital lesions impair object recognition but not object-directed grasping: An fMRI study. *Brain, 126,* 2463–2475.

James, W. J. (1981). *The principles of psychology, Volume 1.* Cambridge, MA: Harvard University Press. (Original work published 1890)

Jarrold, C., Baddeley, A. D., & Phillips, C. (1999). Down syndrome and the phonological loop: The evidence for, and importance of, a specific verbal short-term memory deficit. *Down Syndrome: Research and Practice, 6,* 61–75.

Just, M. A., Carpenter, P. A., & Keller, T. A. (1996). The capacity theory of comprehension: New frontiers of evidence and arguments. *Psychological Review, 103,* 773–780.

Kagan, J. (1981). *The second year.* Cambridge, MA: Harvard University Press.

Kail, R., & Hall, L. K. (2001). Distinguishing short-term memory from working memory. *Memory and Cognition, 29,* 1–9.

Knox, H. A. (1913). The differentiation between moronism and ignorance. *New York Medical Journal, 98,* 564–566.

Lanfranchi, S., Cornoldi, C., & Vianello, R. (2004). Verbal and visuospatial working memory deficits in children with Down syndrome. *American Journal on Mental Retardation, 109,* 456–466.

Logie, R. H., & Pearson, D. G. (1997). The inner eye and the inner scribe of visuo-spatial working memory: Evidence from developmental fractionation. *European Journal of Cognitive Psychology, 9,* 241–257.

Luck, S. J., & Vogel, E. K. (1997). The capacity of visual working memory for features and conjunctions. *Nature, 390,* 279–281.

Lustig, C., May, C. P., & Hasher, L. (2001). Working memory span and the role of proactive interference. *Journal of Experimental Psychology: General, 130,* 199–207.

Marcus, G. F., Vijayan, S., Rao, S. B., & Vishton, P. M. (1999). Rule learning by seven-month-old infants. *Science, 283,* 77–80.

McCall, R. B., & Kagan, J. (1967). Attention in the infant: Effects of complexity, contour, perimeter, and familiarity. *Child Development, 38,* 939–952.

Meltzoff, A. N. (1985). Immediate and deferred imitation in 14- and 24-month-old infants. *Child Development, 56,* 62–72.

Meltzoff, A. N., & Moore, M. K. (1983). Newborn infants imitate adult facial gestures. *Child Development, 54,* 702–709.

Miller, G. A., Galanter, E., & Pribram, K. H. (1960). *Plans and the structure of behavior.* New York: Holt, Reinhart and Winston.

Milner, A. D., & Goodale, M. A. (1995). *The visual brain in actions.* Oxford: Oxford University Press.

Moore, M. K., & Meltzoff, A. N. (2004). Object permanence after a 24-hr delay and leaving the locale of disappearance: The role of memory, space, and identity. *Developmental Psychology, 40,* 606–620.

Mosier, C. E., & Rogoff, B. (1994). Infants' instrumental use of their mothers to achieve their goals. *Child Development, 65,* 70–79.

Mottron, L., Belleville, S., & Menard, E. (1999). Local bias in autistic subjects as evidenced by graphic tasks: Perceptual hierarchization or working memory deficit? *Journal of Child Psychology and Psychiatry and Allied Disciplines, 40,* 743–755.

Munir, F., Cornish, K. M., & Wilding, J. (2000). Nature of the working memory deficit in Fragile-X syndrome. *Brain and Cognition, 44,* 387–401.

Nairne, J. S. (2002). Remembering over the short-term: The case against the standard model. *Annual Review of Psychology, 53,* 53–81.

Nelson, C. A. (1995). The ontogeny of human memory: A cognitive neuroscience perspective. *Developmental Psychology, 31,* 723–738.

Nelson, C. A., Monk, C. S., Lin, J., Carver, L. J., Thomas, K. M., & Truwit, C. L. (2000). Functional neuroanatomy of spatial working memory in children. *Developmental Psychology, 36,* 109–116.

Newcombe, N., Huttenlocher, J., & Learmonth, A. (1999). Infants' coding of location in continuous space. *Infant Behavior and Development, 22,* 483–510.

O'Reilly, R. C., Braver, T. S., & Cohen, J. D. (1999). A biologically based computational model of working memory. In A. Miyake & P. Shah (Eds.), *Models of working memory: Mechanisms of active maintenance and executive control* (pp. 375–411). Cambridge, UK: Cambridge University Press.

Pelphrey, K. A., & Reznick, J. S. (2003). Working memory in infancy. In R. Kail (Ed.), *Advances in child development and behavior* (Vol. 31, pp. 173–227). New York: Academic Press.

Pelphrey, K. A., Reznick, J. S., Goldman, B. D., Sasson, N., Morrow, J., Donahoe, A., et al. (2004). Development of visuospatial short-term memory in the second half of the first year. *Developmental Psychology, 40,* 836–851.

Peterson, L. R., & Peterson, M. J. (1959). Short-term retention of individual verbal items. *Journal of Experimental Psychology, 58*, 193–198.

Phillips, L. H., & Forshaw, M. J. (1998). The role of working memory in age differences in reasoning. In R. H. Logie & K. J. Gilhooly (Eds.), *Working memory and thinking* (pp. 23–43). Hove, UK: Psychology Press.

Piaget, J. (1962). *Play, dreams, and imitation in childhood.* New York: Norton.

Pickering, S. J. (2001). The development of visuo-spatial working memory. *Memory, 9*, 423–432.

Reznick, J. S. (1999). Influences on maternal attribution of infant intentionality. In P. D. Zelazo & J. W. Astington (Eds.), *Developing theories of intention: Social understanding and self-control* (pp. 243–267). Mahwah, NJ: Erlbaum.

Reznick, J. S., Corley, R., & Robinson, J. (1997). A longitudinal twin study of intelligence in the second year. *Monographs of the Society for Research in Child Development, 62*(1, Serial No. 249).

Reznick, J. S., Morrow, J. D., Goldman, B. D., & Snyder, J. (2004) The onset of working memory in infants. *Infancy, 6,* 145–154.

Rose, S. A., Feldman, J. F., & Jankowski, J. J. (2001). Visual short-term memory in the first year of life: Capacity and recency effects. *Developmental Psychology, 37,* 539–549.

Rose, S. A., Feldman, J. F., & Jankowski, J. J. (2003). Infant visual recognition memory: Independent contributions of speed and attention. *Developmental Psychology, 39,* 563–571.

Ross-Sheehy, S., Oakes, L. M., & Luck, S. J. (2003). The development of visual short-term memory capacity in infants. *Child Development, 74*, 1807–1822.

Saffran, J. R., Aslin, R. N., & Newport, E. L. (1996). Statistical learning by 8-month-old infants. *Science, 274,* 1926.

Salthouse, T. A. (1996). The processing-speed theory of adult age differences in cognition. *Psychological Review, 103,* 403–428.

Schwartz, B. B., & Reznick, J. S. (1999). Measuring infant spatial working memory with a windows and curtains delayed-response procedure. *Memory, 7,* 1–17.

Smith, E. E. (2000). Neural bases of human working memory. *Current Directions in Psychological Science, 9,* 45–49.

Sternberg, S. (1966). High speed scanning in human memory. *Science, 153,* 652–654.

Ungerleider, L. G., & Mishkin, M. (1982). Two cortical visual systems. In D. J. Ingle, M. A. Goodale, & R. J. Mansfield (Eds.), *Analysis of visual behavior* (pp. 549–586). Cambridge, MA: MIT Press.

Vicari, S., Caravale, B., Carlesimo, G. A., Casadei, A. M., & Allemand, F. (2004). Spatial working memory deficits in children at ages 3–4 who were low birth weight, preterm infants. *Neuropsychology, 18*, 673–678.

Wilcox, T., Nadel, L., & Rosser, R. (1996). Location memory in healthy preterm and full-term infants. *Infant Behavior and Development, 19,* 309–323.

Willatts, P. (1984). Stages in the development of intentional search by young infants. *Developmental Psychology, 20,* 389–396.

Willatts, P. (1999). Development of means-end behavior in young infants: Pulling a support to retrieve a distant object. *Developmental Psychology, 35,* 651–667.

Zelazo, P. D., Carter, A., Reznick, J. S., & Frye, D. (1997). Early development of executive function: A problem-solving framework. *General Psychology Review, 1,* 198–226.

2

Individual Differences in the Development of Working Memory During Infancy

MARTHA ANN BELL AND KATHERINE C. MORASCH

Developmental scientists have produced data to demonstrate that the prefrontal cortex has a prolonged developmental pattern relative to other brain areas and may not be physiologically mature until young adulthood (Davis, Segalowitz, & Gavin, 2004; Diamond, 2001; Huttenlocher, 1994; Nelson, 1995; Sowell, Thompson, Tessner, & Toga, 2001). This prolonged period of development gives researchers a wide window during which to examine the functional emergence and development of prefrontally mediated cognitive behaviors. Indeed, in the last few years there has been increasing focus on prefrontal cognitive behaviors during early and later childhood (Diamond, Prevor, Callender, & Druin, 1997; Luciana & Nelson, 1998; Segalowitz & Davis, 2004; Wolfe & Bell, 2004). Cognitive skills associated with prefrontal brain areas allow children to keep two or more rules in mind, update memory with constantly changing information, sustain attention over a brief period of time in the face of distraction, and suppress a dominant response tendency (Gerstadt, Hong, & Diamond, 1994), much as adults do on classic prefrontal tasks. Developmental neuroscience studies have shown, however, that the frontal cortex is active and maturing as early as the last half of the first postnatal year (Bell & Fox, 1992; Chugani, 1994). As such, the foundations of these higher order cognitive processes that are developing during early and later childhood may be manifested during infancy. The many skills involved in successful performance on infant delayed-memory search tasks, such as delayed response and A-not-B, may form the foundations of these childhood prefrontal functions (Bell & Adams, 1999; Diamond, 1990; Diamond et al., 1997; Kane & Engle, 2002).

The purpose of this chapter is to examine the development of prefrontal function by focusing on the emergence and progression of the foundations of working memory during infancy. The prefrontal cortex has multiple subdivisions and working memory is a cognitive skill that appears to underlie functioning across all of these prefrontal areas (Duncan & Owen, 2000; Goldman-Rakic, 1987; Levy & Goldman-Rakic, 2000; Luciana & Nelson, 1998). Of course, like other brain areas, the prefrontal cortex does not work in isolation. This area of the brain serves to moderate the activity of other brain areas, such as superior temporal cortex, posterior parietal cortex, anterior cingulate, and others. Prefrontal cortex also receives information from these other areas and, thus, is modulated by this information (Diamond, 2001). Thus, although it is widely accepted that prefrontal cortex plays a vital role in working memory, other brain areas are involved as well (Levy & Goldman-Rakic, 2000).

In our examination of prefrontal function, we highlight our own research on the development of working memory, as well as selectively review the work of others. Our research takes a decidedly psychobiological approach to the study of working memory development as we examine not only task behaviors but also brain electrical activity before and during task performance. The focus of our research program is on individual differences in frontal lobe development, with an emphasis on working memory. Thus, in this chapter we concentrate on some factors we have found to be associated with variations in the development of this type of short-term memory. In the spirit of this volume, we organize our examination of working memory during infancy around the questions outlined in the introduction by the editors of this volume.

What Kind of Memory Are We Studying?

The construct of infant working memory has its basis in traditional cognitive psychology, and perhaps the best known model of working memory is that described by Baddeley and Hitch (1974). Simply put, working memory is defined as an active system for temporarily storing and manipulating information (Baddeley, 1986, 2000; Baddeley & Hitch, 1974). Baddeley's multicomponent model of working memory consists of four aspects—the central executive, the phonological loop, the visuospatial sketchpad, and the episodic buffer. Within this model, the memory processing function is ascribed to the central executive, which provides the interface with information in long-term memory and also coordinates the distribution of the limited resources throughout the memory system by means of attentional control. Memory storage capabilities are disseminated to the phonological loop and the visuospatial sketchpad, whereas the episodic buffer, a recent addition to the original working memory model, encodes, integrates, and retrieves information in the form of conscious awareness (Baddeley, 2000). As we note later in this chapter, working memory tasks are usually delineated along verbal and spatial categories, indicative of the two storage components. Furthermore, verbal and spatial aspects of working memory are uncorrelated, with this functional independence true for children as well as adults (Gathercole, Pickering, Ambridge, & Wearing, 2004).

The construct of working memory has been the focus of a great deal of attention in the adult cognitive literature, and with good reason. Working memory is an essential component for everyday adult cognition because it underlies higher order cognitive processes such as reasoning, planning, cognitive control, problem solving, and decision making (Logie, 1993). Furthermore, individual difference measures of working memory in adulthood are predictive of language comprehension, learning, and fluid intelligence (see Kane & Engle, 2003, for a review).

Engle's Model of Working Memory

In our research program, we focus on the construct of working memory as refined by Engle and colleagues (Barrett, Tugade, & Engle, 2004; Engle, Kane, & Tuholski, 1999; Kane & Engle, 2002, 2003; Unsworth, Schrock, & Engle, 2004). Engle defines working memory as a system consisting of those highly activated long-term memory traces that are active above threshold as short-term memory representational components. Included in this characterization of working memory are the procedures and skills necessary to achieve and maintain that activation, as well as a limited-capacity, domain-free controlled attention component. This executive attention component is perhaps the most intriguing part of Engle's conceptualization of working memory. Although Baddeley's model incorporates a central executive form of attentional control, the focus of the Baddeley model is mainly on the storage capabilities of the phonological loop and visuospatial sketchpad. Engle's focus is on the attentional component.

The attentional capacity highlighted by Engle and colleagues is the capability of maintaining short-term memory representations in the presence of interference or response competition. Without this interference, information, goals, and response plans are easily retrieved from long-term memory. In the face of interference, however, it is likely that incorrect information and inaccurate responses are retrieved (Kane & Engle, 2002). Thus, this executive attention component is not needed for all cognitive processing, but is called into action in circumstances that require inhibition of prepotent responses, error monitoring and correction, and decision making and planning (Engle et al., 1999; Unsworth et al., 2004). As would be expected, this domain-free executive attention ability can be used to predict performance on higher order cognitive tasks (Kane & Engle, 2002).

It is precisely this predictive ability that is the focus of Engle's research. Individual differences in executive attention, called working memory capacity by Engle and colleagues (Engle et al., 1999; Kane & Engle, 2002, 2003; Unsworth et al., 2004), are associated with a wide variety of cognitive abilities, including general fluid intelligence (Engle et al., 1999). It should be emphasized that individual differences in executive attention are revealed only in situations that encourage or require controlled attention. Thus, the individual differences perspective in Engle's model reflects the ability of the individual to apply activation to short-term memory representations, to bring these representations into focus and maintain them, and to do so in the face of interference or distraction (Engle et al., 1999; Kane & Engle, 2003). This suggests that individuals high in this controlled attention ability are more effective at blocking distracting, task-irrelevant information and maintaining a focus on pertinent information than individuals low in attention. Indeed, individuals ranked low on this attentional ability are more likely to break focus and orient to an irrelevant, attention-capturing external cue (Unsworth et al., 2004). Based on human and nonhuman primate literatures, Engle has hypothesized that individual differences in attentional control (i.e., working memory capacity) are associated with individual differences in the functioning of the prefrontal cortex (Engle et al., 1999; Kane & Engle, 2002).These individual differences are considered to be a characteristic of the individual person and do not result from experience (Engle et al., 1999).

Engle asserts that his model is appropriate for research with children (Engle et al., 1999). Indeed, we use Engle's model of working memory because it includes the processes associated with controlled attention such as inhibitory control of prepotent responses, specifies the role of the prefrontal cortex in the process of working memory, and allows for individual differences in working memory based on both the capacity for controlled attention and differences in prefrontal functioning. These individual differences are the focus of our developmental work with infants, and we will return to Engle's model and the notion of controlled attention when we discuss possible mechanisms for individual differences in infant working memory later in this chapter.

How Is Working Memory Measured?

Adult working memory tasks used in research studies are traditionally divided into categories relating to the two storage components of Baddeley's model: verbal working memory and spatial working memory. As noted previously, performance on tasks in these two domains is uncorrelated (Gathercole et al., 2004).

Memory-span tasks classically assess verbal working memory by requiring research participants to remember words while also reading a string of unrelated sentences. The task is also accomplished by having participants listen to the sentences as opposed to reading them. Usually the words to be remembered are the last word of each sentence. A variation of the memory-span task is to have participants solve math problems while remembering words. In this instance, the words to be remembered are presented following each math problem. In each type of memory-span task, the individual must activate short-term memory representations (i.e., keep the words to be remembered in short-term memory), bring these representations into focus and maintain them, and do so in the face of interference or distraction (the sentences or math problems). Responses may either be oral or written (i.e., paper or computer). These are the types of tasks used to assess working memory capacity, the specific focus of Engle's refinement of the classic working memory construct (Kane & Engle, 2002).

Delayed memory tasks usually assess spatial working memory and include the delayed response task, which is perhaps the most consistently used measure of prefrontal functioning (Diamond, 2001; Luciana & Nelson, 1998). The delayed response task has been employed in research with non-human primates, as well as with adults with frontal lobe damage, making it a highly desirable task to use with nonverbal populations. During this task, the research participants are required to remember spatial information across a delay period and update memory representations of that information from trial to trial. As further distraction, participants are not allowed to maintain attentional focus to the spatial information during the delay.

Classic Working Memory Tasks for Infants

As might be expected, delayed memory tasks also are used to assess spatial working memory with nonverbal human infants (e.g., Bell, 2001, 2002; Bell & Fox, 1992, 1997; Diamond, 1985, 1990; Gilmore & Johnson, 1995; Reznick, Morrow, Goldman, & Snyder, 2004; see also chapter 1, this volume). Thus, the classic delayed response task used with nonhuman primates and with brain-damaged human adults, as well as the corollary Piagetian A-not-B task, are the working memory tasks of choice for infant researchers. Working memory allows the infant to maintain online information about where an object is hidden, to update that information on each trial of the task, and to inhibit the prepotent response of reaching or looking to previously rewarded locations. Imposition of a delay increases the interference involved in maintaining and updating spatial memory.

Diamond (1990) reported that both human infants and nonhuman primate infants demonstrated identical developmental progression on delayed response and A-not-B. This was demonstrated in longitudinal assessments from 7.5 months to 12 months of age in human infants and from 50 days to 125 days of age in infant monkeys. The two tasks are very similar, with the only difference being the rule for deciding in which of two hiding wells an attractive toy is to be hidden. In the A-not-B task, the toy is hidden in the same-side well until the infant correctly reaches for the hidden toy for a specified consecutive number of times (usually twice or three times). Then the toy is hidden in the opposite-side well and the pattern is repeated.

Assessment ceases when the infant reaches toward the incorrect side in two reversal, or opposite-well, trials. In delayed response, the hiding pattern varies according to a predetermined schedule regardless of whether or not the infant reaches correctly on any one trial. Assessment ceases when the experimenter reaches the end of the schedule. Thus, the pattern of hidings for A-not-B is infant driven, whereas the pattern of hidings for delayed response is experimenter driven. Again, we emphasize that infants demonstrate identical developmental progression on A-not-B and delayed response (Diamond, 1990). In our research lab, we have always used the A-not-B version of the delayed memory task because of its long tradition in the developmental psychology literature (Wellman, Cross, & Bartsch, 1986). As noted previously, delayed response was originally used with nonhuman primates and brain-damaged human adults, so when we began our work with human infants, fewer human infant delayed response studies were available for comparison.

Because these are delayed memory tasks, it is typical for the mother to hold her infant's hands while the experimenter calls the infant's name to briefly divert the infant's gaze from the hiding site. Under very brief delay conditions, immediately after diverting the infant's gaze the examiner asks, "Where's the toy?" or otherwise allows the infants to search for the hidden toy. Under longer delay conditions, the mother holds the infant's hands while the experimenter calls the infant's name, claps her hands, and counts out the delay period to divert the infant's gaze from the hiding site. After the delay period, the experimenter asks, "Where's the toy?" or otherwise allows the infant to search. Diamond (1985) argued that a distractor to break the infant's gaze is necessary because visual fixation to the correct well can be used to simplify the A-not-B task. Maintaining visual fixation negates the use of working memory.

There are several different ways to score infant performance on these delayed memory tasks, and we have used three in our own research studies using the A-not-B task. One of the most common scoring procedures is to report the maximum amount of delay under which infants can reach correctly on the B (i.e., reversal) trials, or the amount of delay needed in order to observe incorrect reaches on B reversal trials (e.g., Bell & Fox, 1992; Diamond, 1985). Of course, use of this method requires that infants are able to uncover a hidden object, as well as reach correctly when presented with two initial hiding locations on the A trials. Thus, this scoring method yields no data for infants who are just beginning to uncover a completely hidden object or for infants who are successful in searching with only one hiding location.

Second, infants may be assessed on the percentage of correct reaches across the entire testing session, either combining A trials and B trials or calculating separate percentages for each (e.g., Bell, 2002, 2004; Bell & Adams, 1999; Hofstadter & Reznick, 1996). This method would distinguish infants who can uncover a hidden object from infants who cannot yet do so.

Finally, some researchers use an ordinal scale that takes into account a wide range of performance from inability to uncover a completely hidden object to success on the B reversal trials even after a long delay (e.g., Bell, 2001; Bell & Fox, 1997; Kermoian & Campos, 1988). This is an example of an ordinal scale that we have used (Bell & Adams, 1999):

1. Object partially covered with one cloth (i.e., one hiding site)
2. Object completely covered with one cloth (i.e., one hiding site)
3. Object hidden under one of two identical cloths
4. A-not-B with 0 delay
5. A-not-B with 2-second delay
6. A-not-B with 4-second delay

An advantage of the ordinal scale is that performance among 8-month-old infants is normally distributed across these scale levels (Bell & Adams, 1999; Figure 1, p. 231). Variability in performance is crucial to any examination of individual differences.

As seen from this description of A-not-B and delayed response, the delayed memory tasks assessing spatial working memory are necessarily different from memory span tasks used to assess verbal working memory. Because of this, Russell (1998) questioned the capability of the traditional A-not-B task, and thus the delayed response task as well, to accurately assess the construct of working memory. Actually, it is Munakata's (1998) account of the A-not-B task that Russell questioned. As noted, working memory requires refreshing old information while performing operations on new information. Munakata proposed that old memory traces must be suppressed so that novel information can be attended to. Using that explanation of the cognitions required for this delayed memory task, Russell (1998) commented that infant working memory cannot be assessed using the traditional A-not-B task because working memory models traditionally do not call for the suppression of old memory; rather, it must be kept updated in the face of constantly changing information. Russell noted that the A-not-B task with invisible displacement would be a better example of an infant task requiring working memory. During invisible displacement, the infant must keep in memory that an occluded object has been moved from site A to site B under a cup and then use that old information to search under the most recent hiding site.

On the other hand, Engle and colleagues have argued that delayed memory tasks (and they specifically mention delayed response) do involve working memory (Engle et al., 1999; Kane & Engle, 2002). Tasks like the traditional delayed response and its corollary A-not-B require that attention be drawn away from the to-be-recalled information during the delay (i.e., visual gaze is broken). Some infant researchers implement even more distraction by counting out the delay in addition to breaking the infant's gaze to the hiding site (i.e., Bell, 2001; Bell & Fox, 1992, 1997; Diamond, 1985). These types of distractions are not used in short-term memory tasks that require immediate recall. Thus, Engle and colleagues argue that the delayed memory tasks are analogous to the memory span tasks because both types of tasks require that the stimulus be maintained for use in the presence of distraction from the environment as well as in the presence of interference from information from the previous trial (Kane & Engle, 2002). In other words, both types of tasks require working memory.

Contemporary Working Memory Tasks for Infants

A recent advance in working memory methodology with human infants is the creation of a visuospatial working memory task that is considered a valid measure of working memory ability. Looking tasks during infancy, as opposed to reaching tasks (like A-not-B and delayed response), were once assumed to be easier and thus more likely to yield better performance or, even more so, better performance at much younger ages (e.g., Ahmed & Ruffman, 1998; Baillargeon & Graber, 1988). Unfortunately, in many developmental research studies, task differences between the looking and reaching tasks have been so vast as to make direct comparisons of performance unreliable.

Diamond provided the basic behavioral neuroscience evidence that maturation of the dorsolateral prefrontal cortex and corresponding skills of working memory and inhibitory control are major contributors to classic reaching performance on the A-not-B, as well as the delayed response tasks (Diamond, 2001; Diamond et al., 1997). We reasoned that the very same skills of working memory and inhibitory control would be needed on looking versions of the same task and we also added the skill of attention to the mix. Because cognitive skills are the same, with only response modality being different, performance on a reaching version of the A-not-B task should be comparable to a looking version of the task (Bell & Adams, 1999).

At that time, there were two research teams who had compared performance on the classic reaching version of infant working memory with performance on a looking version of the task. The first study used the delayed response version of the working memory task and the second study used the A-not-B version of the task. As noted previously, Diamond (1990) demonstrated identical developmental progression on these two tasks. In a between-subjects design, Hofstadter and Reznick (1996) reported that a cross-sectional group of infants (ages 5, 7, 9, and 11 months) were more likely to search at the correct well on the looking version of delayed response at each age relative to a same-age group of infants' performance on the reaching version. The same testing apparatus was used for each group of infants, with modifications to prevent the infants in the looking group from touching the wells. In spite of the premise that the looking task would be easier, infants did tend to make some search errors during the looking response. Hofstadter and Reznick suggested that looking and reaching may be alternative assessments of the same cognitive construct and, thus, can be considered to be different aspects of the same biological system. Further, they suggested that the pathways from prefrontal cortex that control reaching may be more vulnerable than the pathways from the prefrontal cortex that control looking, thus accounting for more reaching errors.

Whereas Hofstadter and Reznick (1996) reported better performance on a looking version of their working memory task than on the reaching version, this finding is not consistent with the other study comparing reaching and looking. Matthews, Ellis, and Nelson (1996) used a longitudinal design to compare full-term and preterm infants' performance on a battery of cognitive measures that included the classic reaching A-not-B task and a looking version of the task. In contrast to Hofstadter and Reznick, these researchers reported that performance on the looking and reaching versions of the working memory task was essentially the same at each age from approximately 6.5 to 14 months. That is, there was no advantage in performance with the looking version of the task in their longitudinal study. Because of this finding, Matthews et al. (1996) questioned the assumption that looking and reaching in the A-not-B task proceed from different underlying representations. Specifically, they questioned the notion that looking is a more accurate reflection of knowledge, whereas reaching is contaminated from representations of previous trials, a popular hypothesis about infant cognition a few years ago.

Thus, the two studies that had compared reaching and looking performance had different outcomes. It may be, however, that the between-subjects design used by Hofstadter and Reznick (1996) explains the results. As we discuss in the next section, there are several accounts in the developmental literature of individual differences in A-not-B performance among same-age infants (e.g., Bell & Fox, 1992, 1997; Diamond, 1985). Because performance is so variable among same-age infants, we have argued that it is imperative that the research design examining looking performance relative to reaching performance utilize within-subjects methodology (Bell & Adams, 1999).

We were able to support our arguments with data from two cohorts of 8-month-old infants using within-subjects methodology. In each cohort, performance on looking and reaching versions of the A-not-B task was comparable (Bell & Adams, 1999). Performance of individual infants on the looking and reaching scales was examined, and 24% of the infants had duplicate scores on the looking and reaching versions of the task. Similarly, 73% of the infants had looking and reaching scores that were within one ordinal scale level of each other. (We detailed our ordinal scale in a previous paragraph.) In contrast, 11% scored higher on the looking version relative to the reaching version by at least two scale levels, and 16% scored higher on the reaching version by at least two scale levels.

Reznick and colleagues (Pelphrey et al., 2004; chapter 1, this volume) examined the development of working memory in 5.5- to 12-month-old infants using several delayed-memory delayed response tasks. Two tasks manipulated the delay between hiding and search (one requiring a looking response and one requiring a reaching response) and two other tasks challenged the infant with multiple hiding locations (one requiring a look response and one requiring a reach response). When examining the comparability of the test modality within this within-subject research design, working memory performance did not differ for the looking or reaching responses. Thus, the researchers who have utilized a within-subjects research design have all reported no differences in infant working memory between looking and reaching versions of the task. Likewise, Diamond (1995) noted that infant performance on looking and reaching versions of a short-term recognition memory task is similar across task modality. Indeed, the long-held notion that looking may be a better indicator of cognitive ability than reaching is now being questioned in the developmental literature (e.g., Smith, Thelen, Titzer, & McLin, 1999).

How Do We Measure Individual Differences in Working Memory?

As noted at the beginning of this chapter, the focus of our research program is on individual differences in frontal lobe development, and the frontal construct we examine is working memory. In the initial publication of her longitudinal study of A-not-B in human infants, Diamond (1985) noted that errors reaching to the B site on reversal trials occurred at a 10-second delay at 12 months of age. A look at her data (Table 4, p. 877) shows a range of 5 to 12 seconds, demonstrating that a wide range of individual differences led to a group mean of 10 seconds. Our own longitudinal work demonstrates a similar A-not-B error delay range at 12 months of age (2–14 seconds; Bell & Fox, 1992). Thus, this type of delayed memory task yields great variability in performance among infants.

Baseline EEG and Individual Differences in Infant Working Memory

Our initial studies of individual differences in infant working memory utilized baseline electroencephalogram (EEG) recordings as a marker of brain development. There is a rich infant literature dating back to the early 1930s that traces developmental patterns in brain development using baseline EEG recordings (see Bell, 1998, in press, for reviews of this literature). More recent research pairs these baseline recordings with behaviors known to likewise demonstrate developmental patterns and then draw conclusions regarding brain–behavior relations. Baseline EEG recordings are made while the infant is at rest on a parent's lap, or perhaps in an infant chair. In reality, it is the rare infant who will calmly sit on a parent's lap during a baseline EEG recording, so we present the infant with interesting visual information (bouncing balls) to capture attention and aid the infant in sitting still for a brief (1–2 minute) recording. Baseline recordings were used in our initial studies because we concentrated on the reaching version of the A-not-B infant working memory task, and the gross motor movements associated with reaching overwhelm the EEG signal, rendering it full of motor artifact rather than a useful recording of scalp electrical activity.

In a longitudinal study, we have reported that changes in baseline frontal EEG power values from 7 to 12 months of age are associated with changes in reaching spatial working memory (i.e., A-not-B) performance during that same age period (Bell & Fox, 1992). EEG power reflects the excitability of groups of neurons. In the classic infant EEG literature, increasing power values across age are considered a marker of brain maturation (see Bell, 1998, in press; Bell & Fox, 1994, for reviews of this literature). In our study, infants tolerating long delays between hiding of the object and actual manual search by 12 months of age showed changes across age from 7 to 12 months in baseline frontal EEG power. Infants tolerating only short delays by 12 months of age did not. Also, infants tolerating longer delays by 12 months of age exhibited greater left occipital EEG power relative to right occipital power across the entire 6 months of the study. Thus, successful reaching performance in this longitudinal study was associated with age-related changes in frontal EEG power and consistently greater left hemisphere EEG power for occipital EEG power.

In an age-held-constant study, we reported that individual differences in baseline frontal EEG among 8-month-old infants were related to differences in performance on a reaching A-not-B working memory task (Bell & Fox, 1997). Specifically, higher levels of task performance were associated with greater EEG power values at the frontal scalp locations. Higher performance was also associated with a frontal asymmetry, as infants in the high-performance group exhibited greater right frontal EEG power values relative to their left frontal power values. As in the longitudinal study, we reported occipital EEG differences between performance groups, with higher levels of performance associated with greater occipital EEG power values. Thus, it appears that at least in baseline EEG recordings, frontal as well as occipital power values are associated with reaching spatial working memory performance.

Task-Related EEG and Individual Differences in Infant Working Memory

Our initial work necessarily utilized baseline EEG recordings because the gross motor movements required by a reaching task negate the use of task-related EEG recordings. Typical adult protocols do not require gross motor movements during cognitive processing, however. Thus, in the adult psychophysiological literature, EEG is recorded while research participants are engaged in cognitive problems (e.g., Bell & Fox, 2003) and comparisons are made between baseline and task EEG. This task-related EEG gives a more accurate reflection of brain involvement with task performance because it reflects actual neuronal activity associated with cognitive processing. Change in the amount of electrical activity at a specific scalp location from baseline to task is considered indicative of the cortical areas involved in task performance. The EEG has high temporal resolution and is relatively inexpensive and easy to use with infants and children. These characteristics make it a highly desirable brain imaging technique for use with young populations and for relating brain development to changes in behavior (Casey & de Haan, 2002; Taylor & Baldeweg, 2002).

Recall that using a within-subjects research design, we demonstrated comparable performance on reaching and looking delayed-memory A-not-B tasks with two different groups of 8-month-old infants (Bell & Adams, 1999). That study paved the way for utilizing task-related EEG recordings during the infant working memory task where we recorded EEG from 8-month-old infants during baseline and task (Bell, 2001, 2002). Of particular interest was a change in EEG power values from baseline to task because this would be indicative of cortical involvement. In our initial study, only infants with high performance on the looking version of the working memory task exhibited changes in EEG power from baseline to task; the low performers showed no change in EEG from baseline to task. These task-related changes were evident at frontal and posterior scalp locations (Bell, 2001). These data confirmed our previous cognitive neuroscience work associating frontal and posterior function with cognitive performance levels during infancy and strengthened our position that better performance was associated with greater brain maturation.

More intriguing from a neuropsychological point of view is that the EEG recorded during task performance was highly informative (Bell, 2002). We are able to event-mark the EEG record to indicate various aspects of our looking working memory task. For example, when we are displaying the toy to the infant to get her to look at it prior to hiding, we mark that particular portion of the EEG record and label it as the attention component of the task. After the toy is hidden, we break the infant's gaze to the hiding site and count a delay to add further distraction before we allow her to make an eye movement to indicate the toy's location ("Where's the toy?"). We mark this section as the memory component of the task. Finally, when we indicate to the infant that her choice was either correct or incorrect, varying our own facial expression and tone of voice, and show her that the toy is indeed where she looked, or is not, that portion of the record we mark as the reward. We have already shown that the EEG changes from baseline to task. We have been able to further distinguish among the three stages of cognitive activity: attention, memory, and reward. The EEG was most active during the memory portion of the task, the most cognitively challenging phase. Most important, and most exciting for us, was that the EEG distinguished between correct and incorrect eye movement responses (Bell, 2002). These are all findings that are possible only with task-related EEG.

We have completed data collection on a longitudinal study in which we examined the simultaneous development of performance on the reaching and looking versions of the A-not-B working memory task from 5 to 10 months of age (Bell, 2006). The behavioral data from that study are briefly described in the next section. We have just begun to examine the EEG data collecting during the looking working memory task. Specifically, we want to know if these task-related EEG findings that we have just reported are specific to EEG data and working memory tasks at 8 months of age or whether these brain–behavior relations are apparent in both younger and older infants.

How Does Working Memory Develop During the First Postnatal Year?

Two overarching principles underlie the development of infant working memory. Performance on infant working memory tasks increases with age and decreases with challenge (most often demonstrated by increasing the delay between presentation and search). Spatial working memory, as defined by performance on delayed-memory tasks, has been shown to emerge somewhere between 5 and 8 months of age in studies utilizing longitudinal as well as cross-sectional methodology. Working memory performance has been demonstrated to linearly improve until 12 months of age, the usual time when data collection ceases in infant working memory studies utilizing the A-not-B and delayed response tasks (Bell & Fox, 1992; Diamond, 1985; Diamond et al., 1997).

In an elegant longitudinal examination of the development of working memory during infancy, Diamond (1985) demonstrated how very tight manipulations of the delay imposed between hiding and search demonstrates the progression of working memory development. Twenty-five infants were assessed biweekly from 6 to 12 months of age using the classic Piagetian reaching A-not-B task and the amount of delay tolerated increased at a rate of about 2 seconds per month. Diamond reported that in general, infants were able to tolerate a 10-second delay without making errors on the B or reversal trials by their first birthday. More important, infants who made the reaching error on the B trials at a specific delay demonstrated correct performance when the imposed delay was decreased by 2 to 3 seconds on the next set of trials. Likewise, infants who made the classic B error at a specific delay (meaning that they erred only on the B side) demonstrated deteriorated performance when the imposed delay was increased by 2 to 3 seconds (meaning that they erred on the A side as well). Thus, a very narrow range of delay was required to demonstrate the A-not-B error. This characteristic appears to lend credence to the use of this type of delayed memory task to assess the rudiments of working memory during infancy.

We likewise used increasing delays in our own longitudinal assessment of spatial working memory (using the A-not-B task) and baseline EEG reported previously in this chapter (Bell & Fox, 1992). Like Diamond, we reported linear improvement between 7 and 12 months on the infant working memory task with imposed delay. Our findings were specific to a subset of infants, however. Infants who demonstrated age-related changes in frontal EEG activity showed these linear improvements in working memory performance. That is, with age, these infants became more robust to task challenges, such as an increasingly long delay between presentation and search. We interpreted these data as evidence that frontal lobe maturation is a contributing factor to individual differences in the development of working memory across the second half of the first postnatal year.

Reznick and colleagues (Pelphrey et al., 2004; chapter 1, this volume) examined the development of delayed response working memory in infants using several delayed response tasks. Two tasks manipulated the delay between presentation and search (one requiring a look response and one requiring a reach response), and two other tasks challenged the infant with multiple hiding locations (one requiring a gaze response and one requiring a reach response). Although above-chance working memory was observed between 5.5 and 8 months of age, no age-related improvements were observed in this range. Infants between 8 and 12.5 months old, however, demonstrated linear improvement in the percentage of correct trials. In addition, manipulation of the duration of the delay and number of locations both revealed linear improvements with age, although improvement to the delay challenge preceded improvement on the location challenge. As previously noted, working memory performance did not differ for the looking or reaching responses.

Reznick and colleagues (Pelphrey et al., 2004) suggested that three developmental processes were operating up until 8 months of age. First, nonchallenging tasks elicit stable working memory performance. In addition, linear improvement on working memory tasks is elicited from manipulation of the delay between presentation and search. Finally, there is significant variability in the durability of working memory against increases in the number of hiding locations for infants between 5.5 and 8 months of age.

In another investigation, Reznick and colleagues (Reznick et al., 2004; chapter 1, this volume) used the delayed response task in an attempt to identify the onset of infant working memory. Working memory performance in infants between 4.5 and 6.5 months of age was investigated using a looking version of the delayed response task. Successful performance on the delayed response task appeared to reliably emerge by 5.5 months. Although above-chance performance was observed for 5.5-month-old infants, there were no age-related changes. This evidence supports other claims (Bell & Fox, 1992; Diamond, 1985; Diamond et al., 1997; Pelphry et al., 2004) that the major developmental changes in infant working memory commence toward the end of the first postnatal year.

We have completed data collection on a study examining the emergence of working memory in infants from 5 to 10 months of age (Bell, 2006). In this longitudinal investigation, 20 infants were seen monthly in the research lab for assessment on both looking and reaching versions of the A-not-B working memory task. Task performance was scored two different ways, in accord with our discussion of scoring procedures in this chapter: the ordinal scale (see Figure 2.1, top) and the percentage of correct trials (see Figure 2.1, bottom). Preliminary analyses of the behavioral data using the ordinal scale technique indicate that as a group, infants demonstrated better performance on the looking version of the A-not-B task from 5 to 8 months of age and then demonstrated comparable performance on the looking and reaching versions

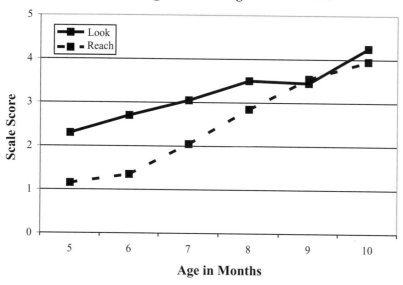

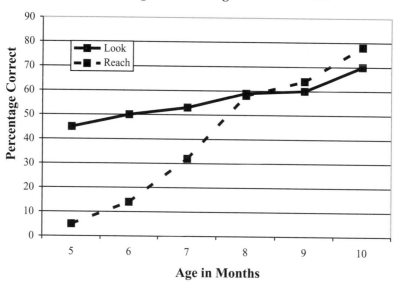

FIGURE 2.1. Comparison of infant performance on looking and reaching versions of the A-not-B task on two measures. Top graph utilizes an ordinal scale. Bottom graph utilizes percentage correct. Adapted from Bell (2006).

of this working memory task at 9 and 10 months of age. When analyzing the data using the percentage of correct trials, a similar pattern emerges. As a group, infants demonstrated better performance on the looking version of the A-not-B task from 5 to 7 months of age and then comparable performance on the looking and reaching versions from 8 to 10 months of age.

These findings are compatible with our earlier work in which we compared looking and reaching performance on the A-not-B working memory task in two cohorts of 8-month-old infants (Bell & Adams, 1999). Furthermore, these data are compatible with what we know about the gross motor abilities of infants. That is, as infants are developing skilled reaching abilities, performance on the looking version of the task is better than performance on the reaching version. Around 8 months of age, however, when reaching behaviors are more developed and skilled, performance on the looking and reaching versions is comparable. Remember that our hypothesis is that the same cognitive skills (i.e., working memory, inhibitory control, attention) are required for both versions of the task. We propose that these data demonstrate the major differences in maturation of brain circuitry associated with the actual task response.

With respect to individual differences in development, our primary focus of that longitudinal study, preliminary analyses of the behavioral data reveal that two groups emerge from this data set. One group of infants performed at a relatively low level on both the looking and reaching versions of the A-not-B task at 5 months and then showed monthly increases in working memory performance on both tasks until 10 months. The other group performed at a relatively high level of performance on the looking version of the task at 5 months and then showed less monthly change in visual working memory performance through 10 months of age. This group demonstrated a more linear increase in performance on the reaching version of the task, however (Bell, 2006). We recorded EEG during looking A-not-B performance and we anticipate that the EEG records will distinguish between these two groups of infants.

What Are the Mechanisms Underlying the Development of Working Memory During Infancy?

Various mechanisms have been proposed to underlie the emergence and development of working memory. Even though we highlight three of these mechanisms separately, in all likelihood they combine to influence working memory development, although it may be that they combine in different ways at different ages (Wolfe & Bell, in press). Other mechanisms, such as language (Gathercole, Willis, Emslie, & Baddeley, 1992; Wolfe & Bell, 2004), also likely impact the development of working memory in preschool children, but because our focus in this chapter is on the first postnatal year, we do not include language in our discussion.

Maturation of the Prefrontal Cortex

Significant changes in working memory processes are clearly identifiable during infancy and early childhood. These changes are inarguably associated with transformations in cortical function and organization. It has been suggested that the most salient modifications in brain anatomy (i.e., growth in brain weight, increased myelination, glucose utilization, and synaptic growth) take place in the first few years of life.

The behavioral neuroscience work accomplished by Diamond and colleagues provided the initial evidence that the maturation and integrity of the dorsolateral prefrontal cortex are involved at some level in successful performance of Piaget's A-not-B reaching task (Diamond & Goldman-Rakic, 1989; Diamond, Zola-Morgan, & Squire, 1989). In her work with human infants, Diamond has emphasized maturation of this brain area (Diamond, 1990; Diamond et al., 1997), as well as the wide range of individual differences among infants in A-not-B performance (Diamond, 1985). Likewise, Nelson (1995) agreed that the dorsolateral prefrontal cortex probably is involved with the memory requirement of the classic A-not-B reaching task. Citing evidence from behavioral neuroscience, neuroimaging, and morphological studies, he noted that this cortical area is likely mature enough by the last half of the first year of life to support memory functions. Nelson also noted that the other skills required for successful performance probably rely on the coordination of dorsolateral and orbital prefrontal areas, the mediodorsal nucleus, and the anterodorsal caudate nucleus.

Haith and Benson (1998) and Johnson (1998) also have noted that the dorsolateral prefrontal cortex likely is involved in A-not-B reaching performance, but have questioned Diamond's strict reliance on frontal lobe maturation as the key mechanism for development. Nevertheless, there is evidence that low birth weight, premature infants display difficulties with spatial working memory when they are assessed 3 to 4 years after birth (Vicari, Caravale, Carlesimo, Casadei, & Allemand, 2004). Likewise, there is electrophysiological evidence for some brain maturation influence on A-not-B reaching task performance. Recall that we (Bell & Fox, 1992) reported that changes in frontal EEG power values from 7 to 12 months of age were associated with changes in A-not-B reaching performance during that same age period.

Dopamine Levels in the Prefrontal Cortex

Diamond et al. (1997) compared the working memory performance of healthy infants and children to the performance of infants and children with the metabolic disorder phenylketonuria (PKU). Infants and children with PKU are unable to convert phenylalanine (Phe) to tyrosine (Tyr), which is the precursor of dopamine. Dopamine neurons that project to the prefrontal cortex are especially sensitive to small decreases in the level of Tyr, leading to the compromise of prefrontal functions. As hypothesized, Diamond reported that children with PKU had lower performance on prefrontal tasks, such as A-not-B, relative to healthy controls. Furthermore, the higher an individual child's Phe level, the worse that child performed on prefrontal working memory tasks. Thus, maturation of the prefrontal cortex may present too simple a mechanism to explain the development of working memory.

Temperament and Self-Regulation

Currently we are examining individual differences in temperament and self-regulation as a possible mechanism for individual differences in the development of working memory. Although this might seem tangential with respect to our discussion of infant working memory thus far, let us explain how we are conceptualizing the association between temperament and working memory (Bell & Wolfe, 2004).

Rothbart and Bates (1998) defined temperament as biologically based individual differences in emotional reactivity and the emergence of self-regulation of that reactivity beginning later in the first year of life. The emergence of these early regulatory processes is facilitated by the development of attention, which may have implications for cognitive development as well (Bush, Luu, & Posner, 2000; Fox, 1994; Posner & Rothbart, 1998; Ruff & Rothbart, 1996). We propose that the most pertinent example of this attentional regulation is the cognitive control infants begin to exhibit on working memory tasks (Diamond, 1990; Diamond et al., 1997).

Recall that the attentional capacity highlighted by Engle in his model of working memory (Engle et al., 1999) is the capability of maintaining short-term memory representations in the presence of interference or response competition. Thus, this executive attention component is not needed for all cognitive processing, but it is needed in circumstances that require inhibition of prepotent responses, error monitoring and correction, and decision making and planning (Engle et al., 1999; Unsworth et al., 2004). These are the skills involved in A-not-B task performance.

Also recall that the individual differences associated with executive attention are the focus of Engle's model of working memory (Engle et al., 1999; Kane & Engle, 2002, 2003; Unsworth et al., 2004). Individual differences in executive attention are evident only in situations that encourage or require controlled attention. This suggests that individuals high in this controlled attention ability (a construct similar to the temperamental aspect of attentional regulation) are more effective at blocking distracting, task-irrelevant information and maintaining a focus on pertinent information than individuals low in attention. Indeed, individuals ranked low on this attentional ability are more likely to break focus and orient to an irrelevant, attention-capturing external cue (Unsworth et al., 2004). Based on human and nonhuman primate literatures, Engle has hypothesized that individual differences in attentional control (i.e., working memory capacity) are associated with individual differences in the functioning of the prefrontal cortex (Engle et al., 1999; Kane & Engle, 2002). These individual differences are considered to be a characteristic of the individual person and do not result from experience (Engle et al., 1999). Temperament, especially during early infancy, is considered to be a characteristic of the individual infant (Rothbart & Bates, 1998). Thus, Engle's attentional control and Rothbart's attentional regulation appear to be similar conceptually.

Furthermore, attentional ability during working memory tasks is noted by Engle to be comparable to the construct of attention described by Posner's anterior attention system, which also includes prefrontal as well subcortical circuitry (Engle et al., 1999). Posner proposed that the anterior attention system regulates both cognitive attention and temperament (i.e., emotion) attention processing (Bush et al., 2000). In adults, this attentional system is characterized by effortful controlled attentional processing. The functioning of this attention system begins to influence behavior during the later half of the first postnatal year (Ruff & Rothbart, 1996). Because the anterior attention system focuses on both the cognitive attention and temperament attention functions of the frontal lobe areas, this may be the functional system that has the ability to connect working memory and temperament processes associated with performance on the A-not-B task.

Researchers have begun to demonstrate some associations between temperament characteristics and cognitive tasks involving working memory in preschool children (Davis, Bruce, & Gunnar, 2002; Gerardi-Caulton, 2000; Wolfe & Bell, 2004). Our own infant studies have yielded correlations between temperament characteristics associated with attentional self-regulation and working memory performance (Bell, 2005). In a group of 8-month-old infants, we reported correlations between temperamental characteristics of activity level and distress to limitations and performance on the A-not-B delayed memory task. We are currently investigating the temperament mechanism of working memory development in a short-term longitudinal study with infants at 5 and 10 months of age. We are collecting multiple measures of working memory and of temperament in an attempt to elucidate what we hypothesize are conceptually based connections between these two sources of individual differences in infant development.

What Are the Issues on the Horizon for the Study of the Development of Working Memory?

The major limitation of these particular methods (A-not-B and delayed response) for measuring infant working memory is that different types of tasks typically are used to assess working memory in older children. That makes direct examination of individual differences from infancy to early childhood less than ideal. As a result, there are no longitudinal investigations of working memory development across infancy and childhood that make direct comparisons on task performance. For example, the longitudinal investigations of Diamond and colleagues (1997) mentioned previously, focusing on the impact of PKU on frontal functioning, have three groups of participants—infants, toddlers, and preschoolers—with longitudinal methodology within each age group, but not across these age groups.

Of course, infants are nonverbal and necessarily must be assessed with the delayed-memory working memory tasks, whereas children are typically assessed with memory-span verbal working memory tasks. Even when delayed memory (i.e., spatial) working memory tasks are used with preschoolers, those tasks are more adultlike in nature than those used with infants. Luciana and Nelson (1998) used the same delayed-memory working memory tasks to compare 4- to 8-year-old children's performance to that of adults. Gathercole and colleagues (2004) made direct comparisons of verbal working memory performance between preschool children and adolescents using the same tasks.

There is one research team, however, who may have found a solution to this problem. Espy, Kaufmann, McDiarmid, and Glisky (1999) used the classic infant A-not-B reaching task with toddler and preschool children between the ages of 23 and 66 months. A 10-second delay was used for all children and age-related effects on correct performance were observed. Age significantly predicted correct performance on the A-not-B task among these children, while accounting for 16% of the variance in performance. Thus, although the A-not-B task has been assumed to be appropriate only for infants, probably due to the strong Piagetian history of the task, it appears to produce age-related differences in young children as well. This is worthy of further investigation.

These are the types of issues that are on the horizon for the study of the development of working memory in infancy and beyond infancy into early childhood. Data are needed that will allow not only for examination of developmental change across this crucial time period, but also for examination of individual differences in development.

References

Ahmed, A., & Ruffman, T. (1998). Why do infants make A not B errors in a search task, yet show memory for the location of hidden objects in a non-search task? *Developmental Psychology, 34,* 441–453.

Baddeley, A. D. (1986). *Working memory.* New York: Oxford University Press.

Baddeley, A. (2000). The episodic buffer: A new component of working memory? *Trends in Cognitive Sciences, 4,* 417–423.

Baddeley, A. D., & Hitch, G. J. (1974). Working memory. In G. Bower (Ed.), *Recent advances in learning and motivation, Volume 8.* New York: Academic Press.

Baillargeon, R., & Graber, M. (1988). Evidence of location memory in 8-month-old infants in a non-search AB task. *Developmental Psychology, 24,* 502–511.

Barrett, L. F., Tugade, M. M., & Engle, R. W. (2004). Individual differences in working memory capacity and dual-process theories of the mind. *Psychological Bulletin, 130,* 553–573.

Bell, M. A. (1998). The ontogeny of the EEG during infancy and childhood: Implications for cognitive development. In B. Garreau (Ed.), *Neuro-imaging in child neuropsychiatric disorders* (pp. 97–111). Berlin: Springer-Verlag.

Bell, M. A. (2001). Brain electrical activity associated with cognitive processing during a looking version of the A-not-B object permanence task. *Infancy, 2,* 311–330.

Bell, M. A. (2002). Infant 6–9 Hz synchronization during a working memory task. *Psychophysiology, 39,* 450–458.

Bell, M. A. (2005). *Individual differences in working memory at 8 months: Contributions from electrophysiology and temperament.* Manuscript under review.

Bell, M. A. (2006). *Looking versus reaching: A longitudinal investigation of infant working memory and EEG.* Manuscript in preparation.

Bell, M. A. (in press). Tutorial on electroencephalogram methodology: EEG research with infants and young children. In D. L. Molfese & V. J. Molfese (Eds.), *Handbook of developmental neuropsychology.* Mahwah, NJ: Erlbaum.

Bell, M. A., & Adams, S. E. (1999). Equivalent performance on looking and reaching versions of the A-not-B task at 8 months of age. *Infant Behavior & Development, 22,* 221–235.

Bell, M. A., & Fox, N. A. (1992). The relations between frontal brain electrical activity and cognitive development during infancy. *Child Development, 63,* 1142–1163.

Bell, M. A., & Fox, N. A. (1994). Brain development over the first year of life: Relations between electroencephalographic frequency and coherence and cognitive and affective behaviors. In G. Dawson & K. W. Fischer (Eds.), *Human behavior and the developing brain* (pp. 314–345). New York: Guilford.

Bell, M. A., & Fox, N. A. (1997). Individual differences in object permanence performance at 8 months: Locomotor experience and brain electrical activity. *Developmental Psychobiology, 31,* 287–297.

Bell, M. A., & Fox, N. A. (2003). Cognition and affective style: Individual differences in brain electrical activity during spatial and verbal tasks. *Brain and Cognition, 53,* 441–451.

Bell, M. A., & Wolfe, C. D. (2004). Emotion and cognition: An intricately bound developmental process. *Child Development, 75,* 366–370.

Bush, G., Luu, P., & Posner, M. I. (2000). Cognitive and emotional influences in anterior cingulate cortex. *Trends in Cognitive Sciences, 4,* 215–222.

Casey, B. J., & de Haan, M. (2002). Introduction: New methods in developmental science. *Developmental Science, 5,* 265–267.

Chugani, H. T. (1994). Development of regional brain glucose metabolism in relation to behavior and plasticity. In G. Dawson & K. W. Fischer (Eds.), *Human behavior and the developing brain* (pp. 153–175). New York: Guilford.

Davis, E. P., Bruce, J., & Gunnar, M. R. (2002). The anterior attention network: Associations with temperament and neuroendocrine activity in 6-year-old children. *Developmental Psychobiology, 40,* 43–56.

Davis, P. L., Segalowitz, S. J., & Gavin, W. J. (2004). Development of response-monitoring ERPs in 7- to 25-year-olds. *Developmental Neuropsychology, 25,* 355–376.

Diamond, A. (1985). Development of the ability to use recall to guide action, as indicated by infants' performance on AB. *Child Development, 56,* 868–883.

Diamond, A. (Ed.). (1990). The development and neural bases of memory functions as indexed by the AB and delayed response tasks in human infants and infant monkeys. *The development and neural bases of higher cognitive functions* (pp. 267–317). New York: New York Academy of Sciences Press.

Diamond, A. (1995). Evidence of robust recognition memory early in life even when assessed by reaching behavior. *Journal of Experimental Child Psychology, 59,* 419–456.

Diamond, A. (2001). A model system for studying the role of dopamine in the prefrontal cortex during early development in humans: Early and continuously treated phenylketonuria. In C. A. Nelson & M. Luciana (Eds.), *Handbook of developmental cognitive neuroscience* (pp. 433–472). Cambridge, MA: MIT Press.

Diamond, A., & Goldman-Rakic, P. S. (1989). Comparison of human infants and rhesus monkeys on Piaget's AB task: Evidence for dependence on dorsolateral prefrontal cortex. *Experimental Brain Research, 74,* 24–40.

Diamond, A., Prevor, M. B., Callender, G., & Druin, D. P. (1997). Prefrontal cortex cognitive deficits in children treated early and continuously for PKU. *Monographs of the Society for Research in Child Development, 62*(4, Serial No. 252).

Diamond, A., Zola-Morgan, S., & Squire, L. R. (1989). Successful performance by monkeys with lesions of the hippocampal formation on AB and object retrieval, two tasks that mark developmental changes in human infants. *Behavioral Neuroscience, 103,* 526–537.

Duncan, J., & Owen, A. M. (2000). Common regions of the human frontal lobe recruited by diverse cognitive demands. *Trends in Neurosciences, 23,* 475–483.

Engle, R. W., Kane, M. J., & Tulholski, S. W. (1999). Individual differences in working memory capacity and what they tell us about controlled attention, general fluid intelligence, and functions of the prefrontal cortex. In A. Miyake & P. Shah (Eds.), *Models of working memory: Mechanisms of active maintenance and executive control* (pp. 102–134). New York: Cambridge University Press.

Espy, K. A., Kaufmann, P. M., McDiamid, M. D., & Glisky, M. L. (1999). Executive functioning in preschool children: Performance on A-not-B and other delayed response format tasks. *Brain and Cognition, 41,* 178–199.

Fox, N. A. (Ed.). (1994). Dynamic cerebral processes underlying emotion regulation. In *The development of emotion regulation: Biological and behavioral considerations* (pp. 152–166). *Monographs of the Society for Research in Child Development, 59*(2–3, Serial No. 240).

Gathercole, S. E., Pickering, S. J., Ambridge, B., & Wearing, H. (2004). The structure of working memory from 4 to 15 years of age. *Developmental Psychology, 40,* 177–190.

Gathercole, S. E., Willis, C. S., Emslie, H., & Baddeley, A. D. (1992). Phonological memory and vocabulary development during the early school years: A longitudinal study. *Developmental Psychology, 28,* 887–898.

Gerardi-Caulton, G. (2000). Sensitivity to spatial conflict and the development of self-regulation in children 24–36 months of age. *Developmental Science, 3,* 397–404.

Gerstadt, C. L., Hong, Y. J., & Diamond, A. (1994). The relationship between cognition and action: Performance of children 3½–7 years on a Stroop-like day-night test. *Cognition, 53,* 129–153.

Gilmore, R. O., & Johnson, M. H. (1995). Working memory in infancy: Six-month-olds' performance on two versions of the oculomotor delayed response task. *Journal of Experimental Child Psychology, 59,* 397–418.

Goldman-Rakic, P. S. (1987). Development of cortical circuitry and cognitive function. *Child Development, 58,* 601–622.

Haith, M. M., & Benson, J. B. (1998). Infant cognition. In W. Damon (Ed.), *Handbook of child psychology* (5th ed., pp. 199–254). New York: Wiley.

Hofstadter, M., & Reznick, J. S. (1996). Response modality affects human infant delayed-response performance. *Child Development, 67,* 646–658.

Huttenlocher, P. R. (1994). Synaptogenesis, synapse elimination, and neural plasticity in human cerebral cortex. In C. A. Nelson (Ed.), *Threats to optimal development: Integrating biological, psychological and social risk factors* (pp. 35–54). Mahwah, NJ: Erlbaum.

Johnson, M. H. (1998). The neural basis of cognitive development. In W. Damon (Ed.), *The handbook of child psychology* (5th ed., pp. 1–49). New York: Wiley.

Kane, M. J., & Engle, R. W. (2002). The role of the prefrontal cortex in working-memory capacity, executive attention, and general fluid intelligence: An individual-differences perspective. *Psychonomic Bulletin and Review, 9,* 637–671.

Kane, M. J., & Engle, R. W. (2003). Working-memory capacity and the control of attention: The contributions of goal neglect, response competition, and task set to Stroop interference. *Journal of Experimental Psychology: General, 132,* 47–70.

Kermoian, R., & Campos, J. J. (1988). Locomotor experience: A facilitator of spatial cognitive development. *Child Development, 59,* 908–917.

Levy, R., & Goldman-Rakic, P. S. (2000). Segregation of working memory functions within the dorsolateral prefrontal cortex. *Experimental Brain Research, 133,* 23–32.

Logie, R. H. (1993). Working memory in everyday cognition. In G. M. Davies & R. H. Logie (Eds.), *Memory in everyday life* (pp. 173–218). Amsterdam: Elsevier Science.

Luciana, M., & Nelson, C. E. (1998). The functional emergence of prefrontally-guided working memory systems in four- to eight-year-old children. *Neuropsychologia, 36,* 273–293.

Matthews, A., Ellis, A. E., & Nelson, C. A. (1996). Development of preterm and full-term infant ability on AB, recall memory, transparent barrier detour, and means-end tasks. *Child Development, 67,* 2658–2676.

Munakata, Y. (1998). Infant perseveration and implications for object permanence theories: A PDP model of the AB task. *Developmental Science, 1,* 161–184.

Nelson, C. A. (1995). The ontogeny of human memory: A cognitive neuroscience perspective. *Developmental Psychology, 31,* 723–738.

Pelphrey, K. A., Reznick, J. S., Davis Goldman, B., Sasson, N., Morrow, J., Donahoe, A., et al. (2004). Development of visuospatial short-term memory in the second half of the 1st year. *Developmental Psychology, 40,* 836–851.

Posner, M. I., & Rothbart, M. K. (1998). Summary and commentary: Developing attentional skills. In J. E. Richards (Ed.), *Cognitive neuroscience of attention: A developmental perspective* (pp. 317–323). Mahwah, NJ: Erlbaum.

Reznick, J. S., Morrow, J. D., Goldman, B. D., & Snyder, J. (2004). The onset of working memory in infants. *Infancy, 6,* 145–154.

Rothbart, M. K., & Bates, J. C. (1998). Temperament. In W. Damon (Series Ed.) & N. Eisenburg (Vol. Ed.), *Handbook of child psychology: Vol 3. Social, emotional, and personality development* (pp. 105–176). New York: Wiley.

Ruff, H. A., & Rothbart, M. K. (1996). *Attention in early development: Themes and variations.* New York: Oxford University Press.

Russell, J. (1998). An odd kind of working memory. *Developmental Science, 1,* 201–202.

Segalowitz, S. J., & Davis, P. L. (2004). Charting the maturation of the frontal lobe: An electrophysiological strategy. *Brain and Cognition, 55,* 116–133.

Smith, L. B., Thelen, E., Titzer, R., & McLin, D. (1999). Knowing in the context of acting: The task dynamics of the A-not-B error. *Psychological Review, 106,* 235–260.

Sowell, E. R., Thompson, P. M., Tessner, K. D., & Toga, A. W. (2001). Mapping continued brain growth and gray matter density reduction in dorsal frontal cortex: Inverse relationships during postadolescent brain maturation. *Journal of Neuroscience, 21,* 8819–8829.

Taylor, M. J., & Baldeweg, T. (2002). Application of EEG, ERP, and intracranial recordings to the investigation of cognitive functions in children. *Developmental Science, 5,* 318–334.

Unsworth, N., Schrock, J. C., & Engle, R. W. (2004). Working memory capacity and the antisaccade task: Individual differences in voluntary saccade control. *Journal of Experimental Psychology: Learning, Memory, and Cognition, 30,* 1302–1321.

Vicari, S., Caravale, B., Carlesimo, G. A., Dasadei, A. M., & Allemand, F. (2004). Spatial working memory deficits in children at ages 3–4 who were low birth weight, preterm infants. *Neuropsychology, 18,* 673–678.

Wellman, H. M., Cross, D., & Bartsch, K. (1986). Infant search and object permanence: A meta-analysis of the A-not-B error. *Monographs of the Society for Research in Child Development, 51*(3, Serial No. 214).

Wolfe, C. D., & Bell, M. A. (2004). Working memory and inhibitory control in early childhood: Contributions from electrophysiology, temperament, and language. *Developmental Psychobiology, 44,* 68–83.

Wolfe, C. D., & Bell, M. A. (in press). The integration of cognition and emotion during infancy and early childhood: Regulatory processes associated with the development of working memory. *Brain and Cognition.*

3

Continuity of Format and Computation in Short-Term Memory Development

LISA FEIGENSON

In their first year of life, infants face the enormous task of making sense of the world around them. Without the ability to store and reason about representations of the individual objects, actions, and sounds in their environment, infants would never accomplish the monumental changes they do. Storing representations of such individuals in memory allows infants to perform computations that, while seemingly simple, are critical to learning about the world. Comparing a scene to one observed earlier, keeping track of the presence of objects even when the objects are temporarily occluded, and making predictions about the outcomes of hidden events are some examples of such computations. The thesis of this chapter is that the short-term memory system that enables infants to store object representations, and many of the computations infants perform over these representations, are continuous throughout the human life span. Infants and adults show similar capacities and similar limitations regarding their ability to represent and reason about objects. At the same time, infants' and adults' short-term memory abilities may differ in some important respects. This chapter explores what is shared and what may differ in early versus mature short-term memory.

First, I would like to lay out some rough definitions. When I talk about short-term memory in this chapter, I am referring to the ability to form and store mental tokens that stand for entities in the outside world. Maintaining these tokens over short durations allows the entities to be thought about even when direct perceptual information is absent, as is the case when objects undergo occlusion. This short-term memory enables infants to represent the presence of entities when those entities might be temporarily hidden (e.g., "There is an object under that blanket") and to store information about those entities (e.g., "The object under the blanket is round and red and striped"). Furthermore, storing representations of more than one item at a time enables infants to compute across an entire scene (e.g., "There are three balls under the blanket"), rather than over just a single item. Here, I suggest that this type of short-term memory in infants corresponds to a system of short-term memory that has been studied in adults (for an argument that *working memory* is a better term for this same system, see chapter 1, this volume). Indeed, one of the most striking observations about this memory system is the extent to which it remains constant throughout development, both in its capacity and in the computations it supports.

I begin with an exploration of the limits on infants' and adults' short-term memory capacity; the evidence I review builds the case that the very same system of memory is relied on across the life span. Second, I examine findings that infants and adults perform similar computations over these short-term memory representations. Both groups compute the continuous and discrete properties of object arrays, and both groups use chunking as a means to recode memory representations into a more efficient format. Third, I address a possible developmental difference in short-term memory, asking whether infants and adults differ in the degree to which their memory computations are driven in top-down versus bottom-up fashion. Finally, I close the chapter by raising some outstanding questions and by suggesting some avenues for future research on short-term memory development.

Short-Term Memory for Object Arrays

Some 25 years ago, pioneers in the newly emerging field of infant cognition demonstrated that, contrary to Piaget's claims, young infants represent and reason about objects. Critically, they do so in ways that go beyond the immediate sensory data available to them. By 5 to 7 months of age, infants represent objects that have been covered by cloths, hidden by screens, or concealed in darkness (e.g., Baillargeon, Spelke, & Wasserman, 1985; Hood & Willats, 1986; Shinskey & Munakata, 2003). That infants have stored representations of these objects in memory is shown by their continued reaching for the objects once hidden, or by their longer looking when objects unexpectedly disappear. Even more impressively, infants reason over these stored representations of objects. For example, when a solid object is placed behind a screen and a second object is launched on a direct path toward it, infants look longer when the second object emerges magically unscathed from the other side of the screen (Baillargeon, 1986). Apparently, infants have reasoned that one solid object cannot pass through another. Because infants' looking times in situations such as these depend on inferred interactions between objects that are hidden rather than visible, we conclude that infants are operating on representations stored in memory rather than operating directly on the immediate sensory data.

Researchers have attempted to characterize the memory systems infants use to reason about such instances of object behavior. One question of interest is whether infants reason over object representations stored in short-term memory or long-term memory.[1] Although the distinction between short- and long-term memory systems has often been controversial, many have suggested that the amount of information stored by each person over long durations is too large and unwieldy to allow sufficiently rapid access for the moment-to-moment comparisons we constantly perform, and which characterize the occlusion events typical of experiments with infants. This problem motivates the existence of a system that is distinct from the larger, long-term memory store. This system holds a limited amount of information in a temporary state of privileged access. Representations held in this short-term memory system can be formed quickly but decay over time, whereas long-term memory representations take longer to form but are far more enduring (see chapters 7–10, this volume). On some models, the information held in short-term memory can come either from the outside world (e.g., storing a representation of an object that is currently visible), or it can come from the activation of a representation previously stored in long-term memory (e.g., thinking about an object that was seen yesterday; Cowan, 2001). In either case, information held in short-term memory is available for immediate processing.

Several factors hint that short-term memory does underlie infants' reasoning about the kinds of object arrays typical of infant cognition research. In such studies, infants receive only brief exposure to a scene before objects are hidden from view, perhaps limiting the extent to which they have the opportunity to store long-term representations. In addition, experiments manipulating the delay between an object's disappearance from view and the moment when infants are allowed to retrieve it reveal that infants' object memories fade rapidly (Diamond, 1990). These factors begin to suggest that short-term memory is the likely locus of infants' object-tracking abilities. However, most studies investigating infants' object representations have not been designed to distinguish the relative contributions of short- versus long-term memory. For example, they have systematically manipulated neither the duration of infants' object exposure nor the interval over which infants must maintain the object representations in memory, at least not in ways that would bear decisively on which memory system is involved. Therefore, the conclusion that many studies of infants' object representations are tapping short-term memory remains tentative.

Short-Term Memory Capacity in Adults

Further evidence is needed. Measuring the capacity of infants' memory is a potential source of such evidence, since capacity differences have traditionally been a distinguishing characteristic of short- versus long-term memory. While long-term memory is usually thought of as unlimited, short-term memory is thought to store only a small amount of information at any one time. This notion of a limited-capacity short-term memory store originated with James (1890) and received significant attention following Miller's (1956) influential postulation of a "magical number seven, plus or minus two." Miller made famous the view of short-term memory as a repository limited by the number of unique items it can hold (approximately seven, in Miller's view), rather than by overall informational load (where information load is influenced by factors such as the complexity of the items). Since then it has been suggested that "seven, plus or minus two" probably over-estimates short-term memory capacity and is likely the by-product of addi-tional mental processes, such as chunking, that allow subjects to recode individual items into groups. A more reasonable estimate, obtained when chunking is prevented, is three to four (Cowan, 2001).

Cowan (2001) reviewed a wide range of experiments probing short-term memory capacity, and finds that most of these produce estimates of three to four items. Space precludes presenting that evidence here, but a summary of a classic experimental series by Sperling (1960) illustrates the type of results obtained. Sperling showed adult subjects 3×4 arrays of letters, presented too briefly for the subjects to store all 12 letters in long-term mem-ory. On whole-report trials, subjects reported the names of all of the letters they could remember; they averaged around 4. On partial-report trials, subjects reported only a subset of the array as specified by an auditory cue. When the cue was heard 2 to 5 seconds after the array had disappeared, sub-jects were able to report an average of 1.3 of the 4 letters in the cued row.[2] Multiplied by the number of rows in the array (3), this again yielded approx-imately 4 as the upper limit on short-term memory capacity.

More recently, short-term memory tasks have produced a similar capacity limit in adults. Halberda, Simons, and Wetherhold (2006) showed subjects a rapidly flashing grid of 32 dots, each of a different luminance value. All but one of the dots maintained its individual luminance value from flash to flash; the remaining dot oscillated between two different values. Subjects had to find the single changing dot. Halberda et al. found that subjects were able to encode the luminance values of a subset of the dots on each flash of the array, store them in memory, and compare them to the dots' luminance values on the next flash. Subjects examined subsets of dots in this way until they located the changing item. By analyzing the number of flashes required to locate the target dot, Halberda et al. estimated that the number of dots subjects could store in short-term memory from a single flash of the array was three.

Other findings strengthen the claim that the capacity limit is defined by the discrete number of items being held in memory, rather than by total informa-tion load. Luck and Vogel (1997) used a change detection task in which sub-jects received a 100-millisecond visual exposure to an array of items, followed 900 milliseconds later by a test array. Subjects had to report whether the two arrays were identical or whether any of the items had changed their features. Luck and Vogel found that performance was at ceiling for arrays containing one to three items, and declined with sets of four or more. Most strikingly, subjects were just as accurate for arrays of items that contained multiple features as for arrays containing just a single feature. Thus, the number of items in the array, and not the number of features in the array, determined subjects' memory capacity.

Several researchers have suggested that there is a similar three-to-four-item capacity limit in attention, prior to the storage of any items in short-term memory (Carey, 2004; Scholl & Leslie, 1999; Trick & Pylyshyn, 1994). This view derives largely from results of the multiple object tracking paradigm. This paradigm was developed by Pylyshyn to examine the process by which a subset of the information in a scene achieves priority for further processing, before its transfer into memory (Pylyshyn, 1994, 2001). In the multiple object tracking task, subjects track several moving onscreen targets amid a field of identical distractors. Because no featural cues distinguish the targets from the distractors, the only way for subjects to succeed is to attend to the targets from the start of each trial (when targets flash briefly to indicate their status) and to keep attending to them in parallel as they move haphazardly through the scene. Subjects perform this task effortlessly with one, two, three, and often four targets. But when asked to track more than four, performance plummets (Pylyshyn & Storm, 1988). Because this task was designed to require little or no memory, many have concluded that the observed limit is grounded in attention. However, more recent evidence disputes the view of a three-to-four-item limit on attention. Experiments by Alvarez and Franconeri (2005) suggest that attentional capacity increases to well above four items when the items move more slowly. Thus it remains to be seen whether an item-based limit on attention will hold.

If such a limit does hold up in purely attentional tasks, is the existence of an identical three-to-four-item limit that constrains both attention and short-term memory purely coincidental? An alternative view has been offered by Cowan (2001), who suggests that there is no structural distinction between attention and short-term memory. Instead, Cowan suggests that in order to reason about remembered items, the items need to be pulled from memory storage into the "focus of attention." This focus of attention can be thought of as activation of the stored items, where activation is required for any sort of conscious processing. Cowan suggests that while memory storage itself is unlimited, only three to four items can be brought into the focus of attention at any given time. Cowan's proposal is controversial but serves to highlight the difficulty in distinguishing between capacity limits on attention versus those on short-term memory.

Measuring Short-Term Memory in Infancy: Recent Advances

We now return to the question of which memory system underlies infants' ability to track and reason about hidden objects. Given that adults can maintain three to four items in short-term memory, a similar limit on infants' abilities would be important in illustrating continuity across development. Recent findings have obtained just such a limit. In a modified version of

Luck and Vogel's (1997) change-detection paradigm, Ross-Sheehy, Oakes, and Luck (2003) presented 10-month-old infants with cycles of simple object arrays appearing simultaneously on a pair of adjacent screens. On every cycle, the arrays appeared on each screen for 500 milliseconds, disappeared for 250 milliseconds, then reappeared for 500 milliseconds. On one of the two screens, one of the objects in the array changed color during the 250-millisecond retention period. On the other screen, none of the objects changed. The arrays cycled such that one screen always displayed an array that changed during the retention period, while the other screen always displayed an array that remained constant (for a more detailed description of their experimental design, see chapter 4, this volume).

Ross-Sheehy et al. (2003) reasoned that since infants generally prefer to look at more complex displays rather than at simple ones, they would spend more time looking at the screen with the changing array than at the screen with the constant array. The ability to notice a change in the array from cycle to cycle depended on storing a representation of the objects in the array, maintaining this representation over the 250 milliseconds when no display was visible, and then comparing it to the next array that appeared. Therefore, a preference for looking at the changing screen implies successful memory retention of the features of all of the objects in the array (since which particular object changed varied randomly from cycle to cycle). Ross-Sheehy and colleagues used this paradigm to probe memory limits by comparing infants' performance with arrays containing different numbers of objects. They found that with one-, two-, three-, and four-object arrays, infants preferred to look at the changing screen. But with six-object arrays, infants showed no such preference. Apparently, 10-month-old infants were unable to represent more than four items at a time and therefore did not discriminate the changing from the unchanging array.

This work, using methods that closely resemble those used to study adults' visual short-term memory, suggests that infants, like adults, can store representations of three to four items at a time. But what about memory for the kinds of real, three-dimensional object arrays used in so many experiments on infant cognition, and which constitute the majority of infants' natural daily experience? Objects in such arrays are likely to be more complex in their shape, shading, and features than the simple squares used by Ross-Sheehy et al. (2003). In addition, objects in a natural scene often undergo complex patterns of motion, sometimes involving periods of occlusion during which they might be hidden for several seconds at a time. Will the three-to-four-item limit of short-term memory also be observed when infants are faced with naturalistic object arrays?

Infants' Short-Term Memory for Naturalistic Object Arrays

The question of exactly how many such hidden objects infants can remember and reason over was first raised by Karen Wynn, who demonstrated that by 5 months of age infants already can represent at least two occluded objects. After seeing a screen hide one object, followed by the addition of a second object behind the screen, infants expected to see two objects when the screen was lifted (Wynn, 1992). Work using similar looking time methods to measure infants' representation of occluded objects has confirmed that infants can remember at least two hidden objects at a time (Kaldy & Leslie, 2003; Koechlin, Dehaene, & Mehler, 1997; Simon, Hespos, & Rochat, 1995; Uller, Huntley-Fenner, Carey, & Klatt, 1999).

My colleagues and I have extended these findings by asking just how many such hidden objects infants can remember. We probed the upper limits of infants' ability to track occluded objects by creating a simple task in which the number of objects infants had to store in memory was parametrically varied. In this "cracker choice" task (Feigenson & Carey, 2005; Feigenson, Carey, & Hauser, 2002), 10- and 12-month-old infants saw two quantities of desirable objects (graham crackers) sequentially placed into a pair of opaque buckets and then were allowed to choose between them. Since determining which bucket contained more crackers required maintaining and comparing representations of the hidden objects, and since adults have been shown to store object representations in short-term memory for durations comparable to those we used (approximately 8–10 seconds; Noles, Scholl, & Mitroff, 2005), we reasoned that our procedure would serve as a naturalistic test of preverbal children's short-term memory.

We started by giving infants a choice between 1 vs. 2, 2 vs. 3, or 3 vs. 4 crackers. Groups of 16 different 10-month-old infants and 16 different 12-month-old infants participated in each of these numerical comparisons. Infants' spontaneous, untrained abilities were revealed by giving each infant just one opportunity to make a choice; thus, the experiment consisted of a single trial for each participant. In our experimental procedure, infants sat on the floor across from an experimenter. The experimenter produced two opaque plastic buckets, showed infants that they were empty, and placed them on the floor approximately 70 cm from infants' starting location and approximately 70 cm from each other. The experimenter then placed crackers one at a time into the buckets, making sure that infants attended to the placement of each cracker. For example, in a 1 vs. 2 choice, the experimenter placed one cracker in one bucket and two crackers one at a time into the other bucket. Which side the presentation began on and which bucket received the greater number of crackers was counterbalanced across participants. The dependent measure was simply which bucket infants chose to walk or crawl to.

Figure 3.1 displays the pattern of infants' spontaneous choices. We found that with choices of 1 vs. 2 and 2 vs. 3 crackers, infants of both age groups successfully chose the bucket containing the greater quantity. Infants failed, however, with a choice of 3 vs. 4 crackers. Infants' failure with this comparison might have been due to either the less discriminable ratio between the quantities, or to the quantities having exceeded the maximum number of

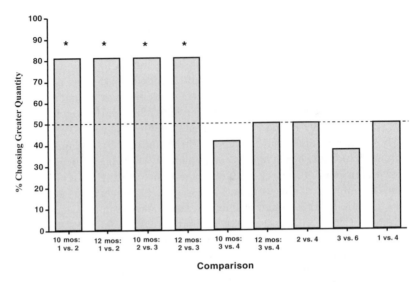

FIGURE 3.1. The percentage of infants choosing the greater of two
quantities. Infants chose the greater quantity with small arrays, but failed
whenever either array contained four or more objects. Reprinted from
Feigenson, L., Carey, S., & Hauser, M. (2002). The representations
underlying infants' choice of more: Object files versus analog magnitudes.
Psychological Science, 13(2), 150–156, copyright (2002), with permission
from Blackwell; and from Feigenson, L., & Carey, S. (2005). On the limits
of infants' quantification of small object arrays. *Cognition, 97,* 295–313,
copyright 2005, with permission from Elsevier.

items infants could hold in memory. Therefore, we next tested new groups
of infants with quantities in a ratio with which we had already observed success (1:2), but which involved more than three items in a single location. We
gave infants a choice between 2 vs. 4, 3 vs. 6, and 1 vs. 4 crackers. Since no
age differences between 10- and 12-month-olds were observed in any of the
previous comparisons we tested, each of the comparisons included 16 infants ranging between 10 and 12 months.

Infants failed to choose systematically with any of these quantities (see
Figure 3.1). This dramatic breakdown in performance illustrates that infants'
ability to remember the hidden objects was determined by the total number of
objects seen, and not by ratio of differences between the two quantities we presented. Infants succeeded only when one, two, or three crackers were placed
in either bucket, and chose entirely at chance when required to remember
larger numbers (Figure 3.1). A variety of control conditions ensured that the
abrupt break in infants' performance was, in fact, due to the number of objects
presented and not to the total presentation duration or complexity (see
Feigenson, Carey, & Hauser, 2002, for details). Thus, it appears that in this task
infants were limited to storing up to three items in each hiding location.

This naturalistic cracker choice task, which required infants to track real, three-dimensional objects undergoing motion and occlusion, revealed the same three-item limit on performance as has been observed in tasks showing infants (Ross-Sheehy et al., 2003) and adults (Halberda et al., 2006; Halberda, Sires, & Feigenson, 2006; Luck & Vogel, 1997) simple, computerized arrays. This suggests that the three-to-four-item capacity limit applies to a range of entities, from grayscale dots to real moving objects. However, one difference between our cracker choice task and previous tasks assessing short-term memory lies in the timing of the presentation. Our cracker task involved sequentially presented objects, whereas previous tasks presented infants and adults with objects that were all visible at once. Therefore, our next step was to ask whether the three-to-four-item capacity limit would be found when real, three-dimensional objects are simultaneously presented.

We addressed this question by again measuring the number of hidden objects infants could remember, but with a simultaneous rather than sequential presentation. In our manual search paradigm, infants searched for objects they had seen an experimenter hide in an opaque box (Feigenson & Carey, 2003, 2005). A group of 12- and 14-month-old infants saw one to four identical balls simultaneously visible atop the box; the balls were then picked up and inserted through a cloth-covered opening in the box's front face. Afterward, infants were allowed to reach in and retrieve the balls. Unbeknownst to the infants, on some trials the experimenter surreptitiously removed a subset of the balls from a concealed opening in the back of the box. We measured infants' continued searching and compared it to their baseline level of searching on trials when the box was expected to be empty. Any increased searching suggests that infants successfully represented and were searching for the remaining object or objects inside the box. In this way, our manual search task serves as a measure of the number of occluded items infants can remember over a relatively short duration.

We probed the limit on the number of objects infants could simultaneously remember via a series of x versus y comparisons. For any x versus y comparison, infants' searching after they saw x balls hidden and had retrieved x of them was contrasted with their searching after they saw y balls hidden and had retrieved only x of them. The logic can be illustrated with a 1 vs. 2 comparison. On one-object trials, infants saw the experimenter hide a single ball in the box, were then allowed to retrieve it, and any subsequent searching into the now-empty box was recorded during the 10 second measurement period that followed (Figure 3.2a). This was compared to the duration of searching on two-object trials, on which infants saw two identical balls hidden and then were allowed to retrieve just one of them. While the experimenter surreptitiously held the remaining ball out of reach for 10 seconds, any searching for the "missing" ball was recorded. After 10 seconds, the experimenter retrieved the remaining ball and showed it to infants, after which the box was once again empty. Any further searching was recorded in a final 10 second measurement period (Figure 3.2b).

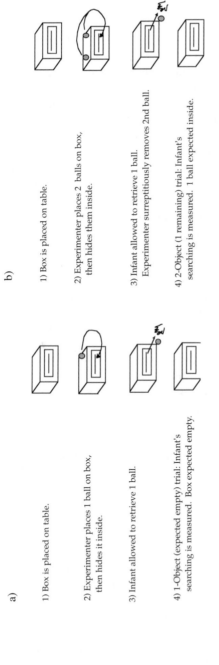

a)

1) Box is placed on table.

2) Experimenter places 1 ball on box, then hides it inside.

3) Infant allowed to retrieve 1 ball.

4) 1-Object (expected empty) trial: Infant's searching is measured. Box expected empty.

b)

1) Box is placed on table.

2) Experimenter places 2 balls on box, then hides them inside.

3) Infant allowed to retrieve 1 ball. Experimenter surreptitiously removes 2nd ball.

4) 2-Object (1 remaining) trial: Infant's searching is measured. 1 ball expected inside.

5) Experimenter "finds" 2nd ball.

6) 2-Object (expected empty) trial: Infant's searching is measured. Box expected empty.

FIGURE 3.2. Presentation sequences illustrating: (a) a one-object trial; (b) a two-object trial. Reprinted from Feigenson, L., & Carey, S. (2003). Tracking individuals via object-files: Evidence from infants' manual search. *Developmental Science, 6*, 568–584, copyright (2003), with permission from Blackwell; and from Feigenson, L., & Carey, S. (2005). On the limits of infants' quantification of small object arrays. *Cognition, 97*, 295–313, copyright 2005, with permission from Elsevier.

If infants were able to remember the correct number of objects hidden in the box, they should search the box only when the box was expected to still contain one or more objects. Therefore, we assessed infants' performance by examining the difference in their searching on trials when the box was expected to contain more objects versus trials when the box was expected to be empty. For example, subtracting search time after infants had seen one object hidden and had retrieved it from search time after infants had seen two objects hidden and had retrieved just one of them creates a difference score. If infants represent two as more than one, this difference score should be positive. We found that when 12- and 14-month-old infants were presented with this task, they succeeded (i.e., had positive difference scores) with 1 vs. 2 and 2 vs. 3 comparisons,[3] but failed with 2 vs. 4 and 1 vs. 4 comparisons (Feigenson & Carey, 2003, 2005). When infants fail, we observe difference scores that are not different from chance (Figure 3.3).

Taken together, the results from the experiments just reviewed using change detection (Ross-Sheehy et al., 2003), cracker choice (Feigenson & Carey, 2005; Feigenson, Carey & Hauser, 2002), and manual search (Feigenson & Carey, 2003, 2005) have yielded identical patterns of results concerning infants' capacity limits. Whether infants saw food or nonfood objects, two-dimensional or three-dimensional objects, sequential or simultaneous presentation, or were asked to approach the larger of two total quantities, to search for hidden objects, or to

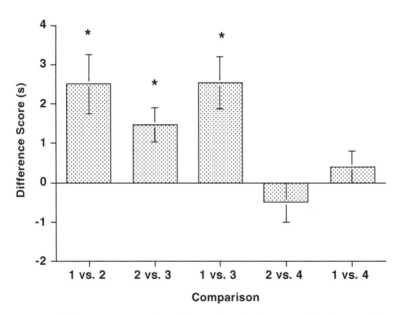

FIGURE 3.3. Difference scores (searching when the box contained more objects minus searching when the box was empty) reflect 12- to 14-month-old infants' capacity to represent and discriminate arrays containing different numbers of objects (Feigenson & Carey, 2003, 2005).

notice changing features in an object array, infants were limited to representing approximately three to four objects at a time in memory.

An important note concerning these observations of short-term memory capacity is that the three-to-four-item limit emerges in situations that require the tracking of objects qua individuals. In contrast, other tasks require infants to represent an array of items as a group whose members are not stored individually, as with a set of 16 dots scattered randomly on a screen. In such tasks, infants have been shown to represent the approximate numerosity of the whole array (Lipton & Spelke, 2003; McCrink & Wynn, 2004; Xu, 2003; Xu & Spelke, 2000; Xu, Spelke, & Goddard, 2005), but likely are not representing the individual dots that comprise the array. It appears that the ability to represent the approximate numerosity of a set containing many items and the ability to represent a small number of discrete individuals are subserved by different mental processes.

Several aspects of infants' performance with small versus large arrays support the view that infants represent them in fundamentally different ways. First, with large numerosities, such as Xu and Spelke's arrays of 16 or 24 dots, infants' success or failure depends on the ratio between to-be-discriminated arrays, rather than on the absolute number of items presented. For example, 6-month-old infants discriminate arrays of 16 from arrays of 32, but not from arrays of 24. We have already seen that for small arrays the reverse is true: It is the absolute number of items that determines performance (Feigenson & Carey, 2003, 2005; Feigenson, Carey, & Hauser, 2002). Second, infants often appear unable to represent the approximate numerosity of arrays containing four or fewer objects when the arrays are controlled for continuous properties that frequently correlate with number (Feigenson, Carey, & Hauser, 2002; Xu, 2003; Xu et al., 2005). In contrast, infants can represent the approximate numerosity of arrays that are controlled for continuous properties when the arrays contain large numbers of items (Lipton & Spelke, 2003; McCrink & Wynn, 2004; Xu, 2003; Xu & Spelke, 2000; Xu et al., 2005). These two divergent patterns of results suggest that two distinct mental systems are available to infants. One of these systems enables the representation of the approximate numerosity of large arrays. The other, which is the focus of the present discussion, allows precise representations of one to four items to be held in short-term memory (for further discussion of this two-system view, see Feigenson, Dehaene, & Spelke, 2004).

Further Evidence of Continuity: Increasing Short-Term Memory Storage via Chunking

Chunking in Adults

Besides claiming that adults have a limited-capacity short-term memory, Miller (1956) also suggested that this capacity could sometimes be increased by condensing information into a more efficient format. Specifically, Miller proposed that individual items could be bound together in memory into chunks whose components were in some way related to each other. If these chunks, rather than the individual items that comprised them, occupied the limited number of available memory slots, then the chunks could later be "unpacked" into their constituent components. Hence, the overall amount of information accessible via short-term memory could effectively be increased.

That chunking can indeed increase memory capacity in this way has been shown in impressive demonstrations of memory enhancement. One particular subject, S.F., was able to increase his memory span to nearly 80 random digits (Ericcson, Chase, & Faloon, 1980). S.F. had an entirely normal memory span at the start of the experiment, but after over 200 hours of laboratory practice he had a span equal to that of professional memory experts. S.F. accomplished this dramatic improvement by developing and perfecting his own idiosyncratic chunking strategy. He associated every three or four digits presented to him with a meaningful unit of information already present in his long-term memory. For example, S.F. remembered the digits 3, 4, 9, and 2 as "3 minutes and 49 point 2 seconds," which he knew was a near-record time to run the mile. The digits 1, 9, 4, and 4 were recalled as "1944, near the end of World War II." Interestingly, even by chunking four-digit strings into discrete chunks, the three-to-four-item limit on short-term memory should have prohibited S.F. from storing any more than three-to-four chunks containing a total of 12 to 16 individual digits. S.F. surpassed this expected limit by creating hierarchical memory entries in which chunks were nested within "superchunks." This extremely efficient collapsing of information accounted for S.F.'s impressive memory abilities. S.F.'s short-term memory enhancement is not an isolated case. Indeed, the finding that adults can use semantic information to increase storage has also been obtained with naive subjects. Typical college students were able to increase their short-term memory for digits over several laboratory sessions by associating groups of digits with preexisting referents, just as S.F. did (Chase & Ericsson, 1981).

A similar chunking mechanism has been found to underlie the exceptional performance of chess experts, who show vastly better memory for the configuration of pieces on a chessboard than do nonexperts. Rather than having a greater number of memory slots in which to store the individual pieces' locations, these experts benefited from the ability to chunk multiple pieces into recognizable formations (Simon & Chase, 1973). Doing so allowed them to store the entire board in terms of only a few formations, the individual components of which could be reconstructed from long-term memory. Support for the explanation that semantic knowledge allowed the formation of chunks comes from experiments testing the memory of expert versus novice players for randomly positioned pieces, as opposed to memory for configurations that might occur in an actual chess game. When presented with random configurations, the recall performance of experts was no better than that of novices (Simon & Chase, 1973).

Thus, the evidence indicates that adults can use existing knowledge to condense individual bits of information into larger chunks. Doing so enables the storage of more total units of information (e.g., more random digits or more locations on a chessboard). This is because short-term memory only has to retain the chunks themselves (e.g., a near-record time for running the mile), since the individual components of these chunks (e.g., 3, 4, 9, 2) already exist in long-term memory. Such a computation is clearly useful, allowing greater speed and efficiency of access to information across a wide variety of situations. But what are the origins of chunking? Is this highly useful strategy a learned one, perhaps acquired during formal education? Or is it available early on, prior to explicit instruction?

Chunking in Infants

My laboratory has addressed this question in a series of studies examining chunking in 14-month-old infants. Infants of this age had previously demonstrated a three-object memory limit in the manual search task, as discussed earlier (Feigenson & Carey, 2003, 2005). The new question was whether infants in this task could be induced to chunk individual items into smaller sets and thereby increase the total number of items remembered. To test this, we presented infants with arrays of identical objects that we then hid inside a box (Feigenson & Halberda, 2004). We used the same 1 vs. 2 and 2 vs. 4 object comparisons as in previous experiments (Feigenson & Carey, 2003, 2005). On 1 vs. 2 comparisons, we asked whether infants searched the box more after seeing two objects hidden and retrieving just one of them (the other was surreptitiously withheld) than they did after seeing one object hidden and retrieving one. Success would indicate the ability to remember at least two objects, and to recognize that two is more than one. On 2 vs. 4 comparisons, we asked whether infants searched the box more after seeing four objects hidden and retrieving just two of them (the other two were surreptitiously withheld) than they did after seeing two objects hidden and retrieving two. Here, success would indicate the ability to remember up to four objects, and the recognition that four is more than two.

Earlier in this chapter, I explained that infants had previously failed at this kind of 2 vs. 4 comparison when four objects were presented in a single line on top of the box. The new manipulation in this study was the spatial arrangement of the objects prior to hiding (see Figure 3.4). On some trials, all of the objects were presented in a single location centered on top of the box (e.g., four objects in a line atop the box). On other trials, the objects were presented on two spatially separated platforms located on either side of the box (e.g., two objects on the left-hand platform, and two on the right-hand platform). Our hypothesis was that this spatial grouping cue would help infants chunk four objects into two sets of two, thereby enabling them to successfully represent a total of four items at once.

We found that this spatial grouping changed the total number of objects infants were able to remember. Although infants succeed at distinguishing

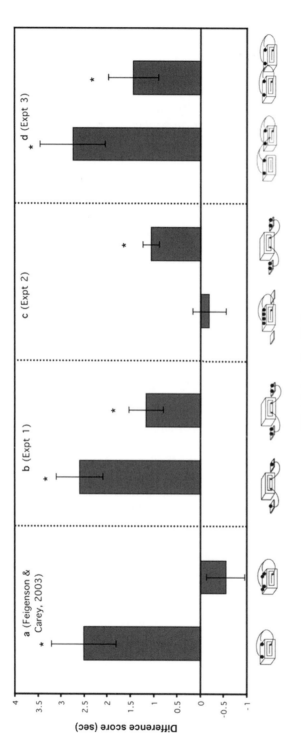

What Infants Saw Hidden

FIGURE 3.4. Difference scores (searching when the box contained more objects minus searching when the box was empty). Difference scores significantly above 0 reflect 14-month-old infants' capacity to remember the correct number of objects in the box. In (a), infants successfully remembered two objects in the box but failed to remember four. In (b), objects were spatially separated into two sets, each containing fewer than three objects. Infants again remembered two objects, and also successfully remembered four objects. In (c), infants' failure to remember four objects and their success at remembering two sets of two was replicated within-subject. In (d), infants remembered the precise location of each set when the sets were hidden in spatially separate locations. Reprinted from Feigenson, L., & Halberda, J. (2004). Infants chunk object arrays into sets of individuals. *Cognition, 91*, 173–190, copyright 2004, with permission from Elsevier.

1 vs. 2 no matter how the objects were arranged, they overcame the three-item short-term memory limit only on trials when the objects were spatially grouped. Only when objects were presented in two distinct groups of two did infants distinguish the hiding of two objects from the hiding of four (Figure 3.4). This pattern reveals two things. First, it replicates our previously reported three-item limit on infants' tracking of occluded objects (Feigenson & Carey, 2003, 2005), showing that infants were unable to store a single four-object array in memory. Second, these results also show that this limit can sometimes be overcome. By chunking representations of individual items into smaller units, infants were able to remember more total objects. The 14-month-old infants represented two chunks, each containing two individual objects. To our knowledge, this is the first demonstration of chunking in infants.

Top-Down Versus Bottom-Up Computations

Initiating Chunking

The data reviewed above suggest that the chunking operations that were classically studied by Miller and others may be both independent of formal training and available quite early in life. If so, this clearly strengthens the case for the continuity of short-term memory throughout the life span, as both the limits on short-term storage and the chunking used to overcome these limits appear to be present in infants as well as in adults. However, there is an important difference between the finding that adults can increase short-term memory capacity and the finding that infants can do so. The adult chunking studies show that adults can use semantic knowledge to condense information. For example, adults can bind multiple individual items together based on existing knowledge (as with the race time example) or can recognize multiple individuals as forming a meaningful gestalt (as with the chess expert example). These computations rely on semantic knowledge that is available for association with the objects in the array. The computations thus can be considered top-down, in the sense that they are driven from the internal knowledge to the external, to-be-chunked items in the world.

Can infants use semantic knowledge to drive chunking? Our developmental results (Feigenson & Halberda, 2004) show that the spatial organization of an array into sets, each of which contains three or fewer items, helps infants overcome the three-to-four-item limit on short-term memory. However, unlike S.F. or the chess experts, infants relied on spatiotemporal rather than semantic information. Furthermore, the computation they performed was bottom-up in the sense that the requisite information for chunking was present in the array itself, rather than in infants' existing knowledge. The spatial arrangement that the experimenter imposed on the array led infants to parse it into smaller sets, rather than infants themselves imposing their knowledge to reorganize their representation of the array. Thus far, it is an open question whether infants can also chunk in a top-down fashion on the basis of stored semantic knowledge.

Experiments in my lab are currently exploring which sources of information infants can use to chunk an array. As in our earlier investigations, we take as evidence for chunking the ability to represent a total of four objects in our manual search task. These previous studies revealed that infants could do so only if they saw the four-object array presented as two spatially separated sets, each containing fewer than three items (Feigenson & Halberda, 2004). In a series of new studies, we replace spatial information with semantic information as the potential basis for chunking. Infants see all four objects in a single line atop the box—a spatial arrangement that has previously led infants to fail. However, we now show infants an array of two cars and two cats, instead of the four identical balls we used in our earlier studies (Feigenson & Carey, 2003, 2005; Feigenson & Halberda, 2004). Given that 14-month-old infants are reported by their parents to be familiar with these entities (and given that most 14-month-olds already know the words *car* and *cat*, or *kitty*; Fenson et al., 1994), we hypothesize that infants may be able to use this semantic knowledge to chunk the four-object array into two sets of two. To ask whether any observed success is based on semantic knowledge of the object categories, as opposed to low-level perceptual differences between the two types of objects, on other trials we present infants with two sets of two objects that are perceptually distinct, yet from unfamiliar categories. If infants fail to represent all four objects when presented with unfamiliar objects, such as two toy shrimp and two toy tanks, but succeed with two cars and two cats, then we can more confidently say that infants are able to use semantic knowledge in a top-down fashion to chunk the array.

Initiating Computations of Discrete and Continuous Quantity

The question of whether infants can initiate top-down computations over object representations is not exclusive to chunking, but also arises for other operations performed over representations being held in memory. An example comes from the work on infants' computations of quantity. Infants have been shown to be capable of computing the discrete number of individual objects in object arrays, showing different looking patterns to expected versus unexpected numbers of objects (Cheries, DeCoste, & Wynn, 2003) or searching a box until the expected number of objects has been retrieved (Feigenson & Carey, 2003). These findings obtain when the total area or volume of the arrays is controlled for. Infants also can compute the total continuous extent contained in an array, showing increased looking when the overall summed area or perimeter of the items in the array changes (Clearfield & Mix, 1999, 2001; Feigenson, Carey, & Hauser, 2002) or choosing to approach an array containing a greater total volume of food over an array containing a smaller total volume, regardless of the number of individual objects involved (Feigenson, Carey, & Spelke, 2002). That these quantity computations operate over the same short-term memory representations discussed above is shown by the conditions under which infants successfully perform them. Infants can compute discrete or continuous quantity over arrays containing small numbers of objects. But when arrays contain four or more objects, infants fail to compute either number or total extent (Feigenson & Carey, 2003, 2005; Feigenson, Carey, & Hauser, 2002; Xu, 2003; Xu et al., 2005). Thus, recognizing the number of objects in an array and recognizing the total extent contained in the array are both the output of computations performed over short-term memory representations of objects. When there are too many objects to be represented in short-term memory, infants fail to compute either number or total extent.

What prompts infants to respond to the discrete (e.g., number of individual objects) versus continuous (e.g., color, total extent) properties of a given object array? Although this question will likely be the focus of many future experiments, one recent set of findings suggests that the features of the objects themselves play a role in determining which dimension of quantity infants represent. A group of 7-month-old infants was habituated to object arrays, then tested with arrays in which either the number of objects or the total surface area had changed (Feigenson, 2005; Feigenson, Carey, & Spelke, 2002). The results revealed that when the array contained objects that were identical in color, pattern, and texture, infants dishabituated to changes in the total area of the array, but not to changes in the number of objects in the array. When the array contained objects that contrasted with each other in color, pattern, and texture, however, infants did just the reverse. They dishabituated to changes in the number of objects in the array but not to changes in total area. In other words, infants appeared able to compute either number or surface area but unable to perform both computations over the same array. Figure 3.5 depicts this double dissociation.

In these experiments, the computation that infants performed (number versus total extent) appeared to be under exogenous control, influenced in a bottom-up fashion based on whether objects in the array had identical properties or not. In contrast, adults can exert top-down control over these computations, choosing whether to represent the number or extent contained in an array even on a trial-by-trial basis (Feigenson & Halberda, in preparation). Thus, infants and adults may differ in the endogenous versus exogenous nature of the quantity computations they can perform.

What Develops?

In the preceding pages, I have tried to build the case that infants and adults share a system for maintaining object representations in short-term memory. This system is capacity limited and can only store representations of three to

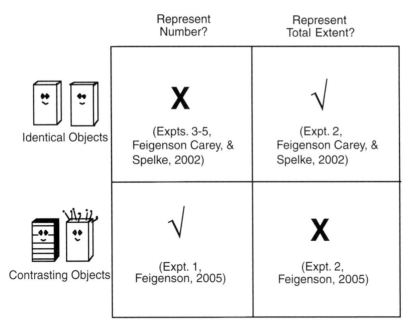

FIGURE 3.5. Double dissociation between array heterogeneity and the computation infants perform over the objects in the array. Reprinted from Feigenson, L. (2005). A double dissociation in infants' representation of object arrays. *Cognition, 95,* B37–B48, copyright 2005, with permission from Elsevier.

four individuals at any one time. Once stored in short-term memory, infants and adults can perform a range of computations over these representations. For example, we have begun to understand the ways in which infants and adults compute quantity, both discrete and continuous, over object arrays. In addition, both infants and adults appear able to reorganize representations of individuals into a hierarchical structure. This chunking of object representations provides a link between limited-capacity short-term memory and the greater storage capacity of long-term memory, and has been shown to enable both infants and adults to overcome the three-to-four-item limit on simultaneous representation. In all of these ways, the representations stored by and the computations performed by infants and adults are strikingly similar.

Where, then, is the development in short-term memory? While I have focused on the respects in which short-term memory may be continuous over development, there may also be important ways in which early versus mature short-term memory differs. I now point to some existing research, some of which is addressed by other chapters in this volume, as well as to avenues for future investigation of short-term memory development.

First, we have already explored some possible differences in short-term memory computations in terms of bottom-up versus top-down processing.

Adults can use semantic knowledge to endogenously initiate the chunking of representations held in short-term memory, and have volition over which dimension of quantity to represent. It remains unclear whether infants also have this ability. To date, infants' computations over object arrays appear to be driven from the bottom up by perceptual information present in the array itself. Even if new research finds that infants can initiate the chunking of an object array in a top-down fashion (for example, by using conceptual knowledge of animals versus vehicles to parse an array into these two categories), the comparative richness of adult knowledge about the world will likely be reflected in developmental differences. If infants do have some top-down control over the chunking of object arrays, this control will almost certainly increase over time. As they come to refine their knowledge of object kinds and categories, infants may gain more ways to parse arrays into chunks and therefore gain more avenues for motivating top-down chunking. Exploring developmental changes in the top-down versus bottom-up execution of short-term memory computations is a promising direction for future research.

In addition, much remains to be understood about the nature of infants' and adults' capacity limits. Although both groups appear able to store up to three to four items in short-term memory, information capacity within each of these three to four available slots is probably not fixed. For example, representing three very complex objects with many features and articulated parts may impose a higher informational load than representing three simple geometric shapes. Alvarez and Cavanaugh (2004) measured this load empirically using a change detection task, and confirmed that the number of objects adults can store depends on the objects' complexity. Adults were able to maintain a larger number of items in visual short-term memory when those items were simple colored squares than when the items were more complex letters or shapes. These results show that although short-term memory can store a maximum number of about four items, the information load of the array can significantly reduce this capacity. This question has yet to be systematically explored in infants, and it raises the possibility that infants and adults may differ in the amount of information they can store in each memory slot. Can infants represent multiple features of three to four complex objects, or are they limited to representing just a few salient properties? Systematically manipulating object complexity will help characterize the subtle limits of short-term memory development.

Finally, while the eventual upper limit on short-term memory appears fixed at three to four items, infants' memory capacity may not reach this limit for some time. In their change detection experiments, Ross-Sheehy et al. (2003) found that 10- and 13-month-old infants detected a changing item contained within a three- or four-item array. But 4- and 6.5-month-old infants could only detect a change with a one-item array, failing with arrays of two and three. A similar pattern has been obtained by Kaldy and Leslie (2005), using a quite different paradigm in which infants are asked to track the shape of three-dimensional objects that move behind occluding screens.

Based on their results, Kaldy and Leslie suggest that 6.5-month-old infants' short-term memory capacity is limited to just one slot. These findings raise the possibility that the capacity of short-term memory increases over the first year of life and reaches asymptote by 10 to 12 months.

This interesting developmental proposal may conflict with previous findings that even by 5 months, infants can successfully track and remember at least two hidden objects at a time (Koechlin et al., 1997; Simon et al., 1995; Wynn, 1992). Ross-Sheehy et al. (2003) suggested that these previous results might not be tapping short-term memory and that, because infants view objects over much longer durations than in the change detection task (several seconds, compared with 500 milliseconds), long-term memory might also be involved. This issue merits deeper exploration. The three-to-four-item limit is observed in tasks involving a wide range of durations, from 500 milliseconds to 30 seconds or more. Does this commonality implicate a single system of memory representation encompassing a wide span of durations? Might there be multiple levels of memory storage that are all limited by a single bottleneck on information processing?

These questions return us to the issues raised by Cowan's (2001) controversial proposal regarding the distinctions between attention, short-term memory, and long-term memory. The developmental evidence reviewed here does not provide definitive answers. Nonetheless, characterizing infants' memory—both its capacities and its limitations—may offer a window into understanding these systems and the interactions between them. As we identify the continuities and discontinuities in representational ability across the life span, we add to the emerging portrait of memory development over time.

Notes

1. Previous work (Feigenson, Carey, & Hauser, 2002; Scholl & Leslie, 1999; Simon, 1997; Uller et al., 1999) has suggested that infants and adults share a system that is dedicated to tracking objects per se, and to storing information about their properties. This "object-file" system enables the creation of a token, or file, that stands for an object in the world and allows it to be represented over changes in spatial location or changes in properties (Kahneman, Treisman, & Gibbs, 1992). While such a system may indeed be in place throughout development, here I make the more general claim that infants and adults share a system for representing discrete items in short-term memory. These items may be objects, but may also be nonobject entities such as sounds or events that are perceived in any sensory modality.

2. Presenting the cue less than 1 second after the array disappeared resulted in much higher capacity limits, which Sperling took as evidence for the existence of a very short-lived, iconic memory store. Iconic memory, which lasts for less than a second, is distinct from the short-term memory that is the focus of the present discussion.

3. Note that this method does not allow us to be certain of the exact number of objects infants represented in the box. For example, for infants who saw three objects hidden, retrieved one of them, and then continued to search, infants may have believed there to be exactly two objects still remaining. Alternatively, it is possible that they represented just one more object in the box or an unspecified number of objects remaining in the box.

References

Alvarez, G. A., & Cavanaugh, P. (2004). The capacity of visual short-term memory is set both by visual information load and by number of objects. *Psychological Science, 15,* 106–111.

Alvarez, G. A., & Franconeri, S. L. (2005). *How many objects can you track?* Paper presented at the annual meeting of the Vision Sciences Society, Sarasota, FL.

Baillargeon, R. (1986). Representing the existence and location of hidden objects: Object permanence in 6- and 8-month old infants. *Cognition, 23,* 21–41.

Baillargeon, R., Spelke, E. S., & Wasserman, S. (1985). Object permanence in five-month-old infants. *Cognition, 20,* 191–208.

Carey, S. (2004). Bootstrapping and the origins of concepts. *Daedalus, 133,* 59–68.

Chase, W. G., & Ericsson, K. A. (1981). Skilled memory. In J. R. Anderson (Ed.), *Cognitive skills and their acquisition* (pp. 141–189). Mahwah, NJ: Erlbaum.

Cheries, E. W., DeCoste, C., & Wynn, K. (2003). *Number Not Area: Infants Use Property Contrasts for Quantifying Objects.* Poster presented at the Society for Research in Child Development, Tampa, FL.

Clearfield, M. W., & Mix, K. S. (1999). Number versus contour length in infants' discrimination of small visual sets. *Psychological Science, 10*(5), 408–411.

Clearfield, M. W., & Mix, K. S. (2001). Infants' use of area and contour length to discriminate small sets. *Journal of Cognition and Development, 2,* 243–260.

Cowan, N. (2001). The magical number 4 in short-term memory: A reconsideration of mental storage capacity. *Behavioral and Brain Sciences, 24,* 87–185.

Diamond, A. (1990). Rate of maturation of the hippocampus and the developmental progression of children's performance on the delayed nonmatching to sample and visual paired comparison tasks. *Annals of the New York Academy of Sciences, 608,* 637–676.

Ericsson, K. A., Chase, W. G., & Faloon, S. (1980). Acquisition of a memory skill. *Science, 208,* 1181–1182.

Feigenson, L. (2005). A double dissociation in infants' representation of object arrays. *Cognition, 95,* B37–B48.

Feigenson, L., & Carey, S. (2003). Tracking individuals via object-files: Evidence from infants' manual search. *Developmental Science, 6,* 568–584.

Feigenson, L., & Carey, S. (2005). On the limits of infants' quantification of small object arrays. *Cognition, 97,* 295–313.

Feigenson, L., Carey, S., & Hauser, M. (2002). The representations underlying infants' choice of more: Object files versus analog magnitudes. *Psychological Science, 13*(2), 150–156.

Feigenson, L., Carey, S., & Spelke, E. (2002). Infants' discrimination of number vs. continuous extent. *Cognitive Psychology, 44*(1), 33–66.

Feigenson, L., Dehaene, S., & Spelke, E. S. (2004). Core systems of number. *Trends in Cognitive Sciences, 8*(7), 307–314.

Feigenson, L., & Halberda, J. (2004). Infants chunk object arrays into sets of individuals. *Cognition, 91,* 173–190.

Feigenson, L., & Halberda, J. (in preparation). *Computations made over set representations.*

Fenson, L., Dale, P. S., Reznick, J. S., Bates, E., Thal, D., Pethick, S. J., et al. (1994). Variability in early communicative development. *Monographs of the Society for Research in Child Development, 242.*

Halberda, J., Simons, D., & Wetherhold, J. (2006). *The flicker-paradigm provides converging evidence for a 3-item limit of visual working memory.* Manuscript submitted for publication.

Halberda, J., Sires, S. F., & Feigenson, L. (2006). Multiple spatially overlapped sets can be enumerated in parallel. *Psychological Science, 17*(7), 572–576.

Hood, B., & Willats, P. (1986). Reaching in the dark to an object's remembered position: Evidence for object permanence in 5-month-old infants. *British Journal of Developmental Psychology, 4,* 57–65.

James, W. (1890). *The principles of psychology.* New York: Henry Holt.

Kahneman, D., Treisman, A., & Gibbs, B. (1992). The reviewing of object files: Object-specific integration of information. *Cognitive Psychology, 24*(2), 175–219.

Kaldy, Z., & Leslie, A. M. (2003). Individuation of objects in 9-month-old infants: Integrating "what" and "where" information. *Developmental Science, 6*(3), 360–373.

Kaldy, Z., & Leslie, A. M. (2005). A memory span of one? Object identification in 6.5-month old infants. *Cognition, 97*(2), 153–157.

Koechlin, E., Dehaene, S., & Mehler, J. (1997). Numerical transformations in five month old human infants. *Mathematical Cognition, 3,* 89–104.

Lipton, J. S., & Spelke, E. S. (2003). Origins of number sense: Large number discrimination in human infants. *Psychological Science, 15,* 396–401.

Luck, S. J., & Vogel, E. K. (1997). The capacity of visual working memory for features and conjunctions. *Nature, 390,* 279–281.

McCrink, K., & Wynn, K. (2004). Large-number addition and subtraction in infants. *Psychological Science, 15,* 776–781.

Miller, G. A. (1956). The magical number seven, plus or minus two: Some limits on our capacity for processing information. *Psychological Review, 63,* 81–97.

Noles, N., Scholl, B. J., & Mitroff, S. R. (2005). The persistence of object file representations. *Perception and Psychophysics, 67*(2), 324–334.

Pylyshyn, Z. W. (1994). Some primitive mechanisms of spatial attention. *Cognition, 50,* 363–384.

Pylyshyn, Z. W. (2001). Visual indexes, preconceptual objects, and situated vision. *Cognition, 80,* 127–158.

Pylyshyn, Z. W., & Storm, R. W. (1988). Tracking multiple independent targets: Evidence for a parallel tracking mechanism. *Spatial Vision, 3*(3), 179–197.

Ross-Sheehy, S., Oakes, L. M., & Luck, S. J. (2003). The development of visual short-term memory capacity in infants. *Child Development, 74,* 1807–1822.

Scholl, B. J., & Leslie, A. M. (1999). Explaining the infant's object concept: Beyond the perception/cognition dichotomy. In E. Lepore & Z. Pylyshyn (Eds.), *What is cognitive science?* (pp. 26–73). Oxford, UK: Blackwell.

Shinskey, J. L., & Munakata, Y. (2003). Are infants in the dark about hidden objects? *Developmental Science, 6,* 273–282.

Simon, H. A., & Chase, W. G. (1973). Skill in chess. *American Scientist, 61,* 393–403.

Simon, T., Hespos, S. J., & Rochat, P. (1995). Do infants understand simple arithmetic? A replication of Wynn (1992). *Cognitive Development, 10,* 253–269.

Simon, T. J. (1997). Reconceptualizing the origins of number knowledge: A "non-numerical" account. *Cognitive Development, 12,* 349–372.

Sperling, G. (1960). The information available in brief visual presentations. *Psychological Monographs, 74.*

Trick, L., & Pylyshyn, Z. (1994). Why are small and large numbers enumerated differently? A limited-capacity preattentive stage in vision. *Psychological Review, 101*(1), 80–102.

Uller, C., Huntley-Fenner, G., Carey, S., & Klatt, L. (1999). What representations might underlie infant numerical knowledge? *Cognitive Development, 14,* 1–36.

Wynn, K. (1992). Addition and subtraction by human infants. *Nature, 358,* 749–750.

Xu, F. (2003). Numerosity discrimination in infants: Evidence for two systems of representation. *Cognition, 89,* B15–B25.

Xu, F., & Spelke, E. S. (2000). Large number discrimination in 6-month old infants. *Cognition, 74,* B1–B11.

Xu, F., Spelke, E. S., & Goddard, S. (2005). Number sense in human infants. *Developmental Science, 8,* 88–101.

4

The Development of Visual Short-Term Memory in Infancy

LISA M. OAKES, SHANNON ROSS-SHEEHY,
AND STEVEN J. LUCK

Short-term storage of visual information is critically important for many cognitive functions. Comparing two items that cannot be simultaneously foveated—for example, deciding which of two cookies is larger—requires that the information about one item (e.g., one cookie) be maintained in a visual short-term memory (VSTM) store while foveating the other item (e.g., the other cookie; Pomplun, Reingold, & Shen, 2001; Pomplun et al., 2001). Similarly, integrating views of the world separated by saccades requires that those views be stored in VSTM (Hollingworth & Henderson, 2002; Irwin, 1991). VSTM is therefore critical for the online use of visual information and is critically important for cognitive development. Given that visual exploration is a primary means of infants' learning about the world, not to mention the enormous number of novel objects they encounter, infants must develop the ability to effectively compare objects online. Consider, for example, an infant presented with a new toy among several familiar toys. Determining that the new toy is similar to one of the old toys requires that he or she be able to compare the features of the new toy with the features of the familiar toys.

Infants must use VSTM to make such comparisons during almost every waking moment. Until 3 months of age, for example, infants require several small saccades to fixate an object such as an attractive toy, and they have difficulty fluidly tracking moving objects (Atkinson, 1984). Integrating that information certainly depends on effectively storing information in VSTM. Similarly, in the occlusion events often used to study cognitive development, infants are exposed to an initial object for a brief period of time (e.g., a few seconds), the object is occluded for a brief period of time (e.g., a few seconds), and then the old or a new object is revealed. Comparing the objects encountered before and after occlusion requires that infants keep the initial object active in VSTM. Thus, limitations in the ability to represent objects in VSTM likely have a large impact on how infants perform in these studies, and a deeper understanding of VSTM in infancy, and how it develops, will provide a deeper understanding of infants' performance on such tasks. Moreover, tracking objects as they are occluded and disoccluded is a common part of infants' everyday experience—VSTM is necessary for infants to recognize, for example, that a ball that rolls under the couch is the same ball that emerges from the other side a short time later.

As is evident from many of the chapters in this volume, psychologists have intensively studied infants' memory abilities for over 30 years, and much work has focused on memory for visual objects, such as faces (e.g., Fagan, 1976) or geometric patterns (e.g., Rose, Gottfried, Melloy-Carminar, & Bridger, 1982). These studies have revealed impressive memory abilities in infancy. For example, infants a few hours old can encode and remember a visually presented stimulus (Slater, Earle, Morison, & Rose, 1985; Slater, Mattock, Brown, Burnham, & Young, 1991), and infants remember visual information for hours or even days (Fagan, 1970, 1973; Rose, 1981). Moreover, infants' representations of objects in memory have been a focus of research in developmental psychology since the time of Piaget (1954). Researchers have asked questions such as whether infants represent objects as being permanent (Baillargeon, 1993) and solid and bounded (Spelke, 1988), as well as whether they use object features to individuate hidden objects (Wilcox & Baillargeon, 1998) and make inferences about how hidden objects interact (Baillargeon, 1993).

However, little work has focused specifically on how infants represent objects in VSTM, or how their VSTM abilities develop (see chapter 3, this volume, for one of the few programs of research explicitly investigating infants' representations of objects in STM). As described later, most work on infants' memory uses tasks that almost certainly involve long-term memory (LTM) systems. Therefore, one challenge for the study of VSTM in infancy is to develop procedures that emphasize VSTM and minimize the role of longer-term memory systems. We have developed such a procedure, and we have begun to study the development of VSTM using this procedure. In this chapter, we first describe what we mean by VSTM and how short-term memory (STM) in our task is related to short-term memory (and working memory) more broadly. We then describe how we have met the challenges of measuring VSTM in infancy and provide a discussion of our procedure. Next we provide data from this procedure that provides an initial description of the development of VSTM over the first year of life and consider the mechanisms that underlie this development. Finally, we discuss the future challenges for this area. Each of the following sections, therefore, addresses one of the questions that provide the unifying themes for this volume.

What Is VSTM?

Psychologists have distinguished between STM and LTM systems for over 100 years (e.g., James, 1890), but our current view of STM comes from work by Baddeley and his colleagues starting in the mid-1970s (Baddeley & Hitch, 1974). The focus of this research was to ask whether the memory system that is used in typical STM tasks is a *working memory* (i.e., a memory system that is used for the temporary storage and manipulation of information in the service of complex tasks). Baddeley and Hitch found that tasks such as reasoning and reading were impaired when STM was filled to capacity by a concurrent task, such as the digit span task. On the basis of these results, they concluded that STM tasks do indeed tap into a working memory system. Moreover, they developed a model of working memory in which modality-specific *slave systems* are used for storing information, and a *central executive* is used to read, write, and manipulate this information.

Baddeley and Logie (1999) described two slave systems used for visual information: the *visual cache,* used for storing visual object identities, and the *visuospatial sketchpad,* used to store spatial information. Much research has used a change-detection paradigm to understand the visual cache and the visuospatial sketchpad in adults (see, e.g., Luck & Vogel, 1997; Phillips, 1974; Simons, 1996; Vogel, Woodman, & Luck, 2001). For example, in the change detection paradigm developed by Luck and Vogel (1997; Vogel et al., 2001), participants are presented with a series of trials during which a sample array and a test array are presented, separated by a 900-millisecond delay (see Figure 4.1A). The two arrays are identical on 50% of trials and differ in terms of one object on the remaining 50% (e.g., the color of one object might change). The participants simply indicate on each trial whether or not the two arrays are identical. Procedures such as asking participants to verbally repeat digits are used to ensure that performance reflects visual rather than verbal memory.

The number of items in each array (the set size) is varied to assess how many items can be stored in VSTM. As shown in Figure 4.1B, Luck and

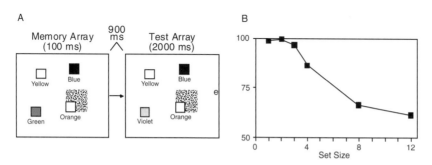

FIGURE 4.1. Schematic of the procedure (A) used by Luck and Vogel (1997) and the results for adults' accuracy at detecting a change for displays of set sizes 2, 3, 4, 8, and 12 (B).

Vogel (1997; Vogel et al., 2001) observed that accuracy in detecting color changes in this task was at ceiling for set sizes 1 through 3 and then declined systematically as set size increased from 4 to 12 items. These results, as well as a more formal quantitative analysis, suggest that adult observers have a VSTM capacity of three to four items (similar storage capacity estimates have been observed for other feature dimensions, such as orientation). Other studies have yielded similar capacity estimates (see review by Cowan, 2001), and complementary results have been obtained using real-world scenes (Hollingworth, Schrock, & Henderson, 2001; Rensink, O'Regan, & Clark, 1997; Simons & Levin, 1997). Moreover, performance is just as accurate for multifeature objects as for single-feature objects. That is, when presented with colored rectangles, adults can remember both the color and the orientation of those rectangles just as easily as they can remember only the color or only the orientation of the rectangles. In fact, adults can remember four-feature objects just as well as single-feature objects. Thus, Luck and Vogel (1997; Vogel et al., 2001) concluded that the features of an object are bound together into an integrated object representation in VSTM—similar results were obtained by Irwin and Andrews (1996) and by Y. Xu (2002).

The goal of our work is to understand the origins of VSTM and how it develops in infancy. Although infants' memory for visually presented objects has been studied for decades, their memory generally been assessed using procedures that recruit LTM systems, and therefore conclusions about VSTM are difficult to draw. Specifically, most studies of infants' memory for visually presented objects have used habituation or novelty preference procedures in which infants are first shown one stimulus for tens of seconds (or more), and then their memory for that stimulus is inferred from the duration of their looking at a novel stimulus in comparison to the duration of their looking at the now familiar stimulus (see chapters 7 and 8, this volume, for a discussion of such procedures). If infants look longer at the novel stimulus, it is assumed they remembered the familiar stimulus. Although these paradigms evaluate memory over a relatively short period of retention (i.e., tens of seconds), they do not isolate the kind of STM systems studied in the adult literature in which the stimuli are presented for a few hundred milliseconds and the retention interval is as short as a tenth of a second. Instead, infants study the familiarization stimulus for tens of seconds (or more), providing plenty of time for LTM encoding, and infants have shown a reliable preference for a novel stimulus after seconds (Diamond, 1995), minutes (Courage & Howe, 2001), or hours and days (Fagan, 1970, 1973; Rose, 1981). For these reasons, previous demonstrations of memory using these tasks probably reflect the use of both STM and LTM stores.

In terms of infants' representations of objects in VSTM, there are two key questions: (1) what features are represented; and (2) how are those features combined to form representations of multifeature objects? Although they do not separate STM and LTM, studies using habituation and familiarization have provided significant insights into infants' representations of visually presented objects (see Kellman & Arterberry, 1998, for a review). Between birth and 3 months, infants represent object identity features such as object color (Bornstein, 1976), orientation (Bornstein, Krinsky, & Benasich, 1986), and shape (Quinn, Slater, Brown, & Hayes, 2001). Between 3 and 5 months, infants can encode and remember location—either the location of an object in relation to a landmark (Quinn, 1994) or the location of an object when it was hidden and then revealed (Newcombe, Huttenlocher, & Learmonth, 1999; Wilcox, Rosser, & Nadel, 1994).

Moreover, in procedures that likely involve LTM, infants can bind features into integrated, multifeature representations. For example, infants familiarized with two compound stimuli (e.g., a red circle and a green square) dishabituated to new feature combinations (e.g., a red square and a green circle; Bushnell & Roder, 1985; Slater et al., 1991; Taga et al., 2002; but see L. B. Cohen, 1973, for a counterexample). Infants must have represented, therefore, not only what features were presented, but also how they were combined. Interestingly, although the ability to bind two object identity features (such as color and orientation) emerges at an early age, the ability to bind object identity and location appears to develop somewhat later. After several familiarization trials in which particular objects were hidden in specific locations, infants between 4 and 5.5 months failed to learn the object-location associations (Mareschal & Johnson, 2003; Newcombe et al., 1999). Catherwood, Skoien, Green, and Holt (1996) did observe that 5-month-old infants could represent the conjunction between an object's color and location, but only when the processing time on each familiarization trial was maximized. It is possible that 5-month-old infants are just beginning to be able to combine information about location and identity and therefore require considerable processing time to do so.

Using a different procedure, Káldy and Leslie (2003) did find clear evidence that by 9 months infants can bind object identity to location. During familiarization, infants were presented with two objects being placed in each of two locations (alternating across trials); thus they could become familiar with the objects in each possible location, but they could not form a single long-term representation of one object on the left and the other object on the right, as in the studies described earlier. During test trials, infants observed the two objects being moved behind occluders placed at the familiar locations. When the occluders were removed, infants looked longer when the objects were in unexpected (e.g., reversed) locations than if the objects were in the expected locations, suggesting that they bound object shape to location. Because infants were shown both possible outcomes during familiarization, this preference does not reflect an LTM representation formed during familiarization. However, because during the test infants had several seconds to learn the relative locations of the objects, these data do not unambiguously rule out the influence of longer term memory systems in infants' binding of object identity and location. What is clear is that the ability to bind together object identity features (e.g., color and orientation) is present early in infancy, but the ability to bind object identity and location develops at 5 months of age or later. However, because these studies of binding used a variety of different methods, this conclusion is tentative.

These studies of infants' object representations in LTM provide the foundation for the study of VSTM in infancy. They demonstrate that, when LTM systems are involved, infants have robust memories for object identities and locations and can bind features of objects from an early age. This work does not directly address, however, how infants represent information in VSTM because the tasks used to study infants' representations of objects have not sufficiently isolated VSTM.

Measuring VSTM in Infancy

Although a number of procedures have been developed to assess infants' memory for visual information, these procedures do not emphasize STM systems. As described earlier, in tasks such as habituation and novelty preference, infants are familiarized with items for tens of seconds (or more) before their memory for those items is assessed. STM systems, however, are assumed to create memory representations rapidly, have a limited capacity, and require active rehearsal to maintain the representations beyond a few seconds. Therefore, we developed a procedure based on the change-detection paradigm developed by Luck and Vogel (1997; see Figure 4.1) that more clearly emphasizes STM systems. As shown in Figure 4.2, infants are shown two simultaneous streams of colored squares that blink on and off repeatedly. On one monitor, the colors of the squares remain constant from cycle to cycle. On the other monitor, the color of one randomly chosen square changes in each new cycle. The displays are presented for a brief period of time (500 milliseconds) and are separated by a brief delay (250 milliseconds). We measure the amount of time infants spend looking at the changing and unchanging streams, and we then compare how much time infants look at the changing stimulus streams relative to the unchanging stream on each trial.

This procedure is a variant of the paired-comparison procedure, which rests on the assumption that given the choice of two similar displays, infants will look longer to the display that imposes a greater information load (typically because it is more novel or complex). In the present context, one display remains constant, imposing a low load, and the other changes, imposing a higher load. Indeed, others have observed that infants prefer to look at stimulus streams that vary compared to stimulus streams that remain the same (Cornell & Heth, 1979; Fantz, 1964). Thus, we expected that infants would prefer to look at the changing displays compared to the nonchanging displays, but only if they could form a memory of the colors and keep those colors active in memory across the 250-millisecond delay.

We evaluated memory capacity by varying the set size. We assessed infants' ability to detect a change with between one and six items in each display.

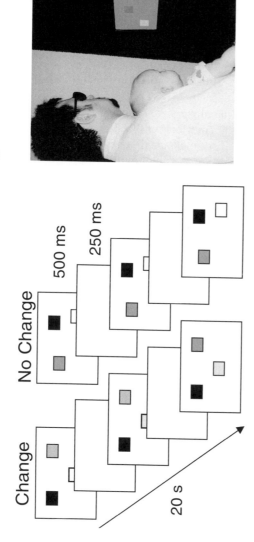

FIGURE 4.2. Schematic depiction of changing and nonchanging stimulus streams used by Ross-Sheehy, Oakes, and Luck (2003) to assess infants' VSTM capacity for object color (A) and a photograph of our experimental setup (B). For each infant, the left-right position of the changing stream was counterbalanced across trials to minimize the effect of side biases on infants' responding (this procedure was used in all of our experiments). Ross-Sheehy et al. (2003) presented infants with changing and nonchanging streams at different set sizes to evaluate developmental changes in infants' VSTM capacity for color (see text for details).

If an infant's memory capacity is greater than or equal to the set size, then the infant should detect the color changes and show a preference for the changing display. When the set size exceeds VSTM capacity, infants should be less likely to detect the change, and the changing and nonchanging displays will become functionally equivalent. Therefore, infants will exhibit significant preferences for changing displays when the set size is within their VSTM capacity, and they will not exhibit significant preferences for changing displays that substantially exceed their VSTM capacity. For example, an infant with a capacity of one item may show a strong preference for the change displays only at set size 1, whereas an infant with a capacity of three items may show strong preferences at set sizes up to 3. Some preference for the changing displays may be observed beyond an infant's capacity because some of the changes can be detected even if only a subset of the items are stored in memory. However, the degree of preference should decline substantially when capacity is exceeded. Thus, this procedure provides a means of assessing changes in the storage capacity of VSTM.

Several aspects of this paradigm were designed to emphasize the use of VSTM and to minimize the contribution of LTM. First, each display was presented for only 500 milliseconds, maximizing the need for rapid memory formation, especially for arrays containing multiple items. Second, although the stimulus arrays were presented for many cycles over a 20-second interval, a given color was not repeated very many times before changing to a different color (in the changing streams). At set size 1, each item was presented only once before being changed. At set sizes 2 and 3, a given color was presented an average of two or three times, respectively, before being changed. The small total exposure duration before a change thus minimized contributions from LTM. In addition, the retention period was only 250 milliseconds, which should be well within the expected duration of STM. Moreover, studies with adults have demonstrated that a 70-millisecond delay is sufficient to prevent the use of iconic memory for accurate change detection (e.g., Rensink et al., 1997), so the 250-millisecond delay used in our procedure should be more than adequate to minimize any contributions from iconic memory. Finally, all of the items were simple colored squares and were therefore highly similar to each other. Such intra- and intertrial similarity leads to substantial interference between LTM representations (Murdock, 1961), minimizing any contribution from LTM.

How does VSTM in infants as assessed in this task relate to the working memory systems proposed by Baddeley? As described earlier, our task emphasizes STM rather than LTM because infants must create memory representations rapidly (in 500 milliseconds), and they need only to maintain the representations for a very brief time (250 milliseconds). In addition, as is discussed in the next section, we have observed that infants have a limited memory capacity in this task. But does this task isolate a working memory system in Baddley's terms? Although our procedure is designed to isolate the visual cache component of Baddeley's working memory model—and is based on a paradigm that isolates the visual cache in adults—it is extremely difficult to demonstrate that the memory system tapped by this procedure in infants is actually a working memory system (i.e., that it is used in the service of cognitive tasks, such as category formation). Consequently, in our work we use the more conservative term *short-term memory* rather than *working memory* to refer to the memory system we are studying. However, it is very likely that we are indeed studying the developmental origins of the adult working memory system (see chapter 1, this volume, for an excellent alternative discussion of a conceptualization of the relationship between working memory and STM in tasks used with infants).

Characterizing VSTM in Infancy

Using the change detection procedure, we have conducted a number of experiments aimed at addressing the following questions: (1) When can infants begin to represent objects in VSTM? (2) How does infants' capacity for object identity in VSTM change over development? (3) How does infants' representation of location in VSTM change over development? (4) How mature are these VSTM representations? These experiments are described in the following subsections.

Can Infants Represent Objects in VSTM?

As a first step, we used our task to assess VSTM for object identity in 4- and 6-month-old infants, using color as the object-defining feature (Ross-Sheehy, Oakes, & Luck, 2003). We examined infants' preferences for changing stimulus streams at set sizes 1, 2, and 3. On each trial, we presented a changing stream on one monitor and a nonchanging stream on the other (both with the same set size), and we measured how long they looked at each screen. We concluded that they detected the change if their *change preference score* (the duration of their looking to the changing stream divided by their total duration of looking) was greater than chance (.50). As illustrated in Figure 4.3, these young infants showed a significant preference for the changing stream only at set size 1. At set sizes 2 and 3, infants looked approximately equally at the changing and nonchanging streams. These results are important because they document that (1) infants as young as 4 months of age can, in fact, represent object features in VSTM, and (2) at this young age, infants' VSTM capacity is limited to one item.

Importantly, in several control experiments we have shown that infants of this age will show systematic preferences in this paradigm when as many as three objects are on the screen as long as VSTM for multiple objects is not required. For example, they will prefer a changing stream if the gap is removed and no memory is required to detect the change (Ross-Sheehy et al., 2003) or if all the items in the stream are the same color and they all change

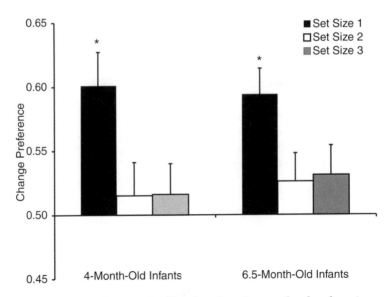

FIGURE 4.3. Four- and 6-month-old infants' preference for the changing streams for set sizes 1, 2, and 3 as reported by Ross-Sheehy et al. (2003, Experiment 2). Scores significantly greater than chance (.50) are indicated by an asterisk, $p < .05$. Error bars indicate +1 SE.

on each cycle (Oakes, Ross-Sheehy, & Luck, 2005). Moreover, they will prefer arrays of three different colors over arrays of three objects all of the same color, which indicates that they can perceive the colors of multiple items presented simultaneously (Oakes et al., 2005). These control experiments rule out the possibility that perceptual and attentional factors significantly limit infants' performance in our paradigm, and they confirm that the failure of the young infants to detect a change in our original experiment was due to limitations in their VSTM capacity.

How Does VSTM Capacity Develop in Infancy?

Our next step was to determine whether VSTM capacity increases during infancy. It may at first seem surprising that young infants can represent only one item in VSTM, but consider that adult capacity for objects of this type is only three to four objects in a similar procedure (Luck & Vogel, 1997). We therefore expect infants' capacity to be quite limited. The important question is, how quickly do infants develop the ability to represent multiple objects in VSTM? In subsequent experiments, we found that 10- and 13-month-old infants significantly preferred the changing stimuli for set sizes 1, 2, and 3, and that 10-month-old infants detected a change at set sizes 2 and 4 but not 6 (Ross-Sheehy et al., 2003; see Figure 4.4).

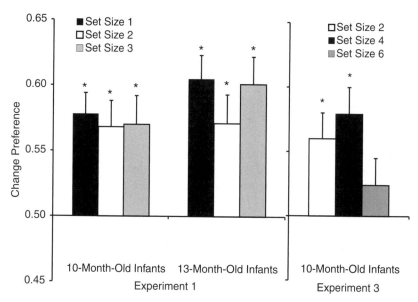

FIGURE 4.4. Ten- and 13-month-old infants' preference for changing streams at set sizes 1, 2, and 3 (Experiment 1, Ross-Sheehy et al., 2003) and 10-month-old infants' preferences for changing streams at set sizes 2, 4, and 6 (Experiment 3, Ross-Sheehy et al., 2003). Scores significantly greater than chance (.50) are indicated by an asterisk, $p < .05$. Error bars indicate +1 SE.

Thus, our results suggest a dramatic change in VSTM capacity for object identity in the second half of the first year of life. Young infants represent the color of only a single object in VSTM, and by 10 months infants can represent the colors of multiple objects in VSTM. Indeed, by 10 months, VSTM capacity allows infants to detect a change when streams contain as many as four items, suggesting that VSTM capacity may be similar to that of adults. Other research, however, suggests that VSTM capacity does not reach adult-like levels until later in childhood (Cowan et al., 2005), and the most important conclusion from our studies is therefore that infants develop from being able to represent only a single object in VSTM at 4 and 6 months to being able to represent multiple objects in VSTM by 10 months.

The timing of this change is important for understanding the underlying neural mechanisms responsible for this development. The parietal cortex, a region thought to be particularly important in determining VSTM capacity (Todd & Marois, 2004; Vogel & Machizawa, 2004), undergoes significant developmental change from 3 to 6 months (Chugani, 1998; Greenough, Black, & Wallace, 1987). The posterior parietal cortex may allow the segregation of feature information into separate object tokens (Baylis, Driver, & Rafal, 1993).

It therefore seems likely that infants would be able to represent multiple objects in VSTM only after this region had undergone significant development and after the development of connections between this and other regions of the brain. It is plausible, therefore, that developmental changes in the parietal lobe set the stage for the changes in capacity that we have observed.

How Does an Infant's VSTM for Object Location Develop?

Our next step was to investigate developmental changes in infants' VSTM representations of features other than color. Specifically, our original results may reflect general capacity changes, or they may reflect specific changes in infants' ability to represent object identity features, such as color. We extended our initial results by examining infants' developing capacity for representing location in VSTM. Assessing developmental changes in location is important for several reasons. First, location is a very different type of property than is color. If the capacity changes we observed for color reflect general changes in VSTM, then we should see similar capacity changes in memory for location. However, if memory for location develops independently of memory for object identity, then capacity for location may show a different time course from capacity for color.

In addition, information about object identity and location are thought to be represented by anatomically separate pathways in the brain (Goodale & Milner, 1992; Ungerleider & Mishkin, 1982), and there is some evidence (at least in LTM) that infants' representation of identity and spatial information develop independently (Mareschal & Johnson, 2003; Mash, Quinn, Dobson, & Narter, 1998). Theories of object individuation have explicitly argued that infants' first object representations are spatiotemporal in nature and that information about object identity is represented only later (i.e., Carey & Xu, 2001; Leslie, Xu, Tremoulet, & Scholl, 1998). Thus, we might predict that infants would show precocious development of capacity for location and that development of capacity for identity would have a slower trajectory. However, others have argued that in fact ventral stream processing, or processing of identity features such as color, develops before dorsal stream processing, or processing of spatiotemporal features such as location (Atkinson, 1998; Johnson, Mareschal, & Csibra, 2001). In this case, we would expect that infants' capacity for object identity would develop more quickly than their capacity for location. Finally, recent evidence suggests that representing multiple object identities depends on a region of cortex in the intraparietal sulcus, part of the dorsal stream (Todd & Marois, 2004). In this case, we should observe similar timing for the developmental changes in infants' representations for location. It is important to note that studies examining the development of the underlying neural structures have not revealed consistent differences for the timing of the development of the ventral and dorsal streams. Conde, Lund, and Lewis (1996), for example, found in monkeys that dorsal regions matured slightly earlier than did ventral regions. Chugani, Phelps, and Mazziotta (2002), using positron emission tomography (PET) in human infants, observed that glucose uptake was similar in temporal (ventral stream) and parietal (dorsal stream) regions of the brain across the first year. It is not clear, therefore, whether ventral and dorsal processing should develop at different times in human infants.

We used a variant of our preferential-looking procedure to examine development of VSTM for location during the same general period as we have observed changes in VSTM for color. We assessed 6- and 12-month-old infants' memory for the locations of one, two, or three objects (see Figure 4.5A: Ross-Sheehy, Oakes, & Luck, 2004). We observed once again that 6-month-old infants significantly preferred the changing stream only at set size 1 (see Figure 4.5B), suggesting that they can represent object location in VSTM, and, like their capacity for color, their capacity is limited to one location. In contrast, 12-month-old infants significantly preferred the changing stream even at set size 3 (see Figure 4.5B). These results are important because they show that (1) infants can represent in VSTM features other than object color; (2) our

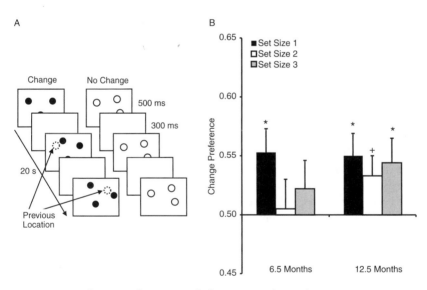

FIGURE 4.5. Schematic depiction of changing and nonchanging streams used by Ross-Sheehy, Oakes, and Luck (2004) to assess infants' VSTM for location (A). On each cycle, the location of one randomly chosen object was changed for the changing streams (the old location is indicated by a dotted circle). Circles, rather than squares, were used to minimize the use of the external contours of each element to form a shape. Six- and 12-month-old infants' preferences for the changing streams at set sizes 1, 2, and 3 are presented in (B). Scores significantly greater than chance (.50) are indicated by an asterisk, $p < .05$; scores marginally greater than chance are indicated by $+$, $p = .07$. Error bars indicate $+1$ SE.

procedure can measure VSTM storage capacity for a variety of features; and (3) like memory capacity for object identity, capacity for location increased dramatically in the second half of the first year of life.

Because we observed the same change in capacity over a similar period of time, it may be tempting to conclude from these studies that VSTM capacity for location and object identity develops at the same rate. However, in these studies we have compared infants at 6 months to infants at 10 or 12 months, and we have observed relatively large changes in capacity. Thus, we have shown that infants 6 months or younger can represent both object identity and object location in VSTM, and that infants' capacity for both types of features changes over the second half of the first year of life. However, additional research is needed to determine whether or not the ability to represent the two types of features develops at the same rate between 6 and 12 months.

How Mature Are Infants' Object Representations in VSTM?

When objects are stored in VSTM, it is important not only to represent what those objects are and where objects are located, but also to link *what* and *where* together, representing where particular objects are located. For example, a child surveying a visual scene needs to be able to remember not only that there was a book and a teddy bear, but that the book was on the left of the couch and the teddy bear was on the right. Such binding may be computationally demanding, however, because it involves integrating information from widely separated brain regions in the dorsal and ventral streams; such integration appears to involve the posterior parietal lobe. For example, Robertson, Treisman, Friedman-Hill, and Grabowecky (1997) found that a patient with bilateral parietal damage was unable to bind under contexts that require the use of spatial information (i.e., when multiple objects were presented simultaneously). Similarly, Shafritz, Gore, and Marois (2002) observed posterior parietal activity when subjects were required to bind features of objects at different locations.

Previous work has demonstrated that adults represent bound objects in VSTM (Luck & Vogel, 1997) and that adults can bind object identity features to locations (Wheeler & Treisman, 2002). That is, adults bind the information about different features into integrated object representations in VSTM. Previous work has established that infants can bind object features (such as color and orientation) in LTM from an early age (Bushnell & Roder, 1985; Slater et al., 1991; Taga et al., 2002), but that the binding of object features to locations develops later (Catherwood et al., 1996; Mareschal & Johnson, 2003). In fact, Káldy and Leslie (2005) have suggested that the binding of location and identity in working memory emerges between 7 and 8.5 months. In our most recent series of experiments, we asked whether infants, like adults, can bind object identity (color) and object location in VSTM (Oakes et al., 2006).

We used a variant of the procedure we previously used to examine VSTM for color and for location individually. Because binding is an issue only in the context of multiple objects, infants were always shown streams containing three objects. The three objects in the nonchanging stream stayed the same on every cycle, just as in our original procedure. In the changing stream, the same three colors and three locations were presented on each cycle, but the color-location bindings changed; that is, the colors swapped locations from cycle to cycle. We call this the *binding-change* stream (see Figure 4.6A). Because every item in the binding-change stream changes in every cycle, it should be trivial to detect a change if one represents the bindings of those colors and locations. However, if one encodes only the particular colors and the particular locations (and not how they are bound), then both the binding-change and the no-change streams will appear to be unchanging, and subjects will be unable to distinguish them. As can be seen in Figure 4.6B, 12.5-month-old infants preferred the binding-change streams, whereas 6.5-month-old infants (who were between 6 and 7 months) did not. Consistent with our other results, the ability to bind color to location develops in the second half of the first year. In addition, we pinpointed this developmental transition when we observed that a group of 7.5-month-old infants (who were between 7 and 8 months) preferred the binding-change stream (see Figure 4.6B), suggesting that the ability to bind color to location

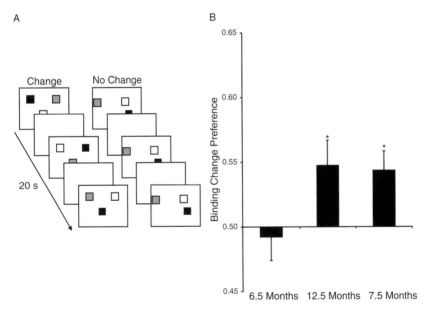

FIGURE 4.6. Schematic depiction of the changing and nonchanging streams used to assess infants' binding of color and location (Oakes, Ross-Sheehy, and Luck, 2006) (A). For the changing streams, the same colors and locations were seen in each cycle; but each color was seen at a different location on each cycle. Thus, the color at each location was different on each reappearance. (B) Scores significantly greater than chance (.50) are indicated by an asterisk, $p < .05$. Error bars indicate $+1$ SE.

emerges rapidly between 6 and 8 months of age. This is exactly the timing of the emergence of this ability predicted by Káldy and Leslie 2005 from their results using very different procedures and stimuli. It is important to remember that we have shown that 6.5-month-old infants can detect a change when presented with three objects at one time—either when no memory is required (Ross-Sheehy et al., 2003) or when all of the objects are the same color (Oakes et al., 2006). Therefore, the observed failure of the youngest infants in our most recent study is not a failure in the ability to detect changes when three items are presented simultaneously, but rather a failure to bind color to location.

Our results provide an important insight into how infants represent information in VSTM. When they first begin to represent object identity and location in VSTM, infants do not appear to bind identity and location. However, this ability rapidly develops between 6 and 8 months. We have also shown that the ability to represent multiple objects in VSTM develops rapidly between 6 and 10 months, consistent with the conclusion that the ability to represent multiple objects and the ability to bind features depend on the same mechanism.

Neural Mechanisms of Developmental Changes in VSTM

The work we have detailed here provides a description of the developmental changes in VSTM, as assessed in one task. However, we believe that these developmental changes are more than descriptive—we believe they also provide insight into the neural mechanisms that underlie developmental changes in VSTM.

Studies of the neural substrates of VSTM using electrophysiological, neuroimaging, and neuropsychological approaches have revealed that VSTM-related neural activity is observed in both prefrontal cortex and posterior cortical regions (see, e.g., De Renzi & Nichelli, 1975; Jonides et al., 1993; Miller, Erickson, & Desimone, 1996). A signature of short-term or working memory is sustained neural activity during the delay period (called *delay activity*). Evidence from single-unit recordings in monkeys and from PET and functional magnetic resonance imaging (fMRI) with humans has revealed that when remembering object identity, there is delay activity in inferotemporal cortex (in the ventral stream) and in prefrontal cortex (J. D. Cohen et al., 1997; Courtney, Ungerleider, Keil, & Haxby, 1997; Miller & Desimone, 1994; Miller et al., 1996). Importantly, the activity in prefrontal cortex, but not inferotemporal cortex, is robust in the face of new, distracting stimuli (Miller & Desimone, 1994; Miller et al., 1996). In other words, it appears that the representations in prefrontal cortex are durable and can be used in the service of additional tasks, whereas the representations in inferotemporal cortex are fragile.

When spatial information is remembered, delay activity is located in the parietal cortex (in the dorsal stream) and in prefrontal cortex (Courtney, Ungerleider, Keil, & Haxby, 1996; McCarthy et al., 1996; Pesaran, Pezaris, Sahani, Mitra, & Andersen, 2002). There is some evidence of a dorsal/ventral distinction in prefrontal cortex (Wilson, O'Scalaidhe, & Goldman-Rakic, 1993), but other studies find evidence that location and object identity are stored together in prefrontal cortex (Rainer, Asaad, & Miller, 1998). In addition, recent ERP and fMRI studies using the change-detection paradigm of Luck and Vogel (1997) have indicated that dorsal stream areas may play a key role in VSTM for object identity when multiple objects must be remembered concurrently. Specifically, the capacity of VSTM for color was strongly related to neural activity in the posterior parietal cortex (Todd & Marois, 2004). Other studies have suggested that the parietal lobe plays a key role in individuating objects (Baylis et al., 1993), which may be necessary when multiple objects are maintained concurrently in VSTM (Raffone & Wolters, 2001). Thus, current evidence suggests that VSTM for object identity in adults may depend on the interplay between the dorsal and ventral streams.

What do our results about the properties and development of object representations in VSTM in infancy tell us about these neural mechanisms? And how can an understanding of these neural mechanisms inform our understanding of the development of this ability? Our results provide several suggestions. First, by age 4 months, neural systems are sufficiently well developed to enable the representation of at least one object identity feature in VSTM, presumably by means of sustained neural activity during the delay period. Sustained neural activity presumably requires some sort of recurrent connections, so our results suggest that some recurrent connections are present by 4 months of age. These findings are consistent with previous studies that have concluded that substantial ventral stream processing is possible within the first 6 months of life (Johnson et al., 2001).

In addition, our results show that by 6 months, and perhaps earlier, infants can represent both object identity features and locations in VSTM, and therefore the neural systems for representing location and identity are both functioning by this point. Recall that, in adults, the dorsal stream is specialized for representing location and the ventral stream is specialized for representing identity; our results therefore suggest that both streams are capable of VSTM storage by 6 months of age. Note, however, that there is some debate about whether the processing of location and identity are anatomically segregated in this manner in young infants (Johnson & Vecera, 1996).

Our results provide no new insights into whether the dorsal or ventral stream develops first. Previous studies have suggested differences in the developmental time course of the dorsal and ventral streams, but the evidence is mixed. Some evidence suggests that the dorsal stream develops before the ventral stream. Mash et al. (1998) found that although both preterm and full-term infants performed well on spatial categorization tasks, only the full-term infants performed well on an object categorization task, consistent with the hypothesis that spatial processing develops first. Similarly, studies have revealed that infants first use spatiotemporal information to individuate objects, and only late in the first year do they use object identity to individuate them (e.g., F. Xu & Carey, 1996). Such differences may be the result of different rates of maturation of the dorsal and ventral streams. For example, neurons in the magnocellular pathway—which provides the main input to the dorsal stream—appear to mature slightly faster than neurons in the parvocellular pathway (Atkinson, 1998; Dobkins, Anderson, & Lia, 1999). However, the difference in maturation rates between magnocellular and parvocellular neurons is small, and the ventral stream receives a substantial input from both the magnocellular and parvocellular pathways (Ferrera, Nealy, & Maunsell, 1994). Thus, it would be premature to conclude that the dorsal stream develops earlier than the ventral stream.

Other evidence indicates that the ventral stream develops before the dorsal stream. For example, Johnson et al. (2001) argued that the ventral stream develops first because there is event-related potential (ERP) evidence for specialization of the ventral stream for face processing by 6 months (suggesting considerable maturation of the ventral pathway), whereas at that same age there is little ERP evidence of dorsal stream involvement in saccadic planning. Although this is a comparison of very different functions of these two processing streams, Johnson et al. took this pattern as consistent with the notion that the ventral stream develops first. Atkinson (1998) drew similar conclusions. Thus, one might expect VSTM for object identity to develop prior to VSTM for location.

We argue that asking whether the dorsal stream develops before the ventral stream or vice versa will not provide a deep insight into the development of VSTM, and in fact a simple dorsal-ventral dichotomy may not be meaningful in this context. These streams contain many distinct cortical areas, and the functional development of these streams presumably unfolds over many months or even years. In contrast to the dorsal-first and ventral-first hypotheses, we propose that it is more fruitful to consider the different types of processes that contribute to VSTM and ask about the functional development of those processes. In particular, a mature VSTM system requires two main abilities: (1) the ability to sustain neural processing in the absence of a stimulus, and (2) the ability to segregate concurrent representations so that they do not interfere with each other and collapse (see Raffone & Wolters, 2001). The ability to sustain neural activity presumably depends on the presence of feedback loops, and we suggest that these loops are present within both the dorsal and ventral streams from an early age, allowing young infants to prefer changing colors or changing locations over nonchanging stimuli as long as the set size is only one object. However, we propose that the ability to segregate concurrent representations develops later. That is, when infants attempt to maintain multiple VSTM representations during the first 6 months, these representations will collide and either terminate or collapse into a single undifferentiated representation. Once infants have developed the ability to segregate these representations, they should be able to show significant change preferences at set sizes greater than one.

In adults, the ability to segregate concurrent representations appears to depend on neural activity in the intraparietal sulcus within the posterior parietal lobe (Todd & Marois, 2004), and the development of this structure may play a key role in determining the development of VSTM capacity. Little is known about when the intraparietal sulcus develops, but some evidence points to dramatic developmental change in the parietal cortex between 3 and 6 months (Gilmore & Johnson, 1998) and general changes in cortical thickness through the first year (Greenough et al., 1987). The intra-parietal sulcus presumably uses spatiotemporal information to segregate concurrent representations, and this information must be linked with infor-mation about object identity in the ventral stream to retain multiple object identities. Thus, the development of connections between this dorsal stream area and the ventral stream may be the key to being able to represent multiple object identities. Representing multiple locations may require connections between the intraparietal sulcus and other dorsal stream areas; alternatively, location information may be intrinsic to the intraparietal sulcus, in which case minimal connectivity would be necessary for this area to maintain mul-tiple locations in VSTM. Thus, we would predict that the ability to store multiple object identities in VSTM would develop at the same time as, or shortly after, the ability to store multiple locations in VSTM.

A similar conjecture has been made in the object individuation literature. Specifically, Carey and Xu (2001) and Leslie and his colleagues (Scholl & Leslie, 1999) separately developed frameworks for understanding develop-mental changes in object representations. These frameworks share the assump-tion that infants first form object indexes or files based on spatiotemporal features alone (in a manner consistent with FINST theory; Pylyshyn, 1994, 2001), and only later in development do they become able to integrate object identity information into those representations.

This conceptualization of VSTM development also fits with our finding that infants become able to bind object identity and location in VSTM be-tween 6 and 8 months. In general, the ability to bind object identities to locations depends on the posterior parietal cortex. As mentioned earlier, pa-tients with bilateral damage to the posterior parietal cortex are unable to bind features when such bindings require spatial information (Robertson et al., 1997), and increased parietal lobe activity is observed in normal subjects engaged in binding features of objects at different locations (Shafritz et al., 2002). Therefore, both the ability to represent multiple objects in VSTM and the ability to bind location and identity may depend on posterior parietal cortex, and both appear to develop at approximately the same time.

Finally, it should be pointed out that we have observed large developmen-tal changes in the second half of the first year of life, exactly the time period when there are substantial changes in prefrontal cortex (Bell, 1998; Diamond, 2002; Johnson, 1995; Nelson, 1995). Specifically, at around 8 months human prefrontal cortex undergoes a rapid phase of synaptogenesis that results in increased connectivity and stability (Bell, 1998; Goldman-Rakic, 1987). Indeed, Carver, Bauer, and Nelson (2000) speculated that changes in frontal lobe functioning at 9 months were related to changes in memory. Because this is an area implicated in representation in STM (Miller et al., 1996; Rowe, Toni, Josephs, Frackowiak, & Passingham, 2000; Smith & Jonides, 1997), developmental changes in prefrontal cortex likely have a large impact on aspects of VSTM. In particular, sustained activity is more robust in prefrontal cortex than in inferotemporal cortex, and so prefrontal cortex development may play an important role in allowing VSTM representations to persist in the face of new stimuli, eyeblinks, saccades, or other potential sources of disruption. Thus, posterior parietal cortex may underlie the ability to form multiple VSTM representations and to bind features together in VSTM, but prefrontal cortex may be necessary to maintain these representations in a dynamic visual environment.

Future Directions

We have described several findings that provide some initial steps toward understanding the development of VSTM in infancy. These studies reveal that 6-month-old infants can represent both object identity and location in VSTM, and they also show that the ability to represent multiple objects and to bind object identity and location develops over the ensuing months. Many questions remain, however, and a full understanding of the development of VSTM depends on answering these questions.

What Are the Developmental Trajectories of Capacity for Object Identity and Location?

Perhaps the most obvious question is whether the ability to represent multiple locations and multiple object identities develops at the same rate between 6 and 10 months. Our experiments identified an age range during which capacity rapidly changes for features such as object color and location. Our results do not, however, determine exactly whether this capacity changes in the same way for both types of features. We know from our studies that capacity for both types of features develops from one item at 6 months to several items by the end of the first year, but we have not yet assessed how capacity for these two types of features changes within this window. It is possible that VSTM capacity for locations develops at a faster rate than VSTM for object identities. For example, we may find that 7- or 8-month-old infants can remember two or three locations, but remembering two or three colors does not emerge until closer to 10 months. This would be consistent with the proposal that the intraparietal sulcus has intrinsic access to spatiotemporal information and can therefore represent multiple locations before it becomes interconnected with ventral stream areas. Alternatively, this connectivity may already be present when the intraparietal sulcus becomes functional, in which case VSTM capacity for location and object identity may develop at the same rate. Therefore, an important step in our understanding of VSTM is to undertake systematic testing of capacity changes between 6 and 12 months for both types of features.

How Does the Ability to Represent Bound Objects Develop?

Our results also delineate the timing of the emergence of binding of object identity and location in VSTM. We found that although 7.5- and 12.5-month-old infants were sensitive to the bindings between color and location, 6.5-month-old infants were not. Thus, this type of binding appears to emerge between 6 and 8 months, exactly as predicted by Káldy and Leslie (2005).

This demonstration is important, but it raises several questions. Note that we assessed the binding of features across visual processing streams—that is, we demonstrated that infants could bind color (a feature processed by the ventral stream) with location (a feature processed by the dorsal stream). It is not surprising that this type of binding emerged after a period during which significant development is thought to occur in the parietal cortex (Gilmore & Johnson, 1998; Johnson, 1997). That is, the posterior parietal lobe appears to be necessary for binding features, particularly when location is important (Robertson et al., 1997). However, what is unknown is whether we have identified the earliest age at which infants can bind any features in VSTM, or whether we have identified the first point at which infants can bind features processed by different visual pathways. Other studies suggest that infants can bind two ventral stream features (such as color and orientation) in LTM at birth (Slater et al., 1991), but even at 5 months infants bind dorsal and ventral features only with difficulty (Catherwood et al., 1996). Binding two object identify features in VSTM may likewise emerge before 7 months, demonstrating that within-stream binding emerges before between-stream binding in VSTM as it apparently does in LTM. Answering this question, therefore, would help to determine whether what develops is a general ability to bind features in VSTM, or whether we have identified the ability to bind dorsal and ventral features in VSTM.

Moreover, if the binding of features depends specifically on the intraparietal sulcus, then we should also observe that infants who can bind features are the same infants who can represent multiple objects in VSTM. That is, we have found that at 6 months infants are unable to detect a change at set sizes greater than one and that they are also unable to bind. We know that 7.5-month-old infants can bind identity and location, but can they also store multiple object identities (or locations) in VSTM? Moreover, is the ability to store multiple objects in VSTM related to the ability to bind features? Answering these questions will provide additional understanding of the mechanisms responsible for developmental changes in the capacity of VSTM.

Summary and Conclusion

We have reported here our initial investigations into the characteristics and development of VSTM in infancy. First, we developed a task that emphasizes STM systems and minimizes the influence of LTM systems. In subsequent studies, we used this task to establish that infants can store object identities and locations in VSTM, that infants' limited VSTM capacity increases rapidly over the first year of life, and that infants can bind object identities and locations by approximately 7 months of age. These findings represent important first steps in our understanding of the development of VSTM, and they bridge significant gaps in our knowledge between adult and infant cognition and between the cognitive and neural bases of the development of memory systems in infancy.

Acknowledgment

The preparation of this chapter and the research reported here were made possible by grants MH64020, MH63001, MH65034, and HD49840. S. R. S. was funded by an individual NRSA predoctoral grant awarded by NIMH.

References

Atkinson, J. (1984). Human visual development over the first 6 months of life: A review and a hypothesis. *Human Neurobiology, 3,* 61–74.

Atkinson, J. (1998). The "where and what" or "who and how" of visual development. In F. Simion & G. Butterworth (Eds.), *The development of sensory, motor and cognitive capacities in early infancy: From perception to cognition* (pp. 3–24). Hove, UK: Psychology Press.

Baddeley, A. D., & Hitch, G. J. (1974). Working memory. In G. H. Bower (Ed.), *The psychology of learning and motivation* (Vol. 8, pp. 47–90). New York: Academic Press.

Baddeley, A. D., & Logie, R. H. (1999). Working memory: The multiple-component model. In A. Miyaki & P. Shah (Eds.), *Models of working memory: Mechanisms of active maintenance and executive control* (pp. 28–61). Cambridge, UK: Cambridge University Press.

Baillargeon, R. (1993). The object concept revisited: New direction in the investigation of infants' physical knowledge. In C. E. Granrud (Ed.). *Visual perception and cognition in infancy.* Hillsdale, NJ: Erlbaum.

Baylis, G. C., Driver, J., & Rafal, R. D. (1993). Visual extinction and stimulus repetition. *Journal of Cognitive Neuroscience, 4,* 453–466.

Bell, M. A. (1998). Frontal lobe function during infancy: Implications for the development of cognition and attention. In J. E. Richards (Ed.), *Cognitive neuroscience of attention: A developmental perspective* (pp. 287–316). Mahwah, NJ: Erlbaum.

Bornstein, M. H. (1976). Infants' recognition memory for hue. *Developmental Psychology, 12*, 185–191.

Bornstein, M. H., Krinsky, S. J., & Benasich, A. A. (1986). Fine orientation discrimination and shape constancy in young infants. *Journal of Experimental Child Psychology, 41*, 49–60.

Bushnell, E. W., & Roder, B. J. (1985). Recognition of color-form compounds by 4-month-old infants. *Infant Behavior and Development, 8*, 255–268.

Carey, S., & Xu, F. (2001). Infants' knowledge of objects: Beyond object files and object tracking. *Cognition, 80*, 179–213.

Carver, L. J., Bauer, P. J., & Nelson, C. A. (2000). Associations between infant brain activity and recall memory. *Developmental Science, 3*, 234–246.

Catherwood, D., Skoien, P., Green, V., & Holt, C. (1996). Assessing the primary moments of infant encoding of compound visual stimuli. *Infant Behavior and Development, 19*, 1–11.

Chugani, H. T. (1998). A critical period of brain development: Studies of cerebral glucose utilization with PET. *Preventative Medicine, 27*, 184–188.

Chugani, H. T., Phelps, M. E., & Mazziotta, J. C. (2002). Positron emission tomography study of human brain functional development. In M. H. Johnson, Y. Munakata, & R. O. Gilmore (Eds.), *Brain development and cognition: A reader* (2nd ed., pp. 101–116). Malden, MA: Blackwell.

Cohen, J. D., Perlstein, W. M., Braver, T. S., Nystrom, L. E., Noll, D. C., Jonides, J., et al. (1997). Temporal dynamics of brain activation during a working memory task. *Nature, 386*, 604–608.

Cohen, L. B. (1973). A two-process model of infant attention. *Merrill-Palmer Quarterly, 19*, 157–180.

Conde, F., Lund, J. S., & Lewis, D. A. (1996). The hierarchical development of monkey visual cortical regions as revealed by the maturation of parvalbumin-immunoreactive neurons. *Developmental Brain Research, 96*, 261–276.

Cornell, E. H., & Heth, C. (1979). Response versus place learning by human infants. *Journal of Experimental Psychology: Human Learning and Memory, 5*, 188–196.

Courage, M. L., & Howe, M. L. (2001). Long-term retention in 3.5-month-olds: Familiarization time and individual differences in attentional style. *Journal of Experimental Child Psychology, 79*, 271–293.

Courtney, S. M., Ungerleider, L. G., Keil, K., & Haxby, J. V. (1996). Object and spatial visual working memory activate separate neural systems in human cortex. *Cerebral Cortex, 6*, 39–49.

Courtney, S. M., Ungerleider, L. G., Keil, K., & Haxby, J. V. (1997). Transient and sustained activity in a distributed neural system for human working memory. *Nature, 386*, 608–611.

Cowan, N. (2001). The magical number 4 in short-term memory: A reconsideration of mental storage capacity. *Behavioral and Brain Sciences, 24*, 87–185.

Cowan, N., Elliott, E. M., Saults, J. S., Morey, C. C., Mattox, S., Hismjatullina, A., et al. (2005). On the capacity of attention: Its estimation and its role in working memory and cognitive aptitudes. *Cognitive Psychology, 51*, 42–100.

De Renzi, E., & Nichelli, P. (1975). Verbal and nonverbal short-term memory impairment following hemispheric damage. *Cortex, 11*, 341–354.

Diamond, A. (1995). Evidence of robust recognition memory early in life even when assessed by reaching behavior. *Journal of Experimental Child Psychology, 59*, 419–456.

Diamond, A. (2002). Normal development of prefrontal cortex from birth to young adulthood: Cognitive functions, anatomy, and biochemistry. In D. T. Stuss & R. T. Knight (Eds.), *Principles of frontal lobe function* (pp. 466–503). London: Oxford University Press.

Dobkins, K. R., Anderson, C. M., & Lia, B. (1999). Infant temporal contrast sensitivity functions (TCSFs) mature earlier for luminance than for chromatic stimuli: Evidence for precocious magnocellular development? *Vision Research, 39*, 3223–3239.

Fagan, J. F. (1970). Memory in the infant. *Journal of Experimental Child Psychology, 9*, 217–226.

Fagan, J. F. (1973). Infants' delayed recognition memory and forgetting. *Journal of Experimental Child Psychology, 16*, 424–450.

Fagan, J. F. (1976). Infants' recognition of invariant features of faces. *Child Development, 47*, 627–638.

Fantz, R. L. (1964). Visual experience in infants: Decreased attention familiar patterns relative to novel ones. *Science, 146*, 668–670.

Ferrera, V. P., Nealy, T. A., & Maunsell, J. H. R. (1994). Responses in macaque visual area V4 following inactivation of the parvocellular and magnocellular LGN pathways. *Journal of Neuroscience, 14*, 2080–2088.

Gilmore, R. O., & Johnson, M. H. (1998). Learning what is where: Oculomotor contributions to the development of spatial cognition. In F. Simion & G. Butterworth (Eds.), *The development of sensory, motor and cognitive capacities in early infancy: From perception to cognition* (pp. 25–47). Hove, UK: Psychology Press.

Goldman-Rakic, P. S. (1987). Development of cortical circuitry and cognitive function. *Child Development, 58*, 601–622.

Goodale, M. A., & Milner, D. A. (1992). Separate visual pathways for perception and action. *Trends in Neuroscience, 15*, 20–25.

Greenough, W. T., Black, J. E., & Wallace, C. S. (1987). Experience and brain development. *Child Development, 58*, 539–559.

Hollingworth, A., & Henderson, J. M. (2002). Accurate visual memory for previously attended objects in natural scenes. *Journal of Experimental Psychology: Human Perception and Performance, 28*, 113–136.

Hollingworth, A., Schrock, G., & Henderson, J. M. (2001). Change detection in the flicker paradigm: The role of fixation position within the scene. *Memory & Cognition, 29*, 296–304.

Irwin, D. E. (1991). Information integration across saccadic eye movements. *Cognitive Psychology, 23*, 420–456.

Irwin, D. E., & Andrews, R. V. (1996). Integration and accumulation of information across saccadic eye movements. In T. Inui & J. L. McClelland (Eds.), *Attention and performance XVI* (pp. 125–155). Cambridge, MA: MIT Press.

James, W. (1890). *The principles of psychology.* New York: Henry Holt.

Johnson, M. H. (1995). The development of visual attention: A cognitive neuroscience perspective. In M. S. Gazzaniga (Ed.), *The cognitive neurosciences* (pp. 735–747). Cambridge, MA: MIT Press.

Johnson, M. H. (1997). *Developmental cognitive neuroscience.* Cambridge, MA: Blackwell.

Johnson, M. H., Mareschal, D., & Csibra, G. (2001). The functional development and integration of the dorsal and ventral visual pathways: A neurocomputational approach. In C. A. Nelson & M. Luciana (Eds.), *The handbook of developmental cognitive neuroscience* (pp. 339–351). Cambridge, MA: MIT Press.

Johnson, M. H., & Vecera, S. P. (1996). Cortical differentiation and neurocognitive development: The parcellation conjecture. *Behavioural Processes, 36,* 195–212.

Jonides, J., Smith, E. E., Koeppe, R. A., Awh, E., Minoshima, S., & Mintun, M. A. (1993). Spatial working memory in humans as revealed by PET. *Nature, 363,* 623–625.

Káldy, Z., & Leslie, A. M. (2003). Identification of objects in 9-month-old infants: Integrating "what" and "where" information. *Developmental Science, 6,* 360–373.

Káldy, Z., & Leslie, A. M. (2005). A memory span of one? Object identification in 6.5-month-old infants. *Cognition, 97,* 153–177.

Kellman, P. J., & Arterberry, M. E. (1998). *The cradle of knowledge: Development of perception in infancy.* Cambridge, MA: MIT Press.

Leslie, A. M., Xu, F., Tremoulet, P. D., & Scholl, B. J. (1998). Indexing and the object concept: Developing "what" and "where" systems. *Trends in Cognitive Sciences, 2,* 10–18.

Luck, S. J., & Vogel, E. K. (1997). The capacity of visual working memory for features and conjunctions. *Nature, 390,* 279–281.

Mareschal, D., & Johnson, M. H. (2003). The "what" and "where" of object representations in infancy. *Cognition, 88,* 259–276.

Mash, C., Quinn, P. C., Dobson, V., & Narter, D. B. (1998). Global influences on the development of spatial and object perceptual categorization abilities: Evidence from preterm infants. *Developmental Science, 1,* 85–102.

McCarthy, G., Puce, A., Constable, R. T., Krystal, J. H., Gore, J. C., & Goldman-Rakic, P. (1996). Activation of human prefrontal cortex during spatial and nonspatial working memory tasks measured by functional MRI. *Cerebral Cortex, 6,* 600–611.

Miller, E. K., & Desimone, R. (1994). Parallel neuronal mechanisms for short-term memory. *Science, 263,* 520–522.

Miller, E. K., Erickson, C. A., & Desimone, R. (1996). Neural mechanisms of visual working memory in prefrontal cortex of the macaque. *Journal of Neuroscience, 16,* 5154–5167.

Murdock, B. B. (1961). The retention of individual items. *Journal of Experimental Psychology, 62,* 618–625.

Nelson, C. A. (1995). The ontogeny of human memory: A cognitive neuroscience perspective. *Developmental Psychology, 31,* 723–738.

Newcombe, N., Huttenlocher, J., & Learmonth, A. (1999). Infants' coding of location in continuous space. *Infant Behavior and Development, 22,* 483–510.

Oakes, L. M., Ross-Sheehy, S., & Luck, S. J. (2006). Rapid development of feature binding in visual short-term memory. *Psychological Science, 17,* 781–787.

Pesaran, B., Pezaris, J. S., Sahani, M., Mitra, P. P., & Andersen, R. A. (2002). Temporal structure in neuronal activity during working memory in macaque parietal cortex. *Nature Neuroscience, 5,* 805–811.

Phillips, W. A. (1974). On the distinction between sensory storage and short-term visual memory. *Perception & Psychophysics, 16,* 283–290.

Piaget, J. (1954). *The construction of reality in the child.* Oxford, UK: Basic Books.

Pomplun, M., Reingold, E. M., & Shen, J. (2001). Investigating the visual span in comparative search: The effects of task difficulty and divided attention. *Cognition, 81,* B57–B67.

Pomplun, M., Sichelschmidt, L., Wagner, K., Clermont, T., Rickheit, G., & Ritter, H. (2001). Comparitive visual search: A difference that makes a difference. *Cognitive Science, 25,* 3–36.

Pylyshyn, Z. W. (1994). Some primitive mechanisms of spatial attention. *Cognition, 50,* 363–384.

Pylyshyn, Z. W. (2001). Visual indexes, preconceptual objects, and situated vision. *Cognition, 80,* 127–158.

Quinn, P. C. (1994). The categorization of above and below spatial relations by young infants. *Child Development, 65,* 58–69.

Quinn, P. C., Slater, A. M., Brown, E., & Hayes, R. A. (2001). Developmental change in form categorization in early infancy. *British Journal of Developmental Psychology, 19,* 207–218.

Raffone, A., & Wolters, G. (2001). A cortical mechanism for binding in visual working memory. *Journal of Cognitive Neuroscience, 13,* 766–785.

Rainer, G., Asaad, W. F., & Miller, E. K. (1998). Selective representation of relevant information by neurons in the primate prefrontal cortex. *Nature, 393,* 577–579.

Rensink, R. A., O'Regan, J., & Clark, J. J. (1997). To see or not to see: The need for attention to perceive changes in scenes. *Psychological Science, 8,* 368–373.

Robertson, L., Treisman, A., Friedman-Hill, S., & Grabowecky, M. (1997). The interaction of spatial and object pathways: Evidence from Balint's syndrome. *Journal of Cognitive Neuroscience, 9,* 295–317.

Rose, S. A. (1981). Developmental changes in infants' retention of visual stimuli. *Child Development, 52,* 227–233.

Rose, S. A., Gottfried, A. W., Melloy-Carminar, P., & Bridger, W. H. (1982). Familiarity and novelty preferences in infant recognition memory: Implications for information processing. *Developmental Psychology, 18,* 704–713.

Ross-Sheehy, S., Oakes, L. M., & Luck, S. J. (2003). The development of visual short-term memory capacity in infants. *Child Development, 74,* 1807–1822.

Ross-Sheehy, S., Oakes, L. M., & Luck, S. J. (2004, May). *Infant spatial short-term memory.* Paper presented at the biennial meeting of the International Conference on Infant Studies, Chicago, IL.

Rowe, J. B., Toni, I., Josephs, O., Frackowiak, R. S. J., & Passingham, R. E. (2000). The prefrontal cortex: Response selection or maintenance within working memory? *Science, 288,* 1656–1660.

Scholl, B. J., & Leslie, A. M. (1999). Explaining the infants' object concept: Beyond the perception/cognition dichotomy. In E. Lepore & Z. Pylyshyn (Eds.), *What is cognitive science?* (pp. 26–73). Oxford, UK: Blackwell.

Shafritz, K. M., Gore, J. C., & Marois, R. (2002). The role of the parietal cortex in visual feature binding. *Proceedings of the National Academy of Science, 99,* 10917–10922.

Simons, D. J. (1996). In sight, out of mind: When object representations fail. *Psychological Science, 7,* 301–305.

Simons, D. J., & Levin, D. T. (1997). Change blindness. *Trends in Cognitive Sciences, 1,* 261–267.

Slater, A., Earle, D., Morison, V., & Rose, D. (1985). Pattern preferences at birth and their interaction with habituation-induced novelty preferences. *Journal of Experimental Child Psychology, 39,* 37–54.

Slater, A., Mattock, A., Brown, E., Burnham, D., & Young, A. (1991). Visual processing of stimulus compounds in newborn infants. *Perception, 20,* 29–33.

Smith, E. E., & Jonides, J. (1997). Working memory: A view from neuroimaging. *Cognitive Psychology, 33,* 5–42.

Spelke, E. S. (1988). The origins of physical knowledge. In L. Weiskrantz (Ed.), *Thought without language: A Fyssen Foundation symposium* (pp. 168–184). New York: Clarendon.

Taga, G., Ikejiri, T., Tachibana, T., Shimojo, S., Soeda, A., Takeuchi, K., et al. (2002). Visual feature binding in early infancy. *Perception, 31,* 273–286.

Todd, J. J., & Marois, R. (2004). Capacity limit of visual short-term memory in human posterior parietal cortex. *Nature, 428,* 751–754.

Ungerleider, L. G., & Mishkin, M. (1982). Two cortical visual systems. In D. J. Ingle, R. J. W. Mansfield, & M. A. Goodale (Eds.), *The analysis of visual behavior* (pp. 549–586). Cambridge, MA: MIT Press.

Vogel, E. K., & Machizawa, M. G. (2004). Neural activity predicts individual differences in visual working memory capacity. *Nature, 428,* 748–751.

Vogel, E. K., Woodman, G. F., & Luck, S. J. (2001). Storage of features, conjunctions, and objects in visual working memory. *Journal of Experimental Psychology, 27,* 92–114.

Wheeler, M. E., & Treisman, A. M. (2002). Binding in short-term visual memory. *Journal of Experimental Psychology: General, 131,* 48–64.

Wilcox, T., & Baillargeon, R. (1998). Object individuation in infancy: The use of featural information in reasoning about occlusion events. *Cognitive Psychology, 37,* 97–155.

Wilcox, T., Rosser, R., & Nadel, L. (1994). Representation of object location in 6.5-month-old infants. *Cognitive Development, 9,* 193–209.

Wilson, F. A. W., O'Scalaidhe, S. P., & Goldman-Rakic, P. S. (1993). Dissociation of object and spatial processing domains in primate prefrontal cortex. *Science, 260,* 1955–1958.

Xu, F., & Carey, S. (1996). Infants' metaphysics: The case of numerical identity. *Cognitive Psychology, 30,* 111–153.

Xu, Y. (2002). Limitations of object-based feature encoding in visual short-term memory. *Journal of Experimental Psychology: Human Perception and Performance, 28,* 458–468.

5

Things to Remember

Limits, Codes, and the Development of Object Working Memory in the First Year

ALAN M. LESLIE AND ZSUZSA KÁLDY

The cognitive revolution of the 1960s had its roots in breakthroughs in the mathematics of machine theory, cybernetics, information, and formal systems associated with Turing, Weiner, von Neumann, Shannon, and Chomsky. For the first time, it was possible through the science of computation to glimpse— at least in principle—a physical basis for mind and mental phenomena. When Miller (1956) published his famous article on memory, it was to proclaim two things that have now become familiar. The first was that we can actually measure mental phenomena without white coats and large machines but, best of all, without embarrassment. The second was that some human memory systems have an astonishingly severe limit. There was also a third finding. Though we can (fairly) easily attach a number to this limit, and measure it in that sense, it is much harder to characterize what exactly are the units that are the subject of this limit. Miller believed the number was around seven; but he quickly showed that it was not seven of Shannon's bits but seven of something else, which he called chunks. The human memory system was not simply a channel carrying input passively but a complex system that actively recoded its throughput, as digits, letters, words, phrases, and so on, according to the goals of the task. The limit of seven reflected the structure of these codes. The twin properties of limit and code still define short-term memory research: how much can be stored and how much of what can be stored.

Miller was not the only pioneer of the cognitive revolution interested in limits. On the other side of the Atlantic, Broadbent (1958) argued that attention too was capacity limited and could be conceptualized as a channel with a limited bandwidth, just as short-term memory could. What are the relations between the limits on attention and on what can be attended to, on the one hand, and the limits of short-term memory, on the other? Are these wholly distinct mechanisms or are they related? As the chapters in this volume testify, these same questions are now being asked by infancy researchers. When do short-term memory and attentional mechanisms emerge in infancy? Do these mechanisms already show the main characteristics of the mature state and, if not, how do they differ, how do they develop toward the mature state, and what is the role of the maturation of the underlying neural systems?

The authors of the previous four chapters focused on the following list of questions:

1. What kind of memory are we studying?
2. What are the methodological challenges and limitations?
3. How does this type of memory change with development?
4. What is the relationship to neuroscientific findings? What do we currently know about the underlying brain mechanisms?

We begin by discussing each of these four questions. We then take a closer look at two central theoretical issues that were raised in chapters 3 and 4: the twin problems of limit and code. Finally, we reflect on the fifth question raised by the editors:

5. What are the main questions for future research?

What Kind of Memory Are We Studying?

The authors of the four previous chapters were asked to characterize the kind of mechanism that they are studying. Each of the four chapters emphasizes a different aspect of the short-term/working memory system. But before we look at these aspects, let's agree on a consistent terminology. Chapter 1 does a great job of clarifying the different terms used in the literature. *Short-term memory* is used to describe the temporary storage of information, with a focus on the actual temporal extent (few seconds). On the other hand, following Baddeley and Hitch (1974), working memory (WM) is the "maintenance of task-relevant information during the performance of a task" that involves more than just storage. In the neuroscience literature, the terms *manipulation* and *maintenance* are used to distinguish the active and passive aspects of this buffer (Courtney, Petit, Haxby, & Ungerleider, 1998). Reznick (chapter 1) argues that we cannot distinguish the storage component from the broader WM concept in infants. In fact, we should not even really be interested in the storage component by itself (which "exists only as a by-product of artificially induced laboratory conditions"). We agree with this view and suggest using the term *working memory* from here on.

The real question of course is not the term, but what we think it covers. An immediate issue: The concept of WM is evolving in the adult literature.

The authors of the four chapters each cite a different new model of WM. For example, Reznick (chapter 1) brings up Nairne's notion of cue salience, Feigenson (chapter 3) mentions Cowan's theory of WM as items in the focus of attention, Oakes, Ross-Sheehy, and Luck (chapter 4) build on Luck and Vogel's findings on visual STM, and Bell and Morasch (chapter 2) refer to Engle, who emphasized the maintenance of items in memory against interference. All of these new approaches question a different aspect of the classic Baddeley model. With this many alternatives at hand, the question arises: Should infancy researchers follow these new models, stick to the classic model, or develop their own? We are definitely in favor of using models that have been proven useful in understanding WM in adults, so the last option does not seem to be so promising. Like the authors of all four chapters, we too implicitly assume a great deal of continuity in the basic structures of WM from infancy to adulthood and expect developmental changes only in quantitative aspects, such as memory capacity, or in what kinds of information get stored. As far as the issue of classic versus more recent models is concerned, we think the classic model in its updated version (Baddeley, 1998, 2003) is still very much alive and doing well.

Notes on Studying Infant WM

Reznick, Oakes et al., and Feigenson all stress the need to clearly distinguish WM from long-term memory. Reznick points out that this distinction is allowed only by those paradigms that use a limited set of experimental stimuli and that in each test probe the infant with a subset of these with replacement. This way, the infant truly has to rely on WM and not a mere recognition of novelty. We think that carefully designed familiarization and test procedures can solve this problem.

For example, in our study on infants' WM (Káldy & Leslie, 2003, 2005), we asked whether infants are able to bind object identity information to an object that changes location (tell *what* was *where*). After being familiarized to a disk and a triangle, infants saw these two objects disappear behind two spatially separated screens. After a 2-second delay, the screens were removed to reveal the two objects in swapped locations. Both 6.5- and 9-month-old infants looked longer at the unexpected (swapped) outcome (see Figure 5.1, panel 1).

Crucially, during both familiarization and test trials, the side of the presentation of the disk and the triangle alternated from trial to trial. This way, infants could not rely on their long-term memories about where a particular object usually was or merely associate a shape feature with a location because both shapes were associated with both locations equally across the experiment. They could only succeed in the task if they could constantly update the content of their WM, exactly as Reznick has suggested. The principle behind this method should be applied in all looking time studies of infant WM: Infants should be familiarized to all the objects and locations

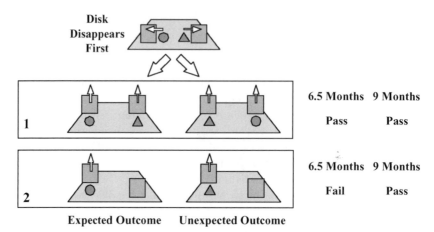

FIGURE 5.1. Summary of main findings of Káldy and Leslie (2003, 2005). Following the logic of violation-of-expectation paradigms, Pass signals that infants looked significantly longer at the unexpected outcome than at the expected outcome, and Fail signals that there was no significant difference between reactions to the two different outcomes. Before the test, infants were systematically familiarized with both of the objects appearing on alternating sides of the stage. Objects were hidden sequentially; in the sequence presented here the first object hidden was the disk on the left. Reprinted from Káldy, Z., & Sigala, N. (2004). The neural mechanisms of object working memory: What is where in the infant brain? *Neuroscience and Biobehavioral Reviews, 28,* 113–121, copyright 2004, with permission from Elsevier. See color plates.

before the final phase of the test, and in that final phase nothing that is novel in itself should appear (see also Tremoulet, Leslie, & Hall, 2000, for further discussion of this point).

One other interesting aspect of our findings was that the younger (6.5-month-old) infants solved the two-screen task in a different way from older ones (9-month-olds). Since in this task objects were hidden sequentially, we could test each group on whether they remembered both objects in the sequence (Figure 5.1, panel 1) or only the last one they had seen (panel 2). Our results showed that 6.5-month-olds did not remember the shape of the first-hidden object, while 9-month-olds did. With this method, we were able to address the question of sampling: namely, whether infants in a multiple-object task are actually tracking all the objects or just a subset of them. Indeed, for 9-month-olds, the effect size in this new experiment was larger than with the removal of both screens, showing that these infants have actually remembered both the first- and the last-hidden object.

Our conclusion was that 9-month-olds are able to bind shape information to two object indexes that followed the objects as they were moved on stage to new locations. They could remember what went where for two distinct individuals: "disk in location 1," "triangle in location 2." The 6.5-month-olds infants could do this too—bind shape information to a representation that indexed a moving object—but they could do so only for a single object. Object identity information was lost or overwritten as soon as attention went to a second object that was moved and hidden. Since we did not find any age effects within our two samples, we estimated that this new ability comes online sometime between 7 and 8.5 months of age (Káldy & Leslie, 2005). Oakes et al. (chapter 4), using a quite different paradigm, report results that match this estimate perfectly. They demonstrated that 7.5-month-old infants could bind color and location information for multiple nonoccluded objects in a rapidly changing stream of images.

We would also like to address here a critical point that Oakes et al. (chapter 4) have expressed about our paradigm. They write, "However, because during the test infants had several seconds to learn the relative locations of the objects, these data do not unambiguously rule out the influence of longer term memory systems in infants' binding of object identity and location." We believe that what they call learning (within an individual trial) is exactly what we call encoding in WM. In their introduction, they list a few examples of everyday scenarios when infants use their visual short-term memory: "Moreover, tracking objects as they are occluded and disoccluded is a common part of infants' everyday experience—VSTM is necessary for infants to recognize, for example, that a ball that rolls under the couch is the same ball that emerges from the other side a short time later." In our opinion, we tested exactly this ability in our infant subjects on each individual trial. If infants were relying on their long-term memory, then presumably they would also remember the trials they had watched previous to the test trial they were currently viewing. Because we alternated the locations of the objects across trials, long-term memory would subject stored object-identity-by-location information to severe proactive interference. Furthermore, we would not expect to see any capacity limit if long-term memory were the storage mechanism tapped by this task.

We think it is much more likely that these two different paradigms provide converging evidence on WM limits. We propose the following hypotheses: (a) infant object WM up to 7 months has a severely restricted capacity of a single item; and (b) this system develops rapidly thereafter, reaching two items by 8 to 9 months and three items by 11 to 12 months. We come back to this proposal later in the chapter.

The Nature of Representations in Infant WM

Reznick (chapter 1) suggests that "a key feature of short-term memory is the notion that an explicit representation is being sustained for some brief duration of time." He argues that looking time studies that rely on the familiar—unfamiliar distinction might reflect the existence of a representation that is not well articulated. In our view, this is not a problem with looking time studies, but one of the essential questions this method can help us solve. When we show a Minnie Mouse doll to an infant, will she remember it as a mouse doll with big round ears and a pink dress, as a black, white, and pink blob, or just as a "thing" (a Spelke object)? These are the kinds of questions that can be asked and answered by figuring out the right kinds of control conditions in further looking time tests. Each of the alternative descriptions of Minnie Mouse is potentially an alternative hypothesis that can be examined. And that is exactly what the evolving literature has been doing—empirically testing the information content of infant representations.

Indeed, both the dialectics of the theoretical controversies in the infant literature and the ingenuity of the designs used are largely directed at questions of determining what properties infants are representing. Clashes of view are invariably centered on exactly such questions. One old example is the series of experiments by Leslie (1982, 1984a, 1984b; Leslie & Keeble, 1987; reviewed in Leslie, 1994) that ruled out a succession of possible spatiotemporal properties of launching events to conclude that infants represent a causal-mechanical property as such when they view launching events (and see also the dissenting views of, e.g., Haith, 1998). One current such controversy is whether infants represent numerosity, individuals, or continuous extent when they track small sets of objects (see chapter 2)? There is nothing unusual about such questions and they are not limited to infant looking time studies. Of course, when we come to study infants, we lack the royal path of language and the ability to instruct our subjects using language. But that is true as well with the study of other species or indeed when we study systems in the adult human that are not dependent upon nor informed by language, such as the visual system. As cases in point, consider the following questions: What properties are represented in V1? Is visual attention structured by space, time, objects, or all of these? What is a visual object? So we do not agree that the question of representation is a special difficulty for infancy studies; rather, it is one of the field's most important topics.

How Should We Study WM in Infants?

Widely Different Methods

A useful way to group the methods that the previous four chapters have discussed is whether they test object location, identity, or number.

- Location of objects: delayed response and peek-a-boo (chapter 1), A-not-B (chapter 2), change detection (chapter 4)
- Identity of objects: change detection (chapter 4)
- Number of objects: cracker choice (foraging) and manual search (chapter 3)

Unfortunately, looking time studies using the violation-of-expectation method are missing from this picture, which is a regrettable shortcoming (just to note a few, besides our own studies discussed above; Mareschal & Johnson, 2003; Wilcox & Baillargeon, 1998; F. Xu & Carey, 1996, etc.). One of the reasons for this omission is that most of the researchers in this field were not using the term *working memory* to describe the system that they have been studying—but this has been changing recently (e.g., Leslie & Káldy, 2001).

Alas, terminology often has a power it should not and it can divide fields that ought to be united. One potentially unifying interest is provided by object cognition itself. Studies of adult attention over the last two decades have given an increasingly important role to objects as an organizing principle (for a review, see Scholl, 2001). Many of these ideas from object-based attention are currently being integrated into the long tradition of study of the object concept in infancy (for an early attempt at this, see Scholl & Leslie, 1999; for recent developments, see chapter 3, this volume). One of the few things that all of the authors in this volume agree on is that something important in regard to object WM develops during the second half of the first year of life. In our opinion, using widely different methods to study these questions is ideal; however, different methods underscore the need for a theory that can connect the results and frame the inevitable puzzles that are the mark of progress.

Ecological Validity

The different tasks that have been used to study infants' WM range in a wide spectrum of ecological validity from the cracker choice task (more valid?) to change detection (less valid?). Violation-of-expectation studies with three-dimensional objects tend to be on the more ecologically valid side. On the other hand, some might argue that change detection with squares flashed for 500 ms might be a straitjacket for infants' abilities. However, there are very good reasons why scientists bring nature into the laboratory. By doing so, we position ourselves so that we can analyze and compare theoretical predictions. The only really important question regarding a method is whether it reveals theoretically meaningful phenomena, and for change detection the answer, as far as we can see, is clearly positive. Ecological validity is only important insofar as it lines up with theoretical validity.

How Does This Type of Memory Change With Development?

As we noted earlier, one of the common themes in chapters 1 through 4 is that WM capacity increases steadily during the first year of life. Improvements can be measured in two separate components: (1) the number of objects or locations that infants can remember, and (2) the length of delay that infants can tolerate. The onset of WM capacity (i.e., remembering at least one object or location over the shortest possible delay) is estimated to be somewhere around 4 months (chapter 4) to 5.5 months (chapter 1). There is a steady improvement in the number of remembered objects and locations up to 12 months (which is the oldest age group tested by the authors of the four chapters). There are a few notable qualifications to this claim. Bell and Morasch (chapter 2) point out (based on a longitudinal study by Bell & Fox, 1992) that they found increasing delay tolerance in the A-not-B task only in those infants whose frontal cortex baseline activity was also increasing during the same period. This points to the importance of longitudinal studies in a field of developmental psychology where we have the advantage that this type of study only requires months and not years.

Here is where we should discuss a particular aspect of Oakes et al.'s (chapter 4) project as well. They studied the different developmental trajectories of remembering object identities, locations, and the binding of identity and location information for multiple objects using a change detection paradigm. The results showed gradual improvements in all three domains between 4 and 12 months of age. However, regarding the third question, binding object identities to locations, we think it is important to raise the issue of sampling. In Oakes et al.'s paradigm, all three objects changed location or identity from one trial to the next, and infants could notice the change by focusing their attention on only one of the objects. We propose a control experiment to test whether infants were sampling the set. In this version, only two of the objects (randomly chosen from the set of three) are swapping their identities (color). Let's say that in Trial 1 infants see red in Location 1, blue in Location 2, and yellow in Location 3. Then in Trial 2, they will again see red in Location 1, but yellow in Location 2 and blue in Location 3. Infants need to track at least two out of three objects to notice the change. If the estimates of power are in the same range as in the original study, then it is possible to conclude that infants in that paradigm can track what is where for multiple objects.

What Is the Relationship to Neuroscientific Findings?
What Do We Currently Know About the Underlying
Brain Mechanisms?

Reznick (chapter 1) rightly points out that most of the pediatric anatomical and neuroimaging studies are not specific enough for developmental psychologists to connect to. He suspects that behavioral researchers will show the way to neuroscientists. We agree with this view, but at the same time, we would like to point out that it is not impossible to make connections between the neurophysiological literature and behavioral studies. The authors of chapters 1 through 4 attempted to make these connections (only Bell and Morasch, chapter 2, were able to rely on results from their own laboratory). We will first summarize these attempts, then outline our take on the neural underpinnings of WM in infants.

Diamond's now classic studies from the 1980s (Diamond, 1985; Diamond & Goldman-Rakic, 1989) showed the importance of the dorsolateral prefrontal (PF) cortex in solving the A-not-B task, the immortal Piagetian test of object-location memory. Indeed, Bell and Morasch (chapter 2) start their discussion of WM as an example of PF functions, implying implicitly that PF involvement is a defining characteristic. (Later on, based on their own studies, they add occipital activity as another factor.) Reznick (chapter 1) cites Diamond as well, along with WM studies with older children that showed posterior parietal and anterior cingulate activity besides PF. The different theories regarding the function of the two visual streams are also prominent. The Goodale-Milner theory asserts that the dorsal stream processes visually guided action, while the ventral stream's main function is object recognition. Reznick uses this hypothesis to explain the performance differences found in infancy studies that measure reaching versus looking behavior. We are inclined to disagree with this hypothesized connection, since both reaching and looking are visually guided behaviors and therefore depend on the dorsal stream. We believe that Oakes et al. (chapter 4) approach the dorsal-ventral question in a fruitful way. They suggest that trying to determine whether the dorsal or the ventral stream develops first based on behavioral data is currently problematic: There is evidence for both possible scenarios. They also suggest that the integration of information from both of the streams is key to the binding of object identity to locations, and we are highly sympathetic to this idea. In fact, we characterized our own results with 9-month-olds (see above) as evidence for dorsal-ventral integration (Káldy & Leslie, 2003). Based on recent adult functional magnetic resonance imaging (fMRI) and event-related potential (ERP) studies, Oakes et al. also argue for a role for the posterior parietal cortex in binding multiple object identities to locations. While this region is definitely involved in remembering object identities (it shows sustained activity during the memory delay), there is also ample evidence that the medial temporal cortex is involved in object-location binding (Milner, Johnsrude, & Crane, 1997; Sommer, Rose, Glascher, Wolbers, & Buchel, 2005).

Our hypothesis for the neural substrates of infant WM differs from the classic model, as we suggest that the PF cortex might not play a central role in object and location memory in infants. Instead, we argue for the involvement of medial temporal structures (Káldy & Leslie, 2003; Káldy & Sigala, 2004). In Káldy and Sigala (2004), we presented a detailed argument based on a comprehensive review of the neuroscience literature. Here we will only briefly summarize the three main lines of research that support our hypothesis: two independent single-cell studies with macaques and an infant ERP study.

First, a subset of neurons in the temporal and PF cortices exhibit object- and/or place-specific delay activity (Suzuki, 1999; Suzuki, Miller, & Desimone, 1997). This delay activity can act as a bridge between the first presentation of the object and the test. Importantly, this activity persists in both the temporal and PF cortices regardless of intervening objects (Suzuki et al., 1997). Prior to this report by Suzuki and her colleagues, only PF neurons were believed to respond in such a way. Survival of a memory trace in the face of subsequent input is a necessary feature of short-term memory (as opposed to iconic memory, for example). So while PF neurons have the same characteristic (as Oakes et al., chapter 4, have pointed out as well), we think it is more parsimonious to suggest that in human infants, in the first year especially, it is the faster maturing temporal area that has the central role.

Second, Baker and his colleagues (Baker, Keysers, Jellema, Wicker, & Perrett, 2001) demonstrated that neurons in the temporal cortex (in the anterior part of the superior temporal sulcus) respond to objects that gradually become occluded. This response is maintained for up to 11 seconds following complete occlusion. Baker et al.'s is the first study to use natural, progressive occlusion of three-dimensional objects; in previous studies of WM in macaques, objects disappeared suddenly on a computer screen. This methodological aspect makes it very relevant for infant studies of object cognition, as infants respond differently to progressive occlusion than to implosive disappearance: Infants only expect object persistence in the case of progressive occlusion. This claim, established almost 40 years ago by Bower (1967), has garnered some new support recently. A high-density ERP study by Kaufman, Csibra, and Johnson (2005) with 6-month-old infants found that activity in the temporal cortex was related to maintaining an object in memory in a naturalistic occlusion situation. There was comparably less activity in this area when, instead of becoming occluded, the object gradually disintegrated. An earlier study by the same research group (Kaufman, Csibra, & Johnson, 2003) measured ERP responses in infants while they were watching a possible and an impossible outcome scenario in a simple object permanence task. Results showed that brain activity was different in the temporal cortex in these two conditions.

The majority of the neuroscientific literature on memory is focused on macaque electrophysiological and adult human imaging studies. Drawing conclusions about mechanisms in the infant brain from these results is notoriously difficult because of the difference in the nature of the tasks. We believe that the temporal cortex hypothesis outlined above is especially attractive, precisely because it has received independent support from high-density ERP studies conducted on young infants. Indeed, the studies by Kaufman et al. (2003, 2005) point the way to linking infant behavioral findings to macaque electrophysiological findings.

Some Theoretical Issues

Motivation and Top-Down Effects

One major problem that none of the authors have discussed is whether the abilities that we test in babies are truly equivalent to adult WM. What constitutes a "task" and "task-relevant information" for an infant? What do adults do in similar paradigms without explicit instructions? We know very little about these issues. Our guess is that some of the gaps in performance between infants and adults would be significantly smaller if adults were tested without verbal instructions (see, e.g., Xu, Carey, & Quint, 2004).

Limits and Codes

The question of how many locations or objects infants can remember has been widely discussed in the present volume and elsewhere. Oakes et al. (chapter 4) present data showing an increase in the number of objects for which infants can track the color in a change detection task. Feigenson (chapter 3) shows that infants have a capacity limit in a two-set counting paradigm of around three to four items. Feigenson then argues that the fact that this number corresponds to the number that has been found in various visual memory tasks in adults (for a summary, see Cowan, 2001) is evidence that infants use the same memory system that adults use. In our work, we also took part in the number game. In Káldy and Leslie (2005) we concluded that somewhere between 7 and 8.5 months of age, infants become capable of remembering the location of two distinct objects.

However, as Feigenson points out, object complexity might complicate the picture and the appealing theory of a fixed number of slots in WM needs to be modified. Alvarez and Cavanagh (2004) questioned the claim that however many short-term memory slots there might be, each slot could hold an essentially unlimited amount of information (Luck & Vogel, 1997). Since Miller's notion of the chunk and the failure of classic information theory to capture memory load in terms of bits, there has never been a good way to measure this load. Alvarez and Cavanagh made an ingenious end run around this problem by taking independent measures of search rate in an attention experiment as proxy for information load in a memory task. When they did this, they found that the greater the information load (slower search rate) for each stimulus item, the fewer items one can hold in memory. Intriguingly, their regression data projected that if the information load of items were zero, short-term memory would still have a maximum capacity of four items. Remarkably, adult short-term memory is limited both by the information load of each item in each slot and by a maximum of four slots. These new ideas need to be researched with infants.

Objects and WM

Although adult WM seems to be fractionated into systems for different kinds of information, such as the phonological loop, the visuospatial sketchpad, and object WM, infant studies have principally focused on object WM. Although none of the chapters addressed the properties of the infant phonological loop, speech processing and word boundary segmentation develop rapidly during the first year. So there is little reason to doubt that infants possess this type of short-term memory system too.

In part, the focus on objects derives from a research tradition stemming from Piaget's work on the object concept. Piaget was concerned not with the question of memory as such but with the question of when infants could be in a position to believe that objects continued to exist behind an occluder. For Piaget this was a matter of fundamentals. He postulated that infants were a sensorimotor system that lacked powers of recall or representation. So although Piaget stressed that infants were active organisms, they could be active only in the limited sense that they could act and react within current stimulation, including the stimulation created by their own actions. This meant that infants would lose an object to the "void," even if they continuously attended to it, if it passed out of sight behind an occluder and the infants had not already activated an action schema while it was still visible. The loss of cognitive contact with the object under these circumstances is, according to his account (Piaget, 1955), the reason infants fail the A-not-B task and subsequently continue to fail invisible displacement tasks. He argued that a belief in the persistence of objects depends upon a mental system that can, as it were, step in for the object that no longer excites by putting a mental representation or image in its place. Piaget argued that this representational intelligence, despite all appearances to the contrary, was not constructed until the last half of the second year.

The contemporary view is now shaped by a more computational understanding of the nature of representation as something basic to any information processing system—one of the legacies of the cognitive revolution—and by a series of landmark experimental studies showing that even very young infants can represent occluded objects (Baillargeon, 1986; Baillargeon, Spelke, & Wasserman, 1985; Diamond, 1988; Spelke, Breinlinger, Macomber, & Jacobson, 1992). Much current research is therefore focused upon identifying and understanding the nature and development of the neurocognitive mechanisms that make this possible.

Object Files and WM

Feigenson in chapter 3 summarizes a rich and fascinating series of experimental findings on the limits of infants' ability to track multiple objects under occlusion. Her studies using measures of looking times, manual search, and foraging behavior produce converging evidence that infants are limited to tracking three individual objects concurrently. This limit, she argues, is strikingly similar to the limit of four items that current studies of visual WM has determined for adults (Alvarez & Cavanagh, 2004; Cowan, 2001). Feigenson then argues that the limit on infants' multiple object tracking reflects their WM limit.

Central to her argument is that infants track objects using internal representations called object files. Kahneman and Treisman (1984) coined this term in developing a new model of adult visual attention (see below). Simon (1997), Leslie, Xu, Tremoulet, and Scholl (1998), and Scholl and Leslie (1999) applied these and related ideas to outline a new theory of infant object concept development that departed radically from previous approaches. We discuss this in more detail below. For now, an object file represents a single object; to represent a set of objects requires a one-to-one corresponding set of object files. These multiple representations are stored in WM and take up multiple memory slots. When available slots run out, the infant loses track of the set. Feigenson skillfully presents convergent findings from a wide range of studies that indicate that the infant numerosity limit on small sets and the infant WM limit are one and the same. She then goes on to provide and consider evidence that infants eventually are able to circumvent these limits by chunking object files in memory. We shall return to the idea of infant chunking below; but lest we move too fast to the first conclusion regarding convergence, we should raise some warning flags.

One Limit or Many?

Could the findings of a limit of three in number and individuation studies and in studies of WM be a simple coincidence? Coincidence should be the last thing a working scientist believes in, so let us be clear what we have in mind here. The question is: Does the infant limit of three (or four) in studies of short-term object identity memory and in studies of object numerosity judgment arise from the very same neurocognitive mechanism? If the answer is yes, then it is no coincidence but a deeply principled finding. On the other hand, if the two limits stem from different neurocognitive mechanisms, then we may only have coincidence. In this regard, it seems that the numbers three or four do crop up as limits across contexts where it is hard to imagine any single common mechanism. For example, FINSTs, a kind of visual index (Pylyshyn, 1989; see below) that allows tracking of multiple objects moving with Brownian motion, are limited in adults to around four. Pylyshyn (2003) argues that FINSTs ("fingers of instantiation") are part of a preattentive mechanism and so their limit would have to be independent of WM. Likewise the subitizing limit in adults is around four and can be observed in tasks that do not demand WM (e.g., the orientation detection task of Sagi & Julesz, 1984). The number of core noun phrases (without prepositions) that verbs can take as arguments is limited to three or four (the verb *bet,* perhaps uniquely, can have four). It is unlikely that this particular limit has anything to do with object WM. Many more arguments can easily be added by way of preposition phrases to make quite intelligible sentences. There may be yet general reasons why three or four are the "magic" numbers in so many different cases without that reason being object WM limits.

Convergence or Divergence?

Some evidence points away from convergence. Oakes et al. (chapter 4) describe evidence from a rapid presentation change-detection paradigm that infant short-term memory limits increase from around one item at 6.5 months to around three (possibly four) items at 12 months. Káldy and Leslie (2003, 2005) used a looking time method that required infants on a trial-by-trial basis to track the changing locations of two differently shaped objects. Infants up to 7 months could remember the identity of only one object following occlusion of the other object. By 8.5 months, infants could robustly remember the identity of two objects. These two sets of studies show a changing WM limit over the second half of the first year, increasing from a severely restricted single item around 6 months to a more adultlike three (or four) items by 12 months. However, there is no evidence from numerosity studies of a similarly changing limit over the same period. The results from both Feigenson's and others' labs (e.g., Simon, Hespos, & Rochat, 1995; Wynn, 1992, 1996; Wynn, Bloom, & Chiang, 2002) seems instead consistent with an unchanging numerosity limit of about three from age 5 or 6 months onward. The available developmental data actually appear to dissociate the small numerosity limit of three and the WM limit of three (or four). We return to this puzzle later.

Object Files: Indexes and Feature Bundles

Because Feigenson and colleagues have made extensive use of the idea of object files in accounting for their findings, let's take a closer look at this idea. Kahneman and Treisman (1984; Kahneman, Treisman, & Gibbs, 1992) introduced the idea of an object file because they perceived a missing link in traditional accounts of object perception. In traditional accounts, bottom-up sensory information is thought to directly activate long-term semantic memory traces; once the appropriate semantic categories have been activated—and only then—can the objects in the scene be identified and tracked. The task of keeping track of objects that change location was conceived of as a search task. Initial contact with an object results in a description in memory that is a combination of the sensory information and the semantic information it activated. When the object moves, the scene must be searched to discover which item in the scene matches this object representation. When an item is found matching the description in memory, then it must be the same object. This traditional view has a long history (and one version of it can be discerned in Piaget's writing). Object representations in the traditional view are essentially feature bundles of one sort or another, including perhaps a semantic category label or a word, activated bottom-up but imposed top-down on sensory input. For Kahneman and Treisman, this view missed important phenomena. For example, objects can be tracked through space without being identified (described); the same object can be tracked through changes in its identification ("It's a bird! It's a plane!"); and two "identical looking" objects can be perceived as distinct if there is a minute spatiotemporal gap between the two, while two radically different looking objects can readily be seen as a single transforming object (frog changes into a prince).

To accommodate such phenomena, Kahneman and Treisman introduced an intermediate level of object representation, which they called the object file. Object files are temporary object representations that interface between sensory information and long-term semantic information. They have two basic functional parts. The first and in many ways most important part of the object file is a continuously updated spatiotemporal code that locates the object corresponding to the object file. This is the indexing function of the object file; the file points at the object it refers to. We can think of this function as the file's "folder"—a container with only (continuously updated) spatiotemporal coordinates written on the folder's tab.

The second basic function of an object file is that the folder can have further information added, taken away, or changed. We can think of this as the sheets of paper that a folder might contain, each sheet having some property written upon it, either from sensory input or from long-term semantic storage. Together, the folder plus any information it may contain is an object file. In thinking about object files, we need to keep clear these two distinct functions. The folder may be empty, but it can still index and track an object without describing that object. In this regard, object file theory distinguishes itself radically from traditional theory. In traditional theory, an object representation is just a bundle of features; it consists of nothing but a sheaf of papers, as it were. Without features, there is no feature bundle; without a bundle, there is no object representation. But an object file can represent and track an object even if its folder is empty.

The way that Kahneman and Treisman thought of an empty object file as tracking an object was analogous to the way that a finger might track a moving object. When one picks out an object in a scene by touching it with one's index finger, the finger picks out the object without describing it. If you see only the finger, you have no idea whether it is touching something red or round or whatever. Instead, the finger helps you find the object by helping you find the object's location. Now imagine: When the object moves, the finger sticks to the object and moves with it.

The concept of the *sticky index* was highlighted and developed in Pylyshyn's FINST theory (Pylyshyn, 1989, 2000). Pylyshyn argued that even spatiotemporal information does not have to be added to a folder; a coordinate code does not have to be written on the folder's tab. We can do without even that much descriptive information. Instead, a simple winner-takes-all network can solve the correspondence problem—matching the mental index to an item in the visual world—without explicitly representing coordinates in the object file (Pylyshyn, 2003).

Howsoever it is implemented in the brain, indexing is an important and necessary function for any organism that tracks objects in real time. Leslie and colleagues chose to use the term *object index* in developing their approach to the infant object concept in order to emphasize this crucial and novel aspect of both object file and FINST theories (Leslie et al., 1998). An object file may or may not contain a feature bundle, but it must minimally contain an index.

We have briefly reviewed object indexing theory because the notion of a representation that does not describe but simply points at the world is an unusual idea with which many readers will not be familiar. It has allowed a new approach to the old problem of the developing object concept. These issues are discussed further in Leslie et al. (1998) and at greater length in Scholl and Leslie (1999; see also Tremoulet et al., 2000; also Krøjgaard, 2004, for an insightful review of more recent developments). Another reason is that indexing is relevant to both limits and chunking.

Are WM Limits Fixed or Do They Change With Development?

Chapters 3 and 4 lead us to a fascinating puzzle. If the WM capacity limit develops over the second half of the first year, why does the small numerosity limit not also develop in lock step? How can older infants exceed the small numerosity limit by chunking if that limit reflects a limit on active object files? How is numerosity information being encoded into WM? Perhaps the data that raise these puzzles will prove unreliable or not sufficiently comprehensive. In this case, as we learn more, the puzzles will simply dissolve. One possibility is that the WM limit of one at 6 months only appears along with an information load. Perhaps infants in numerosity experiments somehow operate with an information load per item that approaches zero. If so, they would be able to display more of their WM capacity, showing up as the numerosity or unloaded-WM limit of three. The upshot would be that the fixed limit on WM does not after all change with development (at least from 5 months onward), while its ability to carry an information load does.

Y. Xu and Chun (2006) have shown that the two different ways in which WM is limited, by total amount of information and by a fixed number of objects (Alvarez & Cavanagh, 2004), may correspond to dissociable neural systems. At least for static unoccluded objects, object WM tasks activate the superior intraparietal sulcus (IPS) together with the lateral occipital complex in a way that correlates to the total amount of information to be retained. The same tasks activate the inferior IPS in a way that indicates that it automatically stores a fixed number of objects (up to four) and tracks their locations. Xu and Chun may have found one of the neural systems underpinning the cognitive distinction between the descriptive information in an object file (the "sheets") and the nondescriptive object index. Indeed, they suggest that inferior IPS is a "spatial indexing mechanism that maintains spatial attention over a fixed number of objects at different spatial locations" (p. 94). It remains to be seen whether inferior IPS implements the sticky indexes required for tracking objects that change location and become occluded. Likewise, it remains to be seen whether superior IPS maintains identity information for moving occluded objects. We therefore do not know how these neural systems relate to those discussed earlier. However, the importance of posterior systems for object WM is again made clear.

These new findings with adults (Alvarez & Cavanagh, 2004; Y. Xu & Chun, 2006) suggest a possible resolution to the puzzle of why infant WM capacity appears to increase between 6 and 12 months (Káldy & Leslie, 2003, 2005; chapter 4, this volume) while the numerosity limit does not. The increase in WM capacity is seen in tasks that require infants to store identity information (shape or color) for the objects. These tasks may tap superior IPS-lateral occipital complex or some other neural system that represents the descriptive information necessary for identification for a subset of the attended objects. The fixed numerosity limit, on the other hand, may reflect inferior IPS (or some other neural system) that indexes objects by location and has a fixed limit of three or four. On this account, it becomes critical to determine whether these dissociable neural systems show differences in their rates of growth and maturation. The identity storing component should show slower growth and maturation, picking up from around 6 months and continuing at least until 12, while the indexing system should grow and mature earlier and more rapidly and change less after 6 months.

One fly in the ointment for this account comes from Feigenson's cracker tracking tasks (Feigenson, Carey, & Hauser, 2002). We had to assume that in numerosity tasks, infants bind near zero information to their object indexes. However, in these tasks infants need to accumulate the continuous extent (size) of each of the objects they track into the containers. They therefore bind size features to the indexes. This seems to be no different from binding shape (Káldy & Leslie, 2003, 2005) or color (Káldy, Blaser, & Leslie, 2006; Ross-Sheehy, Oakes, & Luck, 2003) features. So the puzzle remains.

A resolution of this puzzle will still leave a puzzle about chunking. We still have an infant indexing limit of three together with a capacity to represent two sets of two (four objects). We turn to this in what remains of our chapter.

Can Object Files Be Chunked?

The way in which object files represent numerosity is indirect and implicit. For each object in a set, there is a corresponding object file actively indexing it. Because object files are temporary representations that actively index the location of moving objects, it makes no sense to store object files in long-term storage. Information in the feature bundle might find its way into long-term storage, but the index must be actively maintained in the here and now.

If object files alone are used to implicitly represent the numerosity of sets of objects, there will be a limit to the set size that can be so represented.[1] Moreover, it should be difficult to circumvent this limit, given a need to actively maintain indexes for moving objects and fixed resources. What are the possibilities? If active object files could be placed in long-term storage, there should be no limit on how many can be active; but apparently there is a limit. If object files could be endlessly packed into WM slots, there would be no limit; but again there is. If object files could be packed into WM slots up to a maximum number per slot, then the limit should be the maximum number of object files per slot multiplied by the number of WM slots. On this last account, an adult limit of four and an infant limit of three both suggest that the maximum number of object files per WM slot is about one. So far there is no obvious way to chunk the active object files themselves in order to escape the indexing limit.

Might a single object file index multiple objects? Could a single index point at a collection, like a flock of birds? This seems entirely plausible. Unfortunately there is a cost. Bear in mind that numerosity is represented implicitly by the number of object file indexes. If a single object file is used to index a set of objects, the numerosity represented is not the number of individuals in the set but the number of sets (one). Two such object files would represent two sets, but the number of individuals in each set simply goes unrepresented. Wynn et al. (2002) showed that, in displays where common motion defines distinct collections, infants can distinguish the numerosity of sets of blobs. But indeed, their infants had no idea how many individuals were in each set.

So how do Feigenson's infants not only know that there are two sets of objects but also know how many individuals are in each set? Recall that Feigenson and Halberda (2004) showed that 14-month-old infants will search for two sets of two objects, apparently knowing there are exactly two objects in each of two boxes. Inasmuch as this total of four exceeds the previously established indexing limit of 3, the results are puzzling. Feigenson suggests that the infant chunks the objects into sets. But just how is that done?

Perhaps infants were searching for two total amounts of stuff (Feigenson, Carey, & Spelke, 2002), but that seems unlikely. In a looking time study, Leslie and Chen (in press) familiarized 11-month-old infants with a pair of disks (XX) moved individually from and replaced behind a screen, followed by a pair of triangles (YY) displayed in the same way. Another group were familiarized with a repeating disk-triangle (XY) pair. The infants familiarized with two pairs (XX-then-YY) looked longer when the screen was removed to reveal only a single disk-triangle pair (XY) than did infants familiarized with the single (XY-then-XY) pair. If, however, the screen revealed two pairs, the looking times reversed. Now infants familiarized with the single pair looked longer than infants familiarized with the double pairs. These findings suggest that infants can individuate successive pairs of objects based on sequential shape differences between pairs. We thus have converging evidence from looking time in younger babies that infants chunk.

Representations That Chunk Past the Limit: Integers and Pairs

If infants can track two pairs of objects, how do they track that fourth object when their three object files are already used up? They need to free up an index to track the fourth object, but then they lose track of the object that index was tracking. One possibility is that they employ a code for sets, like SET-OF. When the infant sees a pair of disks followed by a pair of triangles, she might encode this as SET-OF DISKS, SET-OF TRIANGLES. She then looks longer when she detects the discrepancy in the screen revealing only a single disk and a single triangle. However, this sort of representation is equivalent to a singular–plural distinction, and Kouider, Halberda, Wood, and Carey (2006) have found that distinguishing, for example, Set 1 from Set 4 does not develop until 22 months. It seems unlikely that much younger infants employ the SET-OF concept.

We should consider the possibility that infants have another option besides object files for the exact, nonnoisy representation of small numerosities. One possibility that has not been explored in the literature is that infants have the integer representations ONE, TWO, and THREE (but not FOUR) available (for further discussion, see Leslie, Gallistel, & Gelman, in press). Another possibility, also not explored hitherto, is that infants have specific set representations, SINGLETON, PAIR, TRIPLET but not QUADRUPLE (see Leslie & Chen, in press). Either representation, integer or specific-set, would encode small numerosities without a Weber fraction, would chunk object sets so that exactly one, two, or three (but not four) objects can be represented per WM slot, and would allow up to a three-object set to be represented at a point in development (e.g., 6 months) when the infant may have only a single WM slot available. At this time, the literature on discrete number representation has considered only two possibilities, accumulator magnitudes and object files. Perhaps it is time to consider some of the many other possibilities.

Questions for Future Research

The four chapters in this part demonstrate that this is an exciting time in research on infant WM. New findings, new questions, and multiple maturing experimental methods are combining to promise further advances. At the same time, infancy research is making fresh gains by establishing theoretical connections with and exploiting advances being made in the study of adult WM and visual attention. Finally, it is becoming ever clearer just how important neural systems development is in driving cognitive development in infancy.

We already touched on a number of specific questions that are coming into focus and which require new efforts. Here we highlight: What is the relation between the development and maturation of anterior (PF) and posterior (temporal and parietal) brain systems for control of WM and attention, and what are the implications for infant cognitive development (chapter 4)? How does information about objects get bound to information about their locations (chapter 4)? How can we develop paradigms that can be used equally with infants, toddlers, older children, and adults, thus making the comparisons more seamless (chapter 2)? How can we relate WM development to other cognitive abilities (chapter 1)? What is the relation between the numerosity limit and developments in infant object WM (chapter 3)? Does development of infant WM involve an increase in the number of slots or an increase in the information carrying load of each slot with number of slots constant, or is there an increase in both the number of slots and their carrying load? Last century's breakthroughs in understanding the general nature of information machines have opened new perspectives on a very special machine: the mind-brain of the human infant. In this century, the nature of its limits and its codes are sure to remain key topics of investigation.

Note

1. The evidence for a limit comes from multiple object tracking in adults, where the limit is usually around four (Pylyshyn & Storm, 1988; Scholl & Pylyshyn, 1999; Trick & Pylyshyn, 1994a, 1994b; but see Trick, Jaspers-Fayer, & Seth, 2005) and from Feigenson's studies with infants (reviewed in chapter 3), where the limit appears to be three.

References

Alvarez, G. A., & Cavanagh, P. (2004). The capacity of visual short-term memory is set both by visual information load and by number of objects. *Psychological Science, 15,* 106–111.

Baddeley, A. D. (1998). Recent developments in working memory. *Current Opinion in Neurobiology, 8,* 234–238.

Baddeley, A. D. (2003). Working memory: Looking back and looking forward. *Nature Reviews Neuroscience, 4,* 829–839.

Baddeley, A. D., & Hitch, G. (1974). Working memory. In G. A. Bower (Ed.), *The psychology of learning and motivation* (pp. 47–89). New York: Academic Press.

Baillargeon, R. (1986). Representing the existence and the location of hidden objects: Object permanence in 6- and 8-month-old infants. *Cognition, 23,* 21–41.

Baillargeon, R., Spelke, E. S., & Wasserman, S. (1985). Object permanence in five-month-old infants. *Cognition, 20,* 191–208.

Baker, C. I., Keysers, C., Jellema, T., Wicker, B., & Perrett, D. I. (2001). Neuronal representation of disappearing and hidden objects in temporal cortex of the macaque. *Experimental Brain Research, 140,* 375–381.

Bell, M. A., & Fox, N. A. (1992). The relations between frontal brain electrical activity and cognitive development during infancy. *Child Development, 63,* 1142–1163.

Bower, T. G. R. (1967). The development of object permanence: Some studies of existence constancy. *Perception and Psychophysics, 2,* 74–76.

Broadbent, D. E. (1958). *Perception and communication.* London: Pergamon Press.

Courtney, S. M., Petit, L., Haxby, J. V., & Ungerleider, L. G. (1998). The role of prefrontal cortex in working memory: Examining the contents of consciousness. *Philosophical Transactions of the Royal Society of London, Part B, Biological Sciences, 353*, 1819–1828.

Cowan, N. (2001). The magical number 4 in short-term memory: A reconsideration of mental storage capacity. *Behavioral and Brain Sciences, 24*, 87–185.

Diamond, A. (1985). Development of the ability to use recall to guide action, as indicated by infants' performance on A-not-B. *Child Development, 56*, 868–883.

Diamond, A. (1988). Differences between adult and infant cognition: Is the crucial variable presence or absence of language? In L. Weiskrantz (Ed.), *Thought without language* (pp. 335–370). Oxford, UK: Oxford Science Publications.

Diamond, A., & Goldman-Rakic, P. S. (1989). Comparison of human infants and rhesus monkeys on Piaget's AB task: Evidence for dependence on dorsolateral prefrontal cortex. *Experimental Brain Research, 74*, 24–40.

Feigenson, L., Carey, S., & Hauser, M. (2002). The representations underlying infants' choice of more: Object files versus analog magnitudes. *Psychological Science, 13*, 150–156.

Feigenson, L., Carey, S., & Spelke, E. (2002). Infants' discrimination of number vs. continuous extent. *Cognitive Psychology, 44*, 33–66.

Feigenson, L., & Halberda, J. (2004). Infants chunk object arrays into sets of individuals. *Cognition, 91*, 173–190.

Haith, M. M. (1998). Who put the cog in infant cognition? Is rich interpretation too costly? *Infant Behavior and Development, 21*, 167–179.

Kahneman, D., & Treisman, A. (1984). Changing views of attention and automaticity. In R. Parasuraman & D. R. Davies (Eds.), *Varieties of attention* (pp. 29–61). New York: Academic Press.

Kahneman, D., Treisman, A., & Gibbs, B. J. (1992). The reviewing of object files: Object-specific integration of information. *Cognitive Psychology, 24*, 175–219.

Káldy, Z., Blaser, E., & Leslie, A. M. (2006). A new method for calibrating perceptual salience in infants: The case of color vs. luminance. *Developmental Science, 9*, 482–489.

Káldy, Z., & Leslie, A. M. (2003). The identification of objects by 9-month-old infants: Integrating "what" and "where" information. *Developmental Science, 6*, 360–373.

Káldy, Z., & Leslie, A. M. (2005). A memory span of one? Object identification in 6.5-month-old infants. *Cognition, 97*, 153–177.

Káldy, Z., & Sigala, N. (2004). The neural mechanisms of object working memory: What is where in the infant brain? *Neuroscience and Biobehavioral Reviews, 28*, 113–121.

Kaufman, J., Csibra, G., & Johnson, M. H. (2003). Representing occluded objects in the human infant brain. *Proceedings of the Royal Society of London, Part B, Biology Letters, 270(Suppl. 2)*, 140–143.

Kaufman, J., Csibra, G., & Johnson, M. H. (2005). Oscillatory activity in the infant brain reflects object maintenance. *Proceedings of the National Academy of Science, USA, 102*, 15271–15274.

Kouider, S., Halberda, J., Wood, J., & Carey, S. (2006). Acquisition of English number marking: The singular-plural distinction. *Language Learning and Development, 2,* 1–25.

Krøjgaard, P. (2004). A review of object individuation in infancy. *British Journal of Developmental Psychology, 22,* 159–183.

Leslie, A. M. (1982). The perception of causality in infants. *Perception, 11,* 173–186.

Leslie, A. M. (1984a). Infant perception of a manual pick-up event. *British Journal of Developmental Psychology, 2,* 19–32.

Leslie, A. M. (1984b). Spatiotemporal continuity and the perception of causality in infants. *Perception, 13,* 287–305.

Leslie, A. M. (1994). *ToMM, ToBy,* and Agency: Core architecture and domain specificity. In L. Hirschfeld & S. Gelman (Eds.), *Mapping the mind: Domain specificity in cognition and culture* (pp. 119–148). New York: Cambridge University Press.

Leslie, A. M., & Chen, M. L. (in press). Individuation of pairs of objects in infancy. *Developmental Science.*

Leslie, A. M., Gallistel, C. R., & Gelman, R. (in press). Where integers come from. In P. Carruthers (Ed.), *The innate mind: Foundations and future.* Oxford, UK: Oxford University Press.

Leslie, A. M., & Káldy, Z. (2001). Indexing individual objects in infant working memory. *Journal of Experimental Child Psychology, 78,* 61–74.

Leslie, A. M., & Keeble, S. (1987). Do six-month-old infants perceive causality? *Cognition, 25,* 265–288.

Leslie, A. M., Xu, F., Tremoulet, P. D., & Scholl, B. J. (1998). Indexing and the object concept: Developing "what" and "where" systems. *Trends in Cognitive Sciences, 2,* 10–18.

Luck, S. J., & Vogel, E. K. (1997). The capacity of visual working memory for features and conjunctions. *Nature, 390,* 279–281.

Mareschal, D., & Johnson, M. H. (2003). The "what" and "where" of object representations in infancy. *Cognition, 88,* 259–276.

Miller, G. A. (1956). The magical number seven plus or minus two: Some limits in our capacity for processing information. *Psychological Review, 63,* 81–97.

Milner, B., Johnsrude, I., & Crane, J. (1997). Right medial temporal-lobe contribution to object-location memory. *Philosophical Transactions of the Royal Society of London, Part B, Biological Sciences, 352,* 1469–1474.

Piaget, J. (1955). *The child's construction of reality.* London: Routledge and Kegan Paul.

Pylyshyn, Z. (2003). *Seeing and visualizing: It's not what you think.* Cambridge, MA: MIT Press.

Pylyshyn, Z. W. (1989). The role of location indexes in spatial perception: A sketch of the FINST spatial-index model. *Cognition, 32,* 65–97.

Pylyshyn, Z. W. (2000). Situating vision in the world. *Trends in Cognitive Sciences, 4,* 197–207.

Pylyshyn, Z., & Storm, R. (1988). Tracking multiple independent targets: Evidence for both serial and parallel stages. *Spatial Vision, 3,* 179–197.

Ross-Sheehy, S., Oakes, L. M., & Luck, S. J. (2003). The development of visual short-term memory capacity in infants. *Child Development, 74,* 1807–1822.

Sagi, D., & Julesz, B. (1984). Detection versus discrimination of visual orientation. *Perception, 14,* 619–628.

Scholl, B. J. (2001). Objects and attention: The state of the art. *Cognition, 80,* 1–46.

Scholl, B. J., & Leslie, A. M. (1999). Explaining the infant's object concept: Beyond the perception/cognition dichotomy. In E. Lepore & Z. Pylyshyn (Eds.), *What is cognitive science?* (pp. 26–73). Oxford, UK: Blackwell.

Scholl, B. J., & Pylyshyn, Z. W. (1999). Tracking multiple objects through occlusion: Clues to visual objecthood. *Cognitive Psychology, 38,* 259–290.

Simon, T. J. (1997). Reconceptualizing the origins of number knowledge—a non-numerical account. *Cognitive Development, 12,* 349–372.

Simon, T. J., Hespos, S. J., & Rochat, P. (1995). Do infants understand simple arithmetic? A replication of Wynn (1992). *Cognitive Development, 10,* 253–269.

Sommer, T., Rose, M., Glascher, J., Wolbers, T., & Buchel, C. (2005). Dissociable contributions within the medial temporal lobe to encoding of object-location associations. *Learning and Memory, 12,* 343–351.

Spelke, E. S., Breinlinger, K., Macomber, J., & Jacobson, K. (1992). Origins of knowledge. *Psychological Review, 99,* 605–632.

Suzuki, W. A. (1999). The long and the short of it: Memory signals in the medial temporal lobe. *Neuron, 24,* 295–298.

Suzuki, W. A., Miller, E. K., & Desimone, R. (1997). Object and place memory in the macaque entorhinal cortex. *Journal of Neurophysiology, 78,* 1062–1081.

Tremoulet, P. D., Leslie, A. M., & Hall, D. G. (2000). Infant individuation and identification of objects. *Cognitive Development, 15,* 499–522.

Trick, L. M., Jaspers-Fayer, F., & Seth, N. (2005). Multiple-object tracking in children: The "catch the spies" task. *Cognitive Development, 20,* 373–387.

Trick, L. M., & Pylyshyn, Z. (1994a). Cueing and counting: Does the position of the attentional focus affect enumeration? *Visual Cognition, 1,* 67–100.

Trick, L. M., & Pylyshyn, Z. (1994b). Why are small and large numbers enumerated differently? A limited-capacity preattentive stage in vision. *Psychological Review, 101,* 80–102.

Wilcox, T., & Baillargeon, R. (1998a). Object individuation in infancy: The use of featural information in reasoning about occlusion events. *Cognitive Psychology, 37,* 97–155.

Wynn, K. (1992). Addition and subtraction by human infants. *Nature, 358,* 749–750.

Wynn, K. (1996). Infants' individuation and enumeration of actions. *Psychological Science, 7,* 164–169.

Wynn, K., Bloom, P., & Chiang, W. (2002). Enumeration of collective entities by 5-month-old infants. *Cognition, 83,* B55–B62.

Xu, F., & Carey, S. (1996). Infants' metaphysics: The case of numerical identity. *Cognitive Psychology, 30,* 111–153.

Xu, F., Carey, S., & Quint, N. (2004). The emergence of kind-based object individuation in infancy. *Cognitive Psychology, 49*(2), 155–190.

Xu, Y., & Chun, M. M. (2006). Dissociable neural mechanisms supporting visual short-term memory for objects. *Nature, 440,* 91–95.

6

What Infants Can Tell Us About
Working Memory Development

NELSON COWAN

Despite my focus for the past 25 years on theoretical aspects of working memory and its development in adults and elementary school children, my graduate training at the University of Wisconsin, 1974–1980, was in the infant speech perception laboratory of Philip A. Morse, often in collaboration with Lewis A. Leavitt. My graduate research began with questions about whether 4- and 5-month-old infants would show a right-ear advantage for the perception of spoken syllables, as adults do (e.g., Shankweiler & Studdert-Kennedy, 1967), and whether auditory backward recognition masking (Massaro, 1975) could be obtained in infants. However, slight differences in the stimulus arrangement turned out to make enormous differences in the measure of auditory discrimination being pioneered in the laboratory (heart rate deceleration to a change following 15 to 20 repetitions of a prechange sound). Failure of several experiments using that type of measure was followed by the success of conceptually similar investigations with slightly different discrimination measures (Cowan, Suomi, & Morse, 1982; Glanville, Best, & Levenson, 1977). Several hundred infants wiser, I drifted away from infant research, and return to it here with great admiration for exciting advances that have been made through persistent, intrepid work.

I describe a theoretical framework based on adults with which to view the chapters on infants; make tailored observations about each of the chapters individually; and, finally, integrate the points made to form a comparison of answers to the questions that the authors addressed.

Working Memory in Adults as a Backdrop for Infant Research

A Brief History of Working Memory Research

Miller (1956) famously suggested that an individual can remember sets of about seven meaningful units or chunks, no matter whether the units were letters, digits, words, or character combinations (e.g., with the digit string 101–011 counting as only two chunks if 101 is mentally recoded as 5 and 011 as 3, according to a binary system). However, Baddeley, Thomson, and Buchanan (1975) showed that the exact number of verbal list items that could be recalled depended not only on the number of chunks in the list, but also on the spoken duration of the items. Lists of words that could be pronounced more quickly were recalled more successfully than lists of the same number of words that took longer to pronounce. Also, when individuals were asked to pronounce small sets of the words as quickly as possible, those who could pronounce the words faster also could remember more of them. In fact, the number of words a particular person could pronounce in about 2 seconds was a good predictor of the length of list, composed of those same words, that the individual could recall. This was explained with the notion that a phonological form of memory persisted for about 2 seconds unless the memory is refreshed through covert verbal rehearsal, which presumably occurs at about the same rate as speeded overt pronunciation (see Landauer, 1962). The faster the list could be rehearsed, the larger the number of list items that could be kept active until the time of recall, analogous to a juggling act in which balls are kept in the air and not allowed to hit the ground. After that, emphasis in the field of short-term memory shifted from a chunk limit to a time limit, although the concept of a chunk limit was still occasionally investigated in nonverbal domains (e.g., Chase & Simon, 1973; Gobet et al., 2001).

The notion of not only retaining items in short-term memory and then recalling them, but actually combining them for use in diverse types of complex cognition, was the likely basis of the term *working memory* that was used (perhaps coined) by Miller, Galanter, and Pribram (1960) and later expanded upon and made popular by Baddeley and Hitch (1974) in their summary of research on conflicts between tasks.

Working memory limits must be viewed as a strength as well as a limitation. The ability to hold ideas in mind, combine them into new ideas, and manipulate them is an obvious and basic human strength. That it begins in infancy can be illustrated by the finding that infants build expectations about the reemergence of a moving object that disappears behind an opaque obstruction (for a review, see Baillargeon, 2004). That working memory has a small capacity seems to be a human limitation, although it is possible that we would be overwhelmed with too much information to process at once if working memory capacity were unlimited. In the following sections, I discuss the definition and description of working memory and then discuss questions regarding some of its basic properties relevant to infant research.

A Definition and a Simple Model

Miyake and Shah (1999) asked their chapter contributors to define working memory before presenting their own theoretical models of it. The definitions were strikingly different from one another. Some authors provided a general definition, whereas others offered a more specific description, such as a multicomponent system for the storage and manipulation of information (Baddeley & Logie, 1999) or the use of controlled attention to hold and manage information (Engle, Tuholski, Laughlin, & Conway, 1999). My own definition (Cowan, 1999) was more general. I defined working memory as the collection of mental mechanisms that hold information in a temporarily accessible form that can be of use in cognitive tasks. That definition seemed appropriate because multiple mechanisms are involved, and because we are not yet certain of all of the mechanisms.

Cowan (1988, 1995, 1999, 2005) described working memory in a manner illustrated in Figure 6.1. The memory system includes a subset of elements currently in a heightened state of neural activation or accessibility, making the corresponding ideas temporarily very easy to recall. A subset of those active elements is in the focus of attention, which also must include new associations between elements that occupy the focus concurrently. Incoming stimuli activate features in memory automatically, but primarily the physical features (color, shape, tone pitch, and so on). It is true that there is evidence apparently indicating that unattended items can be perceived on a semantic level without the benefit of attention; these include one's own name (Moray, 1959) or word pairs (Eich, 1984) spoken in an unattended auditory channel. However, later evidence suggests that these findings are better explained by the hypothesis that attention sometimes wanders and picks up information that was supposed to be unattended (Conway, Cowan, & Bunting, 2001; Wood, Stadler, & Cowan, 1997).

Within this processing system as conceived by Cowan (1988), activated memory is limited by temporal decay, whereas the focus of attention is limited by the number of chunks that can be held at once: about four chunks on average in adults (see Cowan, 2001). Also, both aspects of working memory are limited by vulnerability to types of interference (the replacement of the relevant active representations by other ones). These proposed limits require further discussion, as does the basis of individual differences.

Do Representations Decay Over Time?

It seems natural to compare forgetting to some inevitable process such as, say, radioactive decay. We can assume that many neurons are involved in the representation of each idea in the brain. It seems reasonable that the

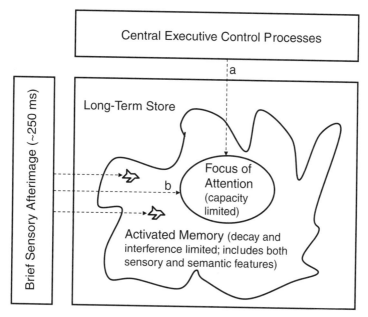

FIGURE 6.1. An illustration of the theoretical framework for the information processing system as described by Cowan (1988, 1995). The focus of attention is controlled by both executive processes (a) and orienting to changed stimuli (b). Whereas the automatic activation of features is only partial, the focus of attention allows a deeper, more semantic perceptual analysis, and it includes new links between memory elements activated concurrently. The theory makes at least two controversial claims about working memory: (1) that activated memory is prone to temporal decay, and (2) that the focus of attention is limited to a small, fixed number of separate chunks.

representation could lose the involvement of some neurons or lose some precision of neural representation and become fuzzy or inexact. If a constant proportion of neurons representing an idea ceased its activity in each unit of time, the number of neurons remaining active in the representation would decay exponentially over time. Simple studies of short-term memory seem to reflect something like exponential decay over time; for example, this is the case in studies in which two tones are presented with a variable delay between them and the participant is to indicate whether the tones differ or not. The notion of short-term memory decay was popular in early theories of information processing (Broadbent, 1958; Brown, 1958, 1959; Peterson & Peterson, 1959), and that tradition was continued by Baddeley et al. (1975) and in Baddeley's following work.

Clearly, the concepts of delay effects and of temporal decay of memory are important topics brought up in chapters 1 through 4 of the present volume.

One simple hypothesis would be that neural activity representing an idea in working memory stays active longer in adults than in infants. However, it is not clear that anything like this simple, temporally based form of memory decay that has been so popular has ever actually been observed, at any age. (This point reinforces a similar one made by Reznick in chapter 1 of this volume.) The problem is that there are a number of other things that can happen over a retention interval to reduce memory. First, as time goes on, the most recent item in a series of items represented in memory can become more blended into previous items and therefore more difficult to retrieve. An analogy is that the last telephone pole in a series seems very distinct from the other poles when you are standing close to the pole, but much less distinct as you continue down the road (cf. Crowder, 1993; Glenberg & Swanson, 1986; Nairne, 2002; Neath & Surprenant, 2003). Second, when the memory task is the comparison of two stimuli then, as the time between them increases, there can be the increasing problem of inappropriate grouping. It may become difficult to compare the two stimuli because the first one in the trial seems to be grouped together with stimuli from previous trials, and not with the second one from the current trial. Third, there can be interference from any stimuli that are used to prevent rehearsal during the retention interval. Fourth, even if there are no interfering stimuli, there can be interference from ideas that the participant may think of during the retention interval, if attention wanders from the task at hand.

A variety of studies now suggest that what has looked like exponential decay is actually nothing of the sort. For example, Cowan, Saults, and Nugent (1997) reexamined the phenomenon of forgetting in a two-tone comparison situation. In order to deal with the grouping issue, we varied not only the time between tones to be compared but also the time between trials. That way, we could examine trials in which the time between tones varied but with a constant ratio between that time and the time between the present trial and the previous one. We observed that memory performance stayed relatively constant from 0 through 6 seconds and then rather suddenly plunged downward by a 12-second intertone interval.

Lewandowsky, Duncan, and Brown (2004) presented letters for serial recall and varied the interresponse time allowed in recall, ranging between 400 and 1,600 milliseconds. This was done with a silent keyboard response along with repetition of a word by the participant to prevent rehearsal, or it was done with spoken recall separated by repetitions of a word to prevent rehearsal. Contrary to what would be expected on the basis of memory decay, there was little or no effect of recall time on recall accuracy. Similarly, Cowan et al. (2006) trained children to speed up their recall in a digit span task and, even though they successfully sped up quite a bit, there was no benefit for recall. Decay does not appear to be an important factor causing forgetting in working memory, according to the recent evidence. (For convergent evidence from event-related potential recordings, see Winkler, Schröger, & Cowan, 2001.)

Is Attention Used to Store Information?

According to the model of information processing shown in Figure 6.1, the focus of attention acts as a temporary information-storage device. In order to test this hypothesis, it is necessary to make a distinction between specific and general interference with memory. For example, consider memory for an array of visual items, as in the infant research described by Oakes, Ross-Sheehy, and Luck (chapter 4, this volume). If there were interference with this memory from another visual object, the origin of this specific interference would be unclear. It could be interference with visual memory in particular, or with a more general storage mechanism such as the focus of attention. However, if there were interference with this visual array memory from some type of stimulus that had little in common with it, with very different memory codes used in the two tasks, then this more general type of interference would lead to a clearer conclusion. It would indicate that attention is used to maintain the visual array and also to carry out the interfering task.

Morey and Cowan (2004) carried out an experiment in this vein. Two arrays of colored squares were to be compared to determine if a probed (encircled) item in the second array had changed color from the first array or not. This task was modeled after Luck and Vogel (1997). However, between the arrays, participants carried out one of several tasks. In the critical condition, the participant was to recite a memory load of seven random digits. This caused a substantial decrease in performance on the visual array comparison task. In a control condition, the participant was to recite his or her own telephone number. This task requires verbal processing but not working memory, and it had little effect on array comparisons compared to no load. Therefore, it can be surmised that the memory faculty that both tasks need is neither visual nor phonological in nature, but something more general. We believe that it is attention that is shared between the array comparison and digit load tasks. Of course, we do not claim that there cannot also be attention-free components in the memory of visual or verbal information.

Despite findings such as those of Morey and Cowan (2004), it is still not clear just what attention does in working memory. It could actually store the information, as Figure 6.1 suggests. An alternative possibility, though, is that storage per se could be nonattentional in nature, but with attention needed to defend the stored information from interference. An example of that latter possibility exists, though it is not yet clear whether the example pertains to working memory. Cowan, Beschin, and Della Sala (2004) tested memory in six densely amnesic individuals (with brain injuries or strokes) and six normal control participants. On each trial, the participant heard a story and then repeated it back to the best of his or her ability. This was followed by a 1-hour delay that was spent either carrying out various psychometric tests or in a quiet, dark room. After the delay, the participant was asked to repeat the story again. Amnesic patients (unlike control participants) recalled almost nothing from the story after an hour of psychometric testing. However, after an hour spent in a quiet, dark room, four of these six patients remembered about 80% of the information from the story. This was the case even on trials in which the participant fell asleep for part of the hour (as evidenced by loud snoring). The patients who benefited from the minimal-interference delay had nontemporal sites of brain lesions, whereas those who did not benefit had temporal sites. One account of the findings is that temporal lobe sites automatically hold information for an indefinite length of time, but only until there is corruption of the memory by interfering stimuli; whereas nontemporal sites that were damaged in the other patients ordinarily reflect the use of attention to defend the memory in the temporal lobe.

Is There a Capacity Limit?

According to the model in Figure 6.1, the focus of attention is limited in adults, usually to somewhere between three to five independent chunks of information at one time. Actually, though, this is a difficult point to test with any certainty. One must show that there is a capacity limit, estimate that limit, and show that it depends on attention. Estimating the capacity limit is the most difficult part because one must make assumptions about what the meaningful units or chunks are, so that the chunks in working memory can be counted. Cowan (2001) considered a wide range of test situations in which it is presumably not possible to combine items into larger chunks and found that performance is limited to about four items in such situations (each of which presumably constitutes a single-item chunk). For example, when lists of words to be recalled are presented along with an articulatory suppression task to block rehearsal and hence grouping, people recall about four items.

Grouping of items into multi-item chunks is difficult also in the visual array comparison task of Luck and Vogel (1997) that forms the basis of research described by Oakes et al. (this volume, chapter 4), because the presentation is brief. In adults, the observed capacity is three to four items whether a cue is present or not. Given the dual-task results of Morey and Cowan (2004), it is very reasonable to hypothesize that this capacity limit is an attentional limit, though it could be that nonattentional processes contribute.

We have explored other ways to investigate capacity limits in adults and have found estimates similar to the limit that Cowan (2001) observed. Cowan, Chen, and Rouder (2004) taught participants pairs of words (e.g., desk–pin) and presented other words as singletons. Then we presented lists of eight words formed from singletons or from learned pairs. With various levels of pairing knowledge, capacity was found to be fixed at about 3.5 chunks (singletons or pairs).

Chen and Cowan (2005) then elaborated on this work in an attempt to reconcile findings indicating that the limit in recall is capacity-based (Miller, 1956) and findings indicating that the limit is time-based (Baddeley et al., 1975).

Word pairs were taught to a criterion of 100% correct cued recall, and to 100% correct indication of the singleton status of other words. These words and word pairs were then used to form lists of varying length. We found that either a capacity limit or a time limit can occur, depending on the manner of testing and scoring. For long lists with free recall or free scoring of serial recall, a chunk limit seemed to apply. Participants recalled lists of 6 learned pairs at the same proportion correct as lists of 6 singletons, and much higher than lists of 12 singletons. However, for shorter lists with strict serial scoring, a time-related limit seemed to apply instead. Participants recalled lists of 4 learned pairs in serial recall only with a proportion correct equivalent to lists of 8 singletons, and much below lists of 4 singletons. We suggested that a capacity-limited mechanism holds the items, in keeping with Miller (1956) and Cowan (2001), but that a phonological rehearsal process greatly helps in the retention of the serial order, in keeping with most other recent work on list recall (see Baddeley, 1986).

There is a wide range of views on capacity limits, which Cowan (2005) summarized. What is interesting about this is that, in the first draft of the paper that eventually became Cowan (2001), some reviewers objected that the concept of capacity was not controversial enough to motivate the commentaries that accompany articles in *Behavioral and Brain Sciences*. It is now clear that this is, indeed, a controversial topic, in terms of both the characterization of the capacity limit and the cause for it. Some researchers disagree on the number of items or chunks encompassed by the capacity limit, others believe instead in only a time limit, and others believe in a modality-specific limit or in no special working memory limit at all; just a single set of rules for all of memory. Length constraints prevent me from going into all of those different theoretical views.

In sum, the simple notion of decay probably should be replaced by a more nuanced notion of interference that can accrue as a function of time, with the amount of interference per unit of time greatly depending on the stimulus situation. The concept of a capacity limit measured in meaningful chunks seems sound despite difficulties in identifying chunks (for a review, see Cowan, 2005). Attention is involved in that capacity limit, but it is still unclear whether attention holds information or only defends storage against the loss of information through interference. Individual differences in working memory also could be discussed here but will be deferred to the next section, as they are part of the discussion of developmental changes during infancy and beyond.

Development of Working Memory in Infancy and Beyond

As a backdrop to assess the chapters of the present volume, it is important to consider what infant research can and cannot tell us. It can tell us what abilities occur relatively early in life and therefore do not depend on an extended period of maturation or training. It can sometimes tell us which abilities co-occur and which ones are independent, and which inabilities put an infant at risk for later learning disabilities. Also, it can indicate which abilities change rapidly over the first year of life. It cannot easily tell us which aspects of ability are innate, given the far-reaching consequences of early experience, with the exception of research on newborns (and, even then, experience in the womb must be taken into account; see, e.g., Kolata, 1984; Morse & Cowan, 1982). Most important, infant research cannot easily tell us about developmental trends from infancy to childhood, except insofar as a common procedure can be devised or a good case can be made for a fair comparison across the very different procedures typically used in infants versus children and adults. The question of what infants know always must be answered with the manner of testing kept in mind.

Each of the chapters on working memory in infancy focuses on an important section of the working memory landscape. The main themes of these chapters now are discussed within the theoretical framework that I have offered.

Chapter 2

Chapter 2, by Bell and Morasch, is notable for its application to infants of leading views of working memory and its individual variation, and for building a methodological bridge between infants and children. I touch these topics in turn.

Working Memory Structure and Its Individual Variation

Chapter 2 seems to adopt two of the major theoretical views of working memory of our time. One is the structural view of working memory proposed by Baddeley and colleagues (e.g., Baddeley, 2000, 2001; Baddeley & Logie, 1999). In this structural view, there are separate modules for the storage of spatial and verbal information (the phonological and visuospatial stores) as well as a recently added module that stores links between elements of different types, the episodic buffer. All of them are regulated by central executive processes. Bell and Morasch also adopt the view about individual differences in working memory proposed by Engle and colleagues (e.g., Engle et al., 1999; Kane, Bleckley, Conway, & Engle, 2001; Kane & Engle, 2002). According to this view, individual and developmental differences in working memory come from differences in the functioning of the frontal lobes, resulting in differences in the ability to control cognition. My own views are not far from these, but there are differences on both accounts.

One difference pertains to the evidence concerning separate visual and spatial modules (Baddeley, 1986). The evidence is not as stark as Bell and

Morasch make out. They say that "verbal and spatial aspects of working memory are uncorrelated, with this functional independence true for children as well as adults," citing Gathercole, Pickering, Ambridge, and Wearing (2004). However, functional independence does not mean an absence of correlation. In structural equation models of performance in children aged 6–7, 8–9, 10–12, and 13–15 years observed by Gathercole et al., the path coefficients between the verbal and spatial memory factors were .41, .32, .33, and .35, respectively; moderate relations well above zero. Functional independence presumably means only that the model worked better with separate verbal and spatial memory factors than with the measures combined into one factor. It is true that a factor reflecting central executive processes was correlated with verbal and spatial memory factors at a much stronger level.

In my recent book (Cowan, 2005) and in older sources (going back to Cowan, 1988), I have explained why I do not favor a modular view but prefer the representation shown in Figure 6.1. My alternative account would state that any type of memory sustains the most interference from additional stimuli with similar features (e.g., verbal interference with verbal memoranda and spatial interference with spatial memoranda). I prefer this formulation because it allows for types of memory that Baddeley's (1986) formulation does not cover. For example, it is unclear in his model how tactile features would be processed, or how speech sounds coming from different spatial locations would be processed. For me, those are just stimuli that activate different physical and sometimes semantic features in memory.

The episodic buffer (Baddeley, 2000) lessens the distinction between our models inasmuch as new links between elements in memory (e.g., new associations between words) can be held in the episodic buffer in his model and in the focus of attention in my model. Another possibility for my model is that these new links can be formed in the focus of attention and then held for a while without effort, as activated memory.

I also doubt that the elegant view of Engle et al. (1999) completely captures the basis of individual differences in working memory. Instead of attributing these totally to differences in the control of attention, I have suggested that a broader function of attention is relevant (Cowan et al., 2005). When the task requires that a goal must be maintained despite prepotent stimuli that work against the goal, as in the A-not-B error that Bell and Morasch discuss, then the focus of attention must zoom in to hold onto the goal with great intensity. In this case, the goal is to recall where the toy was hidden last and not to be swayed by the habit of reaching into one of the containers. This matches Engle's beliefs. However, when the task simply requires multiple elements to be held at once, the focus of attention must zoom out, up to the capacity limit, to allow the elements to be apprehended and held concurrently. An example is memory for visual arrays of objects, as discussed by Oakes et al. (chapter 4, this volume).

Presumably, the focus of attention cannot fully zoom in and zoom out at the same time. Preliminary evidence that multi-item memory and a goal-conflict situation interfere with one another was provided by Bunting and Cowan (2005). We showed that recall of words from a list matching a particular semantic category (e.g., different animal names) was diminished if the words in that category were printed in one color and the probe category word (e.g., the word *animals*) was only occasionally printed in a different color, so as to cause a goal conflict.

Cowan et al. (2005) found that not every successful measure of working memory has to involve the control of attention. It is true that the typical working memory task used for children and adults requires alternate processing and storage of information. Thus, for example, in counting span tasks, a child must indicate how many objects are on each screen and then remember the sum, repeating all of the sums after several screens. That sort of storage-plus-processing task correlates very well with intelligence in adults; much better than does a simple digit span. However, Cowan et al. found just as good basic correlations using tasks that do not require combined storage and processing. This class of tasks was called "scope of attention" tasks because they were thought to index the number of separate items that could be quickly absorbed from a sensory memory into the focus of attention. One example is the visual array comparison task we have already discussed (e.g., Morey & Cowan, 2004), and another example is running memory span (Pollack, Johnson, & Knaff, 1959).

In our version of running span, a string of digits is presented at a rapid 4-per-second rate. The list length ranges from 12 to 20 digits and the list ends unpredictably, after which the participant is to recall as many items as possible from the end of the list, in order (typically recalling the last 3 or 4). In that sort of task, it is impossible to use rehearsal or grouping (Hockey, 1973). Instead, the participant must listen passively and then, presumably, transfer items from the end of the list into a categorical form for recall.

Scope-of-attention tasks based on apprehending information from a stimulus field (e.g., visual array comparisons, running memory span) correlated with verbal and nonverbal intelligence subtests, high school grades, achievement tests, and other working memory tests about as well as did the storage-and-processing tests. So individual differences in working memory may not stem entirely from the control of attention in a goal maintenance state (zoomed in), but also in an apprehension state (zoomed out).

It is not clear that individual differences occur entirely in the frontal lobes. For the array comparison tasks, using a functional magnetic resonance imaging (fMRI) measure, Todd and Marois (2004) found individual differences in more posterior regions of the brain that are related to attention but probably not to its control. Nevertheless, it is quite possible that individual differences in the scope of attention arise at least in part from frontal mechanisms controlling the scope of attention (making it zoom in and out as needed). Vogel, McCollough, and Machizawa (2005), using an event-related potential measure, found that individuals who could recall the most items in an array also were the ones who could do the best job of filtering out irrelevant items; these people could focus efficiently on the relevant items. Cowan, Fristoe, Elliott, Brunner, and Saults (in press) examined measures of both the scope of attention and the control of attention in children and adults, and found them to be partly related and partly independent. They are parts of a multifaceted attention system that varies a great deal among individuals and across ages.

Working Memory: A Bridge Between Infants and Children

One of the most difficult aspects of studying early development is that the same methods generally do not apply across age groups. The thinking of Piaget (for a recent review, see Feldman, 2004) included the notion of vertical décalage, in which the course of development repeats itself at different levels. For example, a baby displays the egocentrism of not remembering that its mother continues to exist when not present, and this egocentrism dissolves with infant maturation; but a young child may display the egocentrism of thinking that the sun exists only to provide light for people. Tied to this is the notion of horizontal décalage. An infant can demonstrate knowledge of the existence of hidden objects through eye movements, and later can do so through hand movements to retrieve the object.

If this description of development is apt, a difficulty for developmental researchers is that tests with different methods can look as if they yield contradictory results. For example, according to Figure 2.1 (chapter 2, this volume), 5-month-old infants tested with looking outperform 7-month-old infants tested with reaching. How, then, is one to make fair comparisons between groups that had to be tested using different methods, such as infants and children?

Given this common problem, it is quite important when continuity can be found between testing methods in infants and young children. Bell and Morasch explained how the A-not-B method could be used in infants and children. They also explained a relation between baseline EEG power and working memory in infants, and it seems likely that this type of response also will be a valid, comparable indicator in children and adults.

There are still some important methodological details to ponder. Infants are distracted in order to avert their gaze from the testing apparatus during a retention interval in the A-not-B paradigm. However, distraction also introduces interference. It might be useful for infant experiments to be carried out, systematically varying the nature of the stimuli used for distraction. For example, distractors could be visual, auditory, or tactile. Visual distraction introduces interference most similar to the visual displays to be remembered. Another possibility is to turn the lights off during the retention interval and back on at the time of test. There is no easy answer to this question of how to impose a distraction period in a valid way, but it seems important to remain aware of the issue.

Chapters 3 and 4

The issues involved in both chapters 3 and 4 is the capacity of visual working memory, and chapter 4 also considers the process of the binding of features to one another within the held objects. It seems helpful to consider
these chapters jointly.

Capacity and Infant Working Memory

Chapters 3 and 4 show a very nice convergence of evidence suggesting that
infants, by 10 months of age, can hold in working memory three or four
objects. There is a slight discrepancy in that Feigenson shows a capacity of
four objects only if the objects form larger groups (chapter 3, Figure 3.1),
whereas Oakes et al. show a capacity of four haphazard, presumably un-
grouped objects by infants of a comparable age (chapter 4, Figure 4.4).
Another discrepancy comes into play if one considers that children in the
lower elementary school years typically display a smaller capacity of only a
little above two of these items, gradually rising with age to the three-plus
items that adults recall on average (Cowan et al., 2005), when tested on
arrays of four items using an array comparison procedure comparable to that
of Luck and Vogel (1997).

These discrepancies make it clear that the various tests of capacity cannot be considered pure indications of capacity alone, which surely must
increase monotonically during infancy and childhood. There are sometimes
simple strategies or behaviors that can be used to work around the capacity
limit, and there are sometimes impediments to performance other than
capacity. For example, consider the infant procedure of Ross-Sheehy, Oakes,
and Luck (2003) shown by Oakes et al. (chapter 4, Figure 4.2). Capacity is
gauged by the detection of changes in the color of one object at a time within
a three-object display. However, imagine what would happen if an infant
attended solely to one of those objects. There would be intermittent changes
in that object, so it would not be necessary to focus on all of the objects in
order to differentiate between a changing and a nonchanging display. In
practice, the infants' attention probably vacillates between the changing and
nonchanging arrays, and a one-item attention fixation seems unlikely. The
actual capacity could be somewhere between one and three items, though.

In the array-comparison procedures applied to older children and adults
(Cowan et al., 2005; Cowan, Fristoe, et al., in press; Luck & Vogel, 1997), it is
possible that there is another limit on performance aside from capacity. It
is possible that apprehension of all items in an array into working memory
is attention demanding and that this process sometimes fails in children
because their attention wanders while an array is presented.

As was briefly mentioned above, evidence linking capacity to the control
of attention in adults was provided by Vogel et al. (2005). They obtained a
lateralized component of event-related electrical potentials that increased as

the size of the array to be remembered increased from two to four objects. This set-size-related increase correlated well with working memory capacity in the same task (Vogel & Machizawa, 2004). Critically, Vogel et al. (2005) presented a situation in which the relevant feature of bars to be remembered was their orientations, and in which only the bars presented in one color were to be remembered. They found that the brains of high-performing individuals responded to arrays that included two relevant (e.g., blue) and two irrelevant (e.g., red) bars in the same way as their brains responded to arrays containing two relevant and no irrelevant bars. In contrast, the brains of low-performing individuals responded to arrays of two relevant and two irrelevant bars in the same way as their brains responded to arrays containing four relevant and no irrelevant bars. Thus, low-span individuals were unable to save working-memory space by excluding the irrelevant items.

Perhaps individuals of this sort have low spans for sets containing only relevant items at least partially because they are unable to adjust the focus of attention to the right breadth at the right time or are in some other way unable to focus on the arrays efficiently. So the capacity estimates that Cowan et al. (2005) obtained in children could underestimate their true maximal abilities. Indeed, Cowan et al. found that estimates of the maximal performance levels of children were closer to the three to four items usually observed as an adult mean.

There is recent neuroimaging evidence in adults from Xu and Chun (2006) on the distinction between the number of items apprehended in working memory (which may be relevant to Feigenson's procedures, described in chapter 3) and identification of those items (which may be relevant to the procedure of Ross-Sheehy et al., 2003, described by Oakes et al. in chapter 4). One area of the posterior cortex (the inferior intraparietal sulcus) displayed increased neural activation as the number of items to be remembered increased, to a limit of four items. However, other areas of the posterior cortex (the superior intraparietal sulcus and the lateral occipital complex) displayed increased neural activation only up to the behavioral limit. This limit can be about four for simple objects, but substantially less than that for more complex objects. One account of the infant data as well as the data on older individuals is that the limit of about four objects changes little across ages from about 10 months of age onward, whereas the complexity-dependent processing limit changes much more with age.

Binding and Infant Working Memory

Another key issue that Oakes et al. raised (chapter 4) was how infants learn to bind features together. For example, in an array-comparison procedure with colored objects, correct performance depends upon more than knowing which colors were present in an array; it depends on knowing whether a particular color appeared at a particular location (provided that the stimuli are designed to allow more than one instance of the same color in an array). A priori, many researchers have expected that holding binding information in working memory requires attention, because the perception of binding requires attention (Treisman & Gelade, 1980). However, the findings of studies with array comparison procedures have indicated that dividing attention surprisingly does not impair performance any more when binding information is required than when it is not required (Allen, Baddeley, & Hitch, 2006; Cowan, Naveh-Benjamin, Kilb, & Saults, 2006; Yeh, Yang, & Chiu, 2005).

Further explanation would help. Binding is needed to detect a change in the associations between items' features in an array (e.g., the correspondence between color and location), but binding is not needed to detect a change to some feature that was not present anywhere in the trial previously (e.g., a new color). Perhaps divided attention affects all types of trials because the binding information is automatically stored, provided that the items themselves are attended and stored. Comparable performance levels are found when binding versus simple item information is tested, provided that these types of trials are put in separate trial blocks designed to equate guessing factors (Cowan, Naveh-Benjamin, et al., 2006). These findings tend to support the suggestion of Oakes et al. (chapter 4) that "if the binding of features depends specifically on the intraparietal sulcus, then we should also observe that infants who can bind features are the same infants who can represent multiple objects in VSTM."

Finally, if bound features are automatically held, this raises the question of the role of attention in working memory, which Feigenson (chapter 3) also raised. It is not necessarily the case that binding information is held attention-free. It could be instead that attention is needed to maintain objects and that this maintenance already includes the feature bindings, or at least some feature bindings such as those between objects and their locations. Such an approach would be consistent with two concepts from cognitive neuroscience: (1) the concept of an object file in working memory (Kahneman, Treisman, & Gibbs, 1992) with its features bound and intact; and (2) the concept that the frontal and parietal lobes of the brain function, respectively, as an anterior attention system largely responsible for controlling attention and a posterior attention system largely responsible for representing attended information such as object files (Cowan, 1995; Posner & Peterson, 1990).

Chapter 1

It is difficult to comment comprehensively on chapter 1 because it is already a broad, integrative review with commentary built in. I endorse Reznick's quest for better definitions and methods to examine working memory in infancy and beyond. I will focus on a consideration of two fundamental questions that he raises: what terms to use for temporary memory in infants, and what the future may hold for infant research.

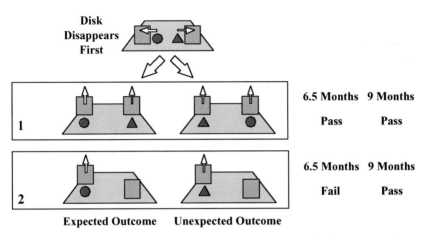

FIGURE 5.1. Summary of main findings of Káldy and Leslie (2003, 2005). Following the logic of violation-of-expectation paradigms, Pass signals that infants looked significantly longer at the unexpected outcome than at the expected outcome, and Fail signals that there was no significant difference between reactions to the two different outcomes. Before the test, infants were systematically familiarized with both of the objects appearing on alternating sides of the stage. Objects were hidden sequentially; in the sequence presented here the first object hidden was the disk on the left. Reprinted from Káldy, Z., & Sigala, N. (2004). The neural mechanisms of object working memory: What is where in the infant brain? *Neuroscience and Biobehavioral Reviews, 28,* 113–121, copyright 2004, with permission from Elsevier.

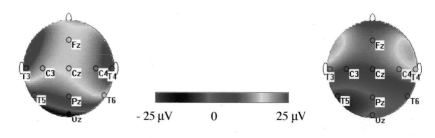

Block 1　　　　　　　　　　　　　　　**Block 2**

FIGURE 8.3. Topographic plots showing the scalp distribution of the positive slow wave (PSW) for Block 1 and Block 2. The PSW is shown as patches of red over the left and right temporal regions when it is maximal (at 1,250 ms).

Terms for Temporary Memory in Infants

Reznick has thoughtfully commented on what it is that one can study in infants. He suggested that the study of cognitive capacity in infancy was a study of working memory and not short-term memory. How would one decide?

The relation between short-term memory and working memory has been thought of in various ways within the recent cognitive psychology and neuroscience literature. According to one perspective, short-term memory is a passive holding device (or set of devices), and working memory is the combination of that holding device along with attention processes that control it (Engle et al., 1999):

short-term memory tasks + use of attention = working memory tasks

According to a slightly different perspective, though, all information has to be held with the help of attention unless some sort of trick is applied, such as covert verbal rehearsal, which can be used to circumvent the attention limit (Barrouillet, Bernardin, & Camos, 2004; Oberauer, Lange, & Engle, 2004). Then one can characterize short-term memory tasks as those in which such a trick is used to circumvent the attention limits:

working-term memory tasks + use of mnemonic strategies
= short-term memory tasks

Our recent work provides some support for the latter formulation. Although simple digit span tasks do not correlate well with intelligence in sixth grade children or adults, who can use rehearsal well, it correlates very well in younger children (Cowan et al., 2005; Hutton & Towse, 2001), who are known to be inefficient in covert verbal rehearsal (Ornstein & Naus, 1978). It is the core capacity that may correlate with intelligence, not the special strategies. It therefore makes perfect sense to assume that the concept being studied in infants is working memory, without the benefit of rehearsal.

What the Future May Hold for Infant Research on Working Memory

Reznick pleaded for methods to study infants' working memory that are flexible, efficient, and valid on an individual-subject basis. I endorse this. Additionally, though, the future of working memory in infancy may involve an expansion of topics. It may cover not only studies of the development of capacity and memory resilience, as noted in all of the chapters of this volume, but also studies of the development of grouping and recoding processes so important for the most efficient use of this capacity (Miller, 1956). The pervasiveness of recoding must not be forgotten. Its role can be illustrated by considering Reznick's comment (chapter 1) that "Baddeley and Hitch's model of working memory . . . to its credit . . . draws a clear distinction between working memory for auditory and visual information." Actually, it does not do this exactly.

To understand why not, consider that when pronounceable visual stimuli are presented to adults, the amount of confusability depends on similarities in their pronunciation, and not primarily in how they look. As a prime example, it is quite difficult to recall, in order, the similar-sounding letters *b, v, t, c, d, p, g* (Conrad, 1964). The reason for this is high confusability, inasmuch as the printed stimuli tend to be mentally converted to a phonological form for covert verbal rehearsal, and these letters sound alike. The Baddeley and Hitch (1974) model is excellent at describing stimuli in terms of their more abstract, phonological versus spatial coding. That theory is less well-suited for explaining why, beyond the phonological code, there is an advantage for spoken as opposed to printed verbal stimuli toward the end of a list (on this modality effect see, e.g., Cowan, Saults, & Brown, 2004; Penney, 1989).

As infants develop, sensory processing may allow them not only a more precise perceptual representation with which to work (Cowan et al., 1982), but also a much richer set of abstract codes with which to retain and mentally manipulate experiences in working memory, for the good of cognition, performance, and social interaction.

A Summary Comparison of Answers to the Five Questions Posed to Authors

There are some striking convergences between chapters, reflecting the zeitgeist, and there are some differences in approaches in answering a few of the five questions.

1. What kind of memory are you studying? What does it permit the infant or young child to do (i.e., what is its function or functional significance)? To what kind of adult memory does it correspond?

Reznick differentiated between short-term memory and working memory, and suggested that infant researchers are studying working memory. The connotation of this distinction is that what is being studied is not some passive storage device, but primarily the attention-demanding retention of key information needed for a task. This opinion seems to mesh well with what the other chapters describe. The A-not-B procedure studied by Bell and Morasch depends on maintaining the goal so as to avoid making a prepotent response, and the procedures described by Feigenson and by Oakes et al. involve apprehending multiple items from a field. The adult research (e.g., Morey & Cowan, 2004) does suggest that this type of memory is attention demanding.

Of course, passive storage is probably also used along with attention in working memory, and the infant findings so far would not be able to distinguish clearly whether any passive type of storage lasts longer as infants get older. There is some indication that, at least in the case of auditory sensory memory for unattended speech sounds, passive storage might persist longer over time with development during elementary school (Cowan, Nugent,

Elliott, & Saults, 2000). However, for the most part, the development of more passive types of short-term memory probably require rehearsal strategies that do not begin in infancy and do not develop fully until middle childhood.

2. How do you measure this type of memory? What are the challenges in measuring it? What are the limitations of the methods we have for measuring it? What are the recent advances (if any) in measuring this type of memory?

A fundamental difference between measures provided by the authors was in the kind of limit imposed. Feigenson, as well as Oakes et al., used procedures in which the number of elements was manipulated to determine the point at which the infant's limit was exceeded. The task was basically to retain the number of items (Feigenson) or to retain the features of each item (Oakes et al.). In contrast, Bell and Morasch, as well as Reznick, described data in which relatively simple stimuli were presented and a time delay with distraction was imposed. In both cases, tough problems must be tackled.

First, according to the theoretical framework depicted in Figure 6.1, the number of items that can be apprehended depends on attention. The recent research I described indicates that we do not yet know what attention does; it could actually hold the information, or it could defend the information against interference. One challenge is to determine the exact role of attention here, both in infant research and beyond.

There are more fundamental challenges in determining the effects of a delay. The delay has to be filled with a distraction that also can cause interference. According to one view, what distinguishes one infant from another (or one age group from another) is the ability to use attention to overcome this interference. The need to attend during a long delay may be a vigilance task. We cannot yet be sure if there is a different component of age differences in responding after a delay that is independent of attention and depends instead on some sort of decay parameter even though, as Reznick noted, there is no clear evidence for a decay process (except perhaps in sensory memory; see Cowan et al., 2000).

3. What do we know about how this type of memory changes with development? What kinds of developmental changes have you (and others) observed?

There seems to be a clear consensus among the researchers that working memory becomes much more robust during the second half of the first year of life. This was true across a wide range of procedures. There are differences between procedures in the detailed nature of the abilities of each age, which can be attributed to differences in task demands, as I have discussed. However, there is more similarity than difference.

4. Why does this type of memory change? What are the mechanisms underlying the development of this type of memory?

The reviewers consistently pointed to developmental maturation of the frontal lobes as a cause of the better control of attention, which in turn allows better maintenance of information in the face of interference.

Although I concur, I tried to emphasize that the attention system should be viewed more as a multicomponent network with a more substantial contribution of posterior regions than some of the researchers noted. Portions of the parietal lobes are involved in the integration of information from the different senses and may reflect the actual seat of attention, as opposed to the frontal lobes, which act more as the controller of attention (Cowan, 1995; Posner & Peterson, 1990). It is not yet clear to what extent age differences in the ability to apprehend multiple items at once depends on maturation of the posterior regions, as opposed to maturation of the frontal regions exerting control over how the posterior regions are used.

The other basis of change in working memory that I have stressed is knowledge, which allows multiple items to be grouped into a single chunk. The process of forming new associations seems close to the binding issue that Oakes et al. brought up. However, we must also consider not only how easily binding can occur, but also what the benefits of already-bound knowledge may be in making working memory efficient.

Actually, it is difficult to imagine that knowledge would form the primary basis of change during the first half of the first year of life, when we know that maturational changes are so predominant (aside from the very real possibility of environmental stimulation being necessary for normal brain maturation). However, knowledge is a secondary factor that should not be ruled out. The kind of knowledge that could be relevant to the tasks that these researchers have used might be very basic, to the point that we might not recognize them as knowledge. Regarding tests with delay periods, for example, infants might have learned that objects that disappear sometimes do reappear. They might even have learned that maintaining attention on the object helps it to reappear; in normal life, if the baby seems interested, parents may be more likely to make the object reappear. Regarding tests with multiple objects to be apprehended, the infant may have learned the link between a certain number of objects and certain patterns that this number of objects can make. Pattern recognition is, in fact, one of the current theories of how the enumeration of small numbers of objects occurs (Logan & Zbrodoff, 2003). Infants also might have to learn very basic things about types and tokens, such as the fact that when a similar shape occurs more than once in different colors, this represents two completely separable objects (unlike, say, an object and its shadow, which represent a single object; or an object that appears first in one place, and then in another place as someone moves it). We still do not know how much of this is innate or learned.

5. What are the questions and issues on the horizon for the study of the development of this type of memory?

All of the chapters seem to point to one major question on the horizon, which is how fair comparisons can be made across age groups, given that different methods seem applicable and impose different processing demands. As I have noted, there are some important leads in this regard, such as the application of infant procedures to older children and adults when it is possible and the use of physiological measures (Bell & Morasch, chapter 2). The question of later development took a different twist for Feigenson (chapter 3), who suggested that a certain basic capacity may reach its mature level by 1 year of age. Clearly, this is a provocative hypothesis that can only be tested when the right methodological bridges between infants and children have been found.

Finally, Reznick (chapter 1) has a vision that working memory observed in infancy will turn out to be related to social regulation and general intelligence, and will turn out to predict and to be involved in various developmental disabilities. An encouraging observation in that regard is that one attention-related process measured in infancy is known to predict later intelligence. In particular, habituation of attention to a familiar object (and in some instances dishabituation to a change) predicts later intelligence and predicts disabilities; for a recent review, see Kavŝek (2004). Although habituation is an attention function, the theory of Sokolov (1963) holds that habituation depends on construction of a neural model of the stimulus in the brain, which would seem to be a working memory function. (For modern support of Sokolov, see Cowan, 1995). Methods for distinguishing between different attention functions in children (Rueda, Posner, & Rothbart, 2005) also might be adapted to infants.

Concluding Remarks

I share with the authors of these four chapters an optimism that methods can be devised to link together the research on infants and children, to begin to construct a developmental psychology of working memory that includes infants. A profound outcome of this endeavor could be a richer understanding of the way in which working memory governs early cognitive development and the grasp of consciousness (cf. Piaget, 1976; Zelazo, 2004).

References

Allen, R., Baddeley, A. D., & Hitch, G. J. (2006). *Is the binding of visual features in working memory resource-demanding? Journal of Experimental Psychology: General, 135,* 298–313.

Baddeley, A. (2000). The episodic buffer: A new component of working memory? *Trends in Cognitive Sciences, 4,* 417–423.

Baddeley, A. (2001). The magic number and the episodic buffer. *Behavioral and Brain Sciences, 24,* 117–118.

Baddeley, A. D. (1986). *Working memory.* Oxford Psychology Series #11. Oxford, UK: Clarendon.

Baddeley, A., & Hitch, G. J. (1974). Working memory. In G. Bower (Ed.), *The psychology of learning and motivation* (Vol. 8, pp. 47–90). New York: Academic Press.

Baddeley, A. D., & Logie, R. H. (1999). Working memory: The multiple-component model. In A. Miyake & P. Shah (Eds.), *Models of working memory: Mechanisms of active maintenance and executive control* (pp. 28–61). Cambridge, UK: Cambridge University Press.

Baddeley, A. D., Thomson, N., & Buchanan, M. (1975). Word length and the structure of short-term memory. *Journal of Verbal Learning and Verbal Behavior, 14,* 575–589.

Baillargeon, R. (2004). Infants' physical world. *Current Directions in Psychological Science, 13,* 89–94.

Barrouillet, P., Bernardin, S., & Camos, V. (2004). Time constraints and resource sharing in adults' working memory spans. *Journal of Experimental Psychology: General, 133,* 83–100.

Broadbent, D. E. (1958). *Perception and communication.* New York: Pergamon Press.

Brown, J. (1958). Some tests of the decay theory of immediate memory. *Quarterly Journal of Experimental Psychology, 10,* 12–21.

Brown, J. (1959). Information, redundancy and decay of the memory trace. In *Mechanisation of thought processes: Proceedings of a symposium held at the National Physical Laboratory on 24, 25, 26, and 27 November, 1958* (pp. 729–752). National Physical Laboratory Symposium Number 10. London: Her Majesty's Stationery Office.

Bunting, M. F., & Cowan, N. (2005). Working memory and flexibility in awareness and attention. *Psychological Research, 69,* 412–419.

Chase, W., & Simon, H. A. (1973). The mind's eye in chess. In W. G. Chase (Ed.), *Visual information processing* (pp. 215–281). New York: Academic Press.

Chen, Z., & Cowan, N. (2005). Chunk limits and length limits in immediate recall: A reconciliation. *Journal of Experimental Psychology: Learning, Memory, and Cognition, 31,* 1235–1249.

Conrad, R. (1964). Acoustic confusion in immediate memory. *British Journal of Psychology, 55,* 75–84.

Conway, A. R. A., Cowan, N., & Bunting, M. F. (2001). The cocktail party phenomenon revisited: The importance of working memory capacity. *Psychonomic Bulletin & Review, 8,* 331–335.

Cowan, N. (1988). Evolving conceptions of memory storage, selective attention, and their mutual constraints within the human information processing system. *Psychological Bulletin, 104,* 163–191.

Cowan, N. (1995). *Attention and memory: An integrated framework.* Oxford Psychology Series, No. 26. New York: Oxford University Press.

Cowan, N. (1999). An embedded-processes model of working memory. In A. Miyake & P. Shah (Eds.), *Models of working memory: Mechanisms of active maintenance and executive control* (pp. 62–101). Cambridge, UK: Cambridge University Press.

Cowan, N. (2001). The magical number 4 in short-term memory: A reconsideration of mental storage capacity. *Behavioral and Brain Sciences, 24,* 87–185.

Cowan, N. (2005). *Working memory capacity.* Hove, UK: Psychology Press.

Cowan, N., Beschin, N., & Della Sala, S. (2004). Verbal recall in amnesiacs under conditions of diminished retroactive interference. *Brain, 127,* 825–834.

Cowan, N., Chen, Z., & Rouder, J. N. (2004). Constant capacity in an immediate serial-recall task: A logical sequel to Miller (1956). *Psychological Science, 15,* 634–640.

Cowan, N., Elliott, E. M., Saults, J. S., Morey, C. C., Mattox, S., Hismjatullina, A., et al. (2005). On the capacity of attention: Its estimation and its role in working memory and cognitive aptitudes. *Cognitive Psychology, 51,* 42–100.

Cowan, N., Elliott, E. M., Saults, J. S., Nugent, L. D., Bomb, P., & Hismjatullina, A. (2006). Rethinking speed theories of cognitive development: Increasing the rate of recall without affecting accuracy. *Psychological Science, 17,* 67–73.

Cowan, N., Fristoe, N. M., Elliott, E. M., Brunner, R. P., & Saults, J. S. (in press). Scope of attention, control of attention, and intelligence in children and adults. *Memory & Cognition.*

Cowan, N., Naveh-Benjamin, M., Kilb, A., & Saults, J. S. (2006). Life-span development of visual working memory: When is feature binding difficult? *Developmental Psychology, 42,* 1089–1102.

Cowan, N., Nugent, L. D., Elliott, E. M., & Saults, J. S. (2000). Persistence of memory for ignored lists of digits: Areas of developmental constancy and change. *Journal of Experimental Child Psychology, 76,* 151–172.

Cowan, N., Saults, J. S., & Brown, G. D. A. (2004). On the auditory modality superiority effect in serial recall: Separating input and output factors. *Journal of Experimental Psychology: Learning, Memory, and Cognition, 30,* 639–644.

Cowan, N., Saults, J. S., & Nugent, L. D. (1997). The role of absolute and relative amounts of time in forgetting within immediate memory: The case of tone pitch comparisons. *Psychonomic Bulletin & Review, 4,* 393–397.

Cowan, N., Suomi, K., & Morse, P. A. (1982). Echoic storage in infant perception. *Child Development, 53,* 984–990.

Crowder, R. G. (1993). Short-term memory: Where do we stand? *Memory & Cognition, 21,* 142–145.

Eich, E. (1984). Memory for unattended events: Remembering with and without awareness. *Memory & Cognition, 12,* 105–111.

Engle, R. W., Tuholski, S. W., Laughlin, J. E., & Conway, A. R. A. (1999). Working memory, short-term memory, and general fluid intelligence: A latent-variable approach. *Journal of Experimental Psychology: General, 128,* 309–331.

Feldman, H. D. (2004). Piaget's stages: The unfinished symphony of cognitive development. *New Ideas in Psychology, 22,* 175–231.

Gathercole, S. E., Pickering, S. J., Ambridge, B., & Wearing, H. (2004). The structure of working memory from 4 to 15 years of age. *Developmental Psychology, 40,* 177–190.

Glanville, B. B., Best, C. T., & Levenson, R. (1977). A cardiac measure of cerebral asymmetries in infant auditory perception. *Developmental Psychology, 13,* 54–59.

Glenberg, A. M., & Swanson, N. C. (1986). A temporal distinctiveness theory of recency and modality effects. *Journal of Experimental Psychology: Learning, Memory, and Cognition, 12,* 3–15.

Gobet, F., Lane, P. C. R., Croker, S., Cheng, P. C.-H., Jones, G., Oliver, I., et al.

(2001). Chunking mechanisms in human learning. *Trends in Cognitive Sciences, 5,* 236–243.

Hockey, R. (1973). Rate of presentation in running memory and direct manipulation of input-processing strategies. *Quarterly Journal of Experimental Psychology (A), 25,* 104–111.

Hutton, U. M. Z., & Towse, J. N. (2001). Short-term memory and working memory as indices of children's cognitive skills. *Memory, 9,* 383–394.

Kahneman, D., Treisman, A., & Gibbs, B. J. (1992). The reviewing of object files: Object-specific integration of information. *Cognitive Psychology, 24,* 175–219.

Kane, M. J., Bleckley, M. K., Conway, A. R. A., & Engle, R. W. (2001). A controlled-attention view of working-memory capacity. *Journal of Experimental Psychology: General, 130,* 169–183.

Kane, M. J., & Engle, R. W. (2002). The role of prefrontal cortex in working-memory capacity, executive attention, and general fluid intelligence: An individual-differences perspective. *Psychonomic Bulletin & Review, 9,* 637–671.

Kavšek, M. (2004). Predicting later IQ from infant visual habituation and dishabituation: A meta-analysis. *Applied Developmental Psychology, 25,* 369–393.

Kolata, G. (1984). Studying learning in the womb. *Science, 225,* 302–303.

Landauer, T. K. (1962). Rate of implicit speech. *Perceptual and Motor Skills, 15,* 646.

Lewandowsky, S., Duncan, M., & Brown, G. D. A. (2004). Time does not cause forgetting in short-term serial recall. *Psychonomic Bulletin & Review, 11,* 771–790.

Logan, G. D., & Zbrodoff, N. J. (2003). Subitizing and similarity: Toward a pattern-matching theory of enumeration. *Psychonomic Bulletin & Review, 10,* 676–682.

Luck, S. J., & Vogel, E. K. (1997). The capacity of visual working memory for features and conjunctions. *Nature, 390,* 279–281.

Massaro, D. W. (1975). Backward recognition masking. *Journal of the Acoustical Society of America, 58,* 1059–1065.

Miller, G. A. (1956). The magical number seven, plus or minus two: Some limits on our capacity for processing information. *Psychological Review, 63,* 81–97.

Miller, G. A., Galanter, E., & Pribram, K. H. (1960). *Plans and the structure of behavior.* New York: Holt, Rinehart and Winston.

Miyake, A., & Shah, P. (Eds.). (1999). *Models of working memory: Mechanisms of active maintenance and executive control.* Cambridge, UK: Cambridge University Press.

Moray, N. (1959). Attention in dichotic listening: Affective cues and the influence of instructions. *Quarterly Journal of Experimental Psychology, 11,* 56–60.

Morey, C. C., & Cowan, N. (2004). When visual and verbal memories compete: Evidence of cross-domain limits in working memory. *Psychonomic Bulletin & Review, 11,* 296–301.

Morse, P. A., & Cowan, N. (1982). Infant auditory and speech perception. In

T. M. Field, A. Huston, H. C. Quay, L. Troll, & G. E. Finley (Eds.), *Review of human development* (pp. 32–61). New York: Wiley.

Nairne, J. S. (2002). Remembering over the short-term: The case against the standard model. *Annual Review of Psychology, 53,* 53–81.

Neath, I., & Surprenant, A. (2003). *Human memory* (2nd ed.). Belmont, CA: Wadsworth.

Oberauer, K., Lange, E., & Engle, R. E. (2004). Working memory capacity and resistance to interference. *Journal of Memory and Language, 51,* 80–96.

Ornstein, P. A., & Naus, M. J. (1978). Rehearsal processes in children's memory. In P. A. Ornstein (Ed.), *Memory development in children* (pp. 69–99). Hillsdale, NJ: Erlbaum.

Penney, C. G. (1989). Modality effects and the structure of short-term verbal memory. *Memory & Cognition, 17,* 398–422.

Peterson, L. R., & Peterson, M. J. (1959). Short-term retention of individual verbal items. *Journal of Experimental Psychology, 58,* 193–198.

Piaget, J. (1976). *The grasp of consciousness: Action and concept in the young child* (S. Wedgwood, Trans.). Cambridge, MA: Harvard University Press. (Originally published in French in 1974)

Pollack, I., Johnson, I. B., & Knaff, P. R. (1959). Running memory span. *Journal of Experimental Psychology, 57,* 137–146.

Posner, M. I., & Peterson, S. E. (1990). The attention system of the human brain. *Annual Review of Neuroscience, 13,* 25–42.

Ross-Sheehy, S., Oakes, L. M., & Luck, S. J. (2003). The development of visual short-term memory capacity in infants. *Child Development, 74,* 1807–1822.

Rueda, M. R., Posner, M. I., & Rothbart, M. K. (2005). The development of executive attention: Contributions to the emergence of self-regulation. *Developmental Neuropsychology, 28,* 573–594.

Shankweiler, D., & Studdert-Kennedy, M. (1967). Identification of consonants and vowels presented to left and right ears. *Quarterly Journal of Experimental Psychology, 19,* 59–63.

Sokolov, E. N. (1963). *Perception and the conditioned reflex.* New York: Pergamon Press.

Todd, J. J., & Marois, R. (2004). Capacity limit of visual short-term memory in human posterior parietal cortex. *Nature, 428,* 751–754.

Treisman, A. M., & Gelade, G. (1980). A feature integration theory of attention. *Cognitive Psychology, 12,* 97–136.

Vogel, E. K., & Machizawa, M. G. (2004). Neural activity predicts individual differences in visual working memory capacity. *Nature, 428,* 749–751.

Vogel, E. K., McCollough, A. W., & Machizawa, M. G. (2005). Neural measures reveal individual differences in controlling access to working memory. *Nature, 438,* 500–503.

Winkler, I., Schröger, E., & Cowan, N. (2001). The role of large-scale memory organization in the mismatch negativity event-related brain potential. *Journal of Cognitive Neuroscience, 13,* 59–71.

Wood, N. L., Stadler, M. A., & Cowan, N. (1997). Is there implicit memory without attention? A re-examination of task demands in Eich's (1984) procedure. *Memory & Cognition, 25,* 772–779.

Xu, Y., & Chun, M. M. (2006). Dissociable neural mechanisms supporting visual short-term memory for objects. *Nature, 440,* 91–95.

Yeh, Y.-Y., Yang, C.-T., & Chiu, Y.-C. (2005). Binding or prioritization: The role of selective attention in visual short-term memory. *Visual Cognition, 12,* 759–799.

Zelazo, P. D. (2004). The development of conscious control in childhood. *Trends in Cognitive Sciences, 8,* 12–17.

PART II

LONG-TERM MEMORY IN INFANCY AND EARLY CHILDHOOD

7

Developmental Aspects of Visual Recognition Memory in Infancy

SUSAN A. ROSE, JUDITH F. FELDMAN,
AND JEFFERY J. JANKOWSKI

Recognition Memory: A Type of Explicit Memory

We have been studying infant visual recognition memory, an early ability that is related to later cognition (McCall & Carriger, 1993; Rose & Feldman, 1995, 1997), an early-emerging form of genuine cognitive ability.

Infant recognition memory has generally been considered a fundamental form of explicit (or pre-explicit) memory (Nelson, 1995, 1997). Until recently, research on infant and adult memory has proceeded along separate but parallel tracks, in large part because differences in methods of study made it difficult to compare findings. Although infant memory is studied exclusively with nonverbal methods, the adult work has used primarily verbal methods. A convergence between the two fields became possible when some infant tasks became recognized as nonverbal analogues of tasks commonly used to study adult memory. In this section, we describe the theoretical distinction between explicit and implicit memory and the neurophysiological basis for explicit memory.

Explicit Versus Implicit Memory

Although it is still a matter of some debate (for overview, see Rovee-Collier, Hayne, & Colombo, 2001), adult memory is not generally considered a unitary ability. Most students of memory recognize at least two major forms: declarative (or explicit) memory and procedural (or implicit) memory (Schacter & Tulving, 1994; Squire, 1987). Explicit memory entails recall or recognition of previously encountered objects or events in a form that is, at least in principle, available to consciousness. There are two major types of explicit memory (Tulving, 1985): semantic memory, which includes memories for facts and general knowledge, and episodic memory, which includes memories that are autobiographical in nature, in that they refer to events one has personally experienced and which are anchored in time and place. Explicit memory is necessary for accruing knowledge about the world, establishing a personal history, and forming a sense of self. Without it, as in the case of amnesia, everything one encounters is experienced as new.

Procedural or implicit memory, on the other hand, is an umbrella category covering a number of disparate forms of memory, all of which share the property of being inaccessible to consciousness. Included here are memories involving knowledge of how to perform skilled activities (such as bike riding and typing), classical conditioning, and memories that are demonstrated by priming. In priming tasks, subjects are typically given brief perceptual exposure to a list of words, and then instructed to complete a word fragment or word stem with the first word that comes to mind. Priming is indicated when participants use previously seen items in their responses more frequently than would be expected by chance and are unaware that they are doing so.

The distinction between explicit and implicit memory was born of early work on adults with amnesia. In a landmark study, Scoville and Milner (1957) found severe loss of memory for recent events in HM, a patient who had his hippocampus removed bilaterally for the treatment of epilepsy. This study was the first to link severe memory loss with damage to the medial temporal lobe. Comprehensive testing of HM showed that perception and other aspects of cognition were otherwise normal. Warrington and Weiskranz (1970) carried out one of the first studies to show a dissociation of explicit and implicit memory systems in severely amnesic patients. They found that such patients failed tests of recognition and recall but succeeded on tests of priming. Similar findings have become commonplace in more recent years, strongly suggesting that there are two distinct memory systems that depend on different brain structures.

The distinction has been further supported by evidence from three sources. First, experimental studies with normal adults have shown dissociations between the two types of memory (for review, see Richardson-Klavehn & Bjork, 1988), with the same experimental manipulations having different effects on tasks of explicit memory (recognition and recall) from those on tasks of implicit memory (such as priming). Second, brain imaging studies with normal adults have shown robust and selective activation in the hippocampal region during tasks of recognition memory (Stark & Squire, 2000). Third, animal models of amnesia have shown that lesions to specific areas in the medial temporal lobe impair recognition and recall but do not affect performance on tasks of implicit memory (see Nelson, 1997; Zola & Squire, 2000).

Infant Visual Recognition as a Form of Explicit Memory: Neuroanatomical Evidence

Visual recognition memory in infants is most frequently measured with the visual paired-comparison (VPC) task. In this task, two identical stimuli are presented side by side for brief viewing (e.g., 5 seconds) and then one of the previously viewed stimuli is presented along with a new one. Typically, subjects prefer to look at the new picture.

Evidence that infant visual recognition memory is a form of explicit memory comes from studies that have used the VPC task in monkeys with brain lesions and adult human patients with acquired amnesia (but see chapter 8, this volume). In both populations, recognition memory has been found to rely on the same brain substrate, namely, the medial temporal lobe and diencephalic structures, including the hippocampus, amygdala, and perirhinal, entorhinal, and parahippocampal cortices (for reviews, see Nelson, 1995; Rovee-Collier et al., 2001).

Monkey Models Implicate the Medial Temporal Lobe in Performance on the VPC Task

In recent years, several investigators have used the VPC paradigm to assess recognition memory in monkeys. In one of the earliest studies in this area, Bachevalier, Brickson, and Hagger (1993) found that recognition memory in rhesus monkeys is (a) normally present by the first month of life, and (b) markedly impaired when the amygdaloid complex, hippocampal formation, and surrounding tissue are lesioned. Such lesions impaired recognition in both newborn and adult monkeys who were given 30 seconds of familiarization and tested at delays of 10 seconds. In a second study, Pascalis and Bachevalier (1999) followed-up a group of monkeys who had neonatal aspiration lesions of the hippocampal formation (including the dentate gyrus, all CA fields, the subicular complex, and the underlying parrahippocampal gyrus). The results showed that the impairment found when they were neonates persisted into adulthood. In the follow-up, monkeys were given 20 seconds of familiarization and tested at delays of 10 seconds, 30 seconds, 1 minute, 2 minutes, 10 minutes, and 24 hours. The lesioned monkeys failed to recognize the objects with delays of 30 seconds or more whereas control monkeys recognized them at all delays, even 24 hours.

In a study designed to examine the effects of damage limited to the *hippocampal region* (the hippocampus proper, the dentate gyrus, and the subiculum), Zola, Squire, Teng, Stefanacci, and Buffalo (2000) employed two different methods to create lesions in a relatively large group of cynomolgus monkeys: radio frequency and ibotenic acid. Each group was tested against controls immediately and after three different delays (10 seconds, 1 minute, 10 minutes). Whereas none of the groups was impaired in immediate memory, both lesioned groups had lower scores than normals at each of the three delays. While this study is commonly cited as evidence of hippocampal involvement in VPC, it can not be considered definitive because many of the monkeys with hippocampal lesions had incidental damage to the caudate nucleus.

Similar impairments to recognition memory were also found, however, with lesions to the *perirhinal cortex* (Buffalo et al., 1999). Here, cynomolgus monkeys with bilateral lesions were presented with stimuli for 25 seconds and then tested for recognition after 4 delays (1 second, 10 seconds, 1 minute, 10 minutes). Their performance was impaired, relative to that of a control group, and like monkeys with lesions in the hippocampal region, the impairment was evident beginning with delays as brief as 10 seconds. Thus, the perirhinal cortex, like other structures of the medial temporal lobe, is important for the formation of memory.

It should be noted that results using VPC parallel those reported with the delayed non-match-to-sample task, long considered the "gold standard" for measuring recognition memory in nonhuman primates. In this task, a single stimulus is presented on each trial and then, following a delay, the old stimulus and a new one are presented side by side. A reward is hidden in a recessed well beneath the new one. The monkey must lift the new stimulus (non-match) to find the reward. Monkeys are trained until they come to systematically select the new stimulus and then are tested with trial-unique stimuli. (Given that the requisite motoric abilities develop earlier in nonhuman primates than in humans, this task has been more widely used with primates than with human infants.) Performance on delayed non-match-to-sample, as on the VPC task, is impaired with lesions to the hippocampal region (e.g., Malkova, Mishkin, & Bachevalier, 1995; Zola et al., 2000), and lesions to the perirhinal cortex (e.g., Buffalo et al., 1999; Malkova et al., 1995; Murray & Mishkin, 1998).

The VPC task has been found to be more sensitive to damage to the medial temporal lobe than the delayed non-match-to-sample task, with performance impaired at shorter delays on VPC than on delayed non-match-to-sample (Buffalo et al., 1999; Zola et al., 2000). Differences between the two tasks were even more striking in the adult monkeys who had been lesioned as neonates (Pascalis & Bachevalier, 1999). Although their performance on the VPC task was impaired at all delays longer than 30 seconds, performance on delayed non-match-to-sample was not impaired at any of the delays, which ranged up to 24 hours.

Overall, these findings show that performance on the VPC task is exquisitely sensitive to damage to the medial temporal lobe.

Human Adults: Amnesia Impairs Performance on the VPC Task

In human adults, recognition is usually tested with verbal procedures. Typically, adults are shown a series of pictures, which are then intermixed with foils; a "yes" or "no" response is required to identify which pictures had been seen earlier.

Recent studies have shown that recognition memory can also be assessed in adults with the VPC task. Fagan and Haiken-Vasen (1997) tested college students and aged populations in the same manner as infants and found that, like infants, both groups showed a novelty preference. Similarly, Manns, Stark, and Squire (2000) also tested adults on recognition with the VPC task, presenting them with 24 pairs of pictures of common objects. After a 5-minute delay, each old target was presented paired with a new one and robust novelty scores were found. Then, 24 hours later, the participants were re-tested for recognition, using the typical adult recognition "yes/no" procedure. Novelty scores from the VPC task correlated significantly with confidence ratings that the items had been seen 24 hours earlier, suggesting that the VPC task is tapping some of the same aspects of recognition memory as standard adult tasks.

The VPC task also passes the amnesia test. That is, adults with amnesia, who have sustained damage to the medial temporal lobe, have considerable difficulty with the VPC task. McKee and Squire (1993) found that, whereas patients with amnesia showed immediate recognition on the VPC task, their performance was significantly impaired, relative to controls, when delays of 2 minutes or more were interposed between familiarization and test. Similar impairments on the VPC task have been found in patients with damage to the perirhinal cortex, where impaired recognition was found with delays as brief as 6 to 10 seconds (Buffalo, Reber, & Squire, 1998).

In sum, the VPC task, which has formed the cornerstone of much of the work on infant cognition, appears to be a sensitive measure of medial temporal lobe function and thus to reflect explicit memory.

Measuring Infant Visual Recognition Memory

VPC Paradigm

The VPC task is the most widely used measure of recognition with infants (Fagan, 1970). In this task, infants are familiarized with two identical stimuli presented side by side (or sometimes, with just a single visual stimulus) and then tested for recognition by simultaneously presenting the old stimulus along with a new one. On test, infants typically look more at the new stimulus; recognition is assessed by the novelty score, defined as the percentage of looking directed to the novel target (Fagan, 1974; Rose & Feldman, 1990).

Preference for the novel stimulus is thought to arise when infants, having completed assimilation of the information in the familiar stimulus, turn their attention to encoding information from the new one. It is presumed that infants form a mental representation of the stimulus during familiarization. This presumption is based on the observation that attention wanes with the repetition of an event and recovers when the event changes. This phenomenon was explained by Sokolov (1963), who proposed a comparator model in which a mental representation is formed over time. When infants first encounter a new stimulus, they try to match it with a stored representation. If a match is found, attention is inhibited. If no match is found, attention remains engaged until enough information is assimilated from the stimulus to render it no longer novel. Thus, preference for a new stimulus can be taken as evidence for a stored representation of the old one (see also the newer work on connectionist models, e.g., Elman et al., 1997).

Habituation Paradigm

Visual recognition memory is sometimes measured with the habituation paradigm. In habituation, a stimulus is repeatedly presented until attention wanes. In the most common variants, trials continue until looking declines to some absolute value (e.g., two successive fixations of less than 4 seconds; see McCall, Kennedy, & Dodds, 1977) or declines to some relative value (e.g., three consecutive trials each 50% shorter than the first three trials). This latter variant is called the infant-controlled procedure (Horowitz, Paden, Bhana, & Self, 1972). Once attention has declined, a new stimulus is introduced. Visual recognition memory is indexed by the extent to which attention recovers (or dishabituates) to the new stimulus. This recovery reflects discrimination of the old from the new and, depending on the length of delay that intervenes before test, immediate or delayed memory.

Challenges to Measuring and Interpreting Visual Recognition Memory

Procedural Factors

Although the VPC task is quite simple and straightforward, there are three procedural issues that need to be kept in mind to ensure that novelty scores reflect processing and recognition memory, and not methodological factors.

First, to ensure that members of each pair are approximately equal in attractiveness at the outset, extensive pretesting is generally done. Here, pairs of stimuli are presented without any prior familiarization to determine if infants look preferentially at one or the other. Only pairs without such an *a priori* preference are selected for the study proper. Second, it is necessary to counteract the effects of side bias (a tendency in some infants to look exclusively, or nearly so, to the right or left). To guard against side bias, the left-right placement of novel and familiar stimuli are reversed midway through the test phase, thereby ensuring that high (or low) novelty scores reflect true preference for one or the other stimulus. Third, to ensure that each infant has an equal opportunity to encode the familiarization stimulus, it is left on display until the infant has actually looked at it for a fixed period of time.

In this way, the "study time," or amount of familiarization time accrued, is held constant across infants.

Interpretative Issues

Using the novelty score as an index of memory seems, at first blush, straightforward. However, it is clear that, a priori, memory could just as well be indexed by a significant preference for the familiar. And indeed, several early studies with infants younger than 2.5 months found a preference for the familiar stimulus (e.g., Hunt, 1970; Hunter, Ross, & Ames, 1982). Hunt proposed a stage theory, in which infants who are first developing the ability to recognize objects take pleasure in the act of recognition itself, with the result that they are most strongly attracted to those objects that have become familiar. This preference was thought to be supplanted by a preference for novelty as the infants got older and the act of recognition became commonplace.

The developmental stage theory was called into question, however, in a set of studies by Rose, Gottfried, Melloy-Carminar, and Bridger (1982). The first of these studies replicated Hunt's early work, finding a shift from familiarity to novelty with increasing age when a fixed familiarization time was used. Three groups of infants (3.5-, 4.5-, and 6.5-month-olds) were presented with a stimulus for 30 seconds. On test, the 3.5-month-olds showed a preference for the familiar; the 4.5-month-olds showed no preference; and the 6.5-month-olds showed a preference for the novel.

In the second study, however, familiarity responses were found in older children as well. Using two age groups, 3.5- and 6.5-month-olds, and study times that varied from 5 to 30 seconds, they found the same sequence of preferences (familiarity → chance → novelty) occurred within each age, with the direction of preference depending on familiarization time. Infants of both ages showed a familiarity response after limited exposure to the stimulus that shifted to a novelty preference after more extended exposure. Specifically, the 3.5-month-olds showed familiarity preferences after 5 and 10 seconds of study time, null preferences after 15 and 20 seconds, and novelty preferences after 30 seconds. The 6.5-month-olds showed the same transition in preferences, but they occurred after briefer familiarization, with familiarity, null, and novelty preferences appearing after 5, 10, and 15 seconds of familiarization, respectively. Thus, the shift occurred at both ages, but occurred with shorter familiarization times at the older age.

Other studies have reported similar shifts. Richards (1997) replicated the findings of Rose et al. (1982) with 3- to 6-month-olds, and Wagner and Sakovits (1986) found a similar shift from familiarity to novelty preferences in 9-month-olds. Hunter and colleagues (Hunter, Ames, & Koopman, 1983; Hunter et al., 1982) reported analogous results on habituation, with infants showing familiarity responses when habituation was interrupted that were supplanted by novelty preferences when habituation was allowed to proceed to completion. Thus, the direction of preference shown on a particular task depends on the age of the infant, the amount of familiarization permitted, and stimulus complexity. Nevertheless, the familiarity response is routinely associated with an incomplete internal representation or engram of the stimulus. With no familiarization at all, one would expect chance responding. Thus, these studies taken together suggest that one sees the following progression during *memory formation*:

chance → familiarity → chance → novelty

Two groups of investigators have shown that the pattern is actually reversed during memory decay, with familiarity responses appearing after long delays (i.e., one or more months). Bahrick and colleagues (Bahrick, 1995; Bahrick, Hernandez-Reif, & Pickens, 1997; Bahrick & Pickens, 1995), using a cross-sectional design to examine the memory of 3-month-olds for object motion, found novelty preferences after delays of 1 minute, null preferences after delays of 1 day and 2 weeks, and familiarity preferences after delays of 1 and 3 months. Courage and Howe (1998, 2001), using a within-subject design, reported a comparable progression during memory decay for infants of the same age, finding novelty, null, and familiarity preferences after delays of 1 minute, 1 week, and 1 month, respectively. These findings are striking, first in revealing the surprising longevity of infant memory traces, and second in revealing that the course of memory decay is exactly the reverse of memory formation.

Based on these findings, Bahrick and colleagues (Bahrick et al., 1997; Bahrick & Pickens, 1995) have proposed a four-phase model of memory decay in which infants' preference for familiar and novel targets change predictably as a function of memory accessibility. In Phase 1 (recent memory), memories are expressed by a novelty response; in Phase 2 (intermediate memories), by null preferences; in Phase 3 (remote memories), by familiarity responses; and in Phase 4 (unavailable or inaccessible memories), by a return to null preferences. Thus, the sequence for *memory decay* is the reverse of the encoding sequence, namely:

novelty → chance → familiarity → chance

Whereas these findings suggest an orderly progression of novelty scores as a function of study time or delay, they also raise a thorny issue about how to interpret an isolated null (chance) response. Traditionally, null preferences have been taken to mean that there is no evidence of memory. However, the results of the above studies indicate that alternative interpretations are possible (see also chapter 8, this volume). On the one hand, null preferences can mean the absence of memory, as when they appear before any encoding has occurred or after the memory trace has entirely decayed. On the other hand, null preferences can reflect an intermediate level of encoding or decay, as when they occur sandwiched between familiarity and novelty preferences.

Recognition memory is most often gauged by novelty scores because they are unambiguous indicators of memory which occur once sufficient encoding has taken place.

Recent Advances in Measuring This Type of Memory

There has been little change in the assessment of infant visual recognition per se, which still relies primarily on behavioral performance on the VPC task. However, recent applications of physiological and electrophysiological methods, in conjunction with VPC, hold promise for elucidating the processes underlying visual recognition memory and isolating the brain areas involved.

The application of physiological methods is seen in the work of Richards (1997), who studied how recognition was affected when familiarization took place during different phases of attention. He used heart rate to define three sequential phases of attention that occur when the infant is looking at something: (a) *orienting*, where heart rate is at baseline; (b) *sustained attention*, in which heart rate decelerates; and (c) *attention termination*, where the heart rate accelerates, returning to baseline. In two studies (Frick & Richards, 2001; Richards, 1997), 14-, 20-, and 26-week-old infants were initially presented with a video of the children's program *Sesame Street*, which was used to elicit the different phases of attention. The video was then interrupted during one or another phase to present a familiarization stimulus. When familiarization occurred during sustained attention, the infants required much less familiarization (5 seconds) to subsequently recognize the stimulus than when familiarization took place during either of the other two phases. Thus, recognition was facilitated when the infants' attentional state was optimized.

The application of electrophysiological methods can be seen in studies of event-related potentials (ERPs) recorded from the scalp. ERPs are electrical activity of the brain that are time locked to the onset of a stimulus. Three components are frequently examined in relation to infant memory. One, the middle latency negative component (Nc), which occurs about 400–800 milliseconds after stimulus presentation, may reflect both attention and memory, particularly recognition of stimuli stored in long-term memory (Carver, Bauer, & Nelson, 2000). The other two components are positive and negative late slow waves (PSW and NSW), occurring 800–1,600 milliseconds after stimulus onset, and are thought to reflect memory updating and detection of novelty (see de Haan, Bauer, Georgieff, & Nelson, 2000).

ERP studies often use an "odd-ball" paradigm, in which some stimuli are presented relatively frequently and others infrequently. Courchesne, Ganz, and Norcia (1981) initially showed that the infant's response to novel and familiar stimuli could be distinguished by the Nc component, which was larger for the novel stimulus, particularly from the frontal and central EEG leads. Although several studies have had similar findings, others have not.

So, for example, deHaan and Nelson (1999) found the Nc component was larger to familiar stimuli—mother's face vs. a stranger's face; familiar toys vs. unfamiliar ones. Bauer and colleagues (Bauer, Wiebe, Carver, Waters, & Nelson, 2003; Carver, Bauer, & Nelson, 2000) also found the Nc component to be larger to photos of familiar event sequences than novel ones. In some of these studies, the PSW was larger for the novel target as well (de Haan & Nelson, 1999), although in others, where the infant's familiarity with the stimuli was more limited, the NSW seem to be particularly sensitive to the difference between familiar and novel targets (Nelson & Collins, 1991, 1992; Richards, 2003). For example, Nelson and Collins (1991, 1992) added a preliminary phase to the oddball paradigm, in which infants were familiarized with two different stimuli. One of these familiar stimuli then occurred frequently (60% of the trials) in the oddball task; the other familiar stimulus occurred infrequently (20% of the trials); and different novel targets appeared on the remaining presentations (20% of the trials). The Nc component did not differ for the three types of stimuli, whereas an NSW distinguished between novel and familiar targets. Richards (2003) found comparable results using a similar presentation sequence, although here age and attentional state also affected the late slow waves to novel targets, which were positive at one age and negative at another.

The relative roles of the early and late components of the ERP in recognition memory are still being worked out. Efforts are currently underway to identify the cortical underpinnings of these ERP components using more sophisticated 128-channel recording systems (Reynolds & Richards, 2005).

Changes in Infant Visual Recognition Memory With Age

In this section, we review some of the dramatic developmental changes in infant visual recognition memory that occur over the first year of life.

Representations Become More Abstract and Flexible

There is considerable evidence that infants' internal representations of stimuli become increasingly abstract and flexible over the first year of life and that the ability to appreciate global and configural information increases.

First, infants' ability to recognize perceptual transformations of stimuli increases over age. For example, by 7 months, if not earlier, infants are able to recognize 2-dimensional versions (pictures and line drawings) of 3-dimensional objects they had seen before (Rose, 1977, 1983). By the latter half of the first year of life, infants are proficient in recognizing protoypes extracted from multiple exemplars of a category (e.g., Rubenstein, Kalakanis, & Langlois, 1999; Sherman, 1985).

Second, reliance on configural information increases over age. This is clearly indicated in a study on face perception from our own lab (Rose, Jankowski, & Feldman, 2002), in which 7- and 12-month-olds were familiarized to a face in full frontal view and then tested with faces that either preserved configural integrity (3/4 poses and profiles) or disrupted configural integrity while preserving featural information (rotations of 160° or 200° and fracturings). While the rotations violated configural integrity by destroying the top-down ordering of features, the fracturings (created by cutting the picture into pieces and pulling the pieces apart) violated configural integrity by destroying the spacing among features. The 7-month-olds recognized 3/4 poses of the familiar face, but none of the other transformations, whereas the 12-month-olds recognized not only the 3/4 poses, but also the profiles and rotations. A subset of the 12-month-olds recognized even the fractured faces. Thus, although the 7-month-olds showed some limited use of configural information in processing faces, the 12-month-olds showed a greater appreciation of this information and more flexible use of it.

Third, proficiency in using impoverished or partial information improves. For example, 12-month-olds were able to integrate information over space and time sufficiently to recognize movement-defined objects (where the object's contour was traced by a moving point source of light), whereas 8-month-olds were unable to so (Rose, 1988; Skouteris, McKenzie, & Day, 1992). By 12-months, infants could also recognize stimuli based on very degraded information. Rose, Jankowski, and Senior (1997) habituated 12-month old infants to line drawings of common objects and then presented them with 33%, 50% or 66% of their contour missing. Recognition was successful even with up to 66% of the contour eliminated. These infants also recognized the complements of 50% contour-deleted figures—that is, figures that had the same global shape but contained none of the original elements (see also Colombo, Freeseman, Coldren, & Frick, 1995; Freeseman, Colombo, & Coldren, 1993; Quinn & Johnson, 2000).

Overall, it is clear then that infants recognize instantiations of objects even when the input is degraded or considerably altered, and where the physical characteristics between the original object and its depiction are quite disparate.

Connectionist models have recently become popular for explaining how recognition can proceed based on partial input (Elman et al., 1997; Mareschal & French, 2000; McClelland, 2000; Shanks, 1997). Such models envision an event or object as represented by a pattern of activity over three types of processing units: input units, which receive information from outside; output units, which send information outside the network; and hidden units, which are used in forming the internal representation. "The behavior of the network is determined by the connection weights between all the units. As the weights change the behavior changes. Hence, learning consists of adjusting the connection weights in the network" (Mareschal & French,

2000, p. 62). When previously learned information is encountered, the spread of activation across the units is repeated, leading to retrieval. In cases like those cited above, where partial information is presented, retrieval occurs if a sufficient number of units are activated.

Retention Increases

Although there has been a great deal of developmental work on immediate recognition memory, there has been surprisingly little systematic work on the development of delayed recognition. Studies of delayed recognition differ in the ages examined, as well as methodological details, such as the number of stimuli presented before recognition is assessed, familiarization times, delay periods, and so forth. Consequently, there are few points of congruence across studies, and it is difficult to obtain a coherent picture of change over age. Nonetheless, despite their differences, one central idea does come across—namely, in all studies, the older the infant, the greater the delay that could be tolerated.

For example, in one study, Cornell (1974) presented faces to two groups, 4-month-olds and 5-to 6-month-olds, using approximately 20 seconds of familiarization, and tested for recognition after two delays, 5 seconds and 2 minutes. While both groups recognized the faces at the 5 second delay, only the older group recognized them after the 2-minute delay. In another study, Rose (1981) presented 6-and 9-month-olds with patterns and faces, using familiarization times ranging from 5 to 20 seconds, and tested both immediately and after a 2–3 minute delay. Infants of both ages recognized the stimuli immediately, but only the 9-month-olds recognized them after the delay. And in a third study, Diamond (1990) presented objects to 4-, 6-, and 9-month-olds, one at a time, in a habituation procedure, and tested for recognition after delays of 10 seconds, 15 seconds, 1 minute, and 10 minutes. The 4-month-olds recognized targets at delays of 10 seconds but not at any of the longer delays, while the 6-month-olds recognized them with delays up to 1 minute, and 9-month-olds recognized them with delays as long as 10 minutes.

Some of the most compelling evidence for recognition over periods as long as days and weeks comes from a set of studies by Fagan (1973). He found that 4- to 5-month-olds given 2 minutes of familiarization could recognize abstract patterns up to 2 days later (Fagan, 1973, Experiment 1) and faces up to 2 weeks later (Fagan, 1973, Experiment 2). Using the habituation paradigm, Pascalis, de Haan, Nelson, and de Schonen (1998) found that 3-month-olds recognized faces over delays ranging up to 24 hours (the longest delay used in this study). As noted earlier, recognition in 3-month-olds has also been demonstrated over a much longer period—up to 3 months (Bahrick & Pickens, 1995; Bahrick et al., 1997; Courage & Howe, 1998, 2001). In these latter studies, unlike those reviewed earlier, the stimuli were particularly engaging, consisting of dynamic rather than static displays. Though memory over such extended delays has not yet been studied developmentally, the findings with dynamic displays suggest that early memory traces may remain viable over considerably longer periods than might have been anticipated.

The amount of information retained in memory also increases with age, as exemplified in a study by Rose and colleagues (Rose, Feldman, & Jankowski, 2001b). They tested memory spans of 1 to 4 items in 5-, 7-, and 12-month olds. After all items of a set were presented, each was successively paired with a new one to test for recognition. Memory capacity, indexed by the highest number of items having a novelty score >55% in any one span, increased over the first year of life. Fewer than 25% of the infants at the two younger ages could hold as many as 3–4 items in mind at once. But nearly half of them could do so by 12 months.

Another indicator of the robustness of infant memory comes from studies showing its resistance to interference. Although this phenomenon has not been studied developmentally, we mention it here because of its considerable importance to memory. Evidence of resistance to interference comes from both VPC and habituation work. In a classic set of studies, this issue was examined in 3- to 4-month-olds using a design with three phases: (1) familiarization (habituation), (2) interference, and (3) test. In the interference phase, the distracter varied in duration (20–40 seconds) and/or similarity to the target. In one of these studies (Cohen, DeLoach, & Pearl, 1977), neither variable had any effect on performance; in the other two, recognition was disrupted only when infants had thoroughly processed the distracters (McCall et al., 1977) or when the distracter was highly similar to the target (Fagan, 1977).

Overall then, recognition memory has been found to be surprisingly robust over periods of minutes, hours, and even weeks, to resist interference, and to remain accessible after delays as long as one and three months. What is lacking is a cohesive body of data on developmental changes in visual recognition memory that details how well, how long, and how much is remembered by infants of different ages.

Factors Influencing Recognition Memory

There is considerable evidence that two behavioral factors, processing speed and attention, influence recognition memory and show dramatic change with age (Rose, Feldman, & Jankowski, 2003b; Rose & Tamis-Lemonda, 1999).

Changes in Processing Speed

Although the definition and scope of speed varies considerably, there is evidence that processing speed plays a central role in performance on VPC tasks. Much of this evidence has been indirect. Some of it comes from the dramatic age-related decreases found in the amount of familiarization time needed for recognition: Older infants need less familiarization time to recognize targets than do younger infants (e.g., Colombo, Mitchell, & Horowitz, 1988; Fagan, 1974; Richards, 1997; Rose, 1980, 1983; Rose et al., 1982). For example, in one study from our own lab (Rose, 1983), 6- and 12-month-olds were given four problems of object recognition, one each with 10, 15, 20, and 30 seconds familiarization. Whereas 6-month-olds achieved significant novelty scores only after the two lengthier familiarization times, the 12-month-olds showed significant novelty scores throughout, even with as little as 10 seconds of familiarization.

Other evidence of the role of processing speed comes from the trade-off found between the amount of time needed to recognize a target and the target's complexity. In an elegant set of studies, Fagan (1970, 1971, 1972, 1974) varied the complexity of the stimuli and the subtlety of the discriminations to be made as well as study times and age. The stimuli, in order of increasing difficulty, were: (a) simple abstract patterns, each very different from the other; (b) patterns made up of the same set of elements arranged differently; and (c) photographs of faces. Whereas the abstract stimuli were recognized by 2- to 3-month olds, the pattern rearrangements were not recognized until infants were 4 months of age, and the faces not until they were 5 to 6 months of age. The difficulty of the task was also reflected in the familiarization time needed for recognition within each age. So, for example, whereas the 5- to 6-month-olds needed less than 4 seconds to recognize the abstract patterns, they needed close to 17 seconds to recognize the more subtle patterns, and as much as 20 to 30 seconds to recognize the faces.

A method of gauging processing speed for individual infants was devised by Rose and colleagues (Orlian & Rose, 1997; Rose, Feldman, & Jankowski, 2002; Rose, Futterweit, & Jankowski, 1999; Rose, Jankowski et al., 2002). In this task, a hybrid of the VPC and habituation tasks, infants see a series of paired faces, one of which remains the same across trials while the other changes. Trials continue until infants reach a criterion of consistent novelty preference, defined as four out of five consecutive trials having a novelty score greater than 55% (with looks directed toward both targets). Using this procedure, an age-related decline in the number of trials to criterion was found in two studies, a cross-sectional study of 5-, 7-, and 9-month-olds (Rose et al., 1999) and a longitudinal study where the same infants were seen at 5, 7, and 12 months (Rose, Feldman et al., 2002). In the longitudinal sample, individual differences in speed of processing were also found to be related to recognition memory: Infants who took more trials to reach criterion had significantly lower novelty scores on a VPC task at all three ages: $r = -.24$, $-.23$, and $-.23$ at 5, 7, and 12 months, respectively (Rose, Feldman, & Jankowski, 2003b). These findings reinforce the notion that processing speed plays an important role in infants' recognition memory.

Additional evidence linking VPC performance with processing speed comes from a longitudinal study showing a relation between infant visual recognition memory at 7 months and processing speed at 11 years (Rose & Feldman, 1995, 1997). The 11-year measures of speed used in this work came from two paper-and-pencil tests (finding As and match-to-sample) and from a computerized battery of tasks (decision time in memory search and match-to-sample tasks, tachistoscopic threshold, and simple and choice reaction times). Infant visual recognition memory remained significantly related to these 11-year speed measures even when IQ was partialed.

Changes in Attention

Two aspects of infant attention have been linked to recognition memory—look duration and shift rate (number of shifts of gaze between stimuli per unit time). Both reflect differences in the way infants distribute their attention when they examine displays. In particular, when examining targets, some infants have characteristically short looks, high shift rates, and widely distributed looks. Others have characteristically long looks, lower shift rates, and more narrowly distributed looks.

There are marked developmental changes in both aspects of attention, with mean and peak looks decreasing systematically over age, and shift rates becoming faster (Axia, Bonichini, & Benini, 1999; Colombo & Mitchell, 1990; Colombo et al., 1988; Rose, Feldman, & Jankowski, 2001a; Rose et al., 1999; Ruff, 1975). In the course of a longitudinal study, Rose et al. (2001a) assessed developmental trajectories for look duration and shift rate. Mean look duration decreased by as much as 40% from 5 to 12 months whereas shift rates increased by as much as 90% over the same period. These changes were independent of stimulus type and characterized performance in both the familiarization and test phase of the VPC task.

More mature patterns of attention (i.e., shorter looks and higher shift rates) are associated with better recognition memory. Colombo and colleagues identified infants as long lookers or short lookers based on their peak (longest) look during a pretest. In a series of studies carried out with 4-month-olds, short lookers were found to have better recognition memory than long lookers across various types of problems (Colombo, 1993; Colombo, Mitchell, Coldren, & Freeseman, 1991; Freeseman et al., 1993). Jankowski and Rose (1997) found similar relations at 5, 7, and 9 months, with short lookers showing better memory for complex geometric forms (made up of the same elements arranged in different configurations) than long lookers, whose responses remained at chance (see also Rose et al., 2001a). Courage and Howe (2001) extended these findings to long-term memory, with short lookers showing better recognition even after 1 month. These results suggest that differences in attention during encoding have important implications for both short-term and long-term recognition.

The strongest suggestion of a causal link between attention and memory comes from a study by Jankowski, Rose, and Feldman (2001). They found that the attentional style of 5-month-old long lookers could be altered, and that this alteration was associated with improved memory. After dividing infants into short and long lookers based on a pretest, a modified familiarization procedure was used to promote shorter looks and more shifts. In this procedure, the quadrants of the stimulus were successively spotlit. The results were dramatic. The long lookers showed shorter looks, more shifts, and a broader distribution of looks. In fact, their attention was now indistinguishable from that of short lookers. Most important, these improvements in attention were accompanied by improved recognition.

Joint Effect of Changes in Processing Speed and Attention

Attention and processing speed, though correlated and theoretically related (Colombo, 1993), nonetheless contribute independently to recognition memory. Rose, Feldman, and Jankowski (2003b), using multiple regression, found independent contributions of attention and processing speed at three ages—5, 7, and 12 months; the two together accounted for 6% to 9% of the variance in visual recognition memory. It is not clear whether the considerable amount of unexplained variance eventually will be explained by other factors, or whether recognition memory will turn out to be largely a "cognitive primitive," reflecting some irreducible characteristic or capability on which individuals differ.

Questions and Issues on the Horizon for the Study of the Development of This Type of Memory

What Is the Developmental Trajectory of Delayed Recognition?

Much of the work in infant recognition memory has been concerned with immediate memory, or memory over very brief delays. This work has concentrated largely on the adequacy of encoding and the nature of the information encoded. While a great deal of work has been done in defining the developmental trajectory of recall (Bauer, 2004), we still have neither an adequate description nor understanding of the developmental course of recognition over extended delays.

Two methodological considerations are critical in order to adequately elucidate developmental changes in retention. First, initial differences in level of encoding must be equated. Since younger infants take longer to encode information than older ones, initial encoding must be equated before age-related differences in retention can be assessed. In many studies, it is often impossible to determine whether developmental changes in recognition memory reflect developmental differences in initial encoding or developmental differences in trace decay. Delay intervals should be introduced only after all infants have had sufficient time to encode the target (i.e., to fully process the initial information).

Second, it is necessary to distinguish between total loss of a memory and its inaccessibility. One way to approach this problem is to determine whether a memory trace that is no longer spontaneously accessible can be reinstated with a retrieval cue. To the extent that information has been encoded, consolidated, stored, and still exists, one should be able to reinstate recognition with a retrieval cue. Although this approach is rarely used in studies of infant recognition memory, the work of Cornell (1979) indicates it holds considerable promise. He found that retrieval cues revealed the existence of memories in 5-month-olds after a period of time when they were no longer demonstrated spontaneously.

Thus, systematic studies introducing varying delays, at different ages, are still needed in this area. Moreover, they must equate encoding and introduce reminders so as to separate genuine forgetting, where the trace has decayed, from retrieval failures.

What Brain Substrates Underlie the Development of Recognition Memory?

The neural underpinnings of recognition memory, which have been described in nonhuman primates and adults, are only beginning to be examined in the human infant. In adults, recognition memory, like other types of explicit memory, has been shown to rely on structures in the medial temporal lobe and their connections with sensory association areas and the prefrontal cortex (see Eichenbaum & Cohen, 2001). Some of these structures are fairly mature at birth. In particular, the vast majority of the cells and connections in the hippocampal formation are already in place at birth in the monkey (Alvarado & Bachevalier, 2000) and by the end of the prenatal period in the human infant. In fact, much of the hippocampus is formed by the 6th month of gestation (Seress, 2001).

However, whereas the hippocampus is fairly well developed at birth, other parts of the medial temporal lobe (e.g., dentate gyrus), are still immature, as are the connections between the medial temporal lobe and the cortical regions implicated in long-term storage. Moreover, even though the hippocampal formation may be anatomically mature, its functional maturity remains in question.

A fuller understanding of the development of recognition memory will require mapping the course of behavioral development onto changes in the development of these basic brain structures. The application of newer ERP techniques, which use a 128-electrode array along with cortical source analysis, promises to be useful for charting brain-behavior relations as they develop (see Reynolds & Richards, 2005).

What Mechanisms Account for the Relation
of Infant Visual Recognition Memory to
Later Cognition?

There are two strong reasons to think that infant visual recognition memory is important to later cognition. First, infants who are expected to have cognitive difficulties later in life, i.e., those at risk, have difficulties on the VPC task. Performance on this task is depressed by a variety of medical risk factors, including prematurity, non-optimal perinatal circumstances (e.g., long labor and low Apgar scores), genetic abnormalities, such as Down syndrome, prenatal exposure to teratogens (e.g., cocaine and PCB), and nutritional deficiency (for overview see Rose, Feldman, & Jankowski, 2003a; Rose, Feldman, & Jankowski, 2004).

Second, infant visual recognition is predictive of later cognitive abilities, including IQ and language. This relation was reviewed in an influential meta-analysis, which reported that the median predictive correlation between infant recognition memory and later cognition is around $r=.45$ (McCall & Carriger, 1993). In our own lab, we have found that recognition memory at 7-months (and, to a lesser extent, at 1-year) was related to IQ at 3, 4, 5, 6, and 11 years, receptive and expressive language at 2.5, 3, 4, and 6 years, and vocabulary at 11 years (for overview, see Rose et al., 2004). These predictive relations were maintained after controlling for socio-economic status, maternal education, and Bayley scores from the first year of life.

What is unclear is how deficits in a simple ability like infant visual recognition memory come to account for later cognition. In beginning to study this issue, we were influenced by Fry and Hale's work with older children (1996), where processing speed influenced working memory which, in turn, influenced intelligence. In our work with infants we found attention, as well as encoding speed, independently predicted visual recognition memory throughout the first year of life (Rose et al., 2003). We assume that the causal arrow goes from attention and speed to visual recognition memory because manipulations that affect attention (Jankowski, Rose, & Feldman, 2001) and speed (Richards, 1997) influence visual recognition memory.

We used these findings to begin to map the structure of infant cognition. In our model, infant cognition is characterized by a cognitive cascade, in which more fundamental or basic abilities underpin more complex ones which, in turn, influence general intelligence. We have evaluated this model using data from four domains of infant information processing: attention, processing speed, visual recognition memory, and representational competence, with attention and speed considered more elementary than memory and representational competence. The cascade model fit the data and the fit was replicated with infant data from both 7 and 12 months. Moreover, these aspects of infant cognition mediated the relation of risk status (preterm birth) to later cognition (Rose et al., 2005b, Rose et al., submitted).

Although we are beginning to learn something about the pathways involved, we still have little knowledge about the intermediaries between infant recognition memory and later IQ. One possible intermediary here is language. Several investigators have documented relations between habituation and the early emergence of representational abilities, such as language and play, which may mediate long term relations between information processing and later cognitive performance (Tamis-LeMonda & Bornstein, 1989). Using data from the first five years of our longitudinal study, we found that language proficiency at 2.5, 3, and 4 years partly mediated relations between novelty preference scores at 7 months and 5 year IQ (Rose, Feldman, Wallace, & Cohen, 1991). While it is far from clear exactly how better recognition leads to expanded language development, there has been speculation that the skills necessary to recognize an object are similar to those needed for perceptual categorization. Perceptual categorization, in turn, has been thought of as a necessary precursor to language acquisition (Slobin, 1985).

Language can not be the only link, however. Other possible mechanisms include later forms of processing speed and memory, both of which are considered to be components of IQ. Indeed, in one longitudinal study, 7-month performance on the VPC task was shown to relate to various measures of speed and memory at 11 years, as assessed with a computerized battery and traditional paper-and-pencil tasks (Rose et al., 1995, 1997). Moreover, the correlation between 7-month visual recognition memory and full-scale IQ at 11 years was reduced from .44 to .28 when controlling for 11-year speed and memory (Rose et al., 1997). Thus, later processing speed and memory are implicated in the link between infant visual recognition memory and later IQ.

Finally, it may be that faster and better execution of lower-level processes, such as recognition memory, leads to the formation of more complete and elaborate cognitive representations, which lead to a richer and broader knowledge base. With a richer knowledge base, newly encountered information will be comprehended and assimilated with greater ease, providing a feedback cycle in which the knowledge base is further expanded. However, there has been no actual test of links between better recognition and faster accrual of knowledge. Further work is needed to elucidate the mechanisms linking better infant recognition to better overall cognitive performance in later childhood.

Acknowledgments

Some of the research reported in this chapter was supported by NIH grants HD 13810, HD 38066, and HD 049491, and by a Social and Behavioral Science Research Grant from the March of Dimes Birth Defects Foundation.

References

Alvarado, M. C., & Bachevalier, J. (2000). Revisiting the maturation of medial temporal lobe memory functions in primates. *Learning and Memory, 7,* 244–256.

Axia, G., Bonichini, S., & Benini, F. (1999). Attention and reaction to distress in infancy: A longitudinal study. *Developmental Psychology, 35,* 500–504.

Bachevalier, J., Brickson, M., & Hagger, C. (1993). Limbic-dependent recognition memory in monkeys develops early in infancy. *Neuroreport, 4,* 77–80.

Bahrick, L. E. (1995). Infant memory for object motion across a period of three months: Implications for a four-phase attention function. *Journal of Experimental Child Psychology, 59,* 343–371.

Bahrick, L. E., Hernandez-Reif, M., & Pickens, J. N. (1997). The effect of retrieval cues on visual preferences and memory in infancy: Evidence for a four-phase attention function. *Journal of Experimental Child Psychology, 67,* 1–20.

Bahrick, L. E., & Pickens, J. N. (1995). Infant memory for object motion across a period of three months: Implications for a four-phase function. *Journal of Experimental Child Psychology, 59,* 343–371.

Bauer, P. J. (2004). Getting explicit memory off the ground: Steps toward construction of a neuro-developmental account of changes in the first two years of life. *Developmental Review, 24,* 347–373.

Bauer, P. J., Wiebe, S. A., Carver, L. J., Waters, J. M., & Nelson, C. A. (2003). Developments in long-term explicit memory late in the first year of life: Behavioral and electrophysiological indices. *Psychological Science, 14,* 629–635.

Buffalo, E. A., Ramus, S. J., Clark, R. E., Teng, E., Squire, L. R., & Zola, S. M. (1999). Dissociation between the effects of damage to perirhinal cortex and area TE. *Learning and Memory, 6,* 572–599.

Buffalo, E. A., Reber, P. J., & Squire, L. R. (1998). The human perirhinal cortex and recognition memory. *Hippocampus, 8,* 330–339.

Carver, L. J., Bauer, P. J., & Nelson, C. A. (2000). Associations between infant brain activity and recall memory. *Developmental Science, 3,* 234–246.

Cohen, L. B., DeLoach, J. S., & Pearl, R. D. (1977). An examination of interference effects in infants' memory for faces. *Child Development, 48,* 88–96.

Cohen, L. B., & Strauss, M. S. (1979). Concept acquisition in the human infant. *Child Development, 50,* 419–424.

Colombo, J. (1993). *Infant cognition: Predicting later intellectual functioning.* Newbury Park, CA: Sage.

Colombo, J., Freeseman, L. J., Coldren, J. T., & Frick, J. E. (1995). Individual differences in infant fixation duration: Dominance of global versus local stimulus properties. *Cognitive Development, 10,* 271–285.

Colombo, J., & Mitchell, D. W. (1990). Individual differences in early visual attention: Fixation time and information processing. In J. Colombo & J. Fagen (Eds.), *Individual differences in infancy: Reliability, stability, prediction* (pp. 193–227). Hillsdale, NJ: Erlbaum.

Colombo, J., Mitchell, D. W., Coldren, J. T., & Freeseman, L. J. (1991). Individual differences in infant visual attention: Are short lookers faster processors or feature processors? *Child Development, 62,* 1247–1257.

Colombo, J., Mitchell, D. W., & Horowitz, F. D. (1988). Infant visual attention in the paired-comparison paradigm: Test-retest and attention-performance relations. *Child Development, 59,* 1198–1210.

Colombo, J., Shaddy, D. J., Richman, W. A., Maikranz, J. M., & Blaga, O. M. (2004). The developmental course of habituation in infancy and pre-school outcome. *Infancy, 5,* 1–38.

Cornell, E. H. (1974). Infants' discrimination of photographs of faces following redundant presentations. *Journal of Experimental Child Psychology, 18,* 98–106.

Cornell, E. H. (1979). Infants' recognition memory, forgetting, and savings. *Journal of Experimental Child Psychology, 28,* 359–374.

Cornell, E. H. (1980). Distributed study facilitates infants delayed recognition memory. *Memory and Cognition, 8*(6), 539–542.

Courage, M. L., & Howe, M. L. (1998). The ebb and flow of infants' attentional preferences: Evidence of long-term recognition memory in 3-month-olds. *Journal of Experimental Child Psychology, 70,* 26–53.

Courage, M. L., & Howe, M. L. (2001). Long-term retention in 3.5-month-olds: Familiarization time and individual differences in attentional style. *Journal of Experimental Child Psychology, 79,* 271–293.

Courchesne, E., Ganz, L., & Norcia, A. M. (1981). Event-related brain potentials to human faces in infants. *Child Development, 52,* 804–811.

de Haan, M., Bauer, P. J., Georgieff, M. K., & Nelson, C. A. (2000). Explicit memory in low-risk infants aged 19 months born between 27 and 42 weeks of gestation. *Developmental Medicine and Child Neurology, 42,* 304–312.

de Haan, M., & Nelson, C. A. (1999). Brain activity differentiates face and object processing in 6-month-old infants. *Developmental Psychology, 35,* 1113–1121.

Diamond, A. (1990). Rate of maturation of the hippocampus and the developmental progression of children's performance on the delayed non-matching to sample and visual paired comparison tasks. In A. Diamond (Ed.), *Development and neural bases of higher cognitive functions: Vol. 608. Annals of the New York Academy of Sciences* (pp. 394–426). New York: Academic Press.

Dougherty, T. M., & Haith, M. M. (1997). Infant expectations and reaction time as predictors of childhood speed of processing and IQ. *Developmental Psychology, 33,* 146–155.

Eichenbaum, H., & Cohen, N. J. (2001). *From conditioning to conscious recollection: Memory systems of the brain.* New York: Oxford University Press.

Elman, J. L., Bates, E. A., Johnson, M. H., Karmiloff-Smith, A., Parisi, D., & Plunkett, K. (1997). *Rethinking innateness: A development (neural networks and connectionist modeling).* Cambridge, MA: MIT Press.

Fagan, J. F. (1970). Memory in the infant. *Journal of Experimental Child Psychology, 9,* 217–226.

Fagan, J. F. (1971). Infants' recognition memory for a series of visual stimuli. *Journal of Experimental Child Psychology, 11,* 244–250.

Fagan, J. F. (1972). Infants' recognition memory for faces. *Journal of Experimental Child Psychology, 14,* 453–476.

Fagan, J. F. (1973). Infants' delayed recognition memory and forgetting. *Journal of Experimental Child Psychology, 16,* 424–450.

Fagan, J. F. (1974). Infant recognition memory: The effects of length of familiarization and type of discrimination task. *Child Development, 45,* 351–356.

Fagan, J. F. (1976). Infants' recognition memory of invariant features of faces. *Child Development, 47,* 627–638.

Fagan, J. F. (1977). Infant recognition memory: Studies of forgetting. *Child Development, 48,* 68–78.

Fagan, J. F., & Haiken-Vasen, J. H. (1997). Selective attention to novelty as a measure of information processing. In J. A. Burack & J. T. Enns (Eds.), *Attention, development, and psychopathology.* New York: Guilford.

Freeseman, L. J., Colombo, J., & Coldren, J. T. (1993). Individual differences in infant visual attention: Four-month-olds' discrimination and generalization of global and local stimulus properties. *Child Development, 64,* 1191–1203.

Frick, J. E., & Richards, J. E. (2001). Individual differences in infants' recognition of briefly presented visual stimuli. *Infancy, 2*(3), 331–352.

Fry, A. F., & Hale, S. (1996). Processing speed, working memory, and fluid intelligence: Evidence for a developmental cascade. *Psychological Science, 7,* 237–241.

Hale, S. (1990). A global developmental trend in cognitive processing speed. *Child Development, 61,* 653–663.

Horowitz, F. D., Paden, L., Bhana, K., & Self, P. (1972). An infant-controlled procedure for studying infant visual fixations. *Developmental Psychology, 7,* 90.

Hunt, J. M. (1970). Attentional preference and experience: I. Introduction. *Journal of Genetic Psychology, 117,* 99–107.

Hunter, M. A., Ames, E., & Koopman, R. (1983). Effects of stimulus complexity and familiarization time on infant preferences for novel and familiar stimuli. *Developmental Psychology, 19,* 338–352.

Hunter, M. A., Ross, H. S., & Ames, E. W. (1982). Preferences for familiar or novel toys: Effects of familiarization time in 1-year-olds. *Developmental Psychology, 18,* 519–529.

Jankowski, J. J., & Rose, S. A. (1997). The distribution of visual attention in infants. *Journal of Experimental Child Psychology, 65,* 127–140.

Jankowski, J. J., Rose, S. A., & Feldman, J. F. (2001). Modifying the distribution of attention in infants. *Child Development, 72,* 339–351.

Kail, R. (1986). Sources of age differences in speed of processing. *Child Development, 57,* 969–987.

Kail, R. (1988). Developmental functions for speeds of cognitive processing. *Journal of Experimental Child Psychology, 45,* 339–364.

Kail, R. (1991). Developmental change in speed of processing during childhood and adolescence. *Psychological Bulletin, 109,* 490–501.

Kail, R., & Salthouse, T. A. (1994). Processing speed as a mental capacity. *Acta Psychologica, 86,* 199–225.

Malkova, L., Mishkin, M., & Bachevalier, J. (1995). Long-term effects of selective neonatal temporal lobe lesions on learning and memory in monkeys. *Behavioral Neuroscience, 109*(2), 212–226.

Manns, J. R., Stark, C. E., & Squire, L. R. (2000). The visual paired-comparison task as a measure of declarative memory. *Proceedings of the National Academy of Sciences U.S.A., 97*(22), 12375–12379.

Mareschal, D., & French, R. (2000). Mechanisms of categorization in infancy. *Infancy, 1,* 59–76.

McCall, R. B., & Carriger, M. S. (1993). A meta-analysis of infant habituation and recognition memory performance as predictors of later IQ. *Child Development, 64,* 57–79.

McCall, R. B., Kennedy, C. B., & Dodds, C. (1977). The interfering effects of distracting stimuli on the infant's memory. *Child Development, 48,* 79–87.

McClelland, J. L. (2000). Connectionist models of memory. In E. Tulving & F. Craik (Eds.), *The Oxford handbook of memory* (pp. 583–596). London: Oxford University Press.

McKee, R. D., & Squire, L. R. (1993). On the development of declarative memory. *Journal of Experimental Psychology: Learning, Memory, and Cognition, 19,* 397–404.

Murray, E. A., & Mishkin, M. (1998). Object recognition and location memory in monkeys with excitotoxic lesions of the amygdala and hippocampus. *Journal of Neuroscience, 18,* 6568–6582.

Nelson, C. A. (1995). The ontogeny of human memory: A cognitive neuroscience perspective. *Developmental Psychology, 31,* 723–738.

Nelson, C. A. (1997). The neurobiological basis of early memory development. In N. Cowan & C. Hulme (Eds.), *The development of memory in childhood* (pp. 41–82). Sussex, UK: Psychology Press.

Nelson, C. A., & Collins, P. F. (1991). Event-related potential and looking-time analysis of infants' responses to familiar and novel events: Implications for recognition memory. *Developmental Psychology, 27,* 50–58.

Nelson, C. A., & Collins, P. F. (1992). Neural and behavioral correlates of visual recognition memory in 4- and 8-month-old infants. *Brain and Cognition, 19,* 105–121.

Orlian, E. K., & Rose, S. A. (1997). Speed vs. thoroughness in infant visual information processing. *Infant Behavior and Development, 20,* 371–381.

Pascalis, O., & Bachevalier, J. (1999). Neonatal aspiration lesions of the hippocampal formation impair visual recognition memory when assessed by paired-comparison task but not by delayed nonmatching-to-sample. *Hippocampus, 9,* 609–616.

Pascalis, O., de Haan, M., Nelson, C. A., & de Schonen, S. (1998). Long-term recognition memory for faces assessed by visual paired comparison in 3- and 6-month-old infants. *Journal of Experimental Psychology: Learning, Memory, and Cognition, 24,* 249–260.

Pascalis, O., & de Schonen, S. (1994). Recognition memory in 3- to 4-day-old human neonates. *NeuroReport, 5,* 1721–1724.

Peterson, B. S., Anderson, A. W., Ehrenkranz, R., Staib, L. H., Tageldin, M., Colson, E., et al. (2003). Regional brain volumes and their later neuro-developmental correlates in term and preterm infants. *Pediatrics, 111*(5), 939–948.

Quinn, P. C., & Johnson, M. H. (2000). Global-before-basic object categorization in connectionist networks and 2-month-old infants. *Infancy, 1,* 31–46.

Reynolds, G. D., & Richards, J. E. (2005). Familiarization, attention, and recognition memory in infancy: An ERP and cortical source localization study. *Developmental Psychology, 41,* 598–615.

Richards, J. E. (1997). Effects of attention on infants' preference for briefly exposed visual stimuli in the paired-comparison recognition-memory paradigm. *Developmental Psychology, 33,* 22–31.

Richards, J. E. (2003). Attention affects the recognition of briefly presented stimuli in infants: An ERP study. *Developmental Science, 6,* 312–328.

Richardson-Klavehn, A., & Bjork, R. A. (1988). Measures of memory. *Annual Review of Psychology, 39,* 475–543.

Rose, S. A. (1977). Infant's transfer of response between two-dimensional and three-dimensional stimuli. *Child Development, 48,* 1086–1091.

Rose, S. A. (1980). Enhancing visual recognition memory in preterm infants. *Developmental Psychology, 16,* 85–92.

Rose, S. A. (1981). Developmental changes in infants' retention of visual stimuli. *Child Development, 52,* 227–233.

Rose, S. A. (1983). Differential rates of visual information processing in fullterm and preterm infants. *Child Development, 54,* 1189–1198.

Rose, S. A. (1988). Shape retention in infancy: Visual integration of sequential information. *Child Development, 56,* 1161–1176.

Rose, S. A., & Feldman, J. F. (1990). Infant cognition: Individual differences and developmental continuities. In J. Colombo & J. W. Fagen (Eds.), *Individual differences in infancy* (pp. 229–245). Hillsdale, NJ: Erlbaum.

Rose, S. A., & Feldman, J. F. (1995). Prediction of IQ and specific cognitive abilities at 11 years from infancy measures. *Developmental Psychology, 31,* 685–696.

Rose, S. A., & Feldman, J. F. (1996). Memory and processing speed in preterm children at 11 years: A comparison with full-terms. *Child Development, 67,* 2005–2021.

Rose, S. A., & Feldman, J. F. (1997). Memory and speed: Their role in the relation of infant information processing to later IQ. *Child Development, 68,* 630–641.

Rose, S. A., Feldman, J. F., Futterweit, L. R., & Jankowski, J. J. (1997). Continuity in visual recognition memory: Infancy to 11 years. *Intelligence, 24,* 381–392.

Rose, S. A., Feldman, J. F., & Jankowski, J. J. (2001a). Attention and recognition memory in the first year of life: A longitudinal study of preterms and full-terms. *Developmental Psychology, 37,* 135–151.

Rose, S. A., Feldman, J. F., & Jankowski, J. J. (2001b). Visual short-term memory in the first year of life: Capacity and recency effects. *Developmental Psychology, 37,* 539–549.

Rose, S. A., Feldman, J. F., & Jankowski, J. J. (2002). Processing speed in the 1st year of life: A longitudinal study of preterm and full-term infants. *Developmental Psychology, 38,* 895–902.

Rose, S. A., Feldman, J. F., & Jankowski, J. J. (2003a). The building blocks of cognition. *Journal of Pediatrics, 143*, S54–S61.

Rose, S. A., Feldman, J. F., & Jankowski, J. J. (2003b). Infant visual recognition memory: Independent contributions of speed and attention. *Developmental Psychology, 39*, 563–571.

Rose, S. A., Feldman, J. F., & Jankowski, J. J. (2004). Infant visual recognition memory. *Developmental Review, 24*, 74–100.

Rose, S. A., Feldman, J. F., & Jankowski, J. J. (2005a). Recall memory in the first three years of life: A longitudinal study of preterms and full-terms. *Developmental Medicine and Child Neurology, 47*, 653–659.

Rose, S. A., Feldman, J. F., Jankowski, J. J., & Van Rossem, R. (2005b). Pathways from prematurity and infant abilities to later cognition. *Child Development, 76*, 1172–1184.

Rose, S. A., Feldman, J. F., Jankowski, J. J., & Van Rossem, R. (submitted). Information processing at 7 and 12 months: Pathways from prematurity to developmental outcome.

Rose, S. A., Feldman, J. F., Wallace, I. F., & Cohen, P. (1991). Language: A partial link between infant attention and later intelligence. *Developmental Psychology, 27*, 798–805.

Rose, S. A., Futterweit, L. R., & Jankowski, J. J. (1999). The relation of affect to attention and learning in infancy. *Child Development, 70*, 549–559.

Rose, S. A., Gottfried, A. W., Melloy-Carminar, P., & Bridger, W. H. (1982). Familiarity and novelty preferences in infant recognition memory: Implications for information processing. *Developmental Psychology, 18*, 704–713.

Rose, S. A., Jankowski, J. J., & Feldman, J. F. (2002). Speed of processing and face recognition at 7 and 12 months. *Infancy, 3*(4), 435–455.

Rose, S. A., Jankowski, J. J., & Senior, G. J. (1997). Infants' recognition of contour-deleted figures. *Journal of Experimental Psychology: Human Perception and Performance, 23*(4), 1206–1216.

Rose, S. A., & Orlian, E. K. (2001). Visual information processing. In L. T. Singer & P. S. Zeskind (Eds.), *Biobehavioral assessment of the infant*. New York: Guilford.

Rose, S. A., & Tamis-Lemonda, C. S. (1999). Visual information processing in infancy: Reflections on underlying mechanisms. In L. Balter & C. S. Tamis-Lemonda (Eds.), *Child psychology: A handbook of contemporary issues* (pp. 64–84). Philadelphia: Psychology Press.

Rovee-Collier, C., Hayne, H., & Colombo, M. (2001). *The development of implicit and explicit memory*. Philadelphia: John Benjamins.

Rubenstein, A. J., Kalakanis, L., & Langlois, J. H. (1999). Infant preferences for attractive faces: A cognitive explanation. *Developmental Psychology, 35*, 848–855.

Ruff, H. A. (1975). The function of shifting fixations in the visual perception of infants. *Child Development, 46*, 657–865.

Schacter, D. L., & Tulving, E. (1994). What are the memory systems of 1994? In D. L. Schacter & E. Tulving (Eds.), *Memory Systems 1994* (pp. 1–38). Cambridge, MA: MIT Press.

Scoville, W. B., & Milner, B. (1957). Loss of recent memory after bilateral hippocampal lesions. *Journal of Neurology, Neurosurgery and Psychiatry, 20*, 11–21.

Seress, L. (2001). Morphological changes of the human hippocampal formation from midgestation to early childhood. In C. A. Nelson & M. Luciana (Eds.), *Handbook of developmental cognitive neuroscience* (pp. 45–58). Cambridge, MA: MIT Press.

Shanks, D. R. (1997). Representation of categories and concepts in memory. In M. A. Conway (Ed.), *Cognitive models of memory* (pp. 111–146). Cambridge, MA: MIT Press.

Sherman, T. (1985). Categorization skills in infants. *Child Development, 56,* 1561–1573.

Skouteris, H., McKenzie, B. E., & Day, R. H. (1992). Integration of sequential information for shape perception by infants: A developmental study. *Child Development, 63,* 1164–1176.

Slater, A., Morison, V., & Rose, D. H. (1984). Habituation of the newborn. *Infant Behavior and Development, 7,* 183–200.

Slobin, D. I. (1985). Cross-linguistic evidence for the language-making capacity. In D. I. Slobin (Ed.), *The cross-linguistic study of language acquisition* (Vol. 2, pp. 1157–1256). Hillsdale, NJ: Erlbaum.

Sokolov, E. N. (1963). *Perception and the conditioned reflex.* Oxford, UK: Pergamon.

Squire, L. R. (1987). *Memory and brain.* New York: Oxford University Press.

Stark, C. E. L., & Squire, L. R. (2000). fMRI activity in the medial temporal lobe during recognition memory as a function of study-test interval. *Hippocampus, 10,* 329–337.

Tulving, E. (1985). How many memory systems are there? *American Psychologist, 40,* 385–398.

Wagner, S. H., & Sakovits, L. J. (1986). A process analysis of infant visual and cross-modal recognition memory: Implications for an amodal code. In L. P. Lipsitt & C. K. Rovee-Collier (Eds.), *Advances in infancy research* (Vol. 4, pp. 195–217). Norwood, NJ: Ablex.

Warrington, E., & Weiskrantz, L. (1970). Amnesia: Consolidation or retrieval? *Nature, 228,* 628–630.

Zola, S. M., & Squire, L. R. (2000). The medial temporal lobe and the hippocampus. In E. Tulving & F. I. M. Craik (Eds.), *The Oxford handbook of memory.* New York: Oxford University Press.

Zola, S. M., Squire, L. R., Teng, E., Stefanacci, L., & Buffalo, E. J. (2000). Impaired recognition memory in monkeys after damage limited to the hippocampal region. *Journal of Neuroscience, 20*(1), 451–463.

8

Neural Mechanisms of Attention and Memory in Preferential Looking Tasks

KELLY A. SNYDER

The Visual Paired Comparison Task: A Measure of Explicit Memory?

The term *preferential looking* refers to a class of behavioral methods that rely on an infant's inherent preference for viewing novel stimuli (i.e., novelty preferences) to provide evidence for learning, memory, or discrimination. Despite wide use of these tasks across different domains of development, there is a long history of debate about how to interpret infants' performance in preferential looking tasks (e.g., Bogartz, Shinskey, & Speaker, 1997). For instance, to what extent do novelty preferences reflect knowledge that the infant has brought to the experiment versus knowledge acquired during the course of the experiment? What is the nature of this knowledge? Is the infant conscious or aware of such knowledge? Does the infant have access to this knowledge for further reasoning and reflection? How flexible is this knowledge, and to what extent can the infant generalize this knowledge across different contexts? One approach to resolving this debate has been to investigate whether the neurobiology underlying novelty preferences reflects brain systems involved in explicit or implicit memory.

The task most widely investigated using this approach has been the visual paired comparison (VPC). By current accounts, the VPC is considered a measure of infants' visual recognition memory (see chapter 7, this volume). I refer to this as the explicit memory hypothesis of novelty preferences. This view holds that there is a one-to-one mapping between the task (VPC) and a competency (i.e., recognition memory), such that infants' performance in the VPC reflects memory per se. That is, despite the fact that look duration is an indirect measure of memory, and memory for a familiar stimulus is most often inferred from longer looking at a novel stimulus, visual preferences are treated as a direct measure of memory (i.e., recognition of the familiar stimulus), and null preferences (equal looking at the novel and familiar stimulus) are treated as failures of memory. As a consequence, developmental differences in infants' performance in the VPC are typically attributed to the development of a single underlying competency, namely recognition memory. Since the VPC can be used with both adults and preverbal infants, such a one-to-one mapping between the VPC and recognition memory would provide researchers with a procedure in which memory could be studied across the life span.

In this chapter, I would like to propose an alternative way of thinking about infants' performance in the VPC. Specifically, instead of interpreting visual preferences as a direct measure of memory, and recognition memory in particular, I would like to propose that infants' performance in the VPC reflects the interaction between visual attention and memory. This view differs from the former in several respects. First, memory is viewed as only one of many processes that may influence infants' performance in the VPC. The implication here is that memory interacts with other processes (e.g., goals, affect, etc.) in guiding visual attention, and so may not always determine visual preferences. Second, the term *memory* in this view does not refer to a specific memory subsystem, such as recognition or explicit memory, but memory in a broader sense as it is implemented in different ways throughout the brain. Thus, while top-down, goal-directed processes over which we have deliberate and voluntary control may guide visual attention in some circumstances, so do bottom-up, automatic processes of which we may be unaware and do not have voluntary control. Third, the goals of the visual attention system are considered to provide an important constraint on the extent to which memory, and indeed what kind of memory, guides visual attention in any particular situation. Thus, in contrast to the explicit memory hypothesis of novelty preferences, I propose that repetition suppression in the visual processing pathway, a phenomenon thought to underlie implicit memory, may direct visual attention toward novel stimuli in preferential looking tasks.

Forms of Memory or Memory Systems?

Graf and Schacter (1985) originally used the terms *explicit* and *implicit* to refer to different forms of memory, as well as the tests that were used to measure them. Explicit memory refers to the ability to deliberately retrieve, or consciously recollect, facts, events, and prior experiences, and is measured by direct tasks that require intentional retrieval such as recall and recognition tests. Implicit memory, on the other hand, refers to facilitation or changes in behavior resulting from involuntary retrieval of prior experience in the absence of conscious awareness and is usually measured by indirect or incidental tests such as word stem completion and repetition priming. It is important to note that these two different forms of memory may simply reflect different retrieval circumstances and do no necessarily imply multiple memory systems in the brain (Schacter & Tulving, 1994).

The task demands of the VPC would appear to make it an implicit memory task, for the simple reason that subjects are not instructed to refer back to a prior study episode, yet prior experience clearly influences their response. There is no evidence that subjects' performance in the task requires deliberate or intentional behavior of any kind, nor is there a way of testing whether infants experience conscious awareness during the test phase of the task. Of course, the lack of evidence for deliberate or intentional retrieval is not itself evidence for the absence of such phenomena. This leads us to a problem at the heart of much research in memory development: Could the VPC measure deliberate, conscious retrieval of information despite the absence of instructions to do so? If so, how can we determine if this is the case? One approach that researchers have used to resolve this problem is to take a memory systems approach to understanding infants' performance in the VPC.

According to most contemporary views of memory, memory consists of multiple systems (but see Roediger, Weldon, & Challis, 1989). The most common nomenclature proposes a primary distinction between explicit (or declarative) and implicit (or nondeclarative) memory systems (e.g., Nelson, 1995; Squire, 1994). The explicit or declarative memory system comprises both semantic (memory for facts) and episodic (memory for personal experiences) memory and is thought to be subserved by a cortico-limbic-diencephalic circuit that includes the hippocampus, entorhinal cortex, anterior and medial-dorsal nuclei of the thalamus, mamillary bodies, ventromedial prefrontal cortex, and modality-specific higher-order areas of the cortex such as visual area TE. The implicit or nondeclarative memory system, on the other hand, comprises multiple independent processes and neural subsystems. Perceptual priming, for example, is thought to reflect experience-induced changes in a cortically based, presemantic perceptual representation system (PRS; e.g., Schacter, Wagner, & Buckner, 2000), whereas procedural memory is thought to depend on a cortical-striatal system.

Evaluation of the Explicit Memory Hypothesis of Novelty Preferences

At the heart of the distinction between explicit and implicit memory is the issue of conscious awareness (Schacter, 1998). Despite researchers' lack of agreement on how to define consciousness (see Willingham & Preuss, 1995), adults' ability to accurately report whether an item occurred during a prior study episode is generally accepted as evidence of conscious awareness and distinguishes explicit from implicit forms of memory. This presents a formidable challenge for the study of early memory development, since infants cannot understand verbal instructions to report their recollective experiences.

Thus, researchers must employ other criteria for distinguishing between explicit and implicit memory in infants. One approach, therefore, has been to focus on the dissociation between brain systems that support explicit and implicit memory in adults.

Using this approach, several researchers have proposed that the VPC is a measure of explicit/declarative or preexplicit memory (McKee & Squire, 1993; Nelson, 1995; Pascalis & Bachevalier, 1999; but see Schacter & Moscovitch, 1984). Evidence from several sources has appeared to support this view, including studies involving amnesic patients, lesion studies of nonhuman primates, and behavioral studies of adults. Much of this evidence has been interpreted as providing support for the view that performance in the VPC depends disproportionately on the hippocampus (see Nelson, 1995; Pascalis & Bachevalier, 1999). A critical evaluation of the evidence from these studies, however, suggests that the hippocampus may not be critical for successful performance in the task.

Neuropsychological Evidence

McKee and Squire (1993) were the first to report that amnesic patients with medial-temporal lobe damage were impaired in the VPC. They found that amnesic patients were impaired, relative to controls, in the VPC at delays of 2 minutes and 1 hour,[1] and concluded that performance in the VPC likely reflects a form of declarative memory mediated by the medial-temporal lobe memory system.

One problem in concluding, from this study, that infants' performance in the VPC is mediated by the hippocampus is that neurological damage in these patients was not confined to the hippocampus. Of the 11 patients tested in this study, only 4 had some degree of hippocampal damage. Four other patients had Korsakoff's syndrome, resulting in damage to the mammillary nuclei, thalamus, and frontal lobes; one patient had bilateral damage to the thalamus; and the remaining two patients were never scanned and so had damage of an unknown locus. Thus, the pattern of impairment observed in these patients cannot be specifically attributed to the hippocampus.

In a more recent study, Pascalis and colleagues tested a patient with discrete hippocampal damage (patient YR) in the VPC at delays of 0, 5, and 10 seconds. YR performed as well as controls at the 0-second delay but was impaired relative to controls at delays of 5 and 10 seconds (Pascalis, Hunkin, Holdstock, Issac, & Mayes, 2004). In a forced-choice recognition memory test, however, YR performed as well as controls at all delays.[2] Based on these findings, the authors argued that performance in the VPC depends on the integrity of the hippocampus, and that the VPC may "provide an indirect index of the ability to show *aware* recognition of studied stimuli" (Pascalis et al., 2004, p. 1294).

The finding that YR was impaired in the VPC at 5-second delays is puzzling given that amnesic patients in McKee and Squire's (1993) study exhibited significant novelty preferences after a 2-minute delay, and recent lesion studies in nonhuman primates (reviewed in the next section) have shown that discrete hippocampal damage does not produce impairments in the VPC at delays less than 1 minute. One possibility is that YR's hippocampal damage was significantly more extensive than that of amnesic patients and nonhuman primates in other studies, and that spared hippocampal tissue in the latter two groups accounts for their enhanced performance relative to YR. Another possibility, however, is that YR's impairment in the VPC is the result of her parietal lobe atrophy. An important function of the parietal lobe is the integration of perceptual information with eye movement plans (Colby, Duhamel, & Goldberg, 1996), a function that may be particularly important for guiding visual attention in the VPC. Considering that YR had no trouble verbally identifying the familiar stimuli in the recognition task, it is possible that YR's impairment in the VPC was the result of disruptions in the integration of stimulus information and visual attention caused by the damage to her parietal lobe.

An important question about the studies reviewed above is whether findings about the neural basis of adults' performance in the VPC generalize to infants. Inferences about the neural basis of infants' performance on the VPC from studies of adults depend on the assumption that the VPC measures the same process in both infants and adults. This assumption is only warranted if (a) the task used with infants and adults is equivalent, and (b) the performance of infants and adults on the task is comparable. Otherwise, there is no reason to suppose that infants and adults are engaging the same cognitive processes, and hence neural circuits, to perform the task.

The task used in the adult studies reviewed above, however, differs from the infant version of the VPC in several respects that may be especially important for interpreting effects of medial-temporal lobe lesions. First, there are differences in the number of items that must be encoded in the infant and adult versions of the VPC. Infants are typically familiarized to a single stimulus, whereas McKee and Squire (1993) required participants to encode 24 different stimuli during the encoding phase of the task. Similarly, Pascalis et al. (2004) tested subjects in 72 trials administered in four sessions over a 1-month period. Thus, the procedures that have been used with adults are much more susceptible to proactive and retroactive interference than the procedure typically used with infants. Second, adults were exposed to each stimulus for a brief period of time (i.e., 5 seconds), whereas the encoding phase in many VPC studies with infants is longer (e.g., 10–20 seconds) and can be as long as several minutes. Third, differences in semantic memory between adults and infants likely affect the way that stimuli are encoded in the first place. Infant studies have used stimuli ranging from abstract patterns to photographs of faces and everyday objects. Depending on the age and experience of the infant, the infant may not have encountered the stimulus before participating in the VPC. In any case, the infant does not likely have a rich semantic representation for the stimulus that would include things such as verbal labels, functions, relations to other objects, and so on. The stimuli used in the adult studies reviewed above, on the other hand, have been pictures of everyday scenes or common objects that adults can readily name, and for which adults have rich semantic representations. Since semantic memory is considered a form of explicit memory, this may represent another fundamental difference in the kinds of processes and representations available to adults compared to infants during encoding.

Thus, differences in the number of stimuli encoded, familiarization times, and semantic memory likely make the nature of the encoding tasks fundamentally different for adults and infants. Critically, encoding in the adult studies but not the infant studies appears to involve (a) interleaved learning (i.e., concurrent learning of multiple stimuli); (b) rapid, single-trial learning (due to the very brief study times); and (c) interactions with pre-existing semantic representations. These encoding circumstances are consistent with proposed hippocampal functioning, which may explain findings that amnesic patients or patients with hippocampal damage are impaired in the adult VPC task. The typical infant VPC, on the other hand, does not seem to require interleaved or rapid, single-trial learning. It is possible, therefore, that the processes and neural circuits underlying infant performance in the VPC may be different from the processes and neural circuits that underlie adults performance in studies using variants of the VPC procedure. Thus, the results of neuropsychological studies of adults may not generalize to infants.

Evidence from Lesion Studies in Nonhuman Primates

Evidence for the explicit memory hypothesis of novelty preferences has also come from lesion studies in nonhuman primates. Early studies showed that large medial-temporal lobe lesions led to impaired performance in the VPC in both infant and mature monkeys at short delays (e.g., Bachevalier, Brickson, & Hagger, 1993), leading to the hypothesis that novelty preferences depend on the hippocampus. It is important to note, however, that the lesions in these early studies encompassed the entire medial-temporal lobe system (i.e., hippocampal formation, entorhinal cortex, perirhinal cortex, and parahippocampal gyrus), as well as the amygdala, so the impairments observed in these animals may not have been caused by damage to the hippocampus per se.

Further studies initially appeared to support the hypothesis that performance in the VPC depended on the hippocampus. Pascalis and Bachevalier (1999) reported that adult monkeys with neonatal aspiration lesions of the hippocampal formation (including the hippocampal cell fields, dentate gyrus, subicular complex, and portions of the parahippocampal gyrus) showed intact performance in the VPC at short delays (10 seconds) but impaired performance relative to controls at longer delays (from 30 seconds to 24 hours). In addition, Zola, Squire, Teng, Stefanacci, and Buffalo (2000) reported that adult monkeys with selective hippocampal lesions (including the hippocampal cell fields, dentate gyrus, and subiculum) showed intact performance in the VPC at 1-second delays but impaired performance relative to controls at delays of 10 seconds, 1 minute, and 10 minutes.[3] One problem with the latter study, however, was that these animals sustained unintended damage to the caudate nucleus that was significantly more extensive (i.e., 38–73%) than the intentional damage to the hippocampus (24% and 33%). This is a critical confound since it raises the question of whether deficits in these animals can be attributed to the medial-temporal lobe system or a cortical-striatal circuit supporting implicit memory.

More recently, Nemanic, Alvarado, and Bachevalier (2004) reported that lesions to different structures within the medial-temporal lobe system impair performance in the VPC in a delay-dependent manner. In this study, perirhinal lesions impaired performance at delays greater than 10 seconds, and parahippocampal lesions impaired performance at delays of 30 seconds or more, but hippocampal lesions did not produce deficits until delays reached 60 seconds. These findings may help explain impairments observed at short delays in the studies reviewed above. For instance, the lesions produced in very early studies encompassed all of these structures (hippocampus, perirhinal cortex, parahippocampal gyrus), suggesting that the impairments observed at short delays were most likely due to damage to perirhinal cortex and not the hippocampus. Similarly, since hippocampal lesions do not appear to create deficits at delays shorter than 60 seconds, the impairment observed at 30-second delays by Pascalis and Bachevalier is most likely due to the inclusion of the parahippocampal area in the lesion and not the hippocampus per se.

Thus, it appears that damage to medial-temporal lobe structures does impair performance in the VPC in adult monkeys, but that the hippocampus is only critical at longer delays. This raises an important point: Performance in the VPC under different delay conditions may be supported by different neural structures. Furthermore, lesions to medial-temporal lobe structures do not impair performance in the VPC at immediate or very short delays. The implication for infant memory research is that immediate performance in the VPC may not depend on the medial-temporal lobe at all. Although damage to visual area TE, a structure implicated in visual perceptual processing, produces impairments in the VPC at very short delays in adult monkeys, the same lesion has no effect on infant monkeys' performance in the VPC (Buffalo et al., 1999; Haggar, Brickson, & Bachevalier, 1985). Thus, there are currently no data regarding the neural structures that may support immediate performance in the VPC in infants.

Given the findings that damage to the medial-temporal lobe system does impair performance in the VPC in adult monkeys, it is tempting to conclude that novelty preferences do, in fact, reflect some form of explicit memory, at least when a long enough delay is imposed between study and test.

Before reaching this conclusion, however, another point is worth consideration: This evidence is based on studies of adult animals. Given changes in the
anatomical and functional maturity of many of the medial-temporal lobe
structures during development, as well as changes in connections between
medial-temporal lobe and other cortical structures, the circuits (and hence
processes) underlying performance in the VPC may change with development. Thus, lesion studies in adult animals ultimately may not inform our understanding of the neurobiology underlying novelty preferences in infants.

Unfortunately, very few studies have examined the neurobiology of VPC
performance in infant monkeys. Early lesion studies reported that infant
monkeys with bilateral medial-temporal lobe lesions failed to show novelty
preferences at short delays (10 seconds) (Bachevalier et al., 1993; Saunders
et al., 1991). The lesions in these early studies, however, encompassed the
entire medial-temporal lobe system as well as the amygdala. Unfortunately,
there have been no studies examining the specific role of these structures in
infant monkeys' performance in the VPC.

Behavioral Evidence

A final source of evidence for the explicit memory hypothesis comes from
a single behavioral study in human adults. Manns, Stark, and Squire (2000)
investigated the relation between preferential looking in the VPC and recognition memory in healthy adults. They found that preferential looking
scores 5 minutes after encoding were correlated with confidence ratings of
recognized items after a 24-hour delay, and concluded that the VPC is a
measure of recognition memory. Note, however, that the task used in this
study had many of the same problems noted earlier. That is, subjects were
given 5 seconds of exposure to each of 24 different colored pictures of common objects during the encoding phase, after which they were tested for
their memory of all 24 objects. Thus, the encoding demands of this task may
reflect processes related to explicit encoding, explaining the correlation
between VPC performance and recognition memory.

An important question about this experiment is the extent to which the
relation between preferential looking and confidence judgments can be
attributed to recognition memory, given that neither recognition accuracy nor
response times were correlated with visual preferences. Snyder (2003) examined the relation between preferential looking scores and confidence judgments in an implicit memory task (i.e., a preference judgments) and found
that preferential looking scores were correlated with confidence judgments in
this task as well. Thus, the relation between preferential looking scores and
confidence judgments may not reflect any particular kind of memory.

In contrast to the evidence for a relation between preferential looking and
recognition memory reviewed above, there is evidence to suggest that adults
recognize stimuli for which they fail to show a novelty preference. For example, McKee and Squire (1993) found that healthy adults did not show novelty
preferences after retention intervals longer 1 hour, yet Manns et al. (2000)

found high recognition accuracy (approximately 84%) for stimuli encountered during the study phase of the VPC after a 24-hour delay. Snyder (2003) examined this pattern directly and found high recognition accuracy (85%) after a 24-hour delay despite no preference in looking behavior in adults. If novelty preferences reflect explicit recognition of the familiar stimulus, then why would novelty preferences and recognition accuracy be dissociated by delay interval? These observations make an explicit memory account of novelty preferences difficult to reconcile with conventional views of recognition memory.

Summary

In summary, the neuropsychological and behavioral evidence from human adults does not fully support the hypothesis that novelty preferences reflect a form of explicit memory dependent on the hippocampus. Patients with amnesia and nonhuman primates with damage to the hippocampus succeed in the VPC when the delay is short. Since damage to the hippocampus in these populations is never absolute, one possibility is that novelty preferences obtained under these conditions are supported by spared tissue. Another possibility is that novelty preferences per se do not depend on the hippocampus, and so the hippocampus is not necessary for novelty preferences. In addition, since adult monkeys with cortical but not hippocampal lesions are also impaired in the VPC, it would appear that the hippocampus is also not sufficient for novelty preferences. These observations argue against a primary role for the hippocampus in preferential looking.

Repetition Suppression in the Occipitotemporal Visual Processing Pathway and Its Role in Visual Attention

Earlier I proposed that the bias toward novelty in preferential looking paradigms reflects an interaction between visual attention and memory. In fact, the preferential processing of new or not recently seen stimuli appears to be an inherent bias of the visual system (Desimone & Duncan, 1995). This bias appears to be mediated by a reduction of neuronal responses in the occipital-temporal visual processing pathway with stimulus repetition, a phenomenon known as repetition suppression. Repetition suppression appears to be an intrinsic property of the visual cortex, as repeated exposure to the same visual stimulus leads to both short- and long-term suppression of neuronal responses to the stimulus (Desimone, 1996). Repetition suppression has been observed in cellular recordings in nonhuman primates (Fahy, Riches, & Brown, 1993; Li, Miller, & Desimone, 1993; Miller, Gochin, & Gross, 1991; Riches, Wilson, & Brown, 1991), as well as event-related potential (ERP) studies (e.g., Begleiter, Porjesz, & Wang, 1993) and brain imaging studies (e.g., Squire et al., 1992) in humans.

Desimone (1996) has proposed that repetition suppression reflects learning about the critical features of a stimulus. As a stimulus is repeated, the population of neurons responding to the stimulus becomes smaller. This decrease in the population of neurons activated by a repeated stimulus reflects a reduction in the responses of cells that were initially activated but were not selective for the features of the stimulus (Li et al., 1993). Thus, repetition suppression may reflect neuronal "tuning" to stimulus features. This type of stimulus memory is considered to be independent of hippocampal functioning and has been found to be long lasting (Fahy et al., 1993; Li et al., 1993), thus providing a plausible alternative to the hypothesized role of the hippocampus in visual preferences. Repetition suppression also occurs during passive fixation (Miller, Gochin, et al., 1991) and in anesthetized monkeys (Vogels, Sary, & Orban, 1995), suggesting that deliberate or voluntary control over visual attention is not necessary for learning to occur. Furthermore, brain imaging studies of humans suggest that repetition suppression plays a role in repetition priming, a form of implicit memory (Buckner et al., 1995; Squire et al., 1992; Ungerleider, 1995).

This model of how memory and visual attention interact suggests a plausible alternative to the hypothesis that novelty preferences depend on the hippocampus and reflect a form of recognition memory. In theory, the reduction in activation to a repeated stimulus would bias the competition for visual processing resources, and hence visual attention, toward a novel stimulus. This is supported by evidence that repetition suppression is sufficient to produce orienting to a novel stimulus in monkeys (Desimone, Miller, Chelazzi, & Lueschow, 1994; Li et al., 1993). Furthermore, since repetition suppression is thought to occur independently of the hippocampus, and has been implicated in perceptual priming, it may account for the observation that patients with amnesia and nonhuman primates with lesions of the medial-temporal lobe succeed in the VPC when the delay is short. Thus, novelty preferences may reflect the effects of repetition suppression on visual attention, independent of the hippocampus.

An important implication of this model is that longer looking to a novel stimulus is merely a consequence of reduced neural responses to previously encoded elements; it does not require explicit awareness, voluntary or deliberate control, or even a comparison between new and previously encoded elements. Thus, memory for a familiar stimulus may influence visual attention in a very indirect sense (i.e., in that the neural activity elicited by the familiar stimulus is reduced, and hence loses the competition for visual attentional resources). In this model, then, memory is an indirect, incidental influence on visual preferences.

The Functional Significance of Preferential Looking

Earlier I proposed that the goals of the visual attention system are an important constraint on the extent to which memory guides visual attention in preferential looking tasks. Understanding these goals may help us to understand otherwise puzzling findings. For instance, if we assume that preferential looking is a direct measure of either memory or discrimination, as most research using the VPC appears to, then the observation that adults show null preferences in the face of intact memory is puzzling. In contrast, if we view preferential looking as merely influenced by memory, but not determined by it, then these findings do not appear contradictory. One implication of this latter view is that the primary function of look duration in preferential looking tasks is not memory or discrimination per se.

Roediger (2003) has argued that although a system may exhibit characteristics of memory, it does not necessarily mean that memory defines the function of the system. An example proposed by Roediger may help clarify this idea: The immune system exhibits characteristics of memory (broadly defined) that are important to the operation of the system, but this does not lead to the conclusion that the immune system exists to perform memory. Instead, the goal of the immune system is to mount a defense against disease. Consequently, one would not consider measures of the relative amounts of antibodies in blood serum a direct measure of memory, since other factors would also contribute to antibody production. Thus, while visual attention in preferential looking tasks clearly exhibits characteristics of memory, it may not be appropriate to define the function of preferential looking in terms of memory per se.

This leads to the question, what are the goals of the visual attention system? As a starting point, it seems reasonable to suppose that the goals of the visual attention system are linked to survival. In order to survive, an organism must be able to interact with and respond to its environment in appropriate ways. At the very least, it must be able to obtain food and avoid harm or predators. This requires the ability to detect (or possibly seek out) things in the environment, make appropriate evaluations (is this food or enemy?), and execute (or fail to inhibit) an appropriate response (eat or run). In this context, it is interesting to note that change is an inherent property of the visual environment, and preferential processing of new or not recently seen stimuli (i.e., change) is an inherent bias of the visual system. Thus, orienting to novel stimuli and the decrement in visual fixation following sufficient exposure to a stimulus that underlies both habituation and novelty preferences may function to distribute attention across events in the environment (for similar arguments, see also Sokolov, 1963). This has clear and obvious adaptive value in that it enables an organism to disengage from irrelevant events in order to alert and respond to relevant ones (e.g., a predator nearby).

Thus, one goal of the visual attention system may be to direct our processing of environmental input to objects and events that have behavioral significance. This suggests an answer to the question posed earlier. That is, adults may fail to show a preference in the VPC despite intact memory for the familiar stimulus because the familiar stimulus has no particular biological significance or relevance to ongoing behavior. This suggests that unlike a recognition memory task, in which the mnemonic status of the stimulus is most relevant in guiding the response, the recency of the information is more relevant in guiding visual attention when there are no explicit task demands (such as in the VPC) and the stimuli are of no inherent interest.

Preferential Looking Procedures: Challenges, Limitations, and Recent Advances

There are two basic preferential looking procedures: habituation-dishabituation, and the VPC. These procedures both rely on the infant's inherent preference for viewing novel stimuli to provide evidence for learning, memory, or discrimination (for a detailed description of these procedures, see chapter 7, this volume). Due to the difference in the test phases of the two procedures, however, the VPC is generally considered to be (a) more sensitive to subtler differences between the familiar and novel stimuli, since the infant may actively compare the two stimuli simultaneously (Cohen & Gelber, 1975); and (b) an easier test of recognition memory since it provides perceptual support for the comparison process. Thus, despite the fact that both paradigms rely on the same dependent measure (i.e., proportion of looking to a novel stimulus) to provide evidence for memory, it is not clear that they engage the same exact cognitive processes. Furthermore, all of the research examining the neural basis of novelty preferences has used the VPC. Thus, our understanding of the neurobiology underlying preferential looking from these studies may not generalize to infants' performance in the habituation-dishabituation procedure.

Challenges and Limitations

One important limitation of preferential looking procedures for the study of infant memory is that there does not appear to be an unambiguous measure of forgetting. Null preferences do not necessarily reflect memory loss since (a) null findings are inconclusive, and (b) memory is confounded with novelty preference in these procedures: The infant must both remember the familiar stimulus and prefer to fixate the novel stimulus (Sophian, 1980). Thus, developmental or group differences in performance may result from differences in either memory or interest, or both. Similarly, null preferences following a delay may result from renewed interest in the familiar stimulus rather than memory loss, and age-related differences in retention may result from changes to preferences as well as memory. Despite these observations, most of the research on age-related differences in memory, as well as recent research on the neural correlates of performance in the VPC involving amnesic patients and nonhuman primates, assumes that null preferences reflect memory loss or impairment.

A significant challenge in using these procedures to study memory development is that many of the parameters, such as length of familiarization and complexity of the stimuli, interact such that certain values of these parameters may be optimal for producing novelty preferences with infants at different ages. For this reason, spurious trends may result when using the same parameter values with infants of different ages, or the same length of familiarization with different stimuli in infants of the same age (Clifton & Nelson, 1976). Thus, our use of these procedures to study change across development is limited, in part, by our lack of knowledge about the relation between procedural parameters, stimulus conditions, and infant variables.

Recent Advances: Electrophysiological Studies with Infants

It is very difficult to dissociate explicit and implicit memory in infants since (a) measures that dissociate these forms of memory tend to rely disproportionately on verbal abilities not present in infants, and (b) brain imaging techniques with the requisite spatial resolution (e.g., fMRI) to assess the participation of neural structures that dissociate different forms of memory (e.g., the hippocampus vs. the striatum) are not feasible for use with infants participating in visual paradigms at this time. One brain imaging method that is appropriate for use with young infants, however, is ERPs.

ERPs reflect the synchronous firing of neuronal populations in response to a discrete event (such as the presentation of a stimulus). They are recorded from electrodes placed on the scalp, are derived from the electroencephalogram, and provide excellent temporal resolution (on the order of milliseconds) of ongoing cognitive processes. There are numerous advantages to using ERPs to study cognitive development. They are noninvasive, do not require the subject to remain motionless for long periods of time, and do not require a behavioral response by the subject. Furthermore, the spatial and temporal information provided by ERPs permits the differentiation of cognitive processes that may not be directly reflected in behavior.

Two major components are typically observed in the infant ERP (see Figure 8.1): a middle-latency negative component (Nc) that peaks between 400 and 800 milliseconds following stimulus onset and is commonly observed over frontocentral scalp regions, and a long-latency slow-wave component that begins around 1,000 milliseconds following stimulus onset and is commonly observed to be maximal over temporal scalp regions. The Nc is thought to reflect aspects of attention and orienting, and the slow wave is thought to reflect aspects of memory (see Nelson, 1994, for review). Since looking time measures reflect the influence of memory on visual attention, ERPs may be especially useful in investigating the neural basis of infants' performance on preferential looking tasks.

Effects of Repetition on Infant Brain Activity

Given the hypothesis that novelty preferences reflect the influence of repetition suppression in the visual processing pathway on visual attention, one

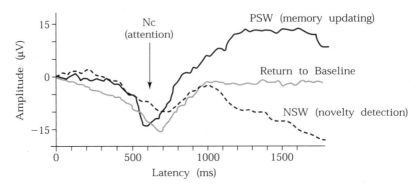

FIGURE 8.1. Illustration of the major ERP components observed in previous ERP studies with infants. Nc, negative component; NSW, negative slow wave; PSW, positive slow wave. Adapted from de Haan and Nelson (1997).

starting point is to examine the effects of stimulus repetition on infant brain activity. Thus, we contrasted the repetition of a familiar stimulus with the repetition of a novel stimulus (Snyder, Webb, & Nelson, 2002). One goal was to see if we would find evidence of repetition suppression using ERPs, and whether repetition effects would be different for familiar versus novel stimuli.

In this study, 6-month-old infants passively viewed alternating pictures of their mother's face and a female stranger's face on a computer screen while their brain activity was recorded. We compared infants' brain activity in response to the first 15 presentations of each face (Block 1) and the second 15 presentations of each face (Block 2). This design allowed us to dissociate memory (i.e., novel vs. familiar) from stimulus repetition (i.e., Block 1 vs. Block 2). We found that the amplitude of the slow wave decreased with repetition for both the familiar and novel face (see Figures 8.2 and 8.3). Thus, repetition of both familiar and novel faces resulted in the reduction of brain activity over temporal scalp regions, a finding consistent with the phenomenon of repetition suppression in the visual processing pathway.

Intracellular recordings in nonhuman primates have shown a functional distinction between repetition suppression in different parts of the visual processing pathway. Specifically, lateral inferotemporal cortex (e.g., visual area TE) exhibits reduced responses for both novel and highly familiar stimuli, whereas perirhinal cortex exhibits reduced responses for novel stimuli only (Baylis & Rolls, 1987; Li et al., 1993; Miller, Li, & Desimone, 1991). Based on these findings, Desimone and colleagues have suggested that lateral inferotemporal cortex may encode and maintain a representation of the immediate visual environment, whereas perirhinal cortex may primarily encode new information. The finding that repetition resulted in reduced brain activity over temporal regions for both novel and familiar faces is consistent

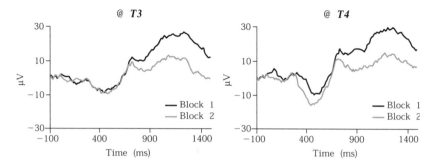

FIGURE 8.2. Grand mean ERP waveforms for Block 1 and Block 2 illustrating the reduction in amplitude of the positive slow wave with repetition. Responses to the familiar and novel face are combined for each block.

with observations of repetition suppression in lateral inferotemporal cortex, suggesting that this effect may reflect the incidental encoding of the visual scene into a perceptual store rather than the encoding of new information per se. This would explain why responses to the mother's face, for which the infant already has extensive experience, exhibited the same effect of repetition as the stranger's face.

Relation Between Infant Brain Activity During Encoding and Preferential Looking at Test

The results of Snyder et al. (2002) reviewed above help to establish evidence of repetition suppression in infants. In a recent study, we examined the relation between infant brain activity during the encoding of a novel stimulus and looking behavior at test (Snyder, Stolarova, & Nelson, 2006).

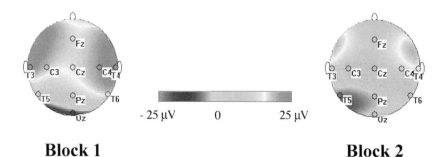

FIGURE 8.3. Topographic plots showing the scalp distribution of the positive slow wave (PSW) for Block 1 and Block 2. The PSW is shown as patches of red over the left and right temporal regions when it is maximal (at 1,250 ms). See color plates.

In addition, we examined whether this relation would be the same or different for faces and objects. This study allowed us to test hypotheses about the neurobiology underlying infant novelty preferences, since the explicit memory hypothesis and repetition suppression hypothesis make different predictions about the observed relation between brain activity during encoding and preferential looking at test.

Both intracellular recordings in nonhuman primates and neuroimaging studies in human adults have shown that recognition is associated with an increase in neural responses in the medial-temporal lobe and prefrontal cortex, whereas priming is associated with a decrease in neural responses in posterior visual areas (Buckner et al., 1998; Schacter & Wagner, 1999; Wagner, Gabrieli, Desmond, & Glover, 1998). Thus, the explicit memory hypothesis would predict that novelty preferences would be associated with increased amplitudes of ERP components over temporal and frontal regions, whereas the repetition-suppression hypothesis would predict that novelty preferences would be associated with decreased amplitudes of components located over posterior and occipitotemporal regions.

In this study, 6-month-olds' brain activity was recorded using a high-density electrode cap during the encoding of a novel object. At test, the familiar and a novel stimulus were presented serially, and the infant was allowed one continuous look at each stimulus. The relation between brain activity at encoding and preferential looking was examined by comparing the ERPs of infants who showed a novelty preference at test (i.e., novelty score ≥55%) and infants who showed a familiarity preference at test (i.e., novelty score ≤55%). Too few infants showed a null preference for further analysis.

The ERP components that showed effects of preference differed for faces and objects. Novelty preferences for faces were associated with a reduction in the amplitude of neural activity over temporal scalp regions (see Figure 8.4),

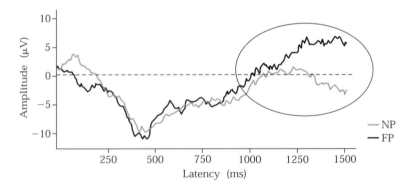

FIGURE 8.4. Grand mean ERP waveforms for infants who showed a novelty preference at test (NP) and infants who showed a familiarity preference at test (FP) at a representative temporal electrode in the vicinity of T3.

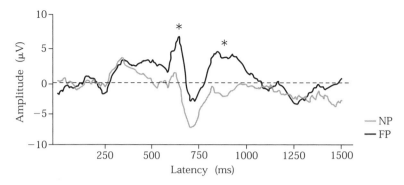

FIGURE 8.5. Grand mean ERP waveforms for infants who showed a novelty preference at test (NP) and infants who showed a familiarity preference at test (FP) at a representative occipitotemporal electrode. Asterisks are shown directly above components that are significantly different between conditions.

and novelty preferences for objects were associated with a reduction in the amplitude of neural activity over occipital-temporal scalp regions (see Figure 8.5). The observed reduction in neural activity over temporal and occipital scalp regions associated with novelty preferences is consistent with the hypothesis that novelty preferences reflect the influence of repetition suppression in the visual processing pathway on visual attention in infants and may thus reflect a form of implicit memory.

Null Preferences Do Not Reflect Memory Loss

Just as novelty preferences are typically interpreted as evidence for recognition of the familiar stimulus, null preferences are typically interpreted as a failure of memory or discrimination. As I noted earlier, however, a null preference may not reflect memory loss, since memory and interest are confounded in preferential looking procedures. Thus, another focus of my research has been to investigate whether null preferences do, in fact, reflect memory loss or an inability to discriminate. One approach I have used is to investigate possible dissociations between looking behavior in the VPC and infant memory as assessed by ERPs. Another approach I have used is to investigate the relation between adults' looking behavior in the VPC and other measures of explicit and implicit memory.

In one study, 6-month-old infants' memory for an object was assessed after a 24-hour delay using two different measures: the VPC and ERPs (Snyder, 2003). Infants who exhibited a null preference in the VPC nevertheless exhibited memory for the familiar stimulus when ERPs were used as the measure of retention. A large negative ERP component observed over posterior scalp regions, putatively labeled the N700, showed this memory

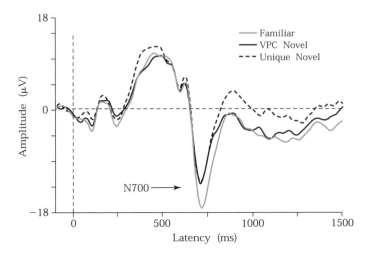

FIGURE 8.6. Grand mean ERP waveforms from a representative posterior electrode showing the effect of familiarity at the N700 component. The N700 peaks later to the familiar stimulus (shaded line), compared to the two novel stimuli (black dotted and black solid lines).

effect and peaked later in response to the familiar object compared to two novel objects, but did not differ in latency for the two novel objects (see Figure 8.6).

Since we used a within-subject design in which infants were first tested in the VPC and then the ERP task at the 24-hour delay, it is possible that the dissociation between looking behavior and ERPs was due to reactivation of the memory for the familiar object in the VPC. To examine this possibility, we tested a second group of infants using the same procedures, except that the VPC contained two completely novel objects. Thus, the infant was not reexposed to the familiar stimulus prior to the ERP task. We observed the same effect of familiarity on the N700 in this second group of infants. The ERP effect observed in the second group of infants could not be due to reactivation of the familiar stimulus, making a stronger case for the argument that the ERP effects observed in the first group reflected residual memory for the familiar stimulus that the VPC was not sensitive enough to detect. Thus, this study provides a source of positive evidence that null effects in the VPC do not reflect memory loss or an inability to discriminate.

The dissociation between VPC performance and infant memory reported here is consistent with previous findings using other measures of retention. For example, Gross, Hayne, Herbert, and Sowerby (2002) reported that infants exhibited retention in a mobile conjugate reinforcement task and a deferred imitation task but showed null preferences for the familiar stimuli from each task in the VPC. Likewise, Wilk, Klein, and Rovee-Collier (2001) compared 3-month-olds' memory in the VPC and mobile conjugate reinforcement paradigm, and found evidence for retention in the mobile conjugate reinforcement measure despite null preferences in the VPC. Thus, there is converging evidence from behavioral and ERP measures that null preferences in the VPC do not necessarily reflect failures of memory or discrimination.

I have also investigated the relation between adults' looking behavior in the VPC and measures of explicit and implicit memory. In one study, adults' memory for an object was assessed following a 24-hour delay using one of three different measures: the VPC, a forced-choice recognition memory task, or a preference task in which participants were asked to indicate which of the two stimuli they liked better (Snyder, 2003). Despite a null preference in the VPC following the 24-hour delay, adults' recognition memory for the familiar stimulus was very high (85%). In addition, adults preferred the novel and familiar objects equally often. The observation that adults exhibited a null preference and equivalent liking of the familiar and novel stimuli provides some support for the idea that null preferences may reflect an intermediate state of memory in which interest in the familiar and novel stimuli are roughly equivalent. Most important, though, adults clearly recognized the familiar object despite exhibiting a null preference. Thus, null preferences in this study clearly do not indicate memory loss or an inability to discriminate.

In summary, the studies reviewed above provide converging evidence for the idea that null preferences do not reflect memory loss or lack of discrimination. Following a long delay, infants still exhibited ERP evidence of memory and adults exhibited highly accurate recognition despite null preferences in the VPC. Converging evidence from these and other studies suggests that null preferences do not provide a measure of memory failure.

Summary

The major findings that have emerged from the work reviewed above are that (a) repetition of a stimulus results in a reduction of neural activity over temporal scalp regions in 6-month-old infants, (b) infant novelty preferences are associated with a reduction in the amplitude of neural activity over temporal and occipital scalp regions during encoding, and (c) both infants and adults show evidence of memory for the familiar stimulus despite exhibiting null preferences when measures other than looking time are used as the measure of retention.

The pattern and topography of the ERP effects observed in the experiments reviewed above are consistent with observations of repetition suppression in inferotemporal cortex from electrophysiological recordings in nonhuman primates and brain imaging studies of human adults, and suggest a common mechanism underlying both repetition of stimuli and novelty preferences. These observations help to establish a possible role for repetition suppression in mediating preferential looking in infants.

Mechanisms of Change in Infants' Performance in Preferential Looking Tasks

Infants' performance in preferential looking tasks changes dramatically during the first year of life. Changes have been observed in infants' ability to encode stimuli of increasing complexity, speed of encoding, retention, and flexibility of the representation (for reviews, see chapter 7, this volume; Bornstein, 1985; Cohen & Gelber, 1975). Changes in infants' performance in preferential looking tasks likely result from complex interactions between neurobiological development and the experience of the infant. Given the enormous changes in the brain during the first few years of life, a complete neurobiological model of memory development must go beyond systems involved in memory and also consider the contribution of systems involved in sensory input, storage, and motor output. Thus I will briefly consider the development of parts of the brain involved in the creation and storage of visual representations (i.e., the visual processing pathway), as well as control over eye movements and their implications for how change occurs.

Visual Processing and Cortical Development

Visual information is processed sequentially along the ventral occipitotemporal pathway. Visual information enters through the retina, travels along the optic nerve to the thalamus, and is then sent on to primary visual cortex (in the occipital lobe), which is the first cortical area to receive visual information. From primary visual cortex, visual processing proceeds sequentially through secondary, tertiary, and association processing areas in the occipital lobe, and then descends through the temporal lobe, culminating in the inferotemporal cortical areas TEO and TE. At each stage in the ventral pathway, the receptive field size of neurons increases, the visual information becomes more highly integrated, and the representation is more complex. Thus, whereas neurons in primary visual cortex have receptive fields restricted to small portions of the retina and are simple edge detectors, a complete representation of a stimulus is synthesized in area TE.

The immaturity of the cortex early in development likely plays a role in age-related changes in infants' performance in preferential looking tasks. For instance, since the visual cortical areas appear to develop hierarchically, with areas earlier in the processing stream (e.g., TEO) developing sooner than areas later in the processing stream (e.g., area TE), the complexity of the information that an infant is able to encode, store, and retrieve is likely to increase with age. The findings that stimulus properties affect rates of habituation and that older infants can detect more subtle differences in change to stimuli, provide some support for this proposal. For example, infants appear to habituate more slowly to more complex stimuli (e.g., Caron & Caron, 1969), suggesting they require more time to adequately encode the stimuli and show larger novelty preferences when the novel and familiar stimuli are more dissimilar looking. Furthermore, these effects interact with age in that young infants (e.g., 3- and 4-month-olds) require a change in more than one dimension (e.g., color, shape) of the familiar stimulus to exhibit a novelty preference at test, whereas by 8 to 12 months a change in one dimension is sufficient (e.g., Cohen, Gelber, & Lazar, 1971; Cohen, 1973). This suggests that either the kind or amount of information that infants encode in preferential looking tasks changes with age, as would be predicted by changes in the visual processing stream with development.

In addition, information stored in the cortex may be especially vulnerable to decay, interference, or retrieval failure during periods of cortical development. Since representations for both explicit and implicit forms of memory are stored in the cortex, one implication of cortical development is that some forms of explicit and implicit memory (e.g., perceptual priming) are equally likely to be affected.

Development of Voluntary Control
Over Eye Movements

An important difference between explicit and implicit memory tasks is that subjects deliberately attempt to match their response (either verbal or motoric) with retrieval of prior study items in an explicit memory task, but are not required to do so in an implicit task. In an implicit task, although subjects may deliberately or voluntarily control their responses (by pushing buttons or speaking), they do not deliberately attempt to use memory to guide these responses. Thus, memory may guide responses in a top-down manner in explicit tasks, whereas it only biases responses in implicit tasks. This raises the question of whether infants have voluntary or deliberate control over their responses (i.e., eye movements) in the VPC task, and whether memory exerts top-down control over looking or simply influences looking in a bottom-up, automatic manner.

In the VPC, eye movements are used to orient toward and visually explore stimuli. Thus, preferential looking behavior relies on the oculomotor system for both sensory input and motor output. Voluntary eye movements, in particular, involve the participation of structures in the frontal cortex that appear to be later developing. The point in development when eye movements come under voluntary control has important implications for preferential looking behavior. If visual fixation and exploration is primarily reflexive, preferential looking behavior may simply reflect the influence of bottom-up, automatic processes (of which novelty is an inherent bias). If eye movements are under voluntary control, on the other hand, infants may be able to use recollective experiences to deliberately guide their looking behavior. Thus, changes in preferential looking behavior with age may reflect, in part, the development of voluntary control over eye movements rather than the infant's ability to encode, remember, and recognize a stimulus.

Visual exploration depends critically on saccadic eye movements, and saccades can be either voluntary or involuntary. The speed, duration, and direction of a saccade are coded by populations of neurons in the brain stem, which project directly to the oculomotor nuclei, controlling the muscles of the eyes. Determining the target location of a saccade and voluntary control over eye movements, on the other hand, involves neurons in the parietal cortex, basal ganglia, and frontal eye fields. Neurons in these three areas project directly to brain stem nuclei, enabling them to initiate or inhibit saccades. The parietal cortex is thought to be critical for determining the target location of the eye movement, whereas the frontal eye fields can override reflexive mechanisms, suggesting it is the critical structure for control of voluntary eye movements.

There is some debate in the literature regarding the age at which voluntary control over eye movements emerges. It has historically been assumed that saccades in young infants are reflexive and not under voluntary control (as cited in Richards, 2001a). Evidence for this view comes primarily from anatomical information and behavioral evidence. Anatomically, the layers of visual cortex mediating voluntary eye movements are relatively immature at birth and undergo significant development over the first 6 months of life (Richards, 2001a). This anatomical information coincides with behavioral evidence that infants between the ages of 2 and 6 months show little to no development in involuntary saccades used for visual tracking, but a significant increase in attention-directed saccades and smooth-pursuit eye movements over this same time period (Richards & Holley, 1999). In contrast to this view, infants as young as 2 to 3 months will make anticipatory eye movements in the visual expectation procedure. Haith, Canfield, and colleagues (Canfield, Smith, Brezsnyak, & Snow, 1997; Wentworth & Haith, 1998) have argued that infants' predictive saccades in this procedure reflect voluntary eye movements and hence the involvement of the frontal eye fields.

Recently, evidence from ERP studies has attempted to resolve this debate, although results have been mixed. Using the spatial cueing task, Richards (2001b) reported saccade-related ERPs over frontal scalp regions in 4.5- and 6-month-old infants, but not in 3-month-olds, and concluded that only in the older infants did saccades involve the frontal eye fields and were, therefore, voluntary. Using the visual expectation procedure, on the other hand, Wentworth, Haith, and Karrer (2001) and Csibra, Tucker, and Johnson (2001) both reported a negative potential over frontal leads in 3- and 4-month-olds that appeared to resemble a negative saccade-related potential observed in adults. In adults, this negative potential is thought to reflect activation of the frontal eye fields or motor potentials in the supplementary eye fields, and hence voluntary eye movements. Thus, these authors concluded that saccades are under voluntary control in 3- and 4-month-old infants.

Development of the Medial-Temporal Lobe System

Although Nelson (1995) has suggested that novelty preferences obtained under immediate test conditions in young infants likely depend disproportionately on the hippocampus, the results of neuropsychological studies and lesion studies in nonhuman primates has shown that damage to the medial-temporal lobe (including the hippocampus) does not impair performance in the VPC at very short delays. Thus, infants' performance in the VPC under immediate test conditions may not depend on the medial-temporal lobe at all.

In general, the observation that older infants require less familiarization time to encode stimuli than younger infants may reflect the contribution of the medial-temporal lobe structures later in development to the encoding portion of the task. This is based on findings that the medial-temporal lobe system is critical for rapid acquisition of information during memory tasks. Note, however, that involvement of the medial-temporal lobe system during encoding does not imply involvement of the system during retrieval. Words activated during a priming task (e.g., word stem completion), for example, may have been initially encoded via the medial-temporal lobe system at some earlier point in time, but successful retrieval during the priming task does not require the medial-temporal lobe. This reflects an additional limitation of lesion studies for investigating the neurobiology underlying performance in the VPC: It is not possible to determine whether the lesion impaired encoding or retrieval. More systematic research examining the interaction of age, familiarization time, length of delay, and location of lesions in infant monkeys is needed to disentangle these issues.

Effects of Experience

Finally, the experience of the infant likely plays an important role in the encoding, storage, and retrieval of information in preferential looking tasks. Earlier I argued that an important difference between the task used with infants and the task that has been used with adults involves semantic memory. By semantic memory, I am referring to perceptual representations of the physical structure of the world, as well as conceptual representations regarding the function, use, and relations between objects. An important difference between adults and infants is that adults have already accumulated a great deal of perceptual and conceptual information about the world, while infants are only beginning to do so. These preexisting perceptual and conceptual representations play a critical role in priming in adults. By several accounts, exposure to a stimulus during the study phase of a priming task results in small changes to a preexisting representation via modifications to connection weights or synaptic efficacies. This helps explain why priming effects seem to last over very long periods of time. When the stimulus is then reencountered during the test phase of the task, the stimulus is processed more fluently (due to stronger connections), resulting in increased reaction time or enhanced likelihood of producing the prime. Thus, priming involves reactivation of a preexisting representation.

Contrast this with an infant's experience in a preferential looking task. Depending on the age of the infants and the stimulus used, infants may not have encountered the stimulus before participating in the task, and may thus have no preexisting perceptual representation for the stimulus. Even if they have, it is unlikely that their perceptual or conceptual representation is adultlike, given the immaturity of the cortex that is thought to store such representations. Thus, the familiarization phase may be more similar to initial learning than to reexposure.

Questions and Issues on the Horizon

The primary goal of this chapter was to examine the hypothesis that infants' performance in the VPC reflects explicit recognition of a familiar stimulus, and that changes in infants' performance in the VPC result from the development of a single underlying competency (i.e., recognition memory). Given the interactions reviewed earlier between age, delay, and location of lesion, a one-to-one mapping between performance on the VPC and a single underlying competency seems unlikely. Instead, it was argued that infants' performance in the VPC reflects the interaction between visual attention and memory, and that memory is but one process that guides visual attention in these tasks. Repetition suppression in the visual processing pathway was proposed as the mechanism that guides visual attention toward a novel stimulus in these tasks. The implication of this latter view is that memory may be an incidental influence on visual attention, and that infants need not be aware that they have seen the familiar stimulus before in order to look longer at a novel stimulus.

It is my hope that the arguments and evidence presented here will reinvigorate the debate about whether infants' performance in preferential looking tasks reflects a form of explicit or implicit memory, since the way we interpret preferential looking is critical to the kinds of knowledge and abilities we ascribe to young infants. Investigating the neurobiology underlying performance on these tasks is one approach to resolving this debate, but many questions remain to be answered. For instance, given the argument that lesion studies in adult animals ultimately may not inform our understanding of the neurobiology underlying novelty preferences in infants, we need more research examining the neurobiology of VPC performance in infant monkeys. In addition, examining interactions among stimulus properties, length of familiarization, delay, and location of lesion could help us understand age-related changes in human infants' performance on preferential looking tasks.

Results from lesion studies provide a good starting point, but converging evidence from additional methodologies is also needed if we wish to provide a full explanatory account of infants' performance in preferential looking tasks, and hence memory development. As was noted earlier, lesion studies may confound processes involved in encoding, storage, and retrieval. It is possible, for example, that medial-temporal lobe structures are involved in the initial encoding of stimuli when study times are brief but are not required for the retrieval of information that produces longer looking toward a novel stimulus during the test phase. Neuroimaging methods, on the other hand, would allow investigators to examine the contribution of different structures during encoding and retrieval, and have been successful in dissociating such processes in other types of memory tasks.

Despite the promise of a neurobiological approach to understanding infants' performance in preferential looking tasks, there remains a very difficult inferential issue that must be addressed. That is, in addition to mapping out the specific parts of the brain that appear to be critical for task performance, we must also figure out the function of these structures early in infancy. For example, the logic of the explicit-memory account of novelty preferences appears to hold that (a) the medial-temporal lobe is critical for explicit memory in adults; (b) the VPC seems to depend on medial-temporal lobe structures; and therefore (c) the VPC likely measures explicit memory. One problem with this line of reasoning is that it assumes that structures like the hippocampus are performing the same function early in infancy as in adulthood. Given changes in the anatomical and functional maturity of many of the medial-temporal lobe structures during development and, perhaps more critically, changes in connections between medial-temporal lobe structures and other cortical structures (e.g., prefrontal cortex), it is possible that the function of these individual structures early in life bears little resemblance to the integrated function of the complete circuit that underlies explicit memory later in life.

Figuring out the function of a structure early in infancy, however, will require going beyond a single task-structure mapping. Instead, studies examining the contribution of a particular structure to performance across different tasks, as well as a principled understanding of the task requirements of these tasks (i.e., what the tasks are actually assessing), are needed to develop an understanding of function. Importantly, without an independent analysis of task requirements, the mapping of structure to function is reduced to a mapping of structure to a bunch of tasks, leaving us with little more than a tautology. In other words, to say that the VPC is dependent on the hippocampus tells us little. What we really want to know is what kind of memory it measures. To answer this, we need to know the function of the hippocampus. If we base the function of the hippocampus on what we think the task measures (i.e., explicit memory), but we base what we think the task measures on the fact that damage to the hippocampus impairs performance on the task, then we are reduced to circular reasoning. Research examining the neurobiology of memory in adults has used multiple tasks, as well as task analysis, to investigate the function of particular brain structures. An understanding of the neurobiology of memory development would benefit greatly from the same approach, but must examine structure-function relations in developing animals and human infants.

Finally, the view that preferential looking reflects the interaction between memory and attention, and that memory is but one influence on looking behavior, raises the question of what other processes influence visual attention in these tasks. For example, the idea that memory for the familiar stimulus and interest in the novel stimulus are confounded in preferential looking paradigms suggests that affective processes may be another influence on visual attention. Thus, a full understanding of the changes in infants' performance in preferential looking tasks will likely involve an understanding of how systems involved in visual processing, oculomotor control, affective modulation of stimulus processing, novelty detection, and learning and memory interact during development.

Acknowledgments

The author wishes to thank Margarita Stolarova, Heather Whitney, Sara Webb, Sandi Wewerka, Alissa Westerlund, Betsy Meehan, Kari Barth, Emily Shunk, and Dana Keufner for help with data collection, Liza Zolot for help with manuscript preparation, and Chad Marsolek for his very helpful comments on an earlier draft of this manuscript.

Notes

1. It is important to note, however, that amnesic patients showed significant novelty preferences at the 2-minute delay and above-chance performance in the recognition memory task.

2. In a forced-choice recognition task, subjects are simultaneously presented with two stimuli, one familiar and one novel, and are asked to identify which stimulus was previously seen.

3. It is interesting to note, however, that animals with radio frequency lesions were impaired at delays of 1 minute and 10 minutes, whereas animals with neurotoxic lesions were impaired at delays of 10 seconds and 10 minutes but showed intact performance at 1-minute delays.

References

Bachevalier, J. M., Brickson, M., & Hagger, C. (1993). Limbic-dependent recognition memory in monkeys develops early in infancy. *Neuroreport, 4*, 77–80.

Baylis, G. C., & Rolls, E. T. (1987). Responses of neurons in the inferior temporal cortex in short term and serial recognition memory tasks. *Experimental Brain Research, 65*, 614–622.

Begleiter, H., Porjesz, B., & Wang, W. (1993). A neurophysiologic correlate of visual short-term memory in humans. *Electroencephalography and Clinical Neurophysiology, 87*, 46–53.

Bogartz, R. S., Shinskey, J. L., & Speaker, C. J. (1997). Interpreting infant looking: The event set × event set design. *Developmental Psychology, 33*, 408–422.

Bornstein, M. H. (1985). Habituation of attention as a measure of visual information processing in human infants: Summary, systematization, and synthesis. In G. Gottlieb & N. A. Krasnegor (Eds.), *The measurement of audition and vision in the first year of postnatal life: A methodological overview* (pp. 253–300). Norwood, NJ: Ablex.

Buckner, R. L., Goodman, J., Burock, M., Rotte, M. Koutstaal, W., Schacter, D., et al. (1998). Functional-anatomic correlates of object priming in humans revealed by rapid presentation event-related fMRI. *Neuron, 20,* 285–296.

Buckner, R. L., Petersen, S. E., Ojemann, J. G., Miezin, F. M., Squire, L. R., & Raichle, M. E. (1995). Functional anatomical studies of explicit and implicit memory retrieval tasks. *Journal of Neuroscience, 15,* 12–29.

Buffalo, E. A., Ramus, S. J., Clark, R. E., Teng, E., Squire, L. R., & Zola, S. M. (1999). Dissociation between the effects of damage to perirhinal cortex and area TE. *Learning and Memory, 6,* 572–599.

Canfield, R. L., Smith, E. G., Brezsnyak, M. E., & Snow, K. L. (1997). Information processing through the first year of life. *Monographs of the Society for Research in Child Development, 62*(2, Serial No. 250).

Caron, A. J., & Caron, R. F. (1969). Degree of stimulus complexity and habituation of visual fixation in infants. *Psychonomic Science, 14,* 78–79.

Clifton, R. K., & Nelson, M. N. (1976). Developmental study of habituation in infants: The importance of paradigm, response system, and state. In T. J. Tighe & R. N. Leaton (Eds.), *Habituation: Perspectives from child development, animal behavior, and neurophysiology* (pp. 159–206). Hillsdale, NJ: Erlbaum, 1976.

Cohen, L. B. (1973). A two process model of infant visual attention. *Merrill-Palmer Quarterly, 19,* 157–180.

Cohen, L. B., & Gelber, E. R. (1975). Infant visual memory. In L. B. Cohen & P. Salapatek (Eds.), *Infant perception: From sensation to cognition,* Vol. 1, (pp. 347–403). New York: Academic Press.

Cohen, L. B., Gelber, E. R., & Lazar, M. A. (1971). Infant habituation and generalization to repeated visual stimulation. *Journal of Experimental Child Psychology, 11,* 379–389.

Colby, C. L., Duhamel, J., & Goldberg, M. E. (1996). Visual, presaccadic, and cognitive activation of single neurons in monkey lateral intraparietal area. *Journal of Neurophysiology, 76,* 2841.

Csibra, G., Tucker, L. A., & Johnson, M. H. (2001). Differential frontal cortex activation before anticipatory and reactive saccades in infants. *Infancy, 2,* 159–174.

de Haan, M., & Nelson, C. (1997). Recognition of the mother's face by 6-month-old infants: A neurobehavioral study. *Child Development, 68,* 187–210.

Desimone, R. (1996). Neural mechanisms for visual memory and their role in attention. *Proceedings of the National Academy of Science, 93,* 13494–13499.

Desimone, R., & Duncan, J. (1995). Neural mechanisms of selective visual attention. *Annual Reviews in Neuroscience, 18,* 193–222.

Desimone, R., Miller, E. K., Chelazzi, L., & Lueschow, A. (1995). Multiple memory systems in the visual cortex. In M. Gazzaniga (Ed.), *The cognitive and neurosciences* (pp. 475–486). Cambridge, MA: MIT Press.

Fahy, F. L., Riches, I. P., & Brown, M. W. (1993). Neuronal activity related to visual recognition memory: Long-term memory and the encoding of recency and familiarity information in the primate anterior and medial inferior rhinal cortex. *Experimental Brain Research, 96,* 457–472.

Graf, P., & Schacter, D. L. (1985). Implicit and explicit memory for new associations in normal and amnesic subjects. *Journal of Experimental Psychology: Learning, Memory, and Cognition, 11,* 501–518.

Gross, J., Hayne, H., Herbert, J., & Sowerby, P. (2002). Measuring infant memory: Does the ruler matter? *Developmental Psychobiology, 40,* 183–192.

Hagger, C., Brickson, M., & Bachevalier, J. (1985). Sparing of visual recognition after neonatal lesions of inferior temporal cortex in infant rhesus monkeys. *Society for Neuroscience Abstracts, 11,* 831.

Li, L., Miller, E. K., & Desimone, R. (1993). The representation of stimulus familiarity in anterior inferior temporal cortex. *Journal of Neurophysiology, 69,* 1918–1929.

Manns, J. R., Stark, C. E. L., & Squire, L. R. (2000). The visual paired-comparison task as a measure of declarative memory. *Proceedings of the National Academy of Sciences, 97,* 12375–12379.

McKee, R. D., & Squire, L. R. (1993). On the development of declarative memory. *Journal of Experimental Psychology: Learning, Memory, and Cognition, 19,* 397–404.

Miller, E. K., Gochin, P. M., & Gross, C. G. (1991). Habituation-like decrease in the responses of neurons in inferior temporal cortex of the macaque. *Visual Neuroscience, 7,* 357–362.

Miller, E. K., Li, L., & Desimone, R. (1991). A verbal mechanism for working and recognition memory in inferior temporal cortex. *Neuroscience Abstracts, 2,* 1377–1379.

Nelson, C. A. (1994). Neural correlates of recognition memory in the first postnatal year. In G. Dawson & K. Fischer (Eds.), *Human behavior and the developing brain* (pp. 269–313). New York: Guilford.

Nelson, C. A. (1995). The ontogeny of human memory: A cognitive neuroscience perspective. *Developmental Psychology, 31,* 723–738.

Nemanic, S., Alvarado, M. C., & Bachevalier, J. (2004). The hippocampal/parahippocampal regions and recognition memory: Insights from visual paired comparison versus object-delayed nonmatching in monkeys. *Journal of Neuroscience, 24,* 2013–2026.

Pascalis, O., & Bachevalier, J. (1999). Neonatal aspiration lesions of the hippocampal formation impair visual recognition memory when assessed by paired-comparison task but not by delayed nonmatching-to-sample task. *Hippocampus, 9,* 609–616.

Pascalis, O., Hunkin, N. M., Holdstock, J. S., Isaac, C. L., & Mayes, A. R. (2004). Visual paired comparison performance is impaired in a patient with selective hippocampal lesions and relatively intact item recognition. *Neuropsychologia, 42,* 1293–1300.

Richards, J. E. (2001a). Cortical indexes of saccade planning in infants. *Infancy, 2,* 123–133.

Richards, J. E. (2001b). Cortical indexes of saccade planning following covert orienting in 20-week-old infants. *Infancy, 2,* 135–157.

Richards, J. E., & Holley, F. B. (1999). Infant attention and the development of smooth pursuit tracking. *Developmental Psychology, 35,* 856–867.

Riches, I. P., Wilson, F. A. W., & Brown, M. W. (1991). The effects of visual stimulation and memory on neurons of the hippocampal formation and the neighboring parahippocampal gyrus and inferior temporal cortex of the primate. *Journal of Neuroscience, 11,* 1763–1779.

Roediger, H. L. (2003). Reconsidering implicit memory. In J. S. Bowers & C. J. Marsolek (Eds.), *Rethinking implicit memory* (pp. 3–18). New York: Oxford University Press.

Roediger, H. L., Weldon, M. S., & Challis, B. H. (1989). Explaining dissociations between implicit and explicit measures of retention: A processing account. In H. L. Roediger III & F. I. M. Craik (Eds.), *Varieties of memory and consciousness: Essays in honour of Endel Tulving* (pp. 3–41). Hillsdale, NJ: Erlbaum.

Saunders, R. C., Richards, R. S., & Bachevalier, J. (1991). *Society for Neuroscience Abstracts, 17,* 133.

Schacter, D. L. (1998). Memory and awareness. *Science, 280,* 59–60.

Schacter, D. L., & Moscovitch, M. (1984). Infants, amnesics, and dissociable memory systems. In M. Moscovitch (Ed.), *Infant memory* (pp. 173–216). New York: Plenum.

Schacter, D. L., & Tulving, E. (1994). What are the memory systems of 1994? In D. L. Schacter & E. Tulving (Eds), *Memory systems of 1994* (pp. 1–38). Cambridge, MA: MIT Press.

Schacter, D. L., & Wagner, A. D. (1999). Medial temporal lobe activations in fMRI and PET studies of episodic encoding and retrieval. *Hippocampus, 9,* 7–24.

Schacter, D. L., Wagner, A. D., & Buckner, R. L. (2000). Memory systems of 1999. In E. Tulving & F. I. M. Craik (Eds.), *Oxford handbook of memory* (pp. 627–643). London: Oxford University Press.

Snyder, K. A. (2003). *Neural mechanisms underlying novelty preferences.* Unpublished doctoral dissertation, University of Minnesota, Minneapolis.

Snyder, K. A., Stolarova, M., & Nelson, C. A. (2006). *Neural correlates of novelty preferences.* Manuscript in preparation.

Snyder, K. A., Webb, S. J., & Nelson, C. A. (2002). Theoretical and methodological implications of variability in infant brain response during a recognition memory paradigm. *Infant Behavior and Development, 25,* 466–494.

Sokolov, Y. N. (1963). *Perception and the conditioned reflex* (S. W. Waydenfeld, Trans.). New York: Macmillan.

Sophian, C. (1980). Habituation is not enough: Novelty preferences, search, and memory in infancy. *Merrill-Palmer Quarterly, 26,* 239–257.

Squire, L. R. (1994). Declarative and nondeclarative memory: Multiple brain systems supporting learning and memory. In D. L. Schacter & E. Tulving (Eds.), *Memory systems* (pp. 203–231). Cambridge, MA: MIT Press.

Squire, L. R., Ojemann, J. G., Miezin, F. M., Petersen, S. E., Videen, T. O., & Raichle, M. E. (1992). Activation of the hippocampus in normal humans: A functional anatomical study of memory. *Proceedings of the National Academy of Sciences, USA, 89,* 1837–1841.

Ungerleider, L. G. (1995). Functional brain imaging studies of cortical mechanisms for memory. *Science, 270,* 769–775.

Vogels, R., Sary, G., & Orban, G. A. (1995). How task-related are the responses of inferior temporal neurons? *Visual Neuroscience, 12,* 207–214.

Wagner, A. D., Gabrieli, J. D. E., Desmond, J. E., & Glover, G. H. (1998). Prefrontal cortex and recognition memory: fMRI evidence for context-dependent retrieval processes. *Brain, 121,* 1985–2002.

Wentworth, N., & Haith, M. M. (1998). Infants' acquisition of spatiotemporal expectations. *Developmental Psychology, 34,* 247–257.

Wentworth, N., Haith, M. M., & Karrer, R. (2001). Behavioral and cortical measures of infants' visual expectations. *Infancy, 2,* 175–195.

Wilk, A. E., Klein, L., & Rovee-Collier, C. (2001). Visual-preference and operant measures of infant memory. *Developmental Psychobiology, 39,* 301–312.

Willingham, D. B., & Preuss, L. (1995). The death of implicit memory. *Psyche: An Interdisciplinary Journal of Research on Consciousness, 2*(15).

Zola, S. M., Squire, L. R., Teng, E., Stefanacci, L., & Buffalo, E. A. (2000). Impaired recognition memory in monkeys after damage limited to the hippocampal region. *Journal of Neuroscience, 20,* 451–463.

9

Infant Memory Development

New Questions, New Answers

HARLENE HAYNE

> *In Psychology, as in Physics there are no pure "facts," if by "facts" are meant phenomena presented nakedly to the mind by nature itself, independent . . . of hypotheses by . . . which the mind examines them, of principles governing the interpretation of experience, and of a systematic framework of existing judgements into which the observer pigeon-holes every new observation.*
> —Jean Piaget (1929, p. 23)

Do you remember your wedding day? The birth of your first child? What about where you left your keys when you came home from the supermarket earlier today or what you need to do tomorrow at work? These everyday memory tasks are universally familiar to adults. In order to function effectively in the world, we frequently reflect on events that have happened in the past (retrospective memory) and plan for events that we know will happen in the future (prospective memory). The fundamental question for memory researchers is, how do these memory skills emerge during the course of human development? That is, do infants or young children think about the past and plan for the future? What memory skills do infants possess at birth and what skills emerge over the course of development? As Piaget articulated decades ago, the way in which we evaluate empirical "facts" in psychology is heavily influenced by our current, theoretical views of the phenomena that we study. In the case of memory development, the way in which we have interpreted data on infant memory skill has been shaped, in large part, by the way in which we think about memory in adults. As our views of adult memory have changed, so have our views of memory development. Over the last decade, the field of cognitive neuroscience has had a major impact on many of our current views about the way in which memory ability might unfold during the course of human development (Bauer, 2004; Hayne, 2004; Nelson, 1995; Rovee-Collier, Hayne, & Colombo, 2001).

Theoretical Models of Long-Term Memory

Figure 9.1 illustrates one way in which researchers working with human adults have viewed the concept of memory. According to this view, memory is not a single process, but rather comprises many different memory systems that are supported by different neural substrates, serve different functions, and operate according to different principles (for reviews, see Gold, 2004; McDonald, Devan, & Hong, 2004; Squire, 2004). Although a large number of memory systems have been proposed, one of the most influential dichotomies has been the nondeclarative (nee procedural) versus declarative memory dichotomy originally proposed by Squire (Squire, 1987, 1994; see Figure 9.1). According to this dichotomy, the nondeclarative memory system supports the retention of skills and habits, priming and perceptual learning, simple classical conditioning, and nonassociative learning. The declarative memory system, on the other hand, is required for the conscious recollection of facts and events and allows for rapid, one-trial learning. Within the declarative memory system, a further distinction has been made between episodic and semantic memory (see Figure 9.1). Broadly defined, episodic memory refers to the recollection of personal experiences (e.g., what "I" did last Christmas) while semantic memory involves the

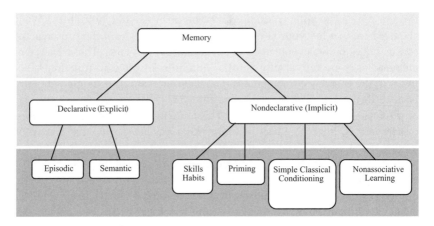

FIGURE 9.1. A memory model based on studies conducted with human adults. Figure redrawn from Squire (1987).

recollection of facts (e.g., Christmas falls on December 25; Tulving, 1972, 1983, 2002).

Although the notion that memory consists of multiple independent processes was originally established through data collected with adults, the same idea has raised fundamental questions about the way in which different long-term memory skills might emerge as the central nervous system matures. The overarching goal of the present chapter is to review what we currently know about infant memory development within the context of the memory model outlined in Figure 9.1. Throughout the chapter, I will describe how views about different kinds of adult memory have raised new questions about the development of long-term memory, particularly during infancy and early childhood.

When Does Long-Term Memory Emerge?

On the basis of the model shown in Figure 9.1, the first question we have to ask is when infants begin to exhibit long-term memory at all. Although many of us now take infant memory ability for granted, for centuries psychologists expressed a relatively dim view of infants' mnemonic capacities. Many experts believed that infants lived exclusively in the world of the here and now and encoded and retained very little of their prior experience. Most contemporary psychologists are well aware of William James' (1890) characterization of infant mental life as a "blooming, buzzing confusion," but what they may not know is that this view was once so pervasive that neonates were rarely given anesthesia during painful medical procedures because it was widely assumed that they would forget the traumatic experience so quickly (for review, see Porter, Grunau, & Anand, 1999).

Over the last four decades, empirical research on memory development has shown that these early notions about infant long-term memory are fundamentally incorrect. We now know that infants are born with a remarkable capacity to encode and retain information. For example, newborn infants recognize the smell of their own mother's breast milk and can discriminate it from the breast milk of another mother by 8 to 10 days after birth (MacFarlane, 1975). Similarly, infants recognize their mother's face by at least 3 to 4 days of age (Bushnell, Sai, & Mullin, 1989; Pascalis, de Schonen, Morton, Deruelle, & Fabre-Grenet, 1995) and the sound of their mother's voice within hours after birth (DeCasper & Fifer, 1980). In fact, subsequent research has shown that maternal voice recognition is based, in large part, on infants' experience with their mother's voice prior to birth (DeCasper & Spence, 1986). Furthermore, a tape recording of the interuterine heartbeat is highly reinforcing to newborn infants, suggesting that infants also recognize at least some characteristics of this stimulus even after they are born (DeCasper & Sigafoos, 1983). In short, infants are born with at least some capacity for long-term memory; many of the long-term memory skills they exhibit at birth involve retention of biologically relevant information that is linked to their survival.

How Do We Measure Infant Memory Development?

As data on long-term memory in newborns continued to accumulate and accrue, the initial research question of whether infants exhibit memory evolved into more sophisticated questions about the characteristics of infants' mnemonic skill. Having established the fact that infants do remember, researchers began to examine what infants remember, how long they remember, and under what conditions they are likely to retrieve and use their memories. Furthermore, researchers began to examine how infants' memories differ from those of adults and in what ways they might also be the same. The next practical problem that researchers had to overcome was how to measure memory development across the infancy period. As research participants, developing infants present some interesting challenges. For example, unlike older children and adults, infants cannot tell experimenters what they remember about a particular stimulus or experience. Instead, researchers must rely on nonverbal aspects of infants' behavior in order to infer if and what they remember. Furthermore, although infants' comprehension of language precedes production by a considerable margin, researchers cannot rely on verbal instructions in tasks designed for infants; instead, they must build nonverbal instructions into the task per se.

In addition to difficulties associated with linguistic immaturity, infants' rapid development has also made it difficult to design a single task that can be used throughout the infancy period. Due to motoric immaturity, for example, some of the tasks that are appropriate for older infants and toddlers cannot be used with newborns. Similarly, due to age-related changes in interest and motivation, some of the tasks that can be used with newborns and young infants cannot be used with older infants and toddlers. Furthermore, throughout the infancy period, infants undergo rapid changes in state. Given this, any task designed to measure memory must be relatively brief or subject loss due to attrition becomes very high.

Despite these constraints, researchers have developed a number of different experimental tasks that can be used to study memory development in participants whose interests, motor ability, and language skills vary quite dramatically.

Visual Paired Comparison Task

The visual paired comparison (VPC) task that is used to study infant memory is based on visual preference techniques originally developed by Fantz (1958) and Berlyne (1958) to study infant perception. These techniques exploit the infant's tendency to orient toward novel stimuli. In a typical perception experiment, the infant is preexposed to a single visual stimulus for a fixed period of time or until his or her looking time to that stimulus decreases to a predetermined level. On the test trial, the infant is then shown a novel stimulus and the familiar stimulus, and looking time to both stimuli is measured.

To the extent that the infant looks more at the novel stimulus than at the familiar stimulus, it is inferred that he or she can discriminate them. When the VPC task is modified to study memory, a delay is inserted between the end of the familiarization phase and the test. Memory for the familiar stimulus is inferred if the infant looks longer at the novel stimulus than at the familiar stimulus during the test. This task was initially used with very young infants, but with minor changes to the familiarization stimuli, it can also be used with older infants, children, and adults (Morgan & Hayne, 2002; Richmond, Sowerby, Colombo, & Hayne, 2004; Robinson & Pascalis, 2004).

Operant Conditioning Procedures

A number of different operant conditioning procedures have been used with preverbal infants, but the two that have been used most commonly are the mobile conjugate reinforcement paradigm and the train paradigm—both of these procedures were originally developed by Rovee-Collier and her colleagues (Hartshorn & Rovee-Collier, 1997; Rovee & Rovee, 1969).

Mobile Conjugate Reinforcement Paradigm

In the mobile conjugate reinforcement paradigm, infants learn to kick their feet to produce movement in an overhead crib mobile. During each session, the infant is placed supine in the crib (2- to 3-month-olds) or is placed in an infant seat inside the crib (6-month-olds). A length of white satin ribbon is connected from the infant's ankle to one of two mobile stands that are secured to opposite sides of the crib; one of these stands supports the mobile and the other stand is empty. Each session consists of three phases. During Phase 1, the mobile is suspended overhead, but the ankle ribbon is attached to the empty stand. In this arrangement, the mobile is visible, but kicks are ineffective in making it move. During Phase 2, the ankle ribbon is attached to the stand that supports the mobile. Kicks of the infant's foot produce movement in the mobile and the degree of mobile movement is directly related to the rate and force of the infant's kicks. During Phase 3, the ankle ribbon is again attached to the empty mobile stand.

Infants' baseline kick rate is assessed during Phase 1 of Session 1 prior to the introduction of the contingency. Learning in the mobile conjugate reinforcement paradigm is defined as a kick rate that exceeds baseline by a factor of at least 1.5 during 2 of any 3 consecutive minutes of training (Phase 2). Immediate retention is assessed during Phase 3 at the conclusion of each session, and long-term retention is assessed during Phase 1 of the test session that can occur days, weeks, or months after the conclusion of training. Memory in this task is evaluated by comparing infant's kick rate during the long-term retention test to his or her kick rate during baseline (baseline ratio) and to his or her kick rate at the end of training, prior to the retention interval (retention ratio). It is important to note that all test periods are conducted under conditions of nonreinforcement; this procedure precludes the opportunity for additional learning (or savings) to occur.

Train Paradigm

The mobile conjugate reinforcement paradigm is ideally suited for 2- to 6-month-old infants, but developmental changes in interest and motivation make it unsuitable for older infants. To overcome this obstacle, Rovee-Collier and her colleagues developed an upward extension of the mobile procedure in which 6- to 18-month-old infants learn to press a lever to make a miniature train move around a track. Like the mobile task, each session in the train task involves three phases. In Phase 1, the lever is inactivated; both the train and the lever are visible, but presses to the lever have no effect on the train. During Phase 2, each press of the lever produces a brief movement in the train. During Phase 3, the lever is again inactivated. As in the mobile task, learning is defined as a press rate that exceeds baseline by a factor of at least 1.5 during 2 of any 3 consecutive minutes of training (Phase 2), and memory is evaluated by comparing the infant's press rate during the long-term retention test to his or her press rate during baseline (baseline ratio) and to his or her press rate at the end of training, prior to the retention interval (retention ratio). Again, in the train paradigm, all test periods occur under conditions of nonreinforcement.

Imitation Tasks

Imitation tasks involve a "monkey see, monkey do" procedure in which an adult demonstrates an action or series of actions and the infant's ability to reproduce those actions is assessed after a delay. In the traditional deferred imitation paradigm that was pioneered by Piaget, infants are not given the opportunity to touch the stimuli or to practice the target actions prior to the test. In an alternative version of this task, commonly referred to as elicited imitation, infants are given an opportunity to practice the actions briefly prior to the retention interval and they are provided with verbal support both during the original demonstration and at the time of the test (e.g., Bauer & Mandler, 1989; chapter 10, this volume; for a comparison of deferred imitation and elicited imitation procedures, see Hayne, Barr, & Herbert, 2003).

On the surface, the procedural differences between the deferred and elicited imitation procedures might seem trivial, but both practice and verbal instructions have been shown to influence infants' imitation performance. For example, the opportunity to practice the target actions at the end of the demonstration session increases the probability that infants will imitate when tested with novel stimuli and increases the effectiveness of a reminder treatment administered after a long delay (Hayne et al., 2003). Similarly, the addition of verbal cues increases the probability that infants will imitate when tested with novel stimuli (Herbert & Hayne, 2000b) and the probability that infants will exhibit retention when tested with the original stimuli after a long delay (Hayne & Herbert, 2004). To make matters more complex, the effects of practice and verbal cues vary as a function of age during the infancy period. For these reasons, we use the standard deferred imitation paradigm in my laboratory unless we are specifically interested in the effects of practice or language cues on measures of long-term retention or generalization.

Piaget (1962) was one of the first psychologists to articulate the relation between imitation and memory. Piaget argued that deferred imitation was a hallmark of mental representation that signaled an infant's ability to form a representation and to recall it after a delay. Piaget's views about infant imitation were based primarily on naturalistic observations of his own three children; Meltzoff was the first investigator to study imitation under highly controlled experimental conditions. In one of his first empirical studies on imitation, Meltzoff (1988) found that, contrary to traditional Piagetian theory, 9-month-old infants exhibited deferred imitation when they were tested after a 24-hour delay. Subsequent research on deferred imitation has shown that newborn infants exhibit imitation of facial gestures (e.g., Meltzoff & Moore, 1977, 1983, 1989, 1994) and that by 6 months of age, infants exhibit deferred imitation of actions with objects (Barr, Dowden, & Hayne, 1996; Collie & Hayne, 1999; Hayne, Boniface, & Barr, 2000). Although these data suggest that Piaget underestimated the age at which infants initially exhibit deferred imitation, they are entirely consistent with Piaget's views about the relation between imitation and long-term memory.

How Does Long-Term Memory Change Over the Course of Development?

Despite differences in a number of task parameters, data collected using the VPC, operant conditioning, and deferred imitation paradigms have yielded a remarkably consistent pattern of results on infant memory development (see Hayne, 2004). On the basis of data collected in a number of different laboratories, it has been possible to derive three general principles of infant memory development based on these experimental procedures. These principles and their experimental support are summarized in Table 9.1 (see also Hayne, 2004).

Older Infants Encode Information Faster

Research conducted using the VPC, operant conditioning, and deferred imitation paradigms has consistently shown that the speed of original encoding increases as a function of age during the infancy period. For example, in the VPC task, younger infants require more exposure to the target stimulus in

Table 9.1   Sample Experimental Support for 3 Basic Principles of Infant Memory Development Derived From Studies Using VPC, Operant Conditioning, and Deferred Imitation Paradigms

Principles of Infant Memory Development	VPC	Operant Conditioning	Deferred Imitation
1. Older infants encode information faster	Fantz, 1964 Rose, 1983 Hunter & Ames, 1988 Morgan, 2003	Davis & Rovee-Collier, 1983 Greco et al., 1986 Hill et al., 1988	Barr et al., 1996 Hayne et al., 2000
2. Older infants remember longer	Rose, 1981 Morgan, 2003	Hartshorn, Rovee-Collier, Gerhardstein, Bhatt, Wondoloski, et al., 1998	Barr & Hayne, 2000 Bauer et al., 2000 Herbert & Hayne, 2000a
3. Older infants exploit a wider range of retrieval cues	Robinson & Pascalis, 2004	Hartshorn, Rovee-Collier, Gerhardstein, Bhatt, Klein, et al., 1998	Hayne et al., 1997 Hayne et al., 2000 Herbert & Hayne, 2000b Hayne, 2006

order to demonstrate a novelty preference during the test (Hunter & Ames, 1988). The inverse relation between age and requisite familiarization time is thought to be due to age-related changes in the speed of original encoding (Rose, 1983; Rose, Gottfried, Melloy-Carminar, & Bridger, 1982).

In a pioneering study originally conducted by Fantz (1964), 2- to 6-month-old infants were familiarized with a series of static visual stimuli. Fantz found that 4- to 6-month-olds exhibited a novelty preference following less exposure to the familiar stimulus than did 3- to 4-month-olds, and 3- to 4-month-olds exhibited a novelty preference following less exposure to the familiar stimulus than did 2- to 3-month-olds. In a similar study with older infants, Rose (1983) found that 6-month-olds required a 15-second exposure to the familiarization stimulus in order to demonstrate a novelty preference, while 12-month-olds required only 10 seconds. The basic finding that older infants recognize stimuli after shorter familiarization times than younger infants has been replicated in a large number of studies using the VPC procedure (e.g., Colombo & Mitchell, 1990; Fagan, 1974; Rose, 1994; Rose, Jankowski, & Feldman, 2002).

In a doctoral study conducted in my laboratory, Morgan (2003) found that age-related changes in the rate of original encoding in the VPC task continue to occur throughout infancy and early childhood. In her task, Morgan familiarized 1- to 5-year-olds with computer-generated cartoon faces. During both the familiarization and the test trials, these faces were animated such that their mouths and eyes moved. These stimuli were designed to be particularly attractive to infants and young children, and subject attrition in the task was close to zero. All participants were tested immediately after original familiarization. Under these conditions, 1-, 2-, and 3-year-olds exhibited a novelty preference after a 10-second familiarization period, but 4- and 5-year-olds exhibited a novelty preference after only a 5-second exposure to the same stimulus. Thus, Morgan's data are highly consistent with prior studies conducted with infants. Furthermore, her task bridges the gap between prior research with infants and the large literature on age-related changes in speed of information processing in school-age children and adolescents (e.g., Kail, 1986, 1993, 2003).

Consistent with studies conducted using the VPC procedure, data collected using operant conditioning procedures have also shown that the speed of original encoding increases as a function of age during the infancy period. In the mobile conjugate reinforcement paradigm, for example, learning is defined as a response rate during acquisition that exceeds that same infant's baseline response rate by a factor of 1.5. When this operational definition of learning is applied to studies of mobile conjugate reinforcement, 2-month-old infants typically learn within 3 to 6 minutes (Davis & Rovee-Collier, 1983), 3-month-olds typically learn within 2 to 3 minutes (Greco, Rovee-Collier, Hayne, Griesler, & Earley, 1986), and 6-month-olds typically learn within 1 minute (Hill, Borovsky, & Rovee-Collier, 1988).

Finally, older infants have also been shown to encode information faster than younger infants in tests of deferred imitation. In two different studies on deferred imitation, 12-, 18-, and 24-month-old infants exhibited retention following a 24-hour delay after observing the target actions modeled only three times over a single 20- to 30-second period; 6-month-olds, on the other hand, required twice as much exposure to the same target actions in order to exhibit imitation following the same delay (Barr et al., 1996; Hayne et al., 2000).

Older Infants Remember Longer

Research conducted using the VPC, operant conditioning, and deferred imitation paradigms have also shown that the duration of long-term memory increases as a function of age during the infancy period. Rose (1981) was the first researcher to compare long-term memory by infants of different ages using the VPC procedure. In her study, 6- and 9-month-old infants were tested either immediately or after a delay. Although infants of both ages exhibited a novelty preference when tested immediately, only the 9-month-olds exhibited a novelty preference after the delay.

Recent research in my laboratory has shown that these age-related changes in retention in the VPC procedure continue to occur throughout early childhood. For example, Morgan (2003) tested 1- to 4-year-olds either immediately after familiarization or after delays ranging from 24 hours to 30 days.

She found that 1-year-olds exhibited a novelty preference when tested immediately, but not after a 24-hour delay; 2-year-olds exhibited a novelty preference after 1 day, but not after 1 week; 3-year-olds exhibited a novelty preference after 1 week, but not after 1 month; and 4-year-olds exhibited a novelty preference after 1 month (see Figure 9.2, left panel).

A more fine-grained analysis of age-related changes in retention during the infancy period per se has been conducted using the mobile conjugate reinforcement and the train paradigms. Because 6-month-old infants perform equivalently when tested with either paradigm (Hartshorn & Rovee-Collier, 1997), it has been possible to combine data from both in order to chart age-related changes in the maximum duration of retention between 2 and 18 months of age. As shown in Figure 9.2 (center panel), age-related changes in the maximum duration of retention occur gradually over this period of development. In addition, although the absolute duration of retention varies across procedures, the pattern of findings obtained with operant conditioning procedures is virtually identical to that obtained with deferred imitation over the same period of development (see Figure 9.2, right panel). Similarly, Bauer and her colleagues have documented age-related changes in long-term memory between the ages of 1 and 2 years in infants tested in the elicited imitation paradigm (Bauer, Wenner, Dropik, & Wewerka, 2000).

Older Infants Exploit a Wider Range of Effective Retrieval Cues

Finally, research conducted using the VPC, operant conditioning, and deferred imitation paradigms has also shown that the range of effective retrieval cues gradually broadens as a function of age across the infancy period. During the early 1970s, Tulving and Thomson (1973; Thomson & Tulving, 1970) published a series of papers in which they argued that a stimulus would serve as an effective retrieval cue if, and only if, it matched the characteristics of a stimulus that had been encoded at the time of the original experience. This relation between encoding and effective retrieval cues is commonly referred to as the encoding specificity hypothesis (Tulving & Thomson, 1973). Although the encoding specificity hypothesis was originally established on the basis of data collected with human adults, some of the best empirical evidence for the hypothesis has come from studies conducted with human infants. The high degree of specificity that characterizes memory retrieval by young infants was originally documented in studies using the mobile conjugate reinforcement paradigm. For example, Hayne, Greco, Earley, Griesler, and Rovee-Collier (1986) trained 2- and 3-month-old infants for two consecutive days with a five-object mobile. Independent groups of infants at each age were tested 24 hours later with a mobile that differed from the training mobile by zero to five objects. Some infants were tested with the original training mobile (zero novel objects) and some infants were tested with a completely novel mobile (five novel objects).

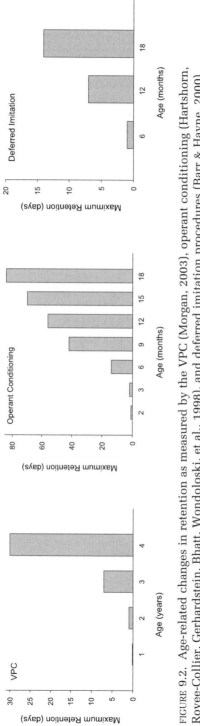

FIGURE 9.2. Age-related changes in retention as measured by the VPC (Morgan, 2003), operant conditioning (Hartshorn, Rovee-Collier, Gerhardstein, Bhatt, Wondoloski, et al., 1998), and deferred imitation procedures (Barr & Hayne, 2000).

Additional groups of infants were tested with mobiles that contained one, two, three, or four novel objects substituted into the original training mobile. Infants of both ages exhibited excellent retention when they were tested with the original training mobile, but they exhibited no retention whatsoever when the test mobile contained more than one novel object.

Subsequent research has shown that this high degree of specificity is also observed in studies of deferred imitation (Hayne et al., 2000; Hayne, MacDonald, & Barr, 1997; Herbert & Hayne, 2000b), and it also extends to aspects of the context in which the original training event takes place (Borovsky & Rovee-Collier, 1990; Butler & Rovee-Collier, 1989; Hayne et al., 2000). Despite the high degree of encoding specificity exhibited by young infants, older infants gradually begin to exploit a wider range of effective retrieval cues. With respect to the environmental context, for example, studies conducted using the VPC, operant conditioning, and deferred imitation paradigms all converge on the view that changes in context become less disruptive to memory retrieval as infants get older. In the VPC task, for example, Robinson and Pascalis (2004) altered the color of the background upon which the target visual stimulus was presented. This change in the background context eliminated retention by 6- and 12-month-olds, but had no effect on retention by 18-month-olds (see Figure 9.3, left panel). Similarly, studies conducted using the mobile conjugate reinforcement and the train paradigms have consistently shown that memory retrieval by 2- to 9-month-old infants is precluded by a change in the environmental context at the time of the retention test. For 12-month-olds, on the other hand, the same changes in the context have no adverse effect on retention (see Figure 9.3, middle panel). Studies conducted using the deferred imitation paradigm have yielded virtually identical results. For example, when infants are shown the demonstration of the target actions in one location (e.g., the lab) and are tested in another (e.g., in their home), 6-month-olds exhibit no retention whatsoever (Hayne et al., 2000). When 12- and 18-month-olds are tested in an altered context, however, their retention is the same as when they are tested in the context in which the original demonstration occurred (Hayne et al., 2000; see Figure 9.3, right panel).

Potential Mechanisms of Changes

What factors might contribute to age-related changes in encoding, retention, and retrieval during the infancy period? Although a definitive answer to this question is not yet possible, it is likely that both maturation and experience play an important role in this process.

Maturation

Although there is mounting evidence that the human brain continues to mature over a prolonged period of development (for reviews, see Dahl &

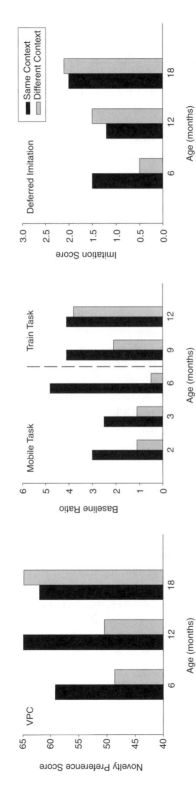

FIGURE 9.3. Age-related changes in the effect of contextual change on infant memory retrieval in the VPC (Robinson & Pascalis, 2004), operant conditioning (Hartshorn, Rovee-Collier, Gerhardstein, Bhatt, Klein, et al., 1998), and deferred imitation procedures (Hayne et al., 2000).

Spear, 2004; Spear, 2000), there is little doubt that it matures very rapidly during infancy and early childhood. In terms of size, the human brain is only 27% of its adult weight at the time of birth; the brain's growth spurt begins during late gestation and extends into childhood (Dobbing & Sands, 1979). The growth of the human brain is due to an increase in a number of different kinds of cells that are involved in learning and memory. For example, during infancy and early childhood, there are marked age-related changes in the myelination of the central nervous system (Casaer, 1993; Kolb & Fantie, 1997). During the course of myelination, glial cells wrap around the axon, providing insulation, which in turn increases the conduction velocity of the neural signal: In an unmyelinated axon, the action potential travels at an average speed of 2 meters per second, while in a myelinated axon, the action potential travels at an average speed of 50 meters per second (Casaer, 1993).

There are also dramatic changes in the growth of dendrites during infancy and early childhood. These dendrites connect one neuron to another, or, in the case of mammalian development, one neuron to thousands of others. Although dendrites begin to develop during the fetal period, the rate of arborization peaks during infancy. In the visual cortex, for example, synaptic density almost doubles between the second and fourth postnatal month and continues to increase until the child's first birthday (Huttenlocher, 1990). Similarly, synaptic density in the frontal cortex also peaks at about 1 year of age (Huttenlocher, 1984).

How might these changes in myelination and arborization contribute to memory development? It is possible that changes in conduction velocity due to myelination may play an important role in the age-related changes in the speed of encoding that occurs during infancy and early childhood. In addition, the speed of memory retrieval increases over the first year of life (Hildreth & Rovee-Collier, 1999); this age-related change may also be due to changes in conduction velocity that are due to myelination. In terms of arborization, it is possible that increased connections between individual neurons play an important role in other aspects of memory development. For example, as neurons in the hippocampus and the cortex become more interconnected, the individual attributes that make up a memory representation may become more integrated, increasing the number of retrieval paths for a particular memory. In theory, a process of this kind could account for age-related changes in the duration of long-term memory and in the flexibility of memory retrieval. Although each of these hypotheses is entirely plausible, a clear understanding of the neural mechanisms involved in memory development awaits further research.

Experience

Some aspects of brain maturation are genetically programmed; however, the ultimate form and function of the brain are a product of genetic potential and experience (Greenough, Black, & Wallace, 1987). In fact, it has been argued that the prolonged period of infancy during human development reflects the important contribution that is made by the environment. In terms of memory, a number of experiential factors may contribute to changes in encoding, retention, and retrieval. For example, young infants typically exhibit retrieval failure when they are tested with new objects or in new contexts. This high degree of specificity is overcome when they are given additional experience with multiple stimuli or in multiple contexts. When 3-month-old infants are trained for three consecutive days with the same stimulus in the mobile conjugate reinforcement paradigm, memory retrieval is precluded by a change in the mobile at the time of the test. This high degree of specificity is overcome, however, if infants are exposed to a variety of mobiles during original encoding (Fagen, Morrongiello, Rovee-Collier, & Gekoski, 1984; Greco, Hayne, & Rovee-Collier, 1990; Hayne, 1996; Hayne et al., 1986). Similarly, if original encoding occurs in a variety of environmental contexts, subsequent retrieval is unaffected by a change in the context at the time of the test (Amabile & Rovee-Collier, 1991; Rovee-Collier & Dufault, 1991). In studies of deferred imitation, the flexibility of memory retrieval is enhanced by providing infants with the opportunity to practice the target actions prior to the retention interval (Hayne et al., 2003) or by providing them with additional verbal cues (Herbert & Hayne, 2000b).

Taken together, research conducted with two different experimental procedures has shown that the range of effective retrieval cues for a particular memory will vary not only as a function of the infant's age, but also as a function of his or her prior experience. The finding that additional experience in the context of an experimental task can extend the range of effective retrieval cues for an infant's memory raises the possibility that infants' experiences outside the experimental context might also facilitate their memory skills. In the course of their daily lives, for example, infants often encounter stimuli that match attributes stored as part of a memory representation. When this occurs, new information encountered at the time of retrieval may be added to the memory representation and the range of subsequent retrieval cues is increased; as an infant's range of experiences expands with development, so does the range of effective retrieval cues for a particular memory.

One potentially important experience for infants' memory development might be the onset of independent locomotion. Rovee-Collier (1996) has argued that as infants begin to move around their environment, they quickly learn that some changes in context are irrelevant: What you learn in one location can be applied to similar events that occur in another. Research in my laboratory has provided empirical support for Rovee-Collier's ecological view. We have found that when chronological age is held constant, crawling status influences the degree to which infants are likely to exploit novel contextual cues. In two studies conducted with 9-month-olds, for example, we found that infants who crawled exhibited excellent retention in a deferred imitation task even when the objects and context were altered at the time of the test. Infants who had not yet crawled, however, exhibited excellent retention on the basic imitation task, but no retention whatsoever when the cues and context were altered (Gross & Hayne, 2004; Herbert, Gross, & Hayne, in press).

What Kind of Memory Do Infants Exhibit?

Taken together, research using the VPC, operant conditioning, and deferred imitation paradigms have yielded a remarkably consistent pattern of findings on age-related changes in encoding, storage, and retrieval during infancy and early childhood (see Figures 9.2 and 9.3). Despite this consistent pattern of data, there has often been debate about the kind of memory that is measured by each memory task. On the one hand, some researchers have argued that all three memory paradigms measure the same kind of memory (Hayne, 2004), while other researchers have argued that one or more of the paradigms differs from the others (Bauer, 1996; Nelson, 1995, 1997). The fundamental question at the heart of this debate is whether any of these procedures provide an adequate measure of declarative memory.

The initial answer to the question of whether infants exhibit declarative memory was decidedly no, at least until late in the first year of life (for review, see Moscovitch, 1984), but two major waves of research forced many experts to reevaluate the characteristics of infants' memory skill. One wave of this research involved studies of human brain maturation. Many of our early assumptions about the characteristics of the human infant brain were based largely on anatomical studies conducted with infant rats. For example, in the highly altricial rat brain, the anatomical structures required for declarative memory (i.e., the medial temporal lobe and the diencephalon) are extremely immature during the infancy period. On the basis of these data, it was inferred that these same structures were also highly immature in the human infant brain (Bachevalier, 1992). More recent research on the human infant brain itself has shown that the medial temporal lobe and the diencephalon are more mature during infancy than we previously assumed (Seress, 2001). These data raise the distinct possibility that declarative memory skill might also begin to emerge very early in development.

The other wave of research that forced many experts to reevaluate the characteristics of infants' memory skill involved evaluating infants' memory performance using strategies previously used in studies conducted with adults. For example, two strategies are commonly used to assign memory tasks to memory systems in studies conducted with adult participants. The first strategy, pioneered by Squire and his colleagues, uses the memory performance of adults who suffer from amnesia as a benchmark for task assignment (for review, see Squire & Schacter, 2002). Using this amnesia filter, amnesic adults are tested on tasks that have been used with infants.

Memory tasks that amnesic adults can perform are considered to require nondeclarative memory, while memory tasks that amnesic adults cannot perform are considered to require declarative memory. What happens when we apply the amnesia filter to studies conducted using the VPC, operant conditioning, and deferred imitation procedures that are commonly used with infants? At least two of these procedures meet the criterion for a declarative memory task. For example, McKee and Squire (1993) tested normal adults and adults who suffered from amnesia using a variation of the VPC task that is used with infants. In the McKee and Squire study, participants were familiarized with a series of magazine photos for 5 seconds each. Independent groups of participants were then tested after a delay of 2 minutes or 1 hour. During the test, participants were presented with pairs of novel and familiar photos, and their visual behavior was recorded. Although normal adults exhibited significant novelty preferences when tested after both delays, adults who suffered from amnesia only exhibited a novelty preference after 2 minutes, and even then the magnitude of their novelty preference was inferior to that exhibited by normal adults. Although the results of their study are often cited as evidence that the VPC task commonly used with infants taps declarative memory skill, a skeptic might argue that McKee and Squire (1993) did not adequately apply the amnesia filter. That is, the VPC procedure used with adult participants in the McKee and Squire (1993) study was different from the procedure typically used with human infants. For example, in the McKee and Squire study, participants studied all of the familiarization stimuli prior to the test; in a typical study conducted with infants, each familiarization trial is followed by a test trial. Thus, whether amnesic adults would struggle with the infant version of the task cannot be determined on the basis of these data alone.

In a study in which researchers used a procedure that more closely resembles the procedure used with infants, Pascalis and his colleagues compared the performance of an adult (YR) with selective hippocampal damage to the performance of age-matched normal adults (Pascalis, Hunkin, Holdstock, Isaac, & Mayes, 2004). Participants were familiarized with a target stimulus and were then tested with that stimulus and a novel one either immediately or after a delay. This procedure was repeated over a series of 24 familiarization and test trials. Consistent with the data reported by McKee and Squire (1993) using a different procedure, the normal adults exhibited a significant novelty preference when tested after a delay, but YR did not. As such, this study provides the most convincing evidence to date that the VPC task commonly used with infants taps declarative memory skill.

The amnesia filter has also been applied to the imitation task commonly used to study memory by preverbal and early verbal infants (McDonough, Mandler, McKee, & Squire, 1995). McDonough et al. tested amnesic patients, patients with frontal lobe damage, and normal adults in a deferred imitation task. To do this, the experimenter modeled a series of three-step actions with everyday objects, and the participants' ability to reproduce those actions was assessed after a 24-hour delay. Both normal adults and adults with frontal lobe damage imitated the target actions during the test, but adults with amnesia did not. In fact, amnesics' reproduction of the target actions did not exceed their baseline performance of the same actions prior to the demonstration. Thus, on the basis of the amnesia filter, these data suggest that the deferred imitation procedure also provides a nonverbal measure of declarative memory.

To date, human adults have not been tested on an analogous version of the operant conditioning procedures typically used with infants. Given this, the amnesia filter is agnostic with respect to assigning these tasks to a particular memory system.

The second strategy that has been used to assign memory tasks to memory systems has been to assess the effect of different independent variables on adults' performance in a particular task. According to this parameter filter, retention on tasks that are thought to tap declarative memory are influenced by independent variables that have no effect on performance in tasks that are thought to tap nondeclarative memory, and vice versa (Tulving, 1983). For example, independent variables such as age, retention interval, study time, and context change have been shown to influence adults' performance on declarative memory tasks, but these same independent variables have little or no effect on adults' performance on nondeclarative tasks (for review, see Rovee-Collier, 1997).

What happens if we apply the parameter filter to studies of infant memory that have been conducted using the VPC, operant conditioning, and imitation procedures? As shown in Table 9.2, infants' performance on all three of these tasks is influenced by age, retention interval, study time, and context change (for review, see Hayne, 2004; Rovee-Collier, 1997). It is important to note that the data summarized in Table 9.2 have been collected in a large number of different laboratories, using a wide range of stimuli, and with infants who range in age from 6 to 24 months of age. These procedural differences make the similarity in the data all the more impressive. In addition to the variables outlined in Table 9.2, infants' performance on operant conditioning tasks is also influenced by interference, level of processing, and serial position—these same variables influence adults' performance on other declarative memory tasks. Similarly, infants' performance on the VPC task is influenced by interference (Cohen, DeLoache, & Pearl, 1977).

In conclusion, if we apply the same strategies that are typically used to assign memory tasks to memory systems in adult participants to work conducted with human infants, then we are forced to conclude that the VPC, imitation, and operant conditioning tasks meet the definition of declarative memory tasks. Given that infants exhibit evidence of retention in each of these tasks by at least 6 months of age, if not earlier, then we must also conclude that the rudiments of declarative memory skill are present by this point in development.

Table 9.2   Sample Studies in Which the Parameter Filter Has Been Applied to Tasks Typically Used to Study Memory in Infancy

Infant Task	Age	Retention Interval	Study Time	Context Change
VPC	Rose, 1981, 1994 Rose et al., 2002 Morgan, 2003	Bahrick & Pickens, 1995 Courage & Howe, 1998, 2001 Morgan, 2003 Richmond et al., 2004	Fagan, 1974 Rose, 1983 Rose et al., 1982 Morgan, 2003 Richmond et al., 2004	Haaf et al., 1996 Robinson & Pascalis, 2004 Richmond et al., 2004
Imitation	Barr et al., 1996 Bauer & Hertsgaard, 1993 Bauer & Wewerka, 1995	Barr & Hayne, 2000 Bauer et al., 2000 Herbert & Hayne, 2000a Klein & Meltzoff, 1999 Meltzoff, 1985, 1995	Barr et al., 1996	Barnat, Klein, & Meltzoff, 1996 Hayne et al., 2000
Operant conditioning	Hartshorn, Rovee-Collier, Gerhardstein, Bhatt, Wondoski, et al., 1998	Hartshorn, Rovee-Collier, Gerhardstein, Bhatt, Klein, et al., 1998	Ohr et al., 1989	Butler & Rovee-Collier, 1989 Borovsky & Rovee-Collier, 1990 Hartshorn, Rovee-Collier, Gerhardstein, Bhatt, Klein, et al., 1998

Do Infants Exhibit Episodic Memory?

Clearly, our views about infant memory have undergone a number of important changes. The initial view that infants were incapable of long-term memory was gradually replaced with the view that infants were born with at least some basic long-term memory skills. Similarly, the view that infants were restricted to nondeclarative memory until late in the first year of life has gradually been replaced by the view that at least some declarative memory skill is possible by 6 months of age and perhaps even earlier. On the basis of the model outlined in Figure 9.1, the next obvious question to address is whether infants exhibit episodic memory and, if so, when this ability emerges during the course of development.

Although both episodic and semantic memory are considered to be part of the declarative memory system, they differ in fundamental ways: Episodic memory is defined as memory for events, while semantic memory is defined as memory for facts. For example, you probably know that Washington, DC, is the capital of the United States (semantic memory), but you probably do not remember where you initially learned this information (episodic memory). In contrast, you may have a vivid memory about where you were when you learned about the bombing of the World Trade Center in New York City or that your tenure had been confirmed. In fact, you can probably visualize who was with you and how the information made you feel. In short, "Episodic memory is about happenings in particular places at particular times, or about *what, where,* and *when*" (Tulving, 2002, p. 3).

Tulving originally coined the term *episodic memory* in 1972, but his views about the features of this system have continued to evolve over more than 30 years (cf. Tulving, 1972, 1983, 2005). As illustrated in Figure 9.1, episodic memory and semantic memory were originally thought to be parallel systems within the declarative system, but more recently Tulving has suggested that the relation may be more hierarchical than parallel, with episodic memory emerging out of semantic memory (Tulving, 2002). In this way, all episodic memories are declarative, but not all declarative memories are episodic.

In addition to the claim that episodic memory is memory for information about the "what, where, and when" of an event, Tulving has recently argued that this system is characterized by two other important features: (1) Episodic memory involves a form of "mental time travel" in which the rememberer actually relives the past event, and (2) episodic memory is accompanied by conscious awareness that does not accompany retrieval of other kinds of memories (see Tulving, 2002). Tulving has also argued that episodic memory is a uniquely human skill (see also Suddendorf & Corballis, 1997) that does not emerge prior to the age of 4 years (see also Perner & Ruffman, 1995).

Tulving's changing views of episodic memory raise new questions for researchers in the area of infant memory development, but in the absence of a suitable nonverbal procedure that can be used with animals and preverbal children, Tulving's claims about the human uniqueness and developmental emergence of episodic memory have been more an article of faith than a matter of science. At first blush, it is difficult to see how we could ever distinguish episodic from semantic memory in a nonverbal organism when both "memory" and "knowledge" are derived from the same event and are expressed without language. In the case of deferred imitation, for example, how can we determine whether an infant remembers the demonstration session that occurred the day before or whether he or she simply knows how to make the objects work on the basis of prior experience? The former alternative would require the kind of recollective experience that is unique to episodic memory, while the latter would not.

Despite the complexity of this issue, episodic memory should not, by definition, require linguistic ability. In the absence of data to the contrary, it is possible that infants reflect on their past in nonverbal terms, traveling back in time to a particularly stressful departure from their primary caregiver or traveling forward in time to an anticipated interaction with an adult who has previously caused the infant pain (e.g., a nurse). By the same token, verbal report per se is not sufficient evidence for episodic memory. When a verbal adult tells us that an apple is a kind of fruit, we have a measure of what that person knows (semantic memory), but no measure of what that same person remembers. Thus, although verbal ability would appear to be neither a necessary nor a sufficient condition for episodic memory, we have yet to develop a suitable nonverbal test of episodic memory that could be used in studies with human infants.

In an attempt to solve this conundrum, Tulving (2005) has offered at least one example of a nonverbal behavior that would meet the requirements for episodic memory. His example is based on a charming Estonian children's story. In the story, a little girl goes to sleep and dreams about a friend's birthday party. At the party, the guests are served a wonderful chocolate pudding, which just happens to be the girl's favorite dessert. Unbeknownst to the little girl, however, guests were required to bring their own spoons to the party. Because she does not have a spoon, the little girl must stand by and watch as others enjoy the pudding. The next night when this same little girl goes to bed, she tucks a spoon under her pillow, just in case she returns to the party in her dreams. According to Tulving (2005), taking the spoon to bed provides a hallmark measure of episodic memory—it signals the little girl's ability to travel both forward and backward in mental time, using a prior experience to plan for a future event. In this way, variations of this "spoon test" could be used as a nonverbal marker for mental time travel and for conscious awareness of a past event—the two essential ingredients for episodic memory.

The Spoon Test in Studies With Nonhuman Animals

The issue of episodic memory has already captured the imagination of researchers working with nonverbal animals. In an elegant series of studies conducted with food-hoarding birds, for example, Clayton and her colleagues have shown that these animals exhibit memory skills that are remarkably similar to those that characterize episodic memory in human adults. In the initial experiments on episodic memory, scrub jays were allowed to cache two kinds of food—wax worms, which are their preferred food but which decay rapidly, and peanuts, which are less preferred but once stored do not decay (Clayton & Dickinson, 1998). When these birds were allowed to recover their cache within hours after the items had been hidden, they searched preferentially for the wax worms. When the opportunity to search was delayed by several days, however, birds preferentially searched for the peanuts. On the basis of these data, Clayton has argued that the scrub jays demonstrate the three *w*'s of episodic memory—what, where, and when. That is, the birds remember what item they had hidden (worms or peanuts), where it had been hidden, and when it had been hidden (hours or days earlier).

Although Clayton's original results provided a compelling demonstration of episodic-like memory in a nonhuman species, not everyone was immediately convinced by the data. Suddendorf and Busby (2003), for example, thought that Clayton's demonstration lacked the critical element of time travel that was inherent in Tulving's definition of episodic memory. In particular, they argued that Clayton had failed to demonstrate that the birds could use their episodic memories to construct future plans—a notion inherent in Tulving's spoon test.

In response to this criticism, Clayton and her colleagues designed another test of episodic memory, but this time the birds had the opportunity to use what they remembered about prior experiences to plan their subsequent cache (Clayton, 2004). In this version of the task, scrub jays were allowed to cache wax worms and peanuts as before, but this time their wax worm cache was always pilfered by another bird. In another condition, wax worms were not pilfered, but they decayed more rapidly than usual, such that whenever the scrub jay returned to the wax worm cache, it was already rotten. Clayton argued that if the birds could use their prior experience with pilfering or decay to plan their future behavior, then they should stop caching wax worms and hide only peanuts. In both conditions, this is exactly what happened. In other words, consistent with Tulving's spoon test, scrub jays used their past experience to plan their subsequent behavior.

Episodic Memory in Human Infants and Young Children

Data collected by Clayton and her colleagues challenge the view that episodic memory is a uniquely human skill and suggest that the essential ingredients for episodic memory can be found even in birds. The finding that episodic memory emerges early in the course of vertebrate evolution raises the distinct possibility that it may also emerge very early during the course of human development. What empirical evidence do we have about the emergence of episodic memory during infancy and early childhood? Is 4 years the boundary for episodic memory, or do children begin to recall the what, when, and where of events much earlier in development?

Some evidence for the early emergence of episodic memory can be found in retrospective studies conducted with verbal children and adults. For example, there is a large database on adults' retrospective reports of their earliest childhood memories. This database has been established in the context of research on childhood amnesia. In an attempt to define the boundary of childhood amnesia, researchers have asked adults to recall their earliest autobiographical memories. Using this technique, it has been repeatedly shown that the average age of earliest autobiographical memory is typically 3.5 years, but it may also be as young as 2 years (Eacott & Crawley, 1998; MacDonald, Uesiliana, & Hayne, 2000; Mullen, 1994; Usher & Neisser, 1993). Furthermore, recent studies have shown that the boundary for childhood amnesia may be even lower than 2 years in studies conducted with children (Peterson, Grant, & Boland, 2005; Tustin, Wright, & Hayne, 2005).

Studies of our earliest autobiographical memories may have important implications for our understanding of episodic memory development. That is, if children and adults can truly recall an event that occurred when they were as young as 2 (and perhaps even younger), then we must conclude that episodic memory begins to emerge much earlier than the age of 4 that has been suggested by Tulving (2002) and others (Perner & Ruffman, 1995). Unfortunately, however, many of the events that participants nominate as their earliest memory play an important part in family stories or have been captured in photographs that can be reviewed and discussed over and over again. Thus, when the participant is recounting the event, we can never be certain that he or she is describing a specific episodic memory or a more generic semantic memory that has been established over multiple retellings. That is, despite the verbal nature of the account, we cannot distinguish what the participant actually remembers from what he or she knows about the same event.

What other ways could we study the development of episodic memory? In light of the data collected by Clayton and her colleagues, my students and I have begun to examine the development of episodic memory using tasks that involve hiding and finding. In one of our tasks, 3- and 4-year-olds were tested in their own homes. The experimenter familiarized the child with seven soft toys (Bert, Ernie, the Count, Mickey Mouse, Donald Duck, Ronald McDonald, and Cookie Monster) and then instructed the child to choose three toys from the original group of seven. Once the child made his or her selections, the experimenter and the child hid the toys in different rooms throughout the house. As the experimenter and the child entered each room, the child was asked to name the room and was instructed to watch carefully as a toy was hidden in a specific location such as under a bed or behind a chair. This sequence of events continued until all of the toys were hidden. Following the hiding portion of the task, the experimenter and the child returned to the living room. To prevent overt rehearsal of the hiding locations, the experimenter read the child two books during the 5-minute retention interval. At the end of the retention interval, the child was asked to name one of the rooms in which a toy was hidden. Once the child provided a room (e.g., the bedroom), he or she was asked to name the toy (e.g., Bert) that was hiding in that room and then to name the specific hiding place (e.g., under the bed). The same sequence of questions was repeated until the child could provide no further information. The child's verbal recall was tape recorded. For each hidden item, a child could recall a total of three pieces of information: the room, the toy, and the exact location of the toy within that room (e.g., under the bed). The audiotapes of verbal recall were transcribed verbatim, and each transcript was coded by two independent observers. For each child, verbal recall was expressed as a proportion of the total number of items that could be recalled. Overall, children recalled a large amount of information ($M = 80.5\%$). Importantly, there was no difference in children's performance as a function of age. That is, children as young as 3 performed as well as 4-year-olds on this episodic memory task. In fact, even when the task was made more difficult by hiding five toys instead of three, there was still no difference in the memory performance of 3-year-olds and 4-year-olds. On the basis of our hiding and finding task, we conclude that, at least by at the age of 3, children are beginning to acquire rudimentary episodic memory skills. In our task, children were highly accurate at recalling the what and where of the event. Furthermore, when they were explicitly asked to do so, children could also recall the order in which the items had been hidden, indicating that they also remembered something about when.

Nonverbal Evidence of Episodic Memory in Infants and Young Children: Avenues for Future Research

There is now mounting evidence that the boundary for the development of episodic memory is likely to be much earlier than previously assumed. Prospective data on hiding tasks suggest that the boundary is at least 3 years, but is it possible that episodic memory might emerge even earlier? Unfortunately, the standard measures of infant long-term memory that have served us so well in the past may be insufficient to examine all of the relevant features of episodic memory. For example, studies of deferred or elicited imitation can tell us about infants' memory for the what and when of an event, but they don't tell us anything about infants' memory for where. Similarly, studies of operant conditioning can tell us about infants' memory for what and where, but not when. Furthermore, none of the tasks currently used with infants provides a suitable measure of prospective memory, another critical feature of Tulving's definition of episodic memory. Ultimately, our ability to track the ontogeny of episodic memory will rely on our ability to establish a nonverbal spoon test that can be used with infants and toddlers. Inspired by Clayton's work with scrub jays, we are currently developing a nonverbal memory task that not only measures participants' memory for the what, when, and where of an event but also examines their ability to use prior knowledge to guide future behavior. Only time (and further research) will tell when the rudiments of episodic memory begin to emerge and how these skills change over course of human development. I predict that episodic memory will emerge substantially earlier than 4 years of age, but that prospective episodic memory skill, in particular, will continue to improve over a very prolonged period of development. These data will have important implications for current theories of the ontogeny and phylogeny of long-term memory, and they will also have important practical implications in settings in which children must rely on their memories, including clinical, legal, and educational contexts.

Conclusion

Throughout this chapter, I have argued that our view of infant memory development is constantly evolving. Over the past two decades, new models of adult memory that emerged from our growing knowledge of the brain have provided a particularly fruitful source of new questions about memory development. Although we may now feel as if we have answered some of our most basic questions, as our knowledge of adult memory continues to accumulate and accrue, it will be prudent for us to continue to evaluate the validity of those answers in light of new findings. In short, we should never become complacent with the state of our knowledge. Only by asking new questions do we have the opportunity to find new answers.

Acknowledgment

Portions of the data reviewed here were supported by a Marsden Grant from the Royal Society of New Zealand to Harlene Hayne.

References

Amabile, T. A., & Rovee-Collier, C. (1991). Contextual variation and memory retrieval at six months. *Child Development, 62,* 1155–1166.

Bachevalier, J. (1992). Cortical versus limbic immaturity: Relationship to infantile amnesia. In M. R. Gunnar & C. A. Nelson (Eds.), *Developmental behavioural neuroscience* (pp. 129–153). Hillsdale, NJ: Erlbaum.

Bahrick, L., & Pickens, J. (1995). Infant memory for object motion across a period of three months: Implications for a four-phase attention function. *Journal of Experimental Child Psychology, 59,* 343–371.

Barnat, S. B., Klein, P. J., & Meltzoff, A. (1996). Deferred imitation across changes in context and object: Memory and generalization in 14-month-old infants. *Infant Behavior and Development, 19,* 241–251.

Barr, R., Dowden, A., & Hayne, H. (1996). Developmental changes in deferred imitation by 6- to 24-month-old infants. *Infant Behavior and Development, 19,* 159–170.

Barr, R., & Hayne, H. (2000). Age-related changes in imitation: Implications for memory development. In C. Rovee-Collier, L. P. Lipsitt, & H. Hayne (Eds.), *Progress in infancy research* (Vol. 1, pp. 21–67). Hillsdale, NJ: Erlbaum.

Bauer, P. J. (1996). What do infants recall of their lives? Memory for specific events by one- to two-year-olds. *American Psychologist, 51,* 29–41.

Bauer, P. J. (2004). Getting explicit memory off the ground: Steps toward construction of a neuro-developmental account of changes in the first two years of life. *Developmental Review, 24,* 347–373.

Bauer, P. J., & Hertsgaard, L. A. (1993). Increasing steps in recall of events: Factors facilitating immediate and long-term memory in 13.5- and 16.5-month-old children. *Child Development, 64,* 1204–1223.

Bauer, P. J., & Mandler, J. M. (1989). One thing follows another: Effects of temporal structure on 1- to 2-year-olds' recall of events. *Developmental Psychology, 25,* 197–206.

Bauer, P. J., Wenner, J. A., Dropik, P. L., & Wewerka, S. S. (2000). Parameters of remembering and forgetting in the transition from infancy to early childhood. *Monographs of the Society for Research in Child Development,* 65(4, Serial No. 263).

Bauer, P. J., & Wewerka, S. S. (1995). One- to two-year-olds' recall of events: The more expressed, the more impressed. *Journal of Experimental Child Psychology, 59,* 475–496.

Berlyne, D. E. (1958). The influence of the albedo and complexity of stimuli on visual fixation in the human infant. *British Journal of Psychology, 56,* 315–318.

Borovsky, D., & Rovee-Collier, C. (1990). Contextual constraints on memory retrieval at six months. *Child Development, 61,* 1569–1583.

Bushnell, I. W. R., Sai, F., & Mullin, J. T. (1989). Neonatal recognition of the mother's face. *British Journal of Developmental Psychology, 7,* 3–15.

Butler, J., & Rovee-Collier, C. (1989). Contextual gating of memory retrieval. *Developmental Psychobiology, 22,* 533–552.

Casaer, P. (1993). Old and new facts about perinatal brain development. *Journal of Child Psychology and Psychiatry, 34,* 101–109.

Clayton, N. S. (2004, December). *Retrospective and prospective cognition in animals: A Western scrub jay's perspective.* Paper presented at the Memory Theme Symposium, University of Otago, Dunedin, New Zealand.

Clayton, N. S., & Dickinson, A. (1998). Episodic-like memory during cache recovery by scrub jays. *Nature, 395,* 272–274.

Cohen, L. B., DeLoache, J. S., & Pearl, R. A. (1977). An examination of interference effects in infants' memory for faces. *Child Development, 48,* 88–96.

Collie, R., & Hayne, H. (1999). Deferred imitation by 6- and 9-month-old infants: More evidence for declarative memory. *Developmental Psychobiology, 35,* 83–90.

Colombo, J., & Mitchell, D. W. (1990). Individual differences in early visual attention: Fixation time and information processing. In J. Colombo & J. Fagen (Eds.), *Individual differences in infancy: Reliability, stability, prediction* (pp. 193–228). Hillsdale, NJ: Erlbaum.

Courage, M. L., & Howe, M. L. (1998). The ebb and flow of infant attentional preferences: Evidence for long-term recognition memory in 3-month-olds. *Journal of Experimental Child Psychology, 70,* 26–53.

Courage, M. L., & Howe, M. L. (2001). Long-term retention in 3.5-month-olds: Familiarization time and individual differences in attentional style. *Journal of Experimental Child Psychology, 79,* 271–293.

Dahl, R. E., & Spear, L. P. (Eds.). (2004). *Adolescent brain development: Vulnerabilities and opportunities.* New York: New York Academy of Sciences.

Davis, J., & Rovee-Collier, C. (1983). Alleviated forgetting of a learned contingency in 8-week-old infants. *Developmental Psychology, 19,* 353–365.

DeCasper, A. J., & Fifer, W. P. (1980). Of human bonding: Newborns prefer their mothers' voices. *Science, 208,* 1174–1176.

DeCasper, A. J., & Sigafoos, A. D. (1983). The intrauterine heartbeat: A potent reinforcer for newborns. *Infant Behavior and Development, 6,* 19–25.

DeCasper, A. J., & Spence, M. J. (1986). Prenatal maternal speech influences newborns' perception of speech sounds. *Infant Behavior and Development, 9,* 133–150.

Dobbing, J., & Sands, J. (1979). Comparative aspects of the brain growth spurt. *Early Human Development, 3,* 79–83.

Eacott, M. J., & Crawley, R. A. (1998). The offset of childhood amnesia: Memory for events that occurred before the age of 3. *Journal of Experimental Psychology: General, 127,* 22–33.

Fagan, J. F. (1974). Infant recognition memory: The effects of length of familiarization and type of discrimination task. *Child Development, 45,* 351–356.

Fagen, J. W., Morrongiello, B. A., Rovee-Collier, C., & Gekoski, M. J. (1984). Expectancies and memory retrieval in 3-month-old infants and adults. *Journal of Experimental Child Psychology, 22,* 272–281.

Fantz, R. L. (1958). Pattern vision in young infants. *Psychological Record, 8,* 43–47.

Fantz, R. L. (1964). Visual experience in infants: Decreased attention to familiar patterns relative to novel ones. *Science, 146,* 668–670.

Gold, P. E. (2004). Coordination of multiple memory systems. *Neurobiology of Learning and Memory, 82,* 230–242.

Greco, C., Hayne, H., & Rovee-Collier, C. (1990). Roles of function, reminding, and variability in categorization by 3-month-olds. *Journal of Experimental Psychology: Learning, Memory, and Cognition, 16,* 617–633.

Greco, C., Rovee-Collier, C., Hayne, H., Griesler, P., & Earley, L. (1986). Ontogeny of early event memory: I. Forgetting and retrieval by 2- and 3-month-olds. *Infant Behavior and Development, 9,* 441–460.

Greenough, W. T., Black, J. E., & Wallace, C. S. (1987). Experience and brain development. *Child Development, 58,* 539–559.

Gross, J., & Hayne, H. (2004, June). *Is there a relation between motor development and cognitive development in human infants?* Paper presented at the International Society for Developmental Psychobiology, Aix-en-Provence, France.

Haaf, R. A., Lundy, B. L., & Codren, J. T. (1996). Attention, recognition, and the effects of stimulus context in 6-month-old infants. *Infant Behavior and Development, 19,* 93–106.

Hartshorn, K., & Rovee-Collier, C. (1997). Infant learning and long-term memory at 6 mos: A confirming analysis. *Developmental Psychobiology, 30,* 71–85.

Hartshorn, K., Rovee-Collier, C., Gerhardstein, P. C., Bhatt, R. S., Klein, P. J., Aaron, F., et al. (1998). Developmental changes in the specificity of memory over the first year of life. *Developmental Psychobiology, 33,* 61–78.

Hartshorn, K., Rovee-Collier, C., Gerhardstein, P. C., Bhatt, R. S., Wondoloski, T. L., Klein, P., et al. (1998). Ontogeny of long-term memory over the first year-and-a-half of life. *Developmental Psychobiology, 32,* 69–89.

Hayne, H. (1996). Categorization in infancy. In C. Rovee-Collier & L. P. Lipsitt (Eds.), *Advances in infancy research* (Vol. 10, pp. 79–120). Norwood, NJ: Ablex.

Hayne, H. (2004). Infant memory development: Implications for childhood amnesia. *Developmental Review, 24,* 33–73.

Hayne, H. (2006). Bridging the gap: The relation between learning and memory during infancy. In M. H. Johnson & Y. Munakata (Eds.), *Attention and performance XXI: Processes of change in brain and cognitive development* (pp. 209–231). London: Oxford University Press.

Hayne, H., Barr, R., & Herbert, J. (2003). The effect of prior practice on memory reactivation and generalization. *Child Development, 74,* 1615–1627.

Hayne, H., Boniface, J., & Barr, R. (2000). The development of declarative memory in human infants: Age-related changes in deferred imitation. *Behavioral Neuroscience, 114,* 77–83.

Hayne, H., Greco, C., Earley, L. A., Griesler, P. C., & Rovee-Collier, C. (1986). Ontogeny of early event memory: II. Encoding and retrieval by 2- and 3-month-olds. *Infant Behavior and Development, 9,* 461–472.

Hayne, H., & Herbert, J. (2004). Verbal cues facilitate memory retrieval during infancy. *Journal of Experimental Child Psychology, 89,* 127–139.

Hayne, H., MacDonald, S., & Barr, R. (1997). Developmental changes in the specificity of memory over the second year of life. *Infant Behavior and Development, 20,* 237–249.

Herbert, J., Gross, J., & Hayne, H. (in press). Crawling is associated with more flexible memory retrieval by 9-month-old infants. *Developmental Science.*

Herbert, J., & Hayne, H. (2000a). The ontogeny of long-term retention during the second year of life. *Developmental Science, 3,* 50–56.

Herbert, J., & Hayne, H. (2000b). Memory retrieval by 18–30-month-olds: Age-related changes in representational flexibility. *Developmental Psychology, 36,* 473–484.

Hildreth, K., & Rovee-Collier, C. (1999). Decreases in the response latency to priming over the first year of life. *Developmental Psychobiology, 35,* 276–290.

Hill, W. H., Borovsky, D., & Rovee-Collier, C. (1988). Continuities in infant memory development over the first half-year. *Developmental Psychobiology, 21,* 43–62.

Hunter, M., & Ames, E. (1988). A multifactor model of infant preferences for novel and familiar stimuli. In C. Rovee-Collier & L. P. Lipsitt (Eds.), *Advances in infancy research* (Vol. 5, pp. 69–95). Norwood, NJ: Ablex.

Huttenlocher, P. R. (1984). Synapse elimination and plasticity in developing in human cerebral cortex. *American Journal of Mental Deficiency, 88,* 488–496.

Huttenlocher, P. R. (1990). Morphometric study of human cerebral cortex development. *Neuropsychologia, 13,* 95–102.

James, W. (1890). *The principles of psychology.* New York: Holt.

Kail, R. (1986). Sources of age differences in speed of processing. *Child Development, 57,* 969–987.

Kail, R. (1993). Processing time decreases globally at an exponential rate during childhood and adolescence. *Journal of Experimental Child Psychology, 56,* 254–265.

Kail, R. (2003). Information processing and memory. In M. H. Bornstein, L. Davidson, C. Keyes, & K. A. Moore (Eds.), *Well-being: Positive development across the life course: Crosscurrents in contemporary psychology* (pp. 269–279). Mahwah, NJ: Erlbaum.

Klein, P. J., & Meltzoff, A. N. (1999). Long-term memory, forgetting, and deferred imitation in 12-month-old infants. *Developmental Science, 2,* 102–113.

Kolb, B., & Fantie, B. (1997). Development of the child's brain and behaviour. In C. R. Reynolds & E. Fletcher-Janzen (Eds.), *Handbook of clinical child neuropsychology* (2nd ed., pp. 17–41). New York: Plenum.

MacDonald, S., Uesiliana, K., & Hayne, H. (2000). Cross-cultural and gender differences in childhood amnesia. *Memory, 8,* 365–376.

MacFarlane, A. J. (1975). Olfaction in the development of social preferences in the human neonate. *Ciba Foundation, Symposia, 33,* 103–117.

McDonald, R. J., Devan, B. D., & Hong, N. S. (2004). Multiple memory systems: The power of interactions. *Neurobiology of Learning and Memory, 82,* 333–346.

McDonough, L., Mandler, J. M., McKee, R. D., & Squire, L. R. (1995). The deferred imitation task as a nonverbal measure of declarative memory. *Proceedings of the National Academy of Science, USA, 92,* 7580–7584.

McKee, R. D., & Squire, L. R. (1993). On the development of declarative memory. *Journal of Experimental Psychology: Learning, Memory, and Cognition, 19,* 397–404.

Meltzoff, A. N. (1985). Immediate and deferred imitation in fourteen- and twenty-four-month-old infants. *Child Development, 56,* 62–72.

Meltzoff, A. N. (1988). Infant imitation and memory: Nine-month-olds in immediate and deferred tests. *Child Development, 56,* 62–72.

Meltzoff, A. N. (1995). What infant memory tells us about infantile amnesia: Long-term recall and deferred imitation. *Journal of Experimental Child Psychology, 59,* 497–515.

Meltzoff, A. N., & Moore, M. K. (1977). Imitation of facial and manual gestures by human neonates. *Science, 198,* 75–78.

Meltzoff, A. N., & Moore, M. K. (1983). Newborn infants imitate adult facial gestures. *Child Development, 54,* 702–709.

Meltzoff, A. N., & Moore, M. K. (1989). Imitation in newborn infants: Exploring the range of gestures imitated and the underlying mechanisms. *Developmental Psychology, 25,* 954–962.

Meltzoff, A. N., & Moore, M. K. (1994). Imitation, memory, and the representation of persons. *Infant Behavior and Development, 17,* 83–99.

Morgan, K. (2003). *A developmental analysis of memory processing.* Doctoral dissertation submitted to the Psychology Department, University of Otago, Dunedin, New Zealand.

Morgan, K., & Hayne, H. (2002, April). *Age-related changes in visual recognition memory from infancy through early childhood.* Paper presented at the International Conference on Infant Studies, Toronto, Canada.

Moscovitch, M. (Ed.). (1984). *Infant memory: Its relation to normal and pathological memory in humans and other animals.* New York: Plenum.

Mullen, M. K. (1994). Earliest recollections of childhood: A demographic analysis. *Cognition, 52,* 55–79.

Nelson, C. A. (1995). The ontogeny of human memory: A cognitive neuroscience perspective. *Developmental Psychology, 31,* 723–738.

Nelson, C. A. (1997). The neurobiological basis of early memory development. In N. Cowan (Ed.), *The development of memory in early childhood* (pp. 41–82). Hove, UK: Psychology Press.

Ohr, P., Fagen, J. W., Rovee-Collier, C., Hayne, H., & Vander Linde, E. (1989). Amount of training and retention by infants. *Developmental Psychobiology, 22,* 69–80.

Pascalis, O., de Schonen, S., Morton, J., Deruelle, C., & Fabre-Grenet, M. (1995). Mother's face recognition by neonates: A replication and an extension. *Infant Behavior and Development, 18,* 79–85.

Pascalis, O., Hunkin, N. M., Holdstock, J. S., Isaac, C. L., & Mayes, A. R. (2004). Visual paired comparison performance is impaired in a patient with selective hippocampal lesions and relatively intact item recognition. *Neuropsychologia, 42,* 1293–1300.

Perner, J., & Ruffman, T. (1995). Episodic memory and autonoetic consciousness: Developmental evidence and a theory of childhood amnesia. *Journal of Experimental Child Psychology, 59,* 516–548.

Peterson, C., Grant, V. V., & Boland, L. D. (2005). Childhood amnesia in children and adolescents: Their earliest memories. *Memory, 13,* 622–637.

Piaget, J. (1929). *The child's conception of the world.* Oxford, UK: Harcourt Brace.

Piaget, J. (1962). *Play, dreams and imitation in childhood.* New York: Norton.

Porter, F. L., Grunau, R. E., & Anand, K. J. S. (1999). Long-term effects of pain in infants. *Developmental and Behavioral Pediatrics, 20,* 253–261.

Richmond, J., Sowerby, P., Colombo, M., & Hayne, H. (2004). The effect of familiarization time, retention interval, and context change on adults' performance in the visual paired-comparison task. *Developmental Psychobiology, 44,* 146–155.

Robinson, A. J., & Pascalis, O. (2004). Development of flexible visual recognition memory in human infants. *Developmental Science, 7,* 527–533.

Rose, S. A. (1981). Lags in the cognitive competence of prematurely born infants. In S. L. Friedman & M. Sigman (Eds.), *Preterm birth and psychological development* (pp. 255–269). New York: Academic Press.

Rose, S. A. (1983). Differential rates of visual information processing in full-term and pre-term infants. *Child Development, 54,* 1189–1198.

Rose, S. A. (1994). Relation between physical growth and information processing in infants born in India. *Child Development, 65,* 889–902.

Rose, S. A., Gottfried, A. W., Melloy-Carminar, P., & Bridger, W. H. (1982). Familiarity and novelty preferences in infant recognition memory: Implications for information processing. *Developmental Psychology, 18,* 704–713.

Rose, S. A., Jankowski, J. J., & Feldman, J. F. (2002). Speed of processing and face recognition at 7 and 12 months. *Infancy, 3,* 435–455.

Rovee, C. K., & Rovee, D. T. (1969). Conjugate reinforcement of infant exploratory behavior. *Journal of Experimental Child Psychology, 8,* 33–39.

Rovee-Collier, C. (1996). Shifting the focus from what to why. *Infant Behavior and Development, 19,* 385–400.

Rovee-Collier, C. (1997). Dissociations in infant memory: Rethinking the development of implicit and explicit memory. *Psychological Review, 104,* 467–498.

Rovee-Collier, C., & Dufault, D. (1991). Multiple contexts and memory retrieval at 3 months. *Developmental Psychobiology, 24,* 39–49.

Rovee-Collier, C., Hayne, H., & Colombo, M. (2001). *The development of implicit and explicit memory.* Amsterdam: Benjamins.

Seress, L. (2001). Morphological changes of the human hippocampal formation from midgestation to early childhood. In C. A. Nelson & M. Luciana (Eds.), *Handbook of developmental cognitive neuroscience* (pp. 45–58). Cambridge, MA: MIT Press.

Spear, L. P. (2000). The adolescent brain and age-related behavioural manifestations. *Neuroscience and Biobehavioral Reviews, 24,* 417–463.

Squire, L. R. (1987). *Memory and brain.* New York: Oxford University Press.

Squire, L. R. (1994). Declarative and nondeclarative memory: Multiple brain systems supporting learning and memory. In D. L. Schachter & E. Tulving (Eds.), *Memory systems 1994* (pp. 203–232). Cambridge, MA: MIT Press.

Squire, L. R. (2004). Memory systems of the brain: A brief history and current perspective. *Neurobiology of Learning and Memory, 82,* 171–177.

Squire, L. R., & Schacter, D. L. (Eds.). (2002). *Neuropsychology of memory* (3rd ed.). New York: Guilford Press.

Suddendorf, T., & Busby, J. (2003). Mental time travel in animals? *Trends in Cognitive Science, 7,* 391–396.

Suddendorf, T., & Corballis, M. C. (1997). Mental time travel and the evolution of the human mind. *Genetic, Social, and General Psychology Monographs, 123,* 133–167.

Thomson, D. M., & Tulving, E. (1970). Associative encoding and retrieval: Weak and strong cues. *Journal of Experimental Psychology, 86,* 255–262.

Tulving, E. (1972). Episodic and semantic memory. In E. Tulving & W. Donaldson (Eds.), *Organization of memory* (pp. 381–403). New York: Academic Press.

Tulving, E. (1983). *Elements of episodic memory.* New York: Oxford University Press.

Tulving, E. (2002). Episodic memory: From mind to brain. *Annual Review of Psychology, 53,* 1–25.

Tulving, E. (2005). Episodic memory and autonoesis: Uniquely human? In H. S. Terrace & J. Metcalfe (Eds.), *The missing link in cognition: Self-knowing consciousnesss in man and animals* (pp. 3–56). New York: Oxford University Press.

Tulving, E., & Thomson, D. M. (1973). Encoding specificity and retrieval processes in episodic memory. *Psychological Review, 80,* 359–380.

Tustin, K., Wright, F., & Hayne, H. (2005, April). *Defining the boundary: Age-related changes in childhood amnesia.* Paper presented at the biennial meeting of the Society for Research in Child Development, Atlanta, GA.

Usher, J. N., & Neisser, U. (1993). Childhood amnesia and the beginnings of memory for four early life events. *Journal of Experimental Psychology: General, 122,* 155–165.

10

In the Language of Multiple Memory Systems

*Defining and Describing Developments in Long-Term
Declarative Memory*

PATRICIA J. BAUER, TRACY DEBOER,
AND ANGELA F. LUKOWSKI

Memory is a fundamental cognitive capacity. Without it, we would live only for the moment. Although we might do well to heed advice to "live for today," appreciation of today is significantly enhanced by the ability to remember yesterday and to anticipate tomorrow. Memory permits these functions by allowing us to store and reflect upon previous experience and use it to guide present as well as future behavior. The continuity afforded by memory is readily apparent as soon as children develop the capacity to use language to share mental experiences. The status of the capacity before language has been a source of active debate. The perspective that infants and preverbal children lack the capacity for storage and retrieval of accessible memory representations is well represented in the traditional (e.g., Piaget, 1952) as well as the contemporary (e.g., K. Nelson & Ross, 1980; Pillemer, 1998; Pillemer & White, 1989) literature. The perspective in this chapter is that the capacity begins to develop well before language and undergoes significant age-related change before first memories are expressed verbally. We develop this perspective by addressing each of the questions posed to contributors to this volume.

What Kind of Memory Is It?

An adequate answer to the question, What kind of memory is it? is absolutely central because, as argued by Bauer (2007), memory is not pudding.

Pudding is a homogeneous entity. When you put a spoon into a bowl of pudding, you draw out pudding. Each new spoonful looks like the last. Comments, characterizations, and truths declared about one spoonful are equally true of the next, and the next, and the next.[1] But memory is not pudding. Rather, there are many different types of memory. One common division of memory—that used to organize this volume—is along a temporal dimension. Some memories are short term, lasting only seconds. Others are long term and may even last a lifetime. A "truth" about short-term memory is that its capacity is limited (i.e., to seven "units" of information, plus or minus two). In contrast, long-term memory is boundless in its capacity. For all practical purposes, there is no upper limit on the amount of information that can be maintained in long-term memory stores. The memories discussed in this chapter are of the long-term variety: They persist for hours, days, weeks, and even months.

If memory were pudding that came in two varieties—vanilla (short-term) and chocolate (long-term)—it would not be important to go beyond the temporal dimension to distinguish the specific "flavor" under consideration. However, at least three different lines of evidence suggest that there are dimensions other than the temporal along which memory differs. Data from patients with focal or localized lesions, from animal models of lesion and disease, and from neuroimaging studies suggest that there are different types of memory that are distinguished by content, function, rules of operation, and neural substrates (e.g., Schacter, Wagner, & Buckner, 2000; Squire, Knowlton, & Musen, 1993). *Declarative* or *explicit* memory—the subject of this chapter—involves conscious recognition or recall. It is devoted to recollection of such things as names, dates, places, facts, and events, and descriptive details about them. These are entities that we think of as being encoded symbolically and that thus can be described with language. Declarative memory is specialized for rapid, even one-trial learning that is not tied to a specific modality or context. As described in more detail in a later section, it is subserved by a multicomponent neural network that includes temporal and cortical structures.

In contrast to declarative memory, *nondeclarative* or *implicit* memory represents a variety of nonconscious abilities, including the capacity for learning skills and procedures, priming, and some forms of conditioning. The content of nondeclarative memory is not names, dates, facts, and events, but finely tuned motor patterns, procedures, and perceptual skills. It is not encoded symbolically and thus is not accessible to language. Nondeclarative memory is characterized as slow (i.e., with the exception of priming, it results from gradual or incremental learning) and inflexible. Different types of nondeclarative memory are subserved by different neural substrates, including the cerebellum and basal ganglia. In addition, the hippocampus—one of the medial temporal lobe structures involved in declarative memory—also is implicated in some nondeclarative tasks.

The distinction between different types of memory is widely accepted in the adult cognitive and cognitive neuroscience communities. In the developmental literature, it is less firmly established, in no small part because of the difficulties evaluating one of the features of declarative memory, namely, its accessibility to consciousness (e.g., C. A. Nelson, 1997; Rovee-Collier, 1997). In adults, conscious access to the contents of memory is assessed verbally. By definition, infants do not speak (in Latin, *infantia* means "inability to speak"). Critically, however, definitions of the construct do not require that it be expressed verbally. Indeed, some scholars have specifically noted that conscious awareness may be expressed nonverbally (e.g., Köhler & Moscovitch, 1997). Empirically, concern about the criterion of consciousness has been addressed by designing tasks that bear other characteristic features of tests of declarative memory—such as requiring acquisition of novel behaviors on the basis of a single trial.

For developmental scientists, the distinction between declarative and nondeclarative memory is vitally important for two major reasons. First, as discussed by Mandler (2004), if we are to make progress in understanding cognitive development, we must be clear about the capacities we are studying. In essence, Mandler's argument is that if we do not know with what kind of knowledge we are dealing, we cannot begin to answer questions regarding the mechanisms by which it was acquired. In other words, if we treat memory as pudding, we cannot hope to discover specific information regarding how it is made. Thus, from a general theoretical perspective, it is important to specify what type of memory we are studying, in order to constrain our theories of how it develops.

Second, the distinction between declarative and nondeclarative forms of memory is important developmentally because the neural structures that contribute to these different types of memory mature at different rates. Specifically, as reviewed by Bauer (2004, 2006, 2007), Carver and Bauer (2001), and C. A. Nelson (1995, 1997, 2000), it seems that the structures that permit some of the different forms of nondeclarative memory are functional at an earlier age, relative to those that permit declarative memory. For example, instrumental conditioning, such as is observed in the mobile conjugate reinforcement paradigm (see Rovee-Collier & Hayne, 2000, for a review) likely depends largely on early developing cerebellum and certain deep nuclei of the brain stem. In contrast, as will be seen in a later section, the temporal-cortical network that supports declarative memory has a slower, longer course of development. The differing rates of development make clear that if we are to fully understand age-related changes in memory, we will need to chart neurodevelopmental changes in the specific structures under question. Our understanding of brain development should constrain our expectations regarding performance as well as inform our interpretation of data. A goal of the balance of this chapter is to evaluate the "fit" between what we know about age-related changes in long-term declarative memory behavior and what we know about the development of the neural substrate responsible for it.

Measuring Long-Term Declarative Memory in Infancy and Early Childhood

In older, verbal children and adults, declarative memory is assessed verbally. For example, study participants are given lists of words to remember and then are asked to recall the list ("Tell me all the words on the list") or make explicit judgments of recognition ("Was the word X on the list?"). Memory for naturally occurring events is studied in much the same way, namely, by asking the participant for a verbal report of the experience.

Because infants do not benefit from the ability to speak, researchers interested in the emergence of long-term declarative memory have developed nonverbal means of assessment. The technique that has been the source of the bulk of the data in this chapter involves infants' imitation of another's actions. Typically, the actions are performed by adults using props. For example, the model may "make a gong" by placing a bar across a support to form a crosspiece, hanging a metal disk from the crosspiece, and using a mallet to hit the disk and make it ring. Although the demonstration may be accompanied by narration of the model's actions, verbal support is not necessary for successful imitation (e.g., Hayne & Herbert, 2004). Thus the task does not require verbal instructions. Nor does it require a verbal response: The measure of memory is behavioral (i.e., imitation).

As summarized in Table 10.1, there are a number of reasons to argue that imitation-based tasks measure declarative memory (see also Bauer, 2005b, 2007, for discussion). First, when infants imitate another's actions on objects, they show that they remember content such as is encoded into declarative memory: *what* happened, *where*, *when*, and even *why*. When they "make a gong," for example, they show that they remember that a disk was suspended from a crosspiece, and that the crosspiece had to be put in place before the disk could be suspended from it (see Travis, 1997, for evidence that infants have some understanding of the *why* or the goal of such sequences). Second, the contents of memories formed in imitation-based tasks are accessible to language. Once children acquire the linguistic capacity to do so, they talk about multistep sequences they experienced as preverbal infants (e.g., Bauer, Kroupina, Schwade, Dropik, & Wewerka, 1998; Cheatham & Bauer, 2005; although see Simcock & Hayne, 2002, for a suggestion to the contrary, and Bauer et al., 2004, for discussion of possible reasons for the negative findings in Simcock & Hayne). Third, although performance is facilitated by multiple experiences (e.g., Bauer, Hertsgaard, & Wewerka, 1995), infants learn and remember on the basis of a single experience (e.g., Bauer & Hertsgaard, 1993). Rapid learning is characteristic of declarative memory.

Fourth and fifth, the memory traces formed in imitation-based tasks are relatively fallible yet flexible. Forgetting sets in as early as 10 minutes after experience of events (Bauer, Cheatham, Strand Cary, & Van Abbema, 2002) and is readily apparent after 48 hours (Bauer, Van Abbema, & de Haan, 1999).

Table 10.1   Imitation-Based Tasks as Measures of Declarative Memory

Feature	Behavior
Content	Memories are elements such as those expressed via verbal narratives, including *what* happened, *where*, *when*, and *why*
Verbal access	The contents of memories formed in imitation-based tasks are accessible to language
One-trial learning	Learning occurs in a single trial (though performance is facilitated by multiple learning trials)
Fallible traces	Forgetting sets in as early as 10 minutes and is readily apparent after 48 hours
Flexible traces	Memories "survive" across changes in the retrieval relative to the encoding context
"Amnesia test"	Individuals with damage to medial temporal structures inflicted as adults or as children are impaired on the task

Memory as tested in imitation-based paradigms also is flexible. Infants show that they remember even when (a) the objects available at the time of retrieval differ in size, shape, color, and/or material composition from those used by the model at the time of encoding (e.g., Bauer & Dow, 1994; Bauer & Fivush, 1992; Lechuga, Marcos-Ruiz, & Bauer, 2001); (b) the appearance of the room at the time of retrieval is different from that at the time of encoding (e.g., Barnat, Klein, & Meltzoff, 1996; Klein & Meltzoff, 1999); (c) encoding and retrieval take place in different settings (e.g., Hanna & Meltzoff, 1993; Klein & Meltzoff, 1999); and (d) the individual who elicits recall is different from the individual who demonstrated the actions (e.g., Hanna & Meltzoff, 1993). Evidence of flexible extension of event knowledge is apparent in infants as young as 9 to 11 months of age (e.g., Baldwin, Markman, & Melartin, 1993; McDonough & Mandler, 1998).

Finally, imitation-based tasks pass the "amnesia test." McDonough, Mandler, McKee, and Squire (1995) tested adults with amnesia (in whom declarative memory processes are impaired) and control participants in an imitation-based task using multistep sequences. Whereas normal adults produced the model's actions even after a delay, patients with amnesia did poorly, performing no better than control participants who had never seen the events demonstrated. Older children and young adults who were rendered amnesic as a result of pre- or perinatal insults also show decreased performance on imitation-based tasks (Adlam, Vargha-Khadem, Mishkin, & de Haan, 2005). These findings strongly suggest that although imitation-based tasks are behavioral rather than verbal, they tap declarative memory.

Development of imitation-based tasks as means of assessing long-term declarative memory in infants and very young children represented a significant advance by allowing empirical tests of long-standing assumptions that declarative memory was a late developmental achievement (see Bauer, 2004, 2005b, 2007, for discussions). As reviewed in the next section, in the 20 years since the tasks have been in use (Bauer & Shore, 1987; Meltzoff,

1995), we have gathered a great deal of descriptive information about developmental differences in declarative memory in infancy. As we begin to face the challenges of *explaining* the age-related changes, we hit one of the limits of the task, however: With any performance-based measure, there is a chasm between overt behavior and the memory representation presumably underlying it. In the case of the study of declarative memory in infancy, this means that it is difficult to know whether younger infants actually remember less than older infants, or whether they are simply less skilled at "showing what they know." Additionally, it is difficult to identify the locus of developmental difference: Relative to older infants, do younger infants encode less, store less, or retrieve less, or perhaps all of the above?

In an attempt to bridge the chasm between behavior and memory representation, we have begun combining measures from imitation-based tasks with event-related potentials (ERPs). ERPs are scalp-recorded electrical oscillations associated with excitatory and inhibitory postsynaptic potentials. Because they are time locked to a stimulus, differences in the latency and amplitude of the response to different classes of stimuli—familiar and novel, for example—can be interpreted as evidence of differential neural processing. Moreover, because they are noninvasive and make no performance demands on the participant (e.g., ERPs to auditory stimuli can be recorded while the participant sleeps), they are ideal for use with human infants. As discussed in a later section, we have used ERPs to determine the locus of both individual and developmental differences in memory. Research thus far has revealed systematic variability in encoding processes and in storage processes, as measured by ERPs; the variability in ERPs is related to variability in performance on imitation-based tasks (see later section). The combination of electrophysiological and behavioral measures is thus allowing us to pave new ground in the study of declarative memory in infancy and very early childhood.

Describing Age-Related Changes in Long-Term Declarative Memory

From nearly 20 years of work on infants' and young children's performance on imitation-based tasks, a number of age-related changes in early long-term declarative memory are apparent (see Bauer, 2004, 2005b, 2006, 2007, for reviews). Two especially salient changes are in the temporal extent of declarative memory and the reliability with which it is observed. We discuss each in turn.

Changes in the Temporal Extent of Declarative Memory

Over the first two years of life, there are pronounced changes in how long memories seemingly last. Importantly, because like any complex behavior,

the length of time over which an event is remembered is multiply determined, there is no "growth chart" function that specifies that children of
x age should remember for y long. Nonetheless, across numerous studies
evidence has emerged that with increasing age, infants tolerate lengthier
retention intervals. Beginning with infants only 6 months of age, Barr,
Dowden, and Hayne (1996) tested recall of a three-step sequence involving
(1) taking a mitten off a puppet's hand; (2) shaking the mitten, which, at the
time of demonstration, held a bell that rang; and (3) replacing the mitten.
The youngest infants remembered an average of one action of the three-step
sequence for 24 hours. In a study by Collie and Hayne (1999), 6-month-old
infants remembered an average of one out of five possible actions over the
same delay. These results signal the "budding" of long-term declarative
memory, at least by 6 months of age. On the other hand, observations that
over 24 hours 6-month-olds apparently remember only a small proportion
of what they observed have not "inspired" researchers to examine retention
over longer intervals.

As schematically illustrated in Table 10.2, by 9 to 11 months of age, the
length of time over which memory for laboratory events is apparent has
increased substantially. Nine-month-olds remember individual actions
over delays of as many as 5 weeks (Carver & Bauer, 1999, 2001). By 10 to
11 months, infants remember for as long as 3 months (Carver & Bauer, 2001;
Mandler & McDonough, 1995), and 13- to 14-month-olds remember over
delays of 4 to 6 months (Bauer et al., 2000; Meltzoff, 1995). By 20 months of
age, children show evidence of memory after as many as 12 months (Bauer
et al., 2000). Clearly, between the latter half of the first year and the middle
of the second year of life, the temporal extent of declarative memory
increases substantially.

Changes in the Reliability of Declarative Memory

Along with changes in the temporal extent of declarative memory come
changes in the reliability with which it is observed in the population.
Age-related increases are especially apparent on the measure of ordered

Table 10.2 Changes in the Temporal Extension of Recall Memory Over the First
Two Years of Life

Age at Exposure (in months)	Time Over Which Memory Is Apparent				
	24 Hours	5 Weeks	3 Months	4–6 Months	12 Months
6	————				
9	————————				
10–11	————————————————			
13–14	————————————————————————		
20	————————————————————————————————

recall of multistep sequences. Whereas a majority of 6-month-old infants re-call the individual actions of a multistep sequence (i.e., 67%), as shown in Table 10.3, only one quarter show evidence of temporally ordered recall (Barr et al., 1996). By 9 months of age, ordered recall is more reliably observed: Almost half of 9-month-olds exhibit ordered reproduction of sequences after a 1-month delay (Bauer, Wiebe, Carver, Waters, & Nelson, 2003; Bauer, Wiebe, Waters, & Bangston, 2001; Carver & Bauer, 1999). By 13 months of age, the substantial individual variability in ordered recall has resolved: Three quarters of 13-month-olds remember the temporal order of multistep sequences after 1 month (Bauer et al., 2000).

Although by the beginning of the second year of life long-term ordered recall is reliably observed over a 1-month delay, as illustrated in Table 10.3, there are further developments over the course of the year. At delays of longer than 1 month, few 13-month-olds show ordered recall. For instance, in Bauer et al. (2000), at delays of 6 months and longer, there was less than a 40% chance that a random selection from the group of 13-month-olds tested would yield a child who remembered temporal order information. In contrast, even after 12 months, two thirds of 20-month-olds showed temporally ordered recall. These data are strongly suggestive of increases in the reliability of long-term declarative memory over the first two years of life.

Explaining Age-Related Changes in Long-Term Declarative Memory

Ultimately, several sources of variance will be implicated in the explanation of age-related changes in long-term declarative memory. They will range from changes in the neural processes and systems and basic mnemonic processes that permit memories to be formed, retained, and later retrieved, to the social forces that shape what children ultimately come to view as important to remember about events and even how they express their mem-ories. For purposes of this review, we focus on "lower-level" mechanisms of

Table 10.3 Changes in the Reliability of Recall Memory
Over the First Two Years of Life

Age at Exposure (in months)	Percentage of Infants Showing Evidence of Ordered Recall After Various Delays			
	24 Hours	1 Month	6 Months	12 Months
6	25%	?		
9		45%	?	
13		78%	39%	39%
20		100%	83%	67%

change—those at the level of neural systems and basic mnemonic processes. We begin with a brief review of the neural network thought to subserve declarative memory in the adult and what is known about its development. We then examine the basic mnemonic processes of encoding, consolidation, storage, and retrieval, and evaluate their contributions to age-related changes in long-term declarative memory (see Bauer, 2004, 2007, for expanded versions of this discussion).

The Neural Substrate of Declarative Event Memory and Its Development

The Substrate of Declarative Memory

In adult humans, the formation, maintenance, and retrieval of declarative memories over the long term depends on a multicomponent neural network involving temporal and cortical structures (e.g., Eichenbaum & Cohen, 2001; Markowitsch, 2000; Zola & Squire, 2000). As schematically illustrated in Figure 10.1, upon experience of an event, sensory and motor inputs are registered in multiple brain regions distributed throughout the cortex (i.e., primary somatosensory, visual, and auditory cortices). Inputs from these primary sensory areas are sent (projected) to sensory association areas that are dedicated to a single modality (somatic sensation, vision, or audition), where they are integrated into whole percepts of what the object or event feels like, looks like, and sounds like, respectively. The unimodal sensory association areas in turn project to polymodal (also termed multimodal) posterior-parietal, anterior-prefrontal, and limbic-temporal association areas where inputs from the different sense modalities converge.

Ultimately, the association areas are the long-term storage sites for memories. Yet between initial registration and commitment to long-term storage there is

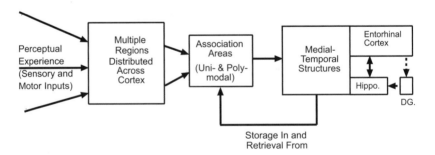

FIGURE 10.1. Schematic representation of the input and output pathways of the hippocampal formation. Hippo, hippocampus; D.G., dentate gyrus. Adapted from Kandel, Schwartz, and Jessell (2000, Figure 62.5, p. 1232) and Zola and Squire (2000, Figure 30.1, p. 487).

substantial additional processing. That processing generally is described as involving integration and stabilization of the inputs from different cortical regions and is thought to be performed by medial temporal lobe structures—in particular, the hippocampus—in concert with the association cortices. Whereas integration and stabilization processes begin upon registration of a stimulus, they do not end there. The process of stabilization of a memory trace, termed *consolidation,* continues for hours, days, months, and perhaps even years. Importantly, throughout the consolidation period, memories are vulnerable to disruption and interference. Eventually, cortical structures alone are responsible for storage of memories over the long term. Prefrontal structures are implicated in the retrieval of memories after a delay. Thus, long-term recall requires multiple cortical regions, including prefrontal cortex; temporal structures; and intact connections between them.

Development of the Neural Network for Declarative Memory

At a general level, the time course of changes in behavior reviewed earlier is consistent with what is known about developments in the temporal-cortical network that supports declarative memory (Bauer, 2002, 2004, 2007; C. A. Nelson, 2000). In the human, many of the medial temporal lobe components of the declarative memory network develop early. As reviewed by Seress (2001), the cells that make up most of the hippocampus are formed early in gestation and by the end of the prenatal period, virtually all have migrated to their adult locations. By approximately 6 postnatal months, the number and density of synapses have reached adult levels, as has glucose utilization in the temporal cortex (e.g., Chugani, 1994).

In contrast to early maturation of most of the hippocampus, development of the dentate gyrus of the hippocampus is protracted (Seress, 2001). It is not until 12 to 15 postnatal months that the morphology of the dentate gyrus appears adultlike. Maximum density of synaptic connections in the dentate gyrus also is reached relatively late. The density of synapses increases dramatically (to well above adult levels) beginning at 8 to 12 postnatal months and reaches its peak at 16 to 20 months. After a period of relative stability, excess synapses are pruned until adult levels are reached at about 4 to 5 years of age (Eckenhoff & Rakic, 1991).

There is reason to believe that the protracted development of the dentate gyrus is consequential. As already noted, information about events and experiences that originally is distributed across regions of cortex converges on medial temporal structures (see Figure 10.1). One of those structures—the entorhinal cortex—provides two "routes" for the transfer of information into the hippocampus. The "long route" (indicated by dotted lines in Figure 10.1) involves projections from entorhinal cortex into the hippocampus, by way of the dentate gyrus; the "short route" (indicated by solid line in Figure 10.1) bypasses the dentate gyrus. Whereas short route processing may support some forms of memory (C. A. Nelson, 1995, 1997), rodent data suggest that adultlike memory behavior depends on processing of information through the dentate gyrus (Czurk, Czh, Seress, Nadel, & Bures, 1997; Nadel & Willner, 1989). This implies that maturation of the dentate gyrus of the hippocampus is a rate-limiting variable in the early development of declarative memory (Bauer, 2002, 2004, 2007; Bauer et al., 2003; C. A. Nelson, 1995, 1997, 2000).

The association areas also develop slowly (Bachevalier, 2001). For instance, it is not until the 7th prenatal month that all six cortical layers are apparent. The density of synapses in prefrontal cortex increases dramatically beginning at 8 postnatal months and peaks between 15 and 24 months. Pruning to adult levels is delayed until puberty (Huttenlocher, 1979; Huttenlocher & Dabholkar, 1997; see Bourgeois, 2001, for discussion). Although the maximum density of synapses may be reached as early as 15 postnatal months, it is not until 24 months that synapses develop adult morphology (Huttenlocher, 1979). Other maturational changes in prefrontal cortex, such as myelination, continue into adolescence, and adult levels of some neurotransmitters are not seen until the second and third decades of life (Benes, 2001).

The network that supports declarative memory can be expected to function as an integrated whole only once each of its components, as well as the connections between them, achieve a level of functional maturity. "Functional maturity" is reached when the number of synapses peaks; "full maturity" is achieved as the number of synapses is pruned to adult levels (Goldman-Rakic, 1987). Adoption of this metric leads to the prediction of (a) emergence of declarative memory by late in the first year of life (with the increase in formation of new synapses in both dentate gyrus and prefrontal cortex), (b) significant development over the second year (continued synaptogenesis through 20 to 24 months), and (c) continued (albeit less dramatic) development for years thereafter (due to protracted selective reduction in synapses both in the dentate gyrus and in the prefrontal cortex).

What are the consequences for behavior of the slow course of development of the network that supports long-term declarative memory? At a general level, we may expect that as the neural substrate develops, the behavior develops as well (and vice versa, of course). More specifically, we may ask how changes in the medial temporal and cortical structures, and their interconnections, produce changes in memory representations. To address this question, we must consider "how the brain builds a memory," and thus, how the "recipe" for a memory might be affected by changes in the underlying neural substrate. In other words, we must consider how developmental changes in the substrate for memory relate to changes in the efficacy and efficiency with which information is encoded and stabilized for long-term storage, in the reliability with which it is stored, and in the ease with which it is retrieved.

Changes in Basic Mnemonic Processes

Encoding

Association cortices are involved in the initial registration and temporary maintenance of experience. Because prefrontal cortex in particular undergoes considerable postnatal development, it is reasonable to assume that there may be changes in encoding processes over the first years of life. Consistent with this suggestion, we have found age-related differences in encoding that are related to age-related differences in long-term recall. In a longitudinal study, relative to when they were 9 months of age, infants at 10 months of age showed more robust encoding and more robust recall. To test encoding, we recorded infants' ERPs as they looked at photographs of props used in multistep sequences to which they had just been exposed, interspersed with photographs of props from novel sequences. The amplitudes of responses to newly encoded stimuli at 10 months were larger than those of the same infants at 9 months; there were no differences in responses to novel stimuli. The differences at encoding were related to differences at recall. One month after each ERP, we used imitation to test long-term recall of the sequences. The infants had higher rates of recall of the sequences to which they had been exposed at 10 months, relative to the sequences to which they had been exposed at 9 months (Bauer et al., 2006).

Age-related differences in encoding do not end at 1 year of age. Relative to 15-month-olds, 12-month-olds require more trials to learn multistep sequences to a criterion (learning to a criterion indicates that the material was fully encoded). In turn, 15-month-olds are slower to achieve criterion relative to 18-month-olds (Howe & Courage, 1997). Indeed, across development, older children learn more rapidly than younger children (Howe & Brainerd, 1989).

Whereas age-related differences in encoding are apparent throughout the first 2 years, they alone do not account for the age trends in long-term declarative memory. Even with levels of encoding controlled statistically (Bauer et al., 2000), by matching (Bauer, 2005a), or by bringing children of different ages to the same learning criterion (Howe & Courage, 1997), older children have higher levels of long-term ordered recall relative to younger children. Findings such as these strongly suggest that changes in postencoding processes also contribute to developmental changes in declarative memory.

Consolidation and Storage

Although separable phases in the life of a memory trace, at the level of analysis available in the existing developmental data, consolidation and storage cannot be effectively separated. For this reason, we discuss them in tandem. As reviewed earlier, medial temporal structures are implicated in the consolidation process by which new memories become "fixed" for long-term storage; cortical association areas are the presumed long-term storage sites.

Even in a mature, intact adult, the changes in synaptic connectivity associated with memory trace consolidation continue for hours, weeks, and even months after an event. Throughout this time, memory traces are vulnerable: Lesions to medial temporal structures inflicted during the consolidation period result in deficits in memory, whereas lesions inflicted after a trace has consolidated do not (e.g., Kim & Fanselow, 1992; Takehara, Kawahara, & Kirino, 2003). Consolidation may be an even more vulnerable process for the developing organism. Not only are some of the neural structures themselves relatively undeveloped (i.e., dentate gyrus and prefrontal cortex), but the connections between them are still being created and thus are not fully effective and efficient. As a consequence, even once children have successfully encoded an event, they remain vulnerable to forgetting. Younger children may be more vulnerable than older children (Bauer, 2005a).

To examine the role of consolidation and storage processes in long-term declarative event memory in 9-month-old infants, Bauer et al. (2003) combined ERP measures of encoding (i.e., immediate ERP tests), ERP measures of consolidation and storage (i.e., 1-week delayed ERP), and deferred imitation measures of recall after 1 month. After the 1-month delay, 46% of the infants showed ordered recall and 54% did not. The differences in long-term recall were not due to differential encoding: Across the groups, infants' ERPs to the old and new stimuli were different, strongly implying that they had encoded the sequences. In spite of apparently successful encoding, at the 1-week delayed recognition test, the infants who would go on to recall the events recognized the familiar props, whereas infants who would not evidence ordered recall did not. Moreover, the size of the difference in the delayed-ERP response predicted recall performance 1 month later. These data strongly imply that at 9 months of age, consolidation and storage processes are a source of individual differences in mnemonic performance.

In the second year of life, there are behavioral suggestions of between-age group differences in consolidation and/or storage processes, as well as a replication of the finding among 9-month-olds that intermediate-term consolidation and/or storage failure relates to recall over the long term. In Bauer et al. (2002), 16- and 20-month-olds were tested for recall of multistep sequences immediately (as a measure of encoding) and after 24 hours. Over the delay, the younger children forgot a substantial amount: They produced only 65% and 57% of the target actions and ordered pairs of actions (respectively) that they had learned just 24 hours earlier. Among the older children, the amount of forgetting was not statistically reliable. These observations suggest age-related differences in the vulnerability of memory traces during the initial period of consolidation.

The vulnerability of memory traces during the initial period of consolidation is related to the robustness of long-term recall. This is apparent from another of the experiments in Bauer et al. (2002), this one involving 20-month-olds only. The children were exposed to sequences and then tested on some of the sequences immediately, some after 48 hours (a delay after which, based on Bauer et al., 1999, some forgetting was expected), and some after 1 month. Although the children exhibited high levels of initial encoding (measured by immediate recall), they showed significant forgetting after both 48 hours and 1 month. The robustness of memory after 48 hours predicted 25% of the variance in recall 1 month later; variability of encoding did not predict significant variance. This finding is a conceptual replication of that observed with 9-month-olds in Bauer et al. (2003). In both cases, the amount of information lost to memory during the period of consolidation predicted the robustness of recall 1 month later.

Retrieval

Retrieval of memories from long-term stores is thought to depend on prefrontal cortex. Because prefrontal cortex undergoes a long period of postnatal development, retrieval processes are a likely candidate source of age-related differences in long-term recall. Unfortunately, there are few data with which to evaluate their contribution because in most studies, there are alternative candidate sources of age-related change. For instance, in studies in which imitation is deferred until after some delay (e.g., Hayne, Boniface, & Barr, 2000; Liston & Kagan, 2002), because no measures of learning are obtained (i.e., no immediate imitation) it is impossible to know whether developmental differences in long-term recall are due to retrieval processes or possibly to encoding processes. Moreover, even when indices of encoding are available, with standard testing procedures, it is difficult to know whether a memory representation is intact but has become inaccessible with the cues provided (retrieval failure) or whether it has lost its integrity and become unavailable (consolidation or storage failure). Implication of retrieval processes as a source of developmental change requires that encoding be controlled and that memory be tested under conditions of high support for retrieval. One study in which these conditions were met was Bauer et al. (2003; i.e., ERPs indicated that the events had been encoded; the suggestion of consolidation and/or storage failure was apparent on a recognition test). The results, described in the preceding section, clearly implicated consolidation and/or storage, as opposed to retrieval.

Another study that permits assessment of the contributions of consolidation and/or storage relative to retrieval processes is Bauer et al. (2000), in which children of multiple ages (13, 16, and 20 months) were tested over a range of delays (1 to 12 months). Because immediate recall of half of the events was tested, measures of encoding are available. There also was high support for retrieval: (a) children were reminded of the sequences both by the props and by verbal labels; and (b) after the test of delayed recall, the ultimate in retrieval support was provided—*the sequences were demonstrated again* and savings in relearning was assessed. When it accrues, savings (a reduction in the number of trials required to relearn a stimulus relative to the number required to learn it initially) is thought to result because the products of relearning are integrated with an existing (though not necessarily accessible) memory trace (Ebbinghaus, 1885/1964). Conversely, absence of savings is attributed to storage failure: There is no residual trace upon which to build. In developmental studies, age differences in relearning would suggest that the residual traces available to children of different ages are differentially intact.

To eliminate encoding processes as a potential source of developmental differences in long-term recall, in a reanalysis of the data from Bauer et al. (2000), subsets of 13- and 16-month-olds and subsets of 16- and 20-month-olds were matched for levels of encoding (as measured by immediate recall; Bauer, 2005a). Performance after the delays then was examined. In both comparisons, the younger children remembered less than the older children. Moreover, in both comparisons, levels of relearning by the older children were higher than those by the younger children (Bauer, 2005a). Together, the findings strongly implicate storage as opposed to retrieval processes as the major source of age-related differences in delayed recall.

Summary

Ultimately, a number of factors will be found to explain age-related variance in long-term declarative memory in the first years of life. At present, developments in the basic mnemonic processes of encoding, consolidation and storage, and retrieval are one of the few sources of change to be evaluated. Examination of their relative contributions implicates consolidation and storage as a major source of developmental change. This conclusion is consistent with the loci of developments in the neural substrate of declarative memory. Late in the first year and throughout the second year of life there are pronounced changes in the temporal lobe structures implicated in integration and consolidation of memory traces. A likely consequence is changes in the efficiency and efficacy with which information is stabilized for storage, with resulting significant behavioral changes in resistance to forgetting.

Are Changes Indicative of Development of a Particular Memory System?

In opening this chapter, we made the argument that the type of memory we study corresponds to long-term declarative (or explicit) memory in adults. We further argued that the age-related functional changes that we see in this type of memory are related to developments in the neural structures and the network that supports it. Yet the functional changes we observe in children's performance on presumably declarative imitation-based tasks are not unlike those charted with other measures. A prime example is conjugate reinforcement: There are similarities in performance on reinforcement and imitation-based tasks (see chapter 9, this volume), even though they are thought to tap different memory systems. At first glance, this may seem counterintuitive: If the tasks assess different memory systems, why the similarities? After describing some of the apparent parallels between the tasks, we discuss their likely sources and their implications for the multiple memory systems perspective.

Conjugate Reinforcement and Imitation: Vanilla and Chocolate Pudding?

In the most commonly used conjugate reinforcement task, a mobile is suspended above an infant's crib or sling seat. Researchers measure the baseline rate of infant kicking and then arrange the testing apparatus such that as the infant kicks, the mobile moves. Infants quickly learn the contingency between their own kicking and the movement of the mobile. Once the conditional response is acquired, a delay is imposed, after which the mobile again is suspended above the infant; the infant's leg is not attached to the mobile. If the posttraining rate of kicking is greater than the baseline rate, memory is inferred (see Rovee-Collier & Hayne, 2000, for a description of this and related procedures).

There are *apparent* similarities in the content, function, and rules by which memory seems to operate in conjugate reinforcement and imitation-based tasks. In both tasks, infants learn about and remember objects. In reinforcement tasks, this is apparent in reduced rates of kicking to mobiles on which some of the elements differ between training and test, thereby demonstrating memory for the objects on the training mobile. In imitation-based tasks, memory for objects is apparent when infants reenact specific actions using props and also when they select from an array the objects previously used to produce a sequence (e.g., Bauer & Dow, 1994). Memory for order information—which elsewhere has been highlighted as clear evidence of recall (e.g., Bauer, 2004, 2005b; Carver & Bauer, 2001)—also seems to be common across the tasks. For instance, Gulya, Rovee-Collier, Galluccio, and Wilk (1998) exposed infants to an ordered "list" of three mobiles. One day later, infants exhibited higher rates of kicking when they saw Mobile 1 before Mobile 2 than they did when they saw Mobile 3 before Mobile 2, thereby showing sensitivity to order information.

There also are apparent similarities across the tasks in the rates of learning: In both tasks learning is relatively rapid and older infants acquire new information at a faster rate than younger infants. In reinforcement tasks, 2- and 3-month-old infants learn the contingency between kicking and the movement of the mobile over two to three 15-minute sessions (Rovee-Collier, 1990). By 6 months of age, learning is accomplished over two or three sessions only 10 minutes in length (e.g., Borovsky & Rovee-Collier, 1990). As noted earlier, rapid—even one-trial—learning also is apparent in imitation-based tasks. Yet younger infants (e.g., 6-month-olds) require more exposures to test sequences than older infants (e.g., 9- and 14-month-olds).

Finally, with regard to the apparent rules by which memory seems to operate, there also seem to be similarities across the tasks. With respect to the elephant in the room of declarative memory—consciousness—neither task can claim a definitive address. The participants in these paradigms do not declare that they are consciously aware that their current behavior is influenced by prior experience. Neither do they verbally express their memories. (Though as noted earlier, once they develop language, children talk about multistep sequences experienced months previously, when they were pre-verbal infants. We are not aware of any evidence of later verbal accessibility of memory for the conjugate-reinforcement training experience.) Moreover, in both paradigms, there seem to be developmental changes in the extent to which memory is context dependent. In reinforcement tasks, young infants show marked decrements in performance if the conditions of training and testing vary even slightly. With increased age, greater deviation is tolerated (see Rovee-Collier & Hayne, 2000, for a review). Hayne and her colleagues have reported similar age-related changes in susceptibility to interference associated with changes in the props used in imitation-based tasks (Hayne, MacDonald, & Barr, 1997; Hayne et al., 2000; Herbert & Hayne, 2000). On the other hand, other laboratories have observed that in imitation-based tasks, memory is robust to changes between the encoding and retrieval contexts (Baldwin et al., 1993; Barnat et al., 1996; Bauer & Dow, 1994; Bauer & Fivush, 1992; Hanna & Meltzoff, 1993; Klein & Meltzoff, 1999; Lechuga et al., 2002; McDonough & Mandler, 1998; Meltzoff, 1988).

Likely Sources of Across-Task Similarities

If reinforcement and imitation-based tasks are indicative of different memory systems, why are there so many apparent similarities between them? There are two answers to this question. First, some of the similarities are delusive. An example is the demonstration of memory for temporal order in the two tasks. In the reinforcement task, sensitivity to temporal order is demonstrated by a higher rate of kicking to a chain of stimuli presented in the same (e.g., Mobile 1 before Mobile 2) relative to a different (i.e., Mobile 3 before Mobile 2) order than originally encountered. The response is not unlike that in another test of nondeclarative or implicit learning, Serial Reaction Time. In Serial Reaction Time tasks, a pattern is established by, for example, a series of lights that are turned on and off in a particular pattern. The participant follows the pattern on a keyboard. As the pattern is repeated, children and adults show facilitated performance in the form of decreased reaction times. If the pattern is changed, performance is disrupted (i.e., longer reaction times; e.g., Thomas & Nelson, 2001). Facilitated and disrupted performance is observed even among participants who profess no awareness that there even was a pattern. This example makes clear that the type of sensitivity to temporal order apparent in the reinforcement task occurs even in the absence of conscious awareness.

Although sensitivity to temporal patterns is sufficient for performance in reinforcement tasks, it is not sufficient for temporally ordered recall of a modeled sequence. In imitation tasks, infants and children watch as a model uses props to demonstrate a sequence of actions. The test of memory for order information is not whether participants increase or decrease their rate of responding when order is violated, but whether they reproduce the temporal order, from memory. The task requires that order information be encoded during presentation of the sequence and then retrieved from memory. In this it is akin to memory for a spoken utterance. Once the utterance is produced, it is no longer perceptually available. The only way it can be reproduced by another is if the other encoded it into memory and then retrieved it. Such tasks cannot be performed by individuals with damage to the neural structures implicated in declarative memory. Whereas individuals with medial temporal lobe amnesia have normal short-term memory for digits and sentences, delays as short as 10 minutes produce severe impairments (e.g., Reed & Squire, 1998). Such individuals also have difficulty on imitation-based tasks (McDonough et al., 1995). In short, careful analysis of task differences makes clear that the demands imposed by reinforcement tasks are in critical ways different from those imposed by imitation-based tasks. Thus, similarities across the task may be more apparent than real.

The second answer to the question of why, if reinforcement and imitation-based tasks are indicative of the operation of different memory systems, there are so many apparent similarities in memory as tested in them, is that we should expect—rather than be surprised by—similarities in mnemonic behavior even as it "crosses" different memory systems. In all its manifestations, memory involves taking in information that is out in the environment at the moment and preserving it beyond its physical duration. The mechanisms by which this feat is accomplished are highly conserved across evolution and within species, across brain regions and systems.

At the cellular and molecular level, the best (indeed, only viable) mechanism for learning and memory is long-term potentiation (LTP). LTP was first discovered in and is best characterized in the hippocampus. Critically, however, it takes place throughout the brain, including in the neocortex, amygdala, neostriatum, cerebellum, and even spinal cord (Eichenbaum & Cohen, 2001). Across brain regions, it operates in the roughly the same manner. Early LTP, which is initiated by brief stimulus exposure (in the form of a high-frequency stimulus train known as a *tetanus*), results in rapid but temporary changes in the probability of synaptic firing. In hippocampal slices, this activation lasts anywhere from 1 to 3 hours. Late LTP is initiated by multiple stimulus chains that result in the synthesis of new proteins, which in turn produce morphological changes, including growth of new dendritic spines on postsynaptic neurons. In hippocampal slices, late LTP can last for 24 hours or more; in intact animals, it can last for days and even weeks. Evidence that LTP is a means by which information is stabilized for long-term storage in the hippocampus comes from mice that have been genetically altered in such a way that late-phase LTP is blocked (see Eichenbaum & Cohen, 2001, for a review). Just like patients with medial temporal lobe damage, the animals have normal short-term memory, but they are unable to consolidate new learning. Assuming that LTP is the fundamental mechanism for learning and memory, the fact that it has been shown to operate in highly similar fashion throughout the brain leads to expectations of similarities, rather than differences, in the factors that affect the encoding, consolidation, and storage of information.

There also is reason to expect similarities in mnemonic behavior at the level of memory systems. The reason is that the same neural structures may participate in multiple memory networks. For instance, as the storage site for most memories, the cerebral cortex is implicated in multiple memory systems. To the extent that declarative and nondeclarative memory tasks share a structure, there may be similarities in function. Importantly, there also are differences in the behavior of a structure as a consequence of the other structures in the network (e.g., Stanton, 2000). In essence, a structure behaves in a particular way as a function of the "crowd" with which it runs. The hippocampus is an excellent case in point. Whereas the hippocampus is classically involved in declarative memory, it also is part of a larger circuit, along with the cerebellum, that mediates modification of adaptive reflexes. As part of these different networks, it is differentially involved in different tasks. We provide illustrations of each of these principles.

Hippocampal Involvement in Different Memory Networks

The involvement of the hippocampus in long-term declarative memory is incontrovertible: Legions of studies have documented that individuals with damage to the hippocampus are impaired on a range and variety of tasks that meet the criterion for tests of declarative memory. Involvement of the hippocampus in declarative memory is further supported by research with animal models and by results from neuroimaging studies (see Eichenbaum & Cohen, 2001; Schacter et al., 2000; Zola & Squire, 2000, for reviews).

There also is strong evidence that the hippocampus is involved in some forms of conditioning, including trace eyeblink conditioning. As illustrated in Figure 10.2A, in trace eyeblink conditioning an organism is presented with an auditory or visual conditioned stimulus (CS) that terminates some number of milliseconds before the onset of a periocular shock or puff of air to the eye (i.e., the unconditioned stimulus, US). Because the CS and US do not overlap, the task requires formation of a short-term memory trace for the CS that persists over the empty interval. Successful trace conditioning critically depends upon the cerebellum, its related circuitry, and the hippocampus (e.g., Krupa, Thompson, & Thompson, 1993; Thompson, 1986). Removing the hippocampus before training abolishes the acquisition of the learned responses (Moyer, Deyo, & Disterhoft, 1990; Solomon, Vander

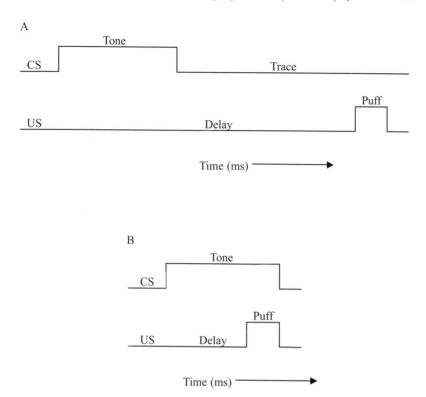

FIGURE 10.2. Schematic representation of the temporal parameters of trace (A) and standard delay (B) conditioning (based on Figure 1 in Herbert, Eckerman, & Stanton, 2003).

Schaaf, Thompson, & Weisz, 1986). On the rare occasion when animals do perform conditioned responses, they are not adaptively timed to avoid the impact of the US (Moyer et al., 1990; Port, Mikhail, & Patterson, 1985; Port, Romano, Steinmetz, Mikhail, & Patterson, 1986).

Within a Memory System, Differential Involvement of the Hippocampus in Different Tasks

Whereas declarative memory depends on the hippocampus (e.g., Squire et al., 1993), different declarative memory tasks may make different demands on the structure. In the context of imitation-based tasks, this point is made via work with a population at risk for memory impairment: infants born to mothers with diabetes. Infants of mothers with diabetes are exposed prenatally to several chronic metabolic risk factors, including iron deficiency, hypoglycemia (low glucose levels), and hypoxemia (insufficient oxygenation of the blood). Although all three of these risk factors impact neurobehavioral development (see Nold & Georgieff, 2004, for review), data from rodents indicate that prenatal iron deficiency *selectively* damages the hippocampus (de Ungria et al., 2000; Jorgenson, Wobken, & Georgieff, 2003; Rao, Tkac, Townsend, Gruetter, & Georgieff, 2003) and alters cellular processes as well (e.g., long-term potentiation: see Jorgensen et al., 2003). The effects of prenatal iron deficiency are apparent on tasks known to be mediated by the hippocampus (e.g., swim distance on the Morris water maze and radial arm maze behavior; Felt & Lozoff, 1996; Schmidt, Waldow, Salinas, & Georgieff, 2004, respectively); they are exacerbated if the animal is also hypoxic (Rao et al., 1999) as is the case in the intrauterine environment of infants of mothers with diabetes.

Using imitation-based tasks, we compared performance of 12-month-old infants of mothers with diabetes to that of a control group (DeBoer, Wewerka, Bauer, Georgieff, & Nelson, 2005). Recall after a 10-minute delay differed between the groups: Infants of mothers with diabetes showed impaired performance on ordered recall, relative to the control group. In contrast, the groups did not differ on immediate imitation (of different sequences). Relative to delayed imitation, immediate imitation may make fewer demands on the hippocampus because the to-be-remembered information is kept active in temporary storage. When imitation must be delayed, the information must be consolidated (a hippocampally mediated process), stored (in distributed cortical areas), and subsequently retrieved.

There also is evidence that the extent of damage to the hippocampus may alter performance on imitation-based tasks. Infants of mothers with diabetes were divided into two groups: those who experienced severe and those who experienced moderate iron deficiency (based on levels of fetal iron stores taken at birth). At 12 months of age, both subgroups showed impaired recall after 10 minutes. The infants in the severely iron deficient group also showed impaired performance when tested immediately. This finding makes the point that the involvement of the hippocampus in declarative memory tasks may be best conceptualized not as simply "on" or "off" but as a continuum of activation with more demanding tasks requiring higher levels of contribution from this structure.

A continuum of hippocampal involvement also is apparent in conditioning tasks. As reviewed earlier, the hippocampus is necessary for normal performance in trace eyeblink conditioning. It also plays a nonessential—though modulatory—role in standard delay conditioning in which an auditory or visual CS overlaps and coterminates with the US (see Figure 10.2, Panel B). In this task, learning is faciliated by induction of LTP in the hippocampus prior to training (Berger, 1984). Conversely, learning is slowed in animals given drugs that interfere with hippocampal function (Moore, Goodell, & Solomon, 1976). Yet lesioned animals eventually learn the contingency such that their performance does not differ from that of controls (e.g., Ivkovich & Stanton, 2001). These data indicate the modulatory role played by the hippocampus, even on a task that is not absolutely dependent on it.

Implications for the Multiple Memory Systems Perspective

There are a number of apparent similarities in performance and developmental changes across tasks thought to tap declarative and nondeclarative memory. Whereas some of the similarities are more apparent than real, others are more substantive. They do not, however, imply that the distinction between different forms of memory is irrelevant for the developmental literature. First, at the cellular and molecular levels, we should expect— rather than be surprised by—similarities in performance across tasks. The basic mechanisms of learning and memory are the same across species, ages, and brain regions: Neurons do not discriminate; they do not know in what type of memory they are participating. Second, a systems-level analysis also leads to the expectation of similarities across tasks. Similarities are to be expected because in some cases, the same structure (e.g., the hippocampus) participates in multiple memory networks. Moreover, within a network, the same structure may play different roles as a function of task demands. As a result of these basic principles, we should expect to find similarities in memory behavior across systems as well as differences in mnemonic behavior within systems.

On the Horizon

The perspective taken in this chapter is that "what develops" in early memory are different memory systems, reasonably specialized for different mnemonic tasks. We argue that the specific type of memory we study corresponds to long-term declarative (or explicit) memory in adults. We further argue that age-related changes in overt behavior that we see in this type of memory across the first years of life are the result (in part) of developments in the neural structures implicated in memory, and in the networks of structures that support different types of memory. With this perspective, a number of undertakings appear on the horizon.

One enterprise for future research is to gain more descriptive information on age-related changes in long-term declarative memory. To date we have learned a great deal about the temporal extent, the robustness, and the reliability of memory in populations of infants and children of different ages. However, we have only begun to learn how changes in the basic mnemonic processes of encoding, consolidation and storage, and retrieval contribute to the observed age-related changes. Future research should be aimed at explicating these processes and the developmental changes therein. In addition, it will be important to further develop conceptual links between age-related changes in these basic processes and developments in the neural substrates that presumably underlie them. The links should guide hypotheses as to the individual and combined contributions of the processes to long-term memory, and how they might change over the course of development (see Bauer, in press, for discussion).

Another avenue for future research is to gain more information about basic brain development in the young human. In the last decade of the 20th century, our knowledge of prenatal brain development and the genetic, cellular, and molecular events that guide it exploded. For example, whereas only a few years ago the means by which neuroblasts navigated their way to the cortex were mysterious indeed, now we have identified a great many of the proteins and signaling systems that accomplish the feat. Over the same period of time, knowledge of postnatal developments also increased, though not as substantially. The task is complicated for obvious practical and ethical reasons. As a result, we must look forward to more powerful imaging techniques of both gray matter and white matter tracts, and to continued progress in research on animal models of human brain development, for insights into development of the neural structures and connections that permit memory for past events.

As we conduct more fine-grained analyses of mnemonic behavior and as we gain more information about neural developments, we will be afforded opportunities for further progress in mapping relations between function and structure. Progress in evaluating relations between structure and function also will be made by making more frequent use in the developmental literature of one of the most powerful techniques in adult neuropsychology—the lesion method. The work described earlier on infants born to mothers with diabetes is an excellent example of this approach. In this population, there is strong reason to believe that there is a relatively focal lesion in the hippocampus. Careful study of the consequences of such lesions for mnemonic behavior in infancy and beyond promises to be very illuminating.

Also needed in the study of relations between structure and function in development are converging tests of relations. At this point, the number of tasks that clearly tap long-term declarative memory in infancy is limited. Development of additional techniques and their use with infants and children in the first years of life is very important in order to test hypotheses regarding the mechanisms of development.

Finally, a task for future research is to begin to determine how different memory networks "talk" to one another. As Eichenbaum and Cohen (2001) pointed out, different memory systems operate in parallel. It is only when we disrupt one or another that we see the "joints" that separate them. In experimental research, we often try to force the joints in order to isolate one particular mnemonic process or system. After completing the nondeclarative serial reaction time task, for example, individuals are typically questioned in a debriefing session to determine whether they had explicit knowledge of the sequence during learning (e.g., Curran, 1997). This process attempts to isolate those who learned nondeclaratively or implicitly, thereby ensuring that the findings were not "contaminated" by explicit awareness. This control is noteworthy in that performance in nondeclarative tasks may be facilitated by declarative learning and memory (in serial reaction time tasks, Curran & Keele, 1993; in trace eyeblink conditioning, Manns, Clark, & Squire, 2000). These examples make clear that the networks that support different types of mnemonic behavior are not isolated from one another. In day-to-day life, organisms make use of the full range of resources available to them to adapt to and thrive in their environments. Developing humans are no exception.

Conclusion

Within a relatively short space of time, the field has moved from considering the mnemonic life of infants and preverbal children as relatively discontinuous with that of older children and adults to recognizing essential continuities in mnemonic processes across the span of development. The change in perspective was made possible by development of nonverbal means of assessing declarative or explicit memory, which in verbal children and adults is typically assessed verbally. Addition of ERPs to the methodological arsenal has allowed for refinement of the description of developmental change. The combination of behavioral and electrophysiological techniques makes it possible to ask questions at the level of overt behavior and at the level of the basic mnemonic processes presumably contributing to it. The new perspective also facilitates the search for explanations of developmental change by closing the distance between levels of analysis. Joint consideration of changes in function and in underlying neural structures brings into sharper focus many of the questions to be addressed in future research and also hints at the form of their answers.

Acknowledgment

The order of authorship of the second and third authors was determined alphabetically. Much of the authors' work discussed was supported by the National Institute of Child Health and Human Development (HD-28425, HD-42483). Additional support for preparation of the chapter was provided by a Doctoral Dissertation Fellowship from the University of Minnesota to Tracy DeBoer and a Kirschstein National Research Service Award to Angela Lukowski (1 F31 MH72110–01).

Note

1. The pudding metaphor is borrowed from Maratsos (1998), who discussed the conceptual pitfalls of considering heterogeneous domains such as language to be essentially homogeneous, or qualitatively the same throughout.

References

Adlam, A.-L. R., Vargha-Khadem, F., Mishkin, M., & de Haan, M. (2005). Deferred imitation of action sequences in developmental amnesia. *Journal of Cognitive Neuroscience, 17*, 240–248.

Bachevalier, J. (2001). Neural bases of memory development: Insights from neuropsychological studies in primates. In C. A. Nelson & M. Luciana (Eds.), *Handbook of developmental cognitive neuroscience* (pp. 365–379). Cambridge, MA: MIT Press.

Baldwin, D. A., Markman, E. M., & Melartin, R. L. (1993). Infants' ability to draw inferences about nonobvious properties: Evidence from exploratory play. *Child Development, 64*, 711–728.

Barnat, S. B., Klein, P. J., & Meltzoff, A. N. (1996). Deferred imitation across changes in context and object: Memory and generalization in 14-month-old children. *Infant Behavior and Development, 19*, 241–251.

Barr, R., Dowden, A., & Hayne, H. (1996). Developmental change in deferred imitation by 6- to 24-month-old infants. *Infant Behavior and Development, 19*, 159–170.

Bauer, P. J. (2002). Long-term recall memory: Behavioral and neurodevelopmental changes in the first 2 years of life. *Current Directions in Psychological Science, 11*, 137–141.

Bauer, P. J. (2004). Getting explicit memory off the ground: Steps toward construction of a neuro-developmental account of changes in the first two years of life. *Developmental Review, 24*, 347–373.

Bauer, P. J. (2005a). Developments in declarative memory: Decreasing susceptibility to storage failure over the second year of life. *Psychological Science, 16*, 41–47.

Bauer, P. J. (2005b). New developments in the study of infant memory. In D. M. Teti (Ed.), *Blackwell Handbook of Research Methods in Developmental Science* (pp. 467–488). Oxford, UK: Blackwell.

Bauer, P. J. (2006). Event memory. In W. Damon (Ed.-in-Chief) & D. Kuhn & R. Siegler (Vol. Eds.), *Handbook of Child Psychology: Vol. 2. Cognition, Perception, and Language* (6th ed., pp. 373–425). New York: Wiley.

Bauer, P. J. (2007). *Remembering the times of our lives: Memory in infancy and beyond.* Mahwah, NJ: Erlbaum.

Bauer, P. J. (in press). Toward a neuro-developmental account of the development of declarative memory. *Developmental Psychobiology.*

Bauer, P. J., Cheatham, C. L., Strand Cary, M., & Van Abbema, D. L. (2002). Short-term forgetting: Charting its course and its implications for long-term remembering. In S. P. Shohov (Ed.), *Advances in psychology research* (Vol. 9, pp. 53–74). Huntington, NY: Nova Science.

Bauer, P. J., & Dow, G. A. (1994). Episodic memory in 16- and 20-month-old children: Specifics are generalized, but not forgotten. *Developmental Psychology, 30*, 403–417.

Bauer, P. J., & Fivush, R. (1992). Constructing event representations: Building on a foundation of variation and enabling relations. *Cognitive Development, 7*, 381–401.

Bauer, P. J., & Hertsgaard, L. A. (1993). Increasing steps in recall of events: Factors facilitating immediate and long-term memory in 13.5- and 16.5-month-old children. *Child Development, 64*, 1204–1223.

Bauer, P. J., Hertsgaard, L. A., & Wewerka, S. S. (1995). Effects of experience and reminding on long-term recall in infancy: Remembering not to forget. *Journal of Experimental Child Psychology, 59,* 260–298.

Bauer, P. J., Kroupina, M. G., Schwade, J. A., Dropik, P. L., & Wewerka, S. S. (1998). If memory serves, will language? Later verbal accessibility of early memories. *Development and Psychopathology, 10,* 655–679.

Bauer, P. J., & Shore, C. M. (1987). Making a memorable event: Effects of familiarity and organization on young children's recall of action sequences. *Cognitive Development, 2,* 327–338.

Bauer, P. J., Van Abbema, D. L., & de Haan, M. (1999). In for the short haul: Immediate and short-term remembering and forgetting by 20-month-old children. *Infant Behavior and Development, 22,* 321–343.

Bauer, P. J., Van Abbema, D. L., Wiebe, S. A., Strand Cary, M., Phill, C., & Burch, M. M. (2004). Props, not pictures, are worth a thousand words: Verbal accessibility of early memories under different conditions of contextual support. *Applied Cognitive Psychology, 18,* 373–392.

Bauer, P. J., Wenner, J. A., Dropik, P. L., & Wewerka, S. S. (2000). Parameters of remembering and forgetting in the transition from infancy to early childhood. *Monographs of the Society for Research in Child Development, 65*(4, Serial No. 263).

Bauer, P. J., Wiebe, S. A., Carver, L. J., Lukowski, A. F., Haight, J. C., Waters, J. M., et al. (2006). Electrophysiological indices of encoding and behavioral indices of recall: Examining relations and developmental change late in the first year of life. *Developmental Neuropsychology, 29,* 293–320.

Bauer, P. J., Wiebe, S. A., Carver, L. J., Waters, J. M., & Nelson, C. A. (2003). Developments in long-term explicit memory late in the first year of life: Behavioral and electrophysiological indices. *Psychological Science, 14,* 629–635.

Bauer, P. J., Wiebe, S. A., Waters, J. M., & Bangston, S. K. (2001). Reexposure breeds recall: Effects of experience on 9-month-olds' ordered recall. *Journal of Experimental Child Psychology, 80,* 174–200.

Benes, F. M. (2001). The development of prefrontal cortex: The maturation of neurotransmitter systems and their interaction. In C. A. Nelson & M. Luciana (Eds.), *Handbook of developmental cognitive neuroscience* (pp. 79–92). Cambridge, MA: MIT Press.

Berger, T. W. (1984). Long-term potentiation of hippocampal synaptic transmission affects rate of behavioral learning. *Science, 224,* 627–630.

Borovsky, D., & Rovee-Collier, C. (1990). Contextual constraints on memory retrieval at six months. *Child Development, 61,* 1569–1583.

Bourgeois, J.-P. (2001). Synaptogenesis in the neocortex of the newborn: The ultimate frontier for individuation? In C. A. Nelson & M. Luciana (Eds.), *Handbook of developmental cognitive neuroscience* (pp. 23–34). Cambridge, MA: MIT Press.

Carver, L. J., & Bauer, P. J. (1999). When the event is more than the sum of its parts: Nine-month-olds' long-term ordered recall. *Memory, 7,* 147–174.

Carver, L. J., & Bauer, P. J. (2001). The dawning of a past: The emergence of long-term explicit memory in infancy. *Journal of Experimental Psychology: General, 130,* 726–745.

Cheatham, C. L., & Bauer, P. J. (2005). Construction of a more coherent story: Prior verbal recall predicts later verbal accessibility of early memories. *Memory, 13,* 516–532.

Chugani, H. T. (1994). Development of regional blood glucose metabolism in relation to behavior and plasticity. In G. Dawson & K. Fischer (Eds.), *Human behavior and the developing brain* (pp. 153–175). New York: Guilford.

Collie, R., & Hayne, H. (1999). Deferred imitation by 6- and 9-month-old infants: More evidence of declarative memory. *Developmental Psychobiology, 35,* 83–90.

Curran, T. (1997). Effects of aging on implicit sequence learning: Accounting for sequence structure and explicit knowledge. *Psychological Research/Psychologische Forschung, 60*(1–2), 24–41.

Curran, T., & Keele, S. W. (1993). Attentional and nonattentional forms of sequence learning. *Journal of Experimental Psychology: Learning, Memory, and Cognition, 19,* 189–202.

Czurkó, A., Czéh, B., Seress, L., Nadel, L., & Bures, J. (1997). Severe spatial navigation deficit in the Morris water maze after single high dose of neonatal X-ray irradiation in the rat. *Proceedings of the National Academy of Science, USA, 94,* 2766–2771.

DeBoer, T., Wewerka, S., Bauer, P. J., Georgieff, M. K., & Nelson, C. A. (2005). Explicit memory performance in infants of diabetic mothers at 1 year of age. *Developmental Medicine and Child Neurology, 47,* 525–531.

de Ungria, M., Rao, R., Wobken, J. D., Luciana, M., Nelson, C. A., & Georgieff, M. K. (2000). Perinatal iron deficiency decreases cytochrome c oxidase (CytOx) activity in selective regions of neonatal rat brain. *Pediatric Research, 48,* 169–176.

Ebbinghaus, H. (1964). *On memory* (H. A. Ruger & C. E. Bussenius, Trans.). New York: Dover. (Original work published 1885)

Eckenhoff, M., & Rakic, P. (1991). A quantitative analysis of synaptogenesis in the molecular layer of the dentate gyrus in the rhesus monkey. *Developmental Brain Research, 64,* 129–135.

Eichenbaum, H., & Cohen, N. J. (2001). *From conditioning to conscious recollection: Memory systems of the brain.* New York: Oxford University Press.

Felt B., & Lozoff, B. (1996). Brain iron and behavior of rats are not normalized by treatment of iron deficiency anemia during early development. *Journal of Nutrition, 126,* 693–701.

Goldman-Rakic, P. S. (1987). Circuitry of primate prefrontal cortex and regulation of behavior by representational memory. In F. Plum (Ed.), *Handbook of physiology, the nervous system, higher functions of the brain* (Vol. 5, pp. 373–417). Bethesda, MD: American Physiological Society.

Gulya, M., Rovee-Collier, C., Galluccio, L., & Wilk, A. (1998). Memory processing of a serial list by young infants. *Psychological Science, 9,* 303–307.

Hanna, E., & Meltzoff, A. N. (1993). Peer imitation by toddlers in laboratory, home, and day-care contexts: Implications for social learning and memory. *Developmental Psychology, 29,* 702–710.

Hayne, H., Boniface, J., & Barr, R. (2000). The development of declarative memory in human infants: Age-related changes in deferred imitation. *Behavioral Neuroscience, 114,* 77–83.

Hayne, H., & Herbert, J. (2004). Verbal cues facilitate memory retrieval during infancy. *Journal of Experimental Child Psychology, 89*(2), 127–139.

Hayne, H., MacDonald, S., & Barr, R. (1997). Developmental changes in the specificity of memory over the second year of life. *Infant Behavior and Development, 20,* 233–245.

Herbert, J. S., Eckerman, C. O., & Stanton, M. E. (2003). The ontogeny of human learning in delay, long-delay, and trace eyeblink conditioning. *Behavioral Neuroscience, 117*(6), 1196–1210.

Herbert, J., & Hayne, H. (2000). Memory retrieval by 18–30-month-olds: Age-related changes in representational flexibility. *Developmental Psychology, 36,* 473–484.

Howe, M. L., & Brainerd, C. J. (1989). Development of children's long-term retention. *Developmental Review, 9,* 301–340.

Howe, M. L., & Courage, M. L. (1997). Independent paths in the development of infant learning and forgetting. *Journal of Experimental Child Psychology, 67,* 131–163.

Huttenlocher, P. R. (1979). Synaptic density in human frontal cortex: Developmental changes and effects of aging. *Brain Research, 163,* 195–205.

Huttenlocher, P. R., & Dabholkar, A. S. (1997). Regional differences in synaptogenesis in human cerebral cortex. *Journal of Comparative Neurology, 387,* 167–178.

Ivkovich, D., & Stanton, M. E. (2001). Effects of early hippocampal lesions on trace, delay, and long-delay eyeblink conditioning in developing rats. *Neurobiology of Learning and Memory, 76,* 426–446.

Jorgenson, L. A., Wobken, J. D., & Georgieff, M. K. (2003). Perinatal iron deficiency alters apical dendritic growth in hippocampal CA1 pyramidal neurons. *Developmental Neuroscience, 25,* 412–420.

Kandel, E. R., Schwartz, J. H., & Jessell, T. M. (2000). *Principles of neural science* (4th ed.). New York: McGraw-Hill.

Kim, J. J., & Fanselow, M. S. (1992). Modality-specific retrograde amnesia of fear. *Science, 256,* 675–677.

Klein, P. J., & Meltzoff, A. N. (1999). Long-term memory, forgetting, and deferred imitation in 12-month-old infants. *Developmental Science, 2,* 102–113.

Köhler, S., & Moscovitch, M. (1997). Unconscious visual processing in neuropsychological syndromes: A survey of the literature and evaluation of models of consciousness. In M. D. Rugg (Ed.), *Cognitive neuroscience* (pp. 305–373). London: UCL Press.

Krupa, D. J., Thompson, J. K., & Thompson, R. F. (1993). Localization of a memory trace in the mammalian brain. *Science, 260,* 989–991.

Lechuga, M. T., Marcos-Ruiz, R., & Bauer, P. J. (2001). Episodic recall of specifics and generalisation coexist in 25-month-old children. *Memory, 9,* 117–132.

Liston, C., & Kagan, J. (2002). Memory enhancement in early childhood. *Nature, 419,* 896.

Mandler, J. M. (2004). Two kinds of knowledge acquisition. In J. M. Lucariello, J. A. Hudson, R. Fivush, & P. J. Bauer (Eds.), *The development of the mediated mind: Sociocultural context and cognitive development. Essays in honor of Katherine Nelson* (pp. 13–32). Mahwah, NJ: Erlbaum.

Mandler, J. M., & McDonough, L. (1995). Long-term recall of event sequences in infancy. *Journal of Experimental Child Psychology, 59,* 457–474.

Manns, J. R., Clark, R. E., & Squire, L. R. (2000). Awareness predicts the magnitude of single-cue trace eyeblink conditioning. *Hippocampus, 10*(2), 181–186.

Maratsos, M. (1998). The acquisition of grammar. In W. Damon (Ed.-in-Chief), & D. Kuhn & R. S. Siegler (Vol. Eds.), *Handbook of child psychology: Vol. 2. Cognition, perception, and language* (5th ed., pp. 421–466). New York: Wiley.

Markowitsch, H. J. (2000). Neuroanatomy of memory. In E. Tulving & F. I. M. Craik (Eds.), *The Oxford handbook of memory* (pp. 465–484). New York: Oxford University Press.

McDonough, L., & Mandler, J. M .(1998). Inductive generalization in 9- and 11-month-olds. *Developmental Science, 1,* 227–232.

McDonough, L., Mandler, J. M., McKee, R. D., & Squire, L. R. (1995). The deferred imitation task as a nonverbal measure of declarative memory. *Proceedings of the National Academy of Sciences, USA, 92,* 7580–7584.

Meltzoff, A. N. (1988). Imitation of televised models by infants. *Child Development, 59,* 1221–1229.

Meltzoff, A. N. (1995). What infant memory tells us about infantile amnesia: Long-term recall and deferred imitation. *Journal of Experimental Child Psychology, 59,* 497–515.

Moore, J. W., Goodell, N. A., & Solomon, P. R. (1976). Central cholinergic blockage by scopolamine and habituation, classical conditioning, and latent inhibition of the rabbit's nictitating membrane response. *Physiological Psychology, 4,* 395–399.

Moyer, J. R., Jr., Deyo, R. A., & Disterhoft, J. F. (1990). Hippocampectomy disrupts trace eye-blink conditioning in rabbits. *Behavioral Neuro-science, 104* (2), 243–252.

Nadel, L., & Willner, J. (1989). Some implications of postnatal maturation of the hippocampus. In V. Chan-Palay & C. Köhler (Eds.), *The hippocampus— new vistas* (pp. 17–31). New York: Alan R. Liss.

Nelson, C. A. (1995). The ontogeny of human memory: A cognitive neuro-science perspective. *Developmental Psychology, 31,* 723–738.

Nelson, C. A. (1997). The neurobiological basis of early memory develop-ment. In N. Cowan (Ed.), *The development of memory in childhood* (pp. 41–82). Hove, UK: Psychology Press.

Nelson, C. A. (2000). Neural plasticity and human development: The role of early experience in sculpting memory systems. *Developmental Science, 3,* 115–136.

Nelson, K., & Ross, G. (1980). The generalities and specifics of long-term memory in infants and young children. In M. Perlmutter (Ed.), *New directions in child development—children's memory* (pp. 87–101). San Francisco: Jossey-Bass.

Nold, J., & Georgieff, M. (2004). Infants of diabetic mothers. *Pediatric Clinics of North America, 51,* 619–637.

Piaget, J. (1952). *The origins of intelligence in children.* New York: Inter-national Universities Press.

Pillemer, D. B. (1998). What is remembered about early childhood events? *Clinical Psychology Review, 18,* 895–913.

Pillemer, D. B., & White, S. H. (1989). Childhood events recalled by children and adults. In H. W. Reese (Ed.), *Advances in child development and behavior* (Vol. 21, pp. 297–340). Orlando, FL: Academic Press.

Port, R. L., Mikhail, A. A., & Patterson, M. M. (1985). Differential effects of hippocampectomy classically conditioned rabbit nictitating membrane response related to interstimulus interval. *Behavioral Neuroscience, 99*(2), 200–208.

Port, R. L., Romano, A. G., Steinmetz, J. E., Mikhail, A. A., & Patterson, M. M. (1986). Retention and acquisition of classical trace conditioned responses by rabbits with hippocampal lesions. *Behavioral Neuroscience, 100*(5), 745–752.

Rao, R., de Ungria, M., Sullivan, D., Wu, P., Wobken, J. D., Nelson, C. A., et al. (1999). Perinatal iron deficiency increases the vulnerability of rat hippocampus to hypoxic ischemic insult. *Journal of Nutrition, 129,* 199–206.

Rao, R., Tkac, I., Townsend, E. L., Gruetter, R., & Georgieff, M. K. (2003). Perinatal iron deficiency alters the neurochemical profile of the developing rat hippocampus. *Journal of Nutrition, 133,* 3215–3221.

Reed, J. M., & Squire, L. R. (1998). Retrograde amnesia for facts and events: Findings from four new cases. *Journal of Neuroscience, 18,* 3943–3954.

Rovee-Collier, C. (1990). The "memory system" of prelinguistic infants. In A. Diamond (Ed.), *The development and neural bases of higher cognitive functions* (pp. 517–536). New York: New York Academy of Science.

Rovee-Collier, C. (1997). Dissociations in infant memory: Rethinking the development of implicit and explicit memory. *Psychological Review, 104,* 467–498.

Rovee-Collier, C., & Hayne, H. (2000). Memory in infancy and early childhood. In E. Tulving & F. I. M. Craik (Eds.), *The Oxford handbook of memory* (pp. 267–282). New York: Oxford University Press.

Schacter, D. L., Wagner, A. D., & Buckner, R. L. (2000). Memory systems of 1999. In E. Tulving & F. I. M. Craik (Eds.), *The Oxford handbook of memory* (pp. 627–643). New York: Oxford University Press.

Schmidt, A. T., Waldow, K. J., Salinas, J. A., & Georgieff, M. K. (2004). The long-term behavioral effects of fetal/neonatal iron deficiency on a hippocampally dependent learning task in the rat [Abstract]. *Pediatric Research, 55,* 279A.

Seress, L. (2001). Morphological changes of the human hippocampal formation from midgestation to early childhood. In C. A. Nelson & M. Luciana (Eds.), *Handbook of developmental cognitive neuroscience* (pp. 45–58). Cambridge, MA: MIT Press.

Simcock, G., & Hayne, H. (2002). Breaking the barrier? Children fail to translate their preverbal memories into language. *Psychological Science, 13,* 225–231.

Solomon, P. R., Vander Schaaf, E. R., Thompson, R. F., & Weisz, D. J. (1986). Hippocampus and trace conditioning of the rabbit's classically conditioned nictitating membrane response. *Behavioral Neuroscience, 100*(5), 729–744.

Squire, L. R., Knowlton, B., & Musen, G. (1993). The structure and organization of memory. *Annual Review of Psychology, 44,* 453–495.

Stanton, M. E. (2000). Multiple memory systems, development and conditioning. *Behavioural Brain Research, 110,* 25–37.

Takehara, K., Kawahara, S., & Kirino, Y. (2003). Time-dependent reorganization of the brain components underlying memory retention in trace eyeblink conditioning. *Journal of Neuroscience, 23,* 9897–9905.

Thomas, K. M., & Nelson, C. A. (2001). Serial reaction time learning in preschool- and school-age children. *Journal of Experimental Child Psychology, 79,* 364–387.

Thompson, R. F. (1986). The neurobiology of learning and memory. *Science, 233,* 941–947.

Travis, L. (1997). Goal-based organization of event memory in toddlers. In P. W. van den Broek, P. J. Bauer, & T. Bourg (Eds.), *Developmental spans in event comprehension and representation: Bridging fictional and actual events* (pp. 111–138). Mahwah, NJ: Erlbaum.

Zola, S. M., & Squire, L. R. (2000). The medial temporal lobe and the hippocampus. In E. Tulving & F. I. M. Craik (Eds.), *The Oxford handbook of memory* (pp. 485–500). New York: Oxford University Press.

11

How Do We Remember?

Let Me Count the Ways

JEAN M. MANDLER

Part II contains an interesting and informative set of chapters. Not only do they lay out some remarkable developments over the past two decades in infant memory research, but they also illuminate the fundamental unsolved issue in the study of infant memory. The chapters show a clear-cut split on the issue of what infant tests of memory measure, and a more nuanced, but nevertheless I believe genuine, split as to the usefulness of differentiating explicit and implicit memory. Underlying this split is the elephant in the room, the ever-disturbing question of how to measure conscious awareness in nonverbal creatures.

The authors of each chapter agree there is a distinction between implicit and explicit memory, but only chapters 8 and 10 make use of it. The authors of both chapters 7 and 9 state that all their research involves only explicit memory. In my commentary, I first provide a brief overview of some of the issues discussed in these chapters. Next, I zero in on the visual paired comparison (VPC) test, which is one of the central arenas of dispute. Then, because the distinction between implicit and explicit memory is crucial to understanding memory, I discuss some refinements that I think are needed in the conceptions of implicit and explicit memory used in these chapters. Finally, I summarize the issues that are still unresolved and offer a tentative assessment of the onset of explicit memory in infancy from the evidence available to us at this time.

The Issues the Chapters Present

Bauer, DeBoer, and Lukowski, in chapter 10, emphasize recall in infancy. Their chapter provides an excellent description of what we have learned in the past 20 years about the development of this kind of explicit memory in the first two years of life. The increase in our understanding of recall in infancy is impressive, much of it due to research coming from Bauer's own lab. I was especially struck by the work assessing the relative contributions to recall of (a) initial encoding, (b) consolidation and storage, and (c) retrieval of the information to awareness, as well as the discussion of the neurological underpinnings of these processes. This research represents a major advance in our knowledge about what is developing during this period of life.

Bauer et al. also make the important point that we should expect commonalities across different memory systems, in that all memory involves taking in information from the environment, storing it, and making use of it at a later time. The fundamental mechanism for doing this, long-term potentiation, happens at the cellular level throughout the brain, and all retention and consolidation of information makes use of it. As Bauer et al. note, neurons do not discriminate which memory system they are a part of, and a number of the same neural structures are involved in different memory networks. For example, the hippocampus is involved in explicit memory, but it is part of a larger circuit that mediates modification of adaptive reflexes and is involved in some kinds of conditioning as well. Bauer et al. provide an excellent summary of how a given brain area such as the hippocampus participates differentially in different tasks involving both implicit and explicit processing.

Both Snyder (chapter 8) and Rose et al. (chapter 7) emphasize recognition rather than recall. Rose et al. describe an impressive amount of research on infants' recognition memory, much of it coming from their own laboratory, and much of it using the VPC task. In this task, two identical pictures are presented side by side and then after a delay one of these pictures is presented again along with a new picture. Longer looking at the new picture is assumed to indicate recognition of the old one. Rose et al. cite monkey models and neuropsychological studies to bolster their claim that this task requires explicit processing; that is, they claim that infants look longer at a novel stimulus in this task because they are *aware* that the old stimulus is familiar (or the new one is not). I discuss some of the ins and outs of this view below, but here I want to note the importance of Rose and her colleagues' work indicating that both attention and processing speed make independent contributions to visual recognition memory, and that individual differences in these variables have long-lasting effects on development.

Chapter 8 also focuses on infant recognition and the VPC test, but Snyder emphasizes that it is more likely to be an implicit than an explicit task. She also summarizes findings from the neuropsychological literature, including some of her own, and comes to the opposite conclusion of that reached by Rose et al. By this point, it should be clear to the reader that there is an important issue yet to be resolved before we can say that we understand infant memory.

Even without mentioning awareness, we are faced with opposing claims on whether the VPC test assesses implicit or explicit memory. As will be clear from the following discussion, Snyder's view of the neuropsychological literature and how to use it is closer to mine than is Rose et al.'s view, but aside from that, I was especially impressed by the wide range of neuropsychological data Snyder brings to bear on the issue. She does not just consider the hippocampus in relation to performance on the VPC test but also the wider issues of the functional significance of the behavior and the processes that may be involved in it—preferential looking, familiarity, novelty, and priming. She describes an important set of infant studies using event-related potentials (ERPs) to measure the effects of repetition of a stimulus on brain activity in various regions. This work helps to clarify the potential processes used in the VPC, including a likely role for repetition suppression in mediating preferential looking.

Hayne (chapter 9), in addition to an interesting presentation on the possible development of episodic (autobiographical) memory, takes on the difficult task of relating three very different tests of memory in infancy to each other: the VPC test, operant conditioning, and deferred imitation. Although she subscribes to the difference between implicit and explicit memory (see Figure 9.1 or the top half of Figure 11.1), she claims that all three of these tests measure explicit memory. I believe there is now general agreement that deferred imitation measures explicit memory. What is at issue, then, is the status of VPC and operant conditioning. Because all three tasks show some commonalities in the way they develop (older infants encode information faster, remember longer, and are less context bound in their performance), Hayne argues they all measure the same kind of memory.

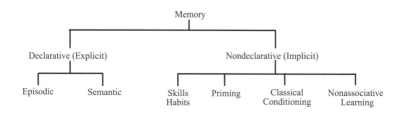

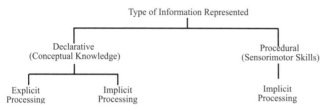

FIGURE 11.1. The bottom half of the figure portrays the separation of declarative and procedural representation from explicit an implicit processing. The top half reproduces Figure 9.1 (this volume), derived from Squire (1994), in which representation and processing are conflated.

However, as Bauer et al. (chapter 10) discuss at length, these commonalities are not sufficient in themselves to differentiate implicit and explicit memory. Hayne realizes this but claims that there are both amnesia tests and "parameter" tests that support her view of the explicit status of memory in these tasks. As Hayne points out, there appears to be no information about amnesic performance on operant conditioning tasks. However, there is a wealth of information on a wide variety of skill learning, habit learning, and classical conditioning tasks that amnesic patients can accomplish, which makes it seem likely that they would succeed at operant conditioning as well. That leaves the VPC task, which I discuss in the next section along with the usefulness of amnesia and parameter tests for evaluating infants' recognition memory.

What Does the Visual Paired Comparison Task Measure?

Here is a 22-year-old quote, rather extensive, but I think as germane today as then:

> Because the terms *recall* and *recognition* often go undefined in the literature, there are serious problems in trying to trace the continuity of memory from infancy to adulthood. . . . In all adult studies the term *recognition* implies consciousness or awareness of prior occurrence. It is assumed that the adult is aware that the item in question has been experienced in his or her personal past. In adults, such recognition is thought to have two components (G. Mandler, 1980). One of these is a familiarity component, caused by repeated exposures during which perceptual integration and organization take place. The other is a retrieval component that involves the search for contextual information, typically concerning when or where the item was experienced in the past. . . . The retrieval process is thought to be the same process that occurs in recall.
>
> Recognition is usually studied in adults by requiring them to make some sort of yes/no judgment as to whether or not they have experienced the item before. They can do this on the basis of sheer familiarity and/or by engaging in a retrieval process such that they can recall the item. Whether one or both components are involved, the ability to make a yes/no judgment requires *awareness* of prior occurrence . . .
>
> The literature on infant recognition has been concerned almost exclusively with the familiarity component. It has not concerned itself by and large with the retrieval component and, to my knowledge, has not even raised the issue of whether or not the infant who demonstrates familiarity with a stimulus has any awareness of "having seen that before." Familiarity with a stimulus is typically measured by habituation (e.g., a decrease in looking time); lack of familiarity is measured by dishabituation (e.g., an increase in looking time). The issue is not that

these measures are fallible (which they are because of the interaction of familiarity with interest or other factors). The point is that measures of habituation and dishabituation do not tap the same process as a yes/no recognition task in which the subject is asked specifically about awareness of the past. (J. M. Mandler, 1984, pp. 77–78)

The message then and now is that adult recognition memory tests are deliberate memory tests requiring explicit judgments. In contrast, the VPC task used in research on infant memory has no explicit requirements. Infants are merely shown an old and a new picture, and looking time at each is measured. I suggested calling the responses shown in VPC *primitive recognition* (a notion based on perceptual learning or perceptual identification as described by Jacoby, 1983; Jacoby & Dallas, 1981), because looking could be based on a modification of the perceptual apparatus itself without requiring retrieval of semantic or episodic information from elsewhere in the system. Each presentation of a stimulus makes it more familiar to the perceptual system, whether or not this familiarity is conscious. The more familiar, the more likely it should be that the infant looks at the new picture.

The logic of this argument was straightforward and even then there was a good deal of evidence to support it, which has increased and been elaborated since then. Today more emphasis would be placed on repetition priming. Repetition priming is a classic example of the implicit learning that takes place in nondeliberate tasks (that is, tasks in which people are not trying to remember the material they are processing). The phenomenon is that a recently presented stimulus (whether picture, word, or object) will be processed more rapidly than a new one. This fact alone should lead to longer looking at a new stimulus in VPC and so might in itself account for successful performance. Adults are usually unaware of their more rapid or fluid responses to previously presented stimuli, and priming occurs whether or not there is explicit recognition memory for what has been presented (Graf, Mandler, & Haden, 1982; Jacoby & Witherspoon, 1982). Indeed, priming can occur when exposures are so brief that people *cannot* be aware of what has been presented; G. Mandler, Nakamura, and van Zandt (1987) showed that even 2 milliseconds of exposure to a stimulus, followed by a mask that cuts off further processing, produces activation that influences later responses to it.

Such results should not be surprising. Perceptual schemas develop through exposure and do not require conceptualization; the results just described suggest that building familiarity does not even require awareness or attention (see J. M. Mandler, 2004, for discussion). Experiencing an event can strengthen a perceptual schema without the attentive conceptual work that enables recall or conscious recognition. A lack of conceptual meaning may be an important consideration in assessing VPC in infancy, given that infants as young as 3 months have been participants. It seems quite likely that in the early months infants look at pictures without much conceptual processing going on (interest is not the same as conceptualization). That is, detailed perceptual processing and perceptual schema formation can take place without conceptual content being aroused, as shown by the fact that 3-month-olds can learn in a few trials to categorize abstract dot patterns or pictures of animals with which they have had no prior experience (e.g., Bomba & Siqueland, 1983; Eimas & Quinn, 1994).

That awareness of prior presentation is not required for priming was also shown by the fact that repetition priming is normal in amnesic patients (e.g., Graf, Squire, & Mandler, 1984; Warrington & Weiskrantz, 1974). These early findings have been consistently confirmed. For example, Cave and Squire (1992) found equivalent facilitation of picture-naming latencies 2 days after a single presentation of pictures to normals and amnesic patients, but the amnesic patients were markedly worse on a yes/no recognition test of the pictures. It seems they had lost awareness of familiarity but not familiarity itself. Cave and Squire concluded that priming and recognition must depend on separate brain systems. (This conclusion is relevant to interpretation of amnesic patients' performance on the VPC test, discussed below.)

Thus, in both normal adults and amnesic patients, recently presented stimuli are primed. Repeated exposure to a stimulus results in both short-term and long-term suppression of neuronal responses to it in the visual cortex; at the neuronal level, repetition suppression appears to be the mechanism responsible for repetition priming (Ungerleider, 1995). As Snyder discusses in chapter 8, repetition suppression occurs even during passive fixation. That is, this characteristic of the visual system appears to be quite general and may apply to unattended as well as to attended information.

These considerations indicate that longer looking at a novel stimulus can result from priming of previously presented stimuli and does not require explicit memory. The question arises, then, why Hayne and Rose et al. insist that VPC is an explicit task. Aside from an understandable desire to relate the recognition tests used in infancy, where it is obviously impossible to ask for explicit judgments, to the tests used with older children and adults, there are also recent amnesic data that the authors of both chapters call upon to bolster their view that the VPC test does measure explicit memory: Some amnesic patients fail to show novelty preferences on it. It is mainly this issue I address here.

It has been frequently assumed that recall and recognition are equivalent measures of explicit memory (e.g., Squire, 1994). However, we have fairly recently learned that at least some amnesic patients with selective hippocampal damage, whose recall processes are seriously compromised, can nevertheless pass a variety of explicit recognition tests (Aggleton et al., 2005; Bastin et al., 2004; Mayes, Holdstock, Isaac, Hunkin, & Roberts, 2002). Such findings invite the conclusion that it is recall that is disrupted by hippocampal damage rather than the familiarity processes that can also enable recognition (e.g., Holdstock et al., 2002).[1] Because explicit recognition tests can be passed via either familiarity or recall and because these two processes typically support each other (G. Mandler, 1980), recognition scores may be lower than normal in hippocampal patients, but they need not be absent.

Because recognition can be mediated by familiarity, it raises the important issue of how to define familiarity. Must it be conscious? Must we be aware that something is familiar for it to produce preferential looking at a novel stimulus? Or is *familiarity* a misleading term, in that it leads us to assume awareness when it is perhaps not warranted? If we use priming as an operational definition of familiarity, on the grounds that it shows the effects of prior experience on current processing, then familiarity does not require awareness. It may be that awareness of familiarity requires recollection, but when this is absent in amnesia, a familiarity process nevertheless still operates.

We know from common experience that familiarity often controls behavior without awareness. We all move about in a familiar world and most of the time we have no awareness of that familiarity. Indeed, if we were continually using our limited conscious capacity to attend to the familiarity of the things around us, we would lose the value of that precious mental asset that enables us to think and plan, communicate, and carry out new projects. It seems more likely that we look longer at newly seen things in an automatic way, not out of a conscious sense of curiosity, unless they are genuinely novel. It may only be in the latter case that we engage in the attentive, elaborative (relational) processing that makes explicit recall and recognition possible.

An example of this principle at work in the laboratory is an experiment by Friedman (1979). In a study of adults' recognition of complex scenes of common places such as kitchens and city streets, as measured by detection of changes in the scenes, she found that both initial fixation time and recognition were a function of the probability of occurrence of the objects in the scene. Changes in plausible but unusual objects in such scenes (e.g., a fireplace in a kitchen or a balloon over a street) were the most likely to be recognized, and changes in the most typical objects were not recognized above chance. These results occurred even though subjects were informed that this was a memory test and that they should carefully inspect every object, because only one object would change. Our perceptual habits are both unconscious and deeply ingrained.

Mack and Rock (1998) call the normal state of perception as we go about the world *inattentional blindness,* in which we cannot report much of what has been seen or heard even immediately after experiencing it. We register and use this information to build the schemas that guide us through the environment, but we retain little of the information in conscious memory (see J. M. Mandler, 2004, for discussion). If it is truly novel or unusual, we engage in the elaborative processing that ensures recallability and explicit recognition (G. Mandler, 1980), and of course we use explicit processes when we are deliberately trying to memorize. However, there appears to be little evidence that we engage in such explicit conceptual processing in most normal activities or in nondeliberate tasks, such as VPC and other repetition priming tasks.

Interestingly, an important exception to this observation about nondeliberate tasks may occur in amnesic patients. Consider the two studies cited by three chapters in this section of the book that have used the VPC test with amnesic patients (McKee & Squire, 1993; Pascalis, Hunkin, Holdstock, Isaac, & Mayes, 2004). The single patient in Pascalis et al. (YR, the same patient as in Mayes et al., 2002) and the several patients in McKee and Squire all showed evidence of explicit recognition memory. YR, one of the relatively few patients studied with lesions restricted to the hippocampus itself (usually termed selective hippocampus damage), passed explicit recognition tests in the normal range. The McKee and Squire patients, who varied considerably in etiology, showed reduced explicit recognition, but still above chance. Yet McKee and Squire found that their patients failed the VPC test at delays of 2 minutes or more between presentation and test, and Pascalis et al. found that YR failed at delays of 5 seconds or more (a puzzling difference). What are we to make of the finding that people with explicit recognition capacity fail the VPC test? Certainly, a likely hypothesis is that the VPC test does not test explicit recognition but implicit recognition instead.[2]

An extensive consideration of possible reasons for failure on the VPC test in conjunction with passing explicit recognition tests was made by Pascalis et al. (2004). They rejected the hypothesis that VPC is more sensitive to familiarity memory deficits than explicit recognition tests, because it seems implausible that a simple test requiring no effort is failed while a more demanding test is passed. They suggested it is more plausible that patients with selective hippocampal damage have preserved familiarity memory processes mediated by the perirhinal cortex and other intact extrahippocampal structures (see Holdstock et al., 2002, for a similar suggestion). They did not discuss whether these familiarity processes are implicit or explicit in nature, although they did suggest that amnesic patients may have a problem with recognition mainly when encoding is "incidental and, therefore, presumably automatic."[3] They also pointed to growing evidence that the hippocampus may not be engaged in familiarity memory (see Rugg & Yonelinas, 2003). Rather, patients with selective hippocampal damage may react to their impaired recollection in the face of normal familiarity memory. The novel items might draw attention, but so might the familiar ones, because the patients are unable to recall why they seem familiar. As Pascalis et al. put it:

> The result would have been the absence of preference for the novel items at the longer delays used in the VPC task. Presumably, at the shortest delay (0 s) YR was still able to recollect why one of a pair of faces was familiar. One implication of this prediction is that normal participants may show reduced novelty preferences when the competing stimulus is familiar, but not recollected. If this is found, then VPC

performance will have been shown to be sensitive to mismatches between recollection and familiarity. This is consistent with the view that hippocampal damage disrupts recollection and recall, but not item familiarity memory. (p. 1298)

Pascalis et al. (2004) also emphasized the related point that amnesic patients are often aware of their memory deficit and if they think their memory is being tested they will attempt to compensate for it. One would not expect compensatory processes in an incidental task. However, when items are presented and tested one at a time (as was the case in their study and in the most comparable experiment in McKee & Squire, 1993), patients rapidly realize that their memory is being tested. The reader will note that if the attention paid to familiar stimuli on the VPC test by amnesic patients is due to attempts to overcome recollective loss, it makes their data irrelevant to evaluating the basis for infant performance on this test.

To summarize, there is still not a large database on performance by amnesic patients on VPC, nor is there consensus on the data that exist. These considerations indicate that there is currently no amnesia test for VPC of the sort that there is for recall. In McDonough, Mandler, McKee, and Squire (1995), we showed that amnesic patients who cannot recall also cannot do deferred imitation. Even under circumstances conducive to repetition priming (the only other way that they might conceivably manage the task), the amnesic patients did not succeed, adding to the evidence that deferred imitation requires recall; priming alone cannot sustain reproduction of observed acts after a delay. In contrast, it is unclear at present what is required (or which brain systems are required) to respond to a novel stimulus on the VPC test.

As all investigators agree, VPC is an indirect test of memory. It could be measuring priming—an implicit process—or novelty preferences, which can be either implicit or explicit processes. Snyder reports in chapter 8 that 6-month-olds who after 24 hours had a null preference in the VPC nevertheless showed memory for the familiar stimulus when ERPs were the measure. Similarly, adults who had a null preference after 24 hours showed very high explicit recognition memory. Such data argue against novelty preferences being a useful measure of explicit memory. Gross, Hayne, Herbert, and Sowerby (2002) found no relation between performance of 6-month-olds on the VPC test and either an explicit test of memory (deferred imitation) or what in my opinion may well be an implicit test, operant conditioning. Available evidence suggests that novelty preferences on VPC and similar tests (and equally, familiarity preferences, which do occur even in adults; see McDonough, Choi, & Mandler, 2003) frequently work outside awareness. A further complicating factor may arise from comparing amnesic VPC data, where all the stimuli typically have some degree of familiarity, to those of young infants, for whom all the stimuli tested may be novel. To make matters even more difficult, as just discussed, amnesic patients' performance on the VPC test quite likely involves attempts to overcome recollective loss, which makes their data ambiguous with respect to the factors involved in infants' performance.

Similar problems arise when considering monkey data. As Rose et al. note (chapter 7), the delayed-nonmatch-to-sample (DNMS) test has long been the gold standard for assessing visual recognition memory in primates. The test is similar to VPC in that a stimulus is first presented and then, following a delay, it is presented again along with a new one. The new object must be chosen in order to receive a food reward. However, the motivational aspects of this task are quite different from VPC. The monkey must deliberately try to remember the old stimulus, and in that sense it is an explicit memory task. There are no requirements at all in VPC, and most likely no attempt to remember, thus producing an implicit task. Results from these two tasks in adult monkeys with lesions to medial temporal lobe structures created in infancy were similar to those reported with human amnesic patients in comparisons of VPC with delayed-match-to-sample (DMS) tasks: The monkeys performed normally on the DNMS test with delays up to 24 hours, but showed no preference for the novel stimulus in the VPC task at any delay longer than 10 seconds (Pascalis & Bachevalier, 1999). Now, one might conclude that the VPC is a more sensitive test of recognition memory than the DNMS, but given the excellent performance on the more demanding DNMS task, as well as its requirement for deliberate memory, a more plausible conclusion would again seem to be that the two tasks are measuring different processes. Deliberate memorizing is, by definition, an explicit memory activity. In contrast, passive looking may result in learning that later enables awareness of having experienced the material before, but a good deal of data suggest that the more common outcome is priming and lack of awareness of what has been seen.

As for what Haynes calls parameter tests, I am dubious that these can be used to differentiate types of infant memory. Haynes states that implicit memory tasks show few differences as a function of age, retention interval, study time, or context change, whereas declarative memory tasks are all influenced by these variables. There are two reasons why this kind of test is problematic when applied to infants. First, it would be truly newsworthy if memory of any kind did not improve during infancy, or vary as a function of retention interval, study time, or context change. Bauer et al. make it clear in chapter 10 why we should expect major developmental changes in the first year or so of life in any kind of memory. In addition, consider the conceptual changes that take place over the course of the first year, all of which must have profound effects on both implicit and explicit memory. Another obvious complicating factor is the likely hypothesis that if explicit memory comes online gradually during the first year, tests such as the VPC (and operant conditioning as well) may initially rely on implicit memory but then become amplified by explicit memory. Currently we have no way of measuring this possibility, because all tests show memory improvement with development in the early stages of life.

Second, the record is mixed on the operation of these variables in implicit and explicit memory. For example, the length of retention of priming effects varies considerably from study to study (e.g., contrast Jacoby & Dallas, 1981, with Graf & Mandler, 1984), some finding it brief and others more long lasting. As for context change, although explicit memory is more robust to context change in adults (e.g., Roediger & Blaxton, 1987), context change is ubiquitously detrimental in memory tasks in young infants, even those that are agreed to be explicit in nature, as both Hayne and Bauer et al. discuss in their chapters. Such difficulties suggest that these variables do not in themselves form a sufficient basis to determine whether a task is an explicit or implicit memory task. As another example, in chapter 9 Hayne describes an experiment from her laboratory, where no differences in explicit memory were found between 3- and 4-year-olds, even across variations in the amount to be remembered. Obviously, lack of an age difference in this or that study is not criterial for saying a task is implicit in nature. Ultimately, conscious awareness of the past is the criterion that must be used. When it is not available, tests of statistical independence seem more useful (e.g., Tulving, Schacter, & Stark, 1982). And in spite of the current uncertainties present in lesion studies and also in brain imaging studies (see Henson, 2005, for review), these would also seem in the long run to provide better evidence.

At this point, therefore, the more conservative view of the VPC test seems to be that there is little evidence that it does test explicit memory, while there is considerable evidence that it need not. Of course, infants *may* be aware that the previously presented stimuli have been seen before (and at some point in development will certainly be), or perhaps they are aware for some stimuli and not others, but we do not yet have convincing evidence that that is the case. One final point on this topic: Many of the infant studies using the VPC test, especially in the early months (e.g., Fagan, 1972), used faces as stimuli. More recent data (Cipolotti et al., 2006) indicate that memory for faces may not be processed by the hippocampus but in a different area of the brain altogether. Gross et al. (2002), using a three-dimensional puppet with which infants had interacted and a new puppet, reported the surprising finding that 6-month-olds completely failed VPC tests with these stimuli. Until we have more information on different kinds of stimuli and their neurological underpinnings, we need to be cautious in our conclusions about infant performance on the VPC test.

In addition, we cannot at present answer the question of whether familiarity with a stimulus requires awareness to qualify as explicit memory. Rose et al. (chapter 7) give an excellent summary of the developmental changes that occur over the first 6 months in response to previously presented stimuli, but given that these changes were found either in habituation or VPC tests, we have no positive evidence that explicit memory was involved. The older the infant, the more likely that explicit memory of something seen before becomes available, but the question is, when does it first begin? From birth?

From 6 months, the age at which we first have evidence of recall memory, as described in chapter 9? What neural development is required? Rose et al. present evidence that "memory" improves as processing speed and attention change, but how much of the behavioral change is due to the onset of a different sort of remembering? How much to increasingly conceptual processing of pictorial stimuli? Rose et al. point out that it is often impossible to determine whether developmental changes in recognition memory reflect developmental differences in initial encoding or developmental differences in trace decay. But we must also consider how much the developmental differences are due to a dawning awareness of the past.

Why We Must Take Account of Both Representation and Processing

If we are to take the distinction between implicit and explicit memory seriously, then we must always specify which kind of memory we are talking about. Hayne is clear about this: She specifies that all the memory studies that have been conducted in infancy are explicit tests; Rose et al. agree about the status of the VPC test. But what then is left for implicit memory? Are infants not primed implicitly the way that adults are? Snyder's research indicates they undergo repetition suppression, like adults. Assuming that they have not been granted dispensation from priming, how should we measure it? In order to do so, I believe that the definitions of implicit and explicit memory provided in these chapters need finer tuning.

A certain vagueness of definitions may be one source of the disagreement these chapters present. For example, although Bauer et al. and Hayne disagree on how to characterize various tests, they both subscribe to a view of memory like that shown in Hayne's chapter in Figure 9.1 (derived from Squire, 1994). For convenience I have reproduced her figure in the top half of Figure 11.1; below it is my suggested revision (adapted from J. M. Mandler, 1998). In Hayne's version we see that declarative versus procedural (now called nondeclarative) and explicit versus implicit have been collapsed. *Declarative* and *procedural* were once terms that applied to the representation of information—for example, people were said to represent declarative and procedural knowledge in different ways. This distinction was sometimes called into question by psychologists who preferred to emphasize processing—asking what kind of processing goes on in acquiring and using different kinds of knowledge. Hence the use of the terms *explicit* and *implicit processing* became common. After a lot of debate on this issue, an unfortunate compromise began to appear, in which the terms became synonymous (e.g., Squire, 1994): Declarative equaled explicit, and procedural (or nondeclarative) equaled implicit, without specifying whether one was talking about representation or processing. Herein lay a source of future miscommunication.

Inspection of the top half of Figure 11.1 makes one problem apparent. Priming, which is subsumed under implicit memory, can also happen with semantic (conceptual) material, which is subsumed under explicit memory. Although, as we have seen, priming does occur with nonsemantic perceptual material (see also Tulving & Schacter, 1990), it can also be shown during ordinary reading, which is a conceptual task. Indeed, one of the first experiments on priming (Meyer & Schvaneveldt, 1971), used a lexical decision task and found semantic (conceptual) priming in the form of faster decisions when two successive words were semantically related, such as *doctor* and *nurse*, than when they were unrelated (see also Murrell & Morton, 1974). Conceptual priming, like repetition priming, is an automatic process that occurs without awareness; it is implicit processing. For example, it occurs even when the primes are masked and thus not available to awareness (Bodner & Masson, 2003; Marcel, 1983). Brain imaging studies have also shown that when subjects are engaging in a deliberate task, they unconsciously apply the task instructions to unseen masked stimuli, thus again demonstrating both perceptual and conceptual processes operating without awareness (Dehaene et al., 1998).

In short, aspects of declarative knowledge that are brought to bear in ordinary reading are often implicitly processed. We definitely need to be sensitive in some fashion to the distinction between procedural and declarative systems and that between implicit and explicit processing (or tasks), such as the way I show in the bottom half of Figure 11.1. As I put it in J. M. Mandler (1998):

> The procedural-declarative distinction has to do with fundamentally different kinds of information that are represented in different ways. This is a *distinction in representational format.* The implicit-explicit distinction, on the other hand, has to do with whether information can be made accessible. This is a *processing distinction.* In the case of procedural knowledge, information is never accessible; we cannot process this kind of information in such a way as to bring it to awareness. In the case of declarative knowledge, the information is stored in a conceptual format and has the potential to be brought to awareness. Whether that happens on a given occasion depends on the particular kind of processing that is carried out. For example, verbal information can be either explicit or implicit depending on attention and elaboration during encoding. (p. 267)

Perhaps not making a distinction between representation and processing is the reason that Hayne believes that all infant memory tests are explicit in nature; if infants are aware of the pictures they are looking at and retain information from them, it must enter the semantic (conceptual) system, and so the resulting knowledge must be explicit. This view does not allow for implicit processing of conceptual material, yet we know that happens from the priming literature just discussed. When one reads *nurse* faster following *doctor*, semantic material, which is being understood by the conceptual system, is being primed. This is not the same as saying it becomes accessible. Implicit memory is not consigned merely to sensorimotor procedures (skills, motor habits, perceptual schemas, and classical conditioning). Priming studies show that any kind of material can be implicitly processed.

Before concluding, it should be noted that the distinctions just discussed inform other realms of cognitive functioning than memory. Research on categorization in infancy has found a number of dissociations reflecting differences between perceptual and conceptual knowledge (J. M. Mandler, 2000). For example, 3- and 6-month-old infants in a few trials learn to categorize pictures of different kinds of animals such as dogs and cats (e.g., Quinn, Eimas, & Rosenkrantz, 1993). However, in a similar paradigm, but using manipulation of objects instead of looking at pictures, 7-month-olds do not react to these perceptual differences, although they easily categorize them at the more global level of animals (J. M. Mandler & McDonough, 1993, 1998a). A related result is that infants do not honor the distinction between dogs and cats for imitation purposes until their second year (J. M. Mandler & McDonough, 1998b). These and similar results are easily explained on the basis of implicit learning of detailed perceptual and motor schemas that enable infants to identify objects in their environment and interact appropriately with them, accompanied by the slow formation of a declarative knowledge base that is less detailed, but accessible for purposes of inductive generalization and recall (J. M. Mandler, 2000). The notion that categorization can come in both implicit and explicit forms has not been without controversy, but no other comprehensive explanation for the various dissociations uncovered in these and related experiments has been forthcoming.

Whether in memory or in categorization, I believe it is vital to respect both the differences between modes of processing (implicit or explicit) and the way that information is represented (procedural or declarative). As another example, there are almost certainly enough differences between neonatal imitation and the deferred imitation that 9-month-old infants exhibit that make it problematic to consider them as two points on a continuum, as Hayne does in chapter 9. The tongue protrusion that neonates show to a tongue (or a pencil) looming toward them appears to be a releasing response that bears little resemblance to the voluntary and effortful attempts of 9-month-old infants to reproduce event sequences. We have evidence that the latter result in explicit memory. It seems unlikely that the former is anything other than implicit processing that contributes to perceptual schema formation and remains inaccessible.

Finally, to the extent that in the first few months of life processing like this is part of sensorimotor learning rather than conceptually mediated encoding, it may not require the hippocampus. Alternatively, as Bauer et al. (chapter 10) point out, the hippocampus may be involved without the cortical circuits yet being formed. Hence, infants may use different brain resources than those used by adults in tasks such as VPC. Adults conceptually (semantically) process the pictures of objects they see, whereas infants in the first few months have at best only begun such conceptual learning.

Conclusion

Somewhat surprisingly, the issue I raised 22 years ago has not yet been resolved. At that time, I said there was no evidence that VPC measures explicit memory and that the test might well be passed by implicit rather than explicit processing. As the preceding discussion makes clear, that judgment still holds in spite of the accumulation of even more neuropsychological data in the interim. Although both Hayne and Rose et al. in their chapters introduce some of that evidence in favor of their view that the VPC is an explicit test of memory, it seems that the issue is rather more complex than would at first appear. At the least, there remain three unresolved questions.

First, is familiarity implicit or explicit? There appears to be consensus that recognition is a dual-process event that can take place either by means of familiarity or recall (often called recollection when recognition is being discussed), or both. There is also consensus that recall (recollection) is an explicit process. What is undecided is the status of familiarity. For some researchers, it is a conscious awareness of prior occurrence (e.g., Squire, 1994). For others, it is understood as "a purely quantitative, 'strength-like' memory signal" (Rugg & Yonelinas, 2003). On this definition (or definition in terms of activation) familiarity need not be conscious. If this is correct, preferential looking in VPC could be implicit, not having to do with a conscious sense that formerly presented pictures seem familiar. Concerning infant performance in VPC, I assume that Hayne and Rose et al. do not suppose that the 3-month-olds who show preferential looking to novel stimuli make use of recall processes. If preferential looking does indeed imply recognition, that leaves familiarity as the route to success. Their view seems to be that this is a conscious process, that infants are aware that a previously presented picture is familiar (or that a new picture is one they have not seen before). Obviously this is a contentious position.

Second, is familiarity (conscious or no) mediated by the hippocampus or does it depend on other regions of the medial temporal lobe? Work by Ranganath and colleagues (2003) used functional magnetic resonance imaging (fMRI) to examine whether the recollection and familiarity processes involved in recognition are supported by different subregions of the medial temporal lobe. They found that encoding activity in the rhinal cortex predicted familiarity-based recognition, whereas activity in the hippocampus and posterior parahippocampal cortex selectively predicted recollection. Rugg and Yonelinas (2003) concluded that current results from neuropsychological, ERP, and fMRI studies of recognition memory strongly support the view that the hippocampus plays a crucial role in the recollective processes involved in recognition and argue for a less important role in familiarity processing. However, as these authors note, there is still considerable debate as to the neural structures mediating familiarity, including the extent to which it may depend on parietal cortex. As far as infants are concerned, Bauer et al. discuss in detail the rather slow process by which the routes to and from the hippocampus to the rhinal and association cortices develop over the course of the first year. The uncertainty that exists in the neuropsychological community over the details of what happens in medial temporal lobe structures as well as other cortical areas adds to the uncertainty that an infancy researcher faces in attempting to determine which processes infants bring to this task.

Third, can the VPC test be passed by processes other than familiarity? The data from the amnesic patients showing explicit recognition memory and failure on the VPC test certainly are an indication that it is not a straightforward memory test. It may be so for normal adults, but what about infants who have not yet developed all of the circuitry that adults depend on? Snyder in chapter 8 provides an alternative by showing that both 6-month-olds' and adults' novelty preferences can be explained in terms of repetition suppression in the visual processing pathway, resulting in repetition priming.

Needless to say, the older the infant, the more likely that explicit memory comes online and may influence VPC, so the issue then becomes, how do we determine when explicit memory becomes available in infancy? At present, our best evidence is in the form of deferred imitation. Hayne's data tell us that it is possible at 6 months. It still seems somewhat tenuous at that age; multiple demonstrations are required, and what is recalled is fragmentary and not very long lasting (Barr, Dowden, & Hayne, 1996; Collie & Hayne, 1999), suggesting that recall processes are just coming online. Before this age, we have no clear evidence of explicit memory. My assumption would be that the declarative representational system is building during the first 6 months, but that in itself does not guarantee explicit access to it.

As far as the temporal extension of recall memory in infancy is concerned, in addition to the evidence that Bauer et al. present, I would add two other findings suggesting that once recall processes come online, memories may be retrieved after considerably longer periods than chapter 10 suggests. Myers, Clifton, and Clarkson (1987) conducted a longitudinal study of auditory localization in infants from 1.5 to 10 months of age. When the children were 3 years old, five of them returned to the laboratory and were questioned about the experimental procedure they had last participated in more than 2 years earlier. When asked about a picture that had been used in the procedure, one of the five children reported correctly that it was a picture of a whale. This finding is particularly interesting not only for the long retention interval (from 10 months to 3 years) but also because the word *whale* was not in his vocabulary until he was 2 years of age.

The other finding was an experiment from McDonough's and my lab, in which 11-month-olds engaged in immediate and 24-hour delayed imitation of eight actions on novel objects. We were able to find 16 of the participants a year later and have them return to the laboratory, where they were given the props used in the earlier modeling (McDonough & Mandler, 1994). One of the actions was performed significantly more often than by a control group of 23-month-olds who had never seen the modeling. We speculated that this finding underestimated the extent of the recall of the experimental group, because the control subjects (being a year older than the original group) spontaneously demonstrated several of the other actions without benefit of seeing them modeled. This situation illustrates one of the disadvantages of the deferred imitation technique for studying long-term memory in infancy; actions within the scope of an 11-month-old may be old hat for a 23-month-old, and if they are demonstrated spontaneously before modeling, they cannot be used as evidence for recall.

This experiment, like the Myers et al. (1987) experiment, which was not designed to systematically study long-term recall memory, nevertheless provided evidence for some recall over very long periods of time by children who had experienced the events as infants less than a year of age. Bauer et al.'s much more systematic work suggests that these early memories are not as robust as later memories, but nevertheless these data indicate the potential for very long-term recall at a very early age. Only further systematic research will answer this question. The chapters in part II indicate how far we have come in understanding memory development in infancy, but there are still a number of questions outstanding to keep us busy over the next decade.

Notes

1. There is not yet a large database of such patients and the findings are not always easy to interpret (see Cipolotti et al., 2006).

2. Note that failure on the VPC test suggests it might be a more sensitive test of hippocampal damage than explicit recognition tests. Indeed, in the abstract of their article, Pascalis and Bachevalier (1999) summarized their results in this way. But that is not the same as saying that the VPC test is a more sensitive test of explicit memory (although these authors appear to reach that conclusion).

3. In the introduction to their article, as Hayne notes, Pascalis et al. (2004) mentioned that one study (Manns, Stark, & Squire, 2000) found that novelty preferences in the VPC task were correlated with later explicit recognition of the nonpreferred stimulus, which is consistent with the view that novelty preference is an indirect index of aware recognition. However, Pascalis et al. did not endorse the view that either familiarity or novelty preferences require awareness. See chapter 8 for data that are contrary to those of Manns et al. and an extended discussion of the difficulties involved in relating novelty preferences to explicit recognition.

References

Aggleton, J. P., Vann, S. D., Denby, C., Dix, S., Mayes, A. R., Roberts, N., et al. (2005). Sparing of the familiarity component of recognition memory in a patient with hippocampal pathology. *Neuropsychologia, 43,* 1810–1823.

Barr, R., Dowden, A., & Hayne, H. (1996). Developmental changes in deferred imitation by 6- to 24-month-old infants. *Infant Behavior and Development, 19,* 159–170.

Bastin, C., Van der Linden, M., Charnallet, A., Denby, C., Montaldi, D., Roberts, N., et al. (2004). Dissociation between recall and recognition memory performance in an amnesic patient with hippocampal damage following carbon monoxide poisoning. *Neurocase, 10,* 330–344.

Bodner, G. E., & Masson, M. E. J. (2003). Beyond spreading activation: An influence of relatedness proportion on masked semantic priming. *Psychonomic Bulletin and Review, 10,* 645–652.

Bomba, P. C., & Siqueland, E. R. (1983). The nature and structure of infant form categories. *Journal of Experimental Child Psychology, 35,* 294–328.

Cave, C. B., & Squire, L. R. (1992). Intact and long-lasting repetition priming in amnesia. *Journal of Experimental Psychology: Learning, Memory, and Cognition, 18,* 509–520.

Cipolotti, L., Bird, C., Good, T., Macmanuse, D., Rudge, P., & Shallice, T. (2006). Recollection and familiarity in dense hippocampal amnesia: A case study. *Neuropsychologia, 44,* 489–506.

Collie, R., & Hayne, H. (1999). Deferred imitation by 6- and 9-month-old infants: More evidence for declarative memory. *Developmental Psychobiology, 35,* 83–90.

Dehaene, S., Nacccache, L., Le Clec'h, G., Koechlin, E., Mueller, M., Dehaene-Lambertz, G., et al. (1998). Imaging unconscious semantic priming. *Nature, 395,* 597–600.

Eimas, P. D., & Quinn, P. C. (1994). Studies on the formation of perceptually based basic-level categories in young infants. *Child Development, 65,* 903–917.

Fagan, J. F. (1972). Infants' recognition memory for faces. *Journal of Experimental Child Psychology, 14,* 453–476.

Friedman, A. (1979). Framing pictures: The role of knowledge in automatized encoding and memory for gist. *Journal of Experimental Psychology: General, 108,* 316–335.

Graf, P., & Mandler, G. (1984). Activation makes words more accessible, but not necessarily more retrievable. *Journal of Verbal Learning and Verbal Behavior, 23,* 553–568.

Graf, P., Mandler, G., & Haden, P. (1982). Simulating amnesic symptoms in normal subjects. *Science, 218,* 1243–1244.

Graf, P., Squire, L. R., & Mandler, G. (1984). The information that amnesic patients do not forget. *Journal of Experimental Psychology: Learning, Memory, and Cognition, 10,* 164–178.

Gross, J., Hayne, H., Herbert, J., & Sowerby, P. (2002). Measuring infant memory: Does the ruler matter? *Developmental Psychobiology, 40,* 183–192.

Henson, R. (2005). A mini-review of fMRI studies of human medial temporal lobe activity associated with recognition memory. *Quarterly Journal of Experimental Psychology, 58B,* 340–360.

Holdstock, J. S., Mayes, A. R., Roberts, N., Cezayirli, E., Isaac, C. L., O'Reilly, R. C., et al. (2002). Under what conditions is recognition spared relative to recall after selective hippocampal damage in humans? *Hippocampus, 12,* 341–351.

Jacoby, L. L. (1983). Perceptual enhancement: Persistent effects of an experience. *Journal of Experimental Psychology: Learning, Memory, and Cognition, 9,* 21–38.

Jacoby, L. L., & Dallas, M. (1981). On the relationship between autobiographical memory and perceptual learning. *Journal of Experimental Psychology: General, 110,* 306–340.

Jacoby, L. L., & Witherspoon, D. (1982). Remembering without awareness. *Canadian Journal of Psychology, 36,* 300–324.

Mack, A., & Rock, I. (1998). *Inattentional blindness.* Cambridge, MA: MIT Press.

Mandler, G. (1980). Recognizing: The judgment of previous occurrence. *Psychological Review, 87,* 252–271.

Mandler, G., Nakamura, Y., & van Zandt, B. J. (1987). Nonspecific effects of exposure on stimuli that cannot be recognized. *Journal of Experimental Psychology: Learning, Memory, and Cognition, 13,* 646–648.

Mandler, J. M. (1984). Representation and recall in infancy. In M. Moscovitch (Ed.), *Infant memory.* New York: Plenum.

Mandler, J. M. (1998). Representation. In W. Damon (Series Ed.) & D. Kuhn & R. Siegler (Eds.), *Handbook of child psychology: Vol. 2. Cognition, perception, and language.* New York: Wiley.

Mandler, J. M. (2000). Perceptual and conceptual processes in infancy. *Journal of Cognition and Development, 1,* 3–36.

Mandler, J. M. (2004). *The foundations of mind: Origins of conceptual thought.* New York: Oxford University Press.

Mandler, J. M., & McDonough, L. (1993). Concept formation in infancy. *Cognitive Development, 8,* 291–318.

Mandler, J. M., & McDonough, L. (1998a). On developing a knowledge base in infancy. *Developmental Psychology, 34,* 1274–1288.

Mandler, J. M., & McDonough, L. (1998b). Studies in inductive inference in infancy. *Cognitive Psychology, 37,* 60–96.

Manns, J. R., Stark, C. E. L., & Squire, L. R. (2000). The visual paired-comparison task as a measure of declarative memory. *Proceedings of the National Academy of Sciences, USA, 97,* 12375–12379.

Marcel, A. J. (1983). Conscious and unconscious perception: Experiments on visual masking and word recognition. *Cognitive Psychology, 15,* 197–237.

Mayes, A. R., Holdstock, J. S., Isaac, C. L., Hunkin, N. M., & Roberts, N. (2002). Relative sparing of item recognition memory in a patient with adult-onset damage limited to the hippocampus. *Hippocampus, 12,* 325–340.

McDonough, L., Choi, S., & Mandler, J. M. (2003). Understanding spatial relations: Flexible infants, lexical adults. *Cognitive Psychology, 46,* 229–259.

McDonough, L., & Mandler, J. M. (1994). Very long-term recall in infants: Infantile amnesia reconsidered. *Memory, 2,* 339–352.

McDonough, L., Mandler, J. M., McKee, R. D., & Squire, L. (1995). The deferred imitation task as a nonverbal measure of declarative memory. *Proceedings of the National Academy of Sciences, USA, 92,* 7580–7584.

McKee, R. D., & Squire, L. R. (1993). On the development of declarative memory. *Journal of Experimental Psychology: Learning, Memory, and Cognition, 19,* 397–404.

Meyer, D. E., & Schvaneveldt, R. W. (1971). Facilitation in recognizing pairs of words: Evidence of a dependence between retrieval operations. *Journal of Experimental Psychology, 90,* 227–234.

Murrell, G. A., & Morton, J. A. (1974). Word recognition and morphemic structure. *Journal of Experimental Psychology, 102,* 963–968.

Myers, N., Clifton, R., & Clarkson, M. (1987). When they were very young: Almost-threes remember two years ago. *Infant Behavior and Development, 10,* 123–132.

Pascalis, O., & Bachevalier, J. (1999). Neonatal aspiration lesions of the hippocampal formation impair visual recognition memory when assessed by paired-comparison task but not by delayed nonmatching-to-sample task. *Hippocampus, 9,* 609–616.

Pascalis, O., Hunkin, N. M., Holdstock, J. S., Isaac, C. L., & Mayes, A. R. (2004). Visual paired comparison performance is impaired in a patient with selective hippocampal lesions and relatively intact item recognition. *Neuropsychologia, 42,* 1293–1300.

Quinn, P. C., Eimas, P. D., & Rosenkrantz, S. L. (1993). Evidence for representations of perceptually similar natural categories by 3-month-old and 4-month-old infants. *Perception, 22,* 463–475.

Ranganath, C., Yonelinas, A. P., Cohen, M. X., Dyb, C. J., Tomb, S. M., & D'Esposito, M. (2003). Dissociable correlates of recollection and familiarity within the medial temporal lobes. *Neuropsychologia, 42,* 2–13.

Roediger, H. L. I., & Blaxton, T. A. (1987). Effects of varying modality, surface features, and retention interval on priming in word fragment completion. *Memory and Cognition, 15,* 379–388.

Rugg, M. D., & Yonelinas, A. P. (2003). Human recognition memory: A cognitive neuroscience perspective. *Trends in Cognitive Sciences, 7,* 313–319.

Squire, L. R. (1994). Declarative and nondeclarative memory: Multiple brain systems supporting learning and memory. In D. L. Schacter & E. Tulving (Eds.), *Memory systems 1994.* Cambridge, MA: MIT Press.

Tulving, E., & Schacter, D. L. (1990). Priming and human memory systems. *Science, 247,* 301–306.

Tulving, E., Schacter, D. L., & Stark, H. (1982). Priming effects in word-fragment completion are independent of recognition memory. *Journal of Experimental Psychology: Learning, Memory, and Cognition, 8,* 336–342.

Ungerleider, L. G. (1995). Functional brain imaging studies of cortical mechanisms for memory. *Science, 270,* 769–775.

Warrington, E. K., & Weiskrantz, L. (1974). The effects of prior learning on subsequent retention in amnesic patients. *Neuropsychologia, 12,* 419–428.

12

To Have and Have Not

What Do We Mean When We Talk About Long-Term Memory Development?

NORA S. NEWCOMBE AND STACIE L. CRAWLEY

When we look at babies in their cradles or their car seats or their parents' arms, we wonder what they make of their experience, and what they will retain of what goes on around them. Opinions on this issue vary widely, with some observers claiming that early memories vanish quickly, if they are ever formed at all, and others arguing that infant memories are formed easily, are retained forever, and are profoundly influential on adult personality. While researchers are working hard on understanding early memory, extreme points of view coexist in popular sources. In a few cases, this public discourse has involved citation of professional papers—although sometimes in opposite ways. For example, Carolyn Rovee-Collier's extensive work with the mobile conjugate reinforcement paradigm has been used both to bolster the notion that babies forget and to support the idea of lifelong influence of infant experience.

On the forgetting side, one father keeping a blog on his infant son cited Hill, Borovsky, and Rovee-Collier (1988):

> I am fascinated by everything about Owen's development. Now that he is sitting up on his own and crawling, the next step he has been working on is going from a sitting position to crawling. This has been a challenge for him, and no matter how close we are to him, he seems to quickly end up in a face-plant when he tries this. So, poor little Owen sits, thinks about crawling, even sways forward a little, but chickens out almost every time. It got me thinking about infant memory and how long the memories of the face-plants would last for Owen

before he got brave enough to try again. I found this interesting study on infant memory development which basically says there's 2–3 weeks before babies forget. Well, we must have reached that mark, because Owen is now moving from sitting to crawling with ease, just since this morning. Ah, the sweet freedom of having Owen sit and play and remain stationary is gone. (http://www.bloggingbaby.com/entry/1234000457048991/)

Owen's father interprets Rovee-Collier's work as telling him about forgetting. On the other hand, on a Web page advancing the view that infants form long-lasting memories from the start of life, including influential memories of birth and of circumcision, David B. Chamberlain, PhD, also cites work by Rovee-Collier (as well as by Patricia Bauer and Andrew Meltzoff):

[T]wo- and three-year-old children [can recall] specifics of their birth when they are first able to speak. This evidence, published in magazines for childbirth educators and parents in 1981, was never taken seriously in scientific circles. Ironically, for the last 16 years, we have had memory experts denying birth memory while new waves of three-year-olds were proving them wrong! ... What the experimental psychologists have [now] managed (against heavy odds) to prove is that children age three, age two, and age one are all capable of both immediate and long-term recall of specific events in their lives. Infants tested at two, four, and six months can recall details about hidden objects, their location, and size. . . . The old belief that infants are mentally incompetent has isolated them and delayed discovery of their elementary abilities. More importantly, this belief has obscured the evidence for higher perception, telepathic communication, and subtle forms of knowing which we have discovered in various forms of psychotherapy. With another big barrier down, perhaps parents and professionals will be able to meet real babies more often.

While it is always gratifying to have the public interested in science, the ease with which the same evidence can be used to contrasting ends is humbling. Some psychologists may be tempted to dismiss these uses of their work as the consequence of misunderstanding, poor communication, or people having axes to grind, but before we wave away these comments as inconsequential, we should consider what message we are transmitting. For several decades, much research in cognitive development, including infant memory development, has revolved around the question of when children of age x have ability y, and how they get it. Such a question seems simple and potentially answerable, but it masks quagmires of uncertainty. Most notably, what do we mean by *have*; how do we ascertain if "ability y" is a natural kind, that is, a productive analytic entity about whose nature it makes sense to inquire; and can we say how they get it in a fashion that does not involve infinite regress, reductionism, invocation of homunculi, or appeal to abstract principles that are hard to translate into specifics? We organize our commentary around these three questions, beginning with the second one because there is a great deal to say about the nature of memory abilities. There are many different kinds of memory, most notably explicit and implicit memory and, within explicit memory, semantic and episodic memory. (These distinctions are ones that Owen's father and Dr. Chamberlain do not take into account.) We go on to discuss what we mean when we speak of children having an ability at a certain age, and finally to discuss the question of mechanism.

Before tackling this agenda, however, we want to begin by applauding what the authors of the four chapters in part II have accomplished, and what Lisa Oakes and Patricia Bauer have achieved in assembling this book. The contributors all report exciting, ingenious, and thoughtful research programs on infants' and young children's long-term memory. Collectively, this work gives us a "great leap forward" toward an understanding of when memory develops, what develops in memory, how memory develops, and why certain memory abilities develop at specific points in development. The volume appears at an important time for taking stock of knowledge about infant memory, because knowledge in the area has been exploding. In Figure 12.1 we have charted the number of papers per year appearing on the topic, as judged by a search of the PsychInfo database for past decades beginning with 1901–1910. Clearly, active interest in the topic did not begin until around 1971, despite the early pioneering work of Robert Fantz. There was an acceleration of interest beginning in 1981, but only in the past 15 years or so have we seen real waves of excitement about research in infant memory. As points of contact with cognitive psychology and cognitive neuroscience grow, and methodological advances come at an accelerating pace, it is an excellent moment to evaluate what we know and what we need to find out about early memory development.

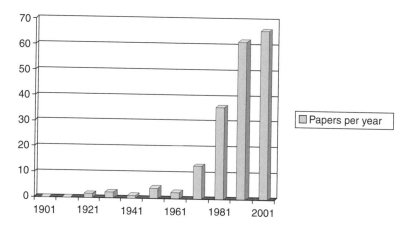

FIGURE 12.1. The number of papers per years on infant memory, as judged by a search of the psychinfo database, for past decades beginning with 1901–1910.

Kinds of Memory: Explicit and Implicit Memory in Infancy

As recently as 20 years ago or so, investigators drew few distinctions between types of memory in infancy and early childhood, or perhaps distinguished primarily between recognition and recall (e.g., Brody, 1981). However, during the 1980s there was a revolution in the adult memory literature leading to the view, now widely accepted, that there are crucial distinctions to be drawn between explicit (or declarative) memory and implicit (or procedural) memory, and that these different types of memory systems are supported by different neural substrates, serve different functions, and operate according to different rules (for examples of recent discussions, see Schacter, Wagner, & Buckner, 2000; Squire, 2004). *Explicit* memory refers to the recognition or recall of objects or events that are available to consciousness. In contrast, *implicit* memory refers to memory that is inaccessible to consciousness. Included under the umbrella of implicit memory are several different kinds of memory, including motor skills (e.g., how to ride a bicycle), classical conditioning, and priming.

The distinction between explicit and implicit memory is harder to work with in investigating infant memory than in examining adult memory. Explicit memory is available to consciousness and, in adult research, is often assessed through verbal reports. Because infants cannot speak, researchers are challenged with designing procedures that tap explicit memory but do not require verbal instruction or verbal expression. Naturally, there can be debate as to whether this goal has been successfully accomplished. This book contains two pairs of chapters on two techniques that investigators have claimed tap explicit memory in infancy: the visual paired comparison (VPC) task and imitation-based tasks. In each case, there has been debate concerning whether the nonverbal procedures used are actually assessing explicit memory and hence about when we first see evidence of explicit memory in human development. The chapters also touch, although in a less focused way, on a third technique about whose meaning there has also been controversy, namely the mobile reinforcement paradigm. In this section, we assess the state of the current evidence.

Does Visual Paired Comparison Index Explicit Memory?

The VPC task used to study infant memory is based on visual preference techniques originally developed to examine infant perception (Fantz, 1958). This technique capitalizes on an infant's tendency to orient toward novel stimuli. In the VPC task, an infant is preexposed to a single visual stimulus for a fixed period of time. After a short delay, the infant is shown a new stimulus and the old stimulus, and the looking time to both stimuli are measured.

If the infant looks longer at the new stimulus, it is inferred that he or she can discriminate the stimuli, and, more important, has a memory of the old stimulus.

Conflicts in Evaluating the Evidence

Rose, Feldman, and Jankowski (chapter 7) argue that VPC is a measure of explicit memory, dependent on the medial temporal lobe and diencephalic structures, including the hippocampus. In contrast, Snyder (chapter 8) argues that performance on VPC may reflect an interaction between visual attention and memory, and may actually reflect implicit memory. Rose et al. cite three lines of neuropsychological evidence to support their argument that the VPC task is a measure of explicit memory, each of which is critically analyzed and reinterpreted by Snyder. The first line of evidence comes from studies with nonhuman primates. Early studies with monkeys showed that large medial-temporal lobe lesions led to impaired performance in VPC in both infant and adult monkeys (Bachevalier, Brickson, & Hagger, 1993). Further studies have supported this conclusion (Pascalis & Bachevalier, 1999; Zola et al., 2000). A second line of evidence comes from studies showing that amnesic patients exhibit impaired performance on the VPC task, suggesting that the VPC reflects a form of explicit memory mediated by a medial-temporal substrate (McKee & Squire, 1993). A third line of evidence comes from behavioral studies with adults. Adults show preferential looking in VPC just as infants do, and, more important, their preferences for novelty in VPC were correlated with their confidence ratings regarding traditional recognition responses after a 24-hour delay (Manns, Stark, & Squire, 2000).

This is a seemingly robust array of data, but Snyder points out many problems with each of the studies in the edifice. First, studies of both humans and monkeys with damage to the hippocampus turn out not to involve damage exclusively confined to that area. Second, the VPC task used in studies with normal and brain-damaged adults varied significantly from the task used with infants. Adults were required to encode 24 different stimuli at acquisition compared to infants' single stimulus encoding; they were given significantly less time to encode stimuli than infants; and, inevitably, the fact that the stimuli were already known to the adults (but not to the infants) most likely affected the way in which the stimuli were encoded at acquisition and led to the engagement of different processes and neural circuits in adults compared to infants. In light of this evidence, Snyder suggests that the neuropsychological and behavioral data cited by Rose and colleagues do not support their view that novelty preferences in VPC constitute a measure of explicit memory dependent on the hippocampus. Rather, infants' performance in the VPC may be the result of repetition suppression in the visual processing pathway, suggesting that performance in VPC is a measure of implicit memory. There is evidence that the visual system may be biased to the processing of new or not recently seen stimuli, with an associated reduction of neuronal responses in the visual processing pathway with stimulus repetition (Desimone & Duncan, 1995).

There is some hope that recent work measuring the neurophysiological processes that underlie infants' novelty preference in the VPC may provide new understanding of the nature of the memory tapped by the task. Event-related potentials (ERPs) are a measure of the electrical activity of the brain time locked to the presentation of a stimulus. They are recorded from electrodes placed on the scalp and provide fine-grained temporal resolution of ongoing cognitive processes. ERPs are an excellent tool to use with infants because no physical response from the infant is required. The use of ERPs in conjunction with VPC potentially provides a better understanding of what brain areas are involved in infants' preferential looking. The two sides in the debate over whether infants' novelty preferences indicate explicit memory or result from repetition suppression predict different ERP results. An explicit memory interpretation would predict that novelty preferences would be associated with increased amplitudes of ERP components over anterior frontal-temporal regions, whereas an implicit memory interpretation would predict that novelty preferences would be associated with decreased amplitudes of ERP components over posterior occipitotemporal regions.

Unfortunately, results from currently available ERP studies of this issue do not produce clear results. Infants show increased amplitudes in some ERP components when viewing familiar stimuli (Bauer, Wiebe, Carver, Waters, & Nelson, 2003; Carver, Bauer, & Nelson, 2000; de Haan & Nelson, 1999), which is not a pattern predicted by either side in the debate. However, this research was not specifically aimed at evaluating the VPC task. More recently, Snyder, Stolarova, and Nelson (2006) showed that preference for novel faces was associated with decreases in electrical activity over the temporal regions and preference for novel objects was associated with decreased brain activity in the occipitotemporal region. Snyder and colleagues argued that these decreases in neural activity support the hypothesis that novelty preferences reflect the influence of repetition suppression in the visual pathway and reflect a form of implicit memory. ERPs clearly hold promise of clarifying the brain bases and essential nature of VPC, but this one study cannot be conclusive. More studies focused on the issue are needed.

Dual Processes in Infant Recognition Memory

One of the exciting aspects of chapters 7 and 8 is that both of them make extensive use of data from a variety of literatures using different techniques and different study populations, rather than being confined simply to behavioral studies of infants. However, somewhat oddly, neither chapter considered the large and potentially highly relevant body of knowledge on recognition memory in normal adults. There is a long-standing and still-raging debate in this literature concerning dual-process versus single-process models of recognition memory. Dual-process theorists argue that adult recognition memory judgments are jointly determined by feelings of familiarity and by specific recollection (for recent views, see Diana, Reder, Arndt, & Park, 2006; Rotello, Macmillan, & Reeder, 2004; Yonelinas, 2002). For example, in remember/know paradigms, adults are asked to judge whether they simply "know" (based on feelings of familiarity) or specifically "remember" (recall specific details) when making a recognition judgment. These memory processes may differ in speed (e.g., Hintzman & Caulton, 1997) and specificity of information retrieved (Gardiner, Gawlik, & Richardson-Klavehn, 1994), and they may be supported by different neural mechanisms (Aggleton & Brown, 1999; Curran, 2000; Rugg & Yonelinas, 2003). Single-process theorists, on the other hand, suggest that recognition memories simply differ in strength, so that, for example, "remember" responses are made to well-encoded items and "know" responses to less well-known ones (Dunn, 2004; McClelland & Chappell, 1998; Shiffrin & Steyvers, 1997; Slotnick & Dodson, 2005; Wixted & Stretch, 2004).

These positions have consequences for understanding VPC. If single-process theorists are correct, then VPC performance may well indicate explicit memory in infants. However, the memory might be rather a weak one, especially because differential looking at the two stimuli in this paradigm does not require a definitive yes-no response. If dual-process theorists are correct, performance on the VPC task, like performance on standard recognition tests, might be based on a blend of processes, supported in part, or at times, by explicit recollection and also, or at other times, by familiarity. Working out the consequences of dual-process theory of recognition for infant performance in the VPC depends on how one thinks about familiarity. Although older dual-process theories argued that familiarity might be based on implicit memory (e.g., Jacoby & Kelley, 1992; Jacoby, Lindsay, & Toth, 1992), most current dual-process theories do not take this position. If feelings of familiarity are based on explicit memory, as they are in contemporary views, then it is natural to suppose that VPC performance would also index explicit memory. Note, though, that looking in VPC need not involve a recollection component. Thus, the consequences of both single- and dual-process views of adult recognition memory in their current forms would be to suggest that VPC indexes explicit memory, but also to warn us against assuming that such ability is equivalent to adult memory because the explicit memories might either be weak (in single-process terms) or lacking in recollection (in dual-process terms). (This matter is discussed further shortly, in the section What Does It Mean to Have an Ability?)

Let us pause, however, to consider whether there might in fact be a familiarity process based on implicit memory that is difficult to discern in adults because they have learned to use implicit memory in support of explicit judgments. There are some indications in the literature that this could be true. For example, in at least one individual with early hippocampal damage, recollection ability was impaired while familiarity-based recognition apparently was not (Bachevalier & Vargha-Khadem, 2005). Furthermore, preschool children seem not to use perceptual fluency (also called processing fluency) as a guide to explicit memory judgments, although this mnemonic strategy appears in elementary school children (Drummey & Newcombe, 1995; Guttentag & Dunn, 2003). If one pursues this idea, it could be that a truly implicit process is available in infants and young children to guide behavior in VPC, as Snyder postulates.

It is an understatement to say that future research is needed. Right now, we know almost nothing about the nature of familiarity, recollection, and implicit processing in memory in infancy and childhood. The main point we are trying to make here is that developmentalists need to be aware of the single- and dual-process theories of recognition (and controversy regarding them).

No Bottom Line Yet on the VPC

We believe the debate as to what form of memory the VPC indexes is not yet resolved. But there is reason for optimism that it can be settled, perhaps soon, by further data collection that focuses on task comparability, careful control (or at least assessment) of areas of brain damage in lesion studies, the further study of behavior in infant monkeys with both intact and lesioned brains, and the utilization of distinctions and insights from the large literature on recognition memory in normal adults. In fact, it is a measure of the scientific maturity of the field of infant memory to see focused and rigorous controversy of the kind we read in chapters 7 and 8.

Does Deferred Imitation Index Explicit Memory?

The VPC task derived from Fantz's early work, and was already well established in the infant memory literature when the explicit-implicit distinction burst on the scene from the adult memory literature. By contrast, it was only in the late 1970s and the early 1980s that we became aware of the imitative abilities of infants (Meltzoff & Moore, 1977, 1983), and still later that we learned that infants would imitate actions even with an intervening delay (Meltzoff, 1988), that toddlers could imitate multistep sequences (Barr, Dowden, & Hayne, 1996; Bauer & Mandler, 1989), and that initial imitation by the infant was not necessary to see retention of the adult's action (Meltzoff, 1995). The appealing feature of imitation-based tasks for assessing early memory is that the measures do not require verbal instructions or a verbal response; rather, memory is inferred from a behavioral response. One limitation to these types of tasks, however, is that they require physical and motor maturity on the part of the infant, so they cannot be used with babies younger than 6 months (at the extreme lower limit).

There are several reasons to argue that imitation-based tasks measure explicit memory. First, explicit memory is the conscious recognition or recall of the content of an experience. Infants' ability to reproduce another person's actions fits this bill. Second, although this measure is nonverbal, the contents of these memories are accessible to language once it begins to be learned (e.g., Bauer, Kroupina, Schwade, Dropik, & Wewerka, 1998). Third, infants learn and remember on the basis of a single experience, which is a characteristic of explicit memory (Bauer & Hertsgaard, 1993). Fourth, memory as tested in the imitation-based task is flexible. For example, infants are able to imitate actions when objects at the time of retrieval are different in various characteristics such as size, shape, and color from the objects used at time of encoding (e.g., Bauer & Dow, 1994). Fourth, imitation-based tasks pass the amnesia test. McDonough, Mandler, McKee, and Squire (1995) tested adults with amnesia and control participants in an imitation-based task using multistep sequences. Normal adults were able to perform the model's actions after a delay, whereas the amnesic patients performed poorly. Last, imitation-based tasks pass the parameter filter. This strategy involves assessing the effect of different independent variables on adults' performance on particular tasks. Variables that are thought to influence explicit memory have no effect on implicit memory and vice versa (Richardson-Klavehn & Bjork, 1988; Tulving, 1983). Several studies have shown that similar variables known to affect adults' explicit memory such as age, retention interval, and context change affect infants' memory in imitation-based tasks (see Hayne, 2004, for a review). This evidence suggests that imitation-based tasks are measures of a form of explicit memory.

The Conjugate Mobile Reinforcement Paradigm

Hayne (chapter 9) discusses data from the Rovee-Collier paradigm, but research using it is not her major focus. However, Rovee-Collier (1997) has argued at length that infants' behavior in this paradigm indexes explicit memory, and Hayne clearly subscribes to the same view. The evidence is somewhat indirect, however, largely involving analogies and parallelisms between studies of adults' explicit memory and how infants behave with the mobiles. The case is persuasive but not closed, and Bauer, DeBoer, and Lukowski (chapter 10) argue that although reinforcement tasks and imitation-based tasks share similar content, function, and rules of operation, reinforcement tasks, unlike imitation-based tasks, may tap implicit rather than explicit memory. For example, in reinforcement paradigms, the test of infants' memory for order information is whether they change their rate of responding when temporal order is violated. In imitation-based tasks, on the other hand, temporal order must be encoded during the time of encoding; that is, the order can be reproduced only if it is encoded into memory. One problem in evaluating what kind of memory is tapped by operant learning is that there do not appear to be studies with amnesic adults, imaging studies, or studies with nonhuman animals. The case on whether the mobile conjugate reinforcement paradigm assesses explicit memory remains open.

Interim Summary

Where does this body of data leave the overall question of the developmental origins of explicit memory? There is strong reason to suppose that deferred imitation depends on explicit memory, but uncertainty remains regarding the nature of VPC and the mobile paradigm. Hence, because deferred imitation cannot be used with infants too young to grasp and manipulate objects, we lack definitive evidence regarding explicit memory in the first 6 months of life. Furthermore, and in the big picture more importantly, the earliest appearance of an ability is not equivalent to its robust presence. We should be careful about concluding that explicit memory is present by 6 months or perhaps even earlier, while neglecting data suggesting that it strengthens and changes in subsequent months and years. We say more about this matter shortly.

A Cautionary Note: Implicit Memory Is Not Permafrost

The focus of these chapters is on when we can first see evidence of explicit memory in infants. The interest is a natural one, since conscious recall seems a hallmark of our everyday existence. But note that popular interest in the retention of infant experience does not focus exclusively on explicit remembering. If the birth process or circumcision affect us, they pretty clearly do not do so because we can consciously or verbally discuss these experiences (although a small minority may claim they can). More plausibly, it might be that what we experience as infants affects our emotions— what we like, what we fear, how trusting or gregarious we are—in an implicit way.

Implicit memory is often conceptualized as more basic and robust than explicit memory, for instance, as not showing developmental change (e.g., Greenbaum & Graf, 1989; Naito, 1990) and as evident even when explicit memory is lacking, both in amnesics (e.g., Schacter, 1983) and in children (Drummey & Newcombe, 1995; Newcombe & Fox, 1994). There is sometimes also an implication that it does not decay, and yet we know relatively little about how long implicit memory lasts. In the adult literature, the issue has not been very much addressed—"long" delays in these experiments are often no longer a few hours, but a few studies have shown that implicit memory does seem to decline over longer intervals such as weeks or months (Goshen-Gottstein & Kempinsky, 2001; Willingham & Dumas, 1997). In the developmental literature, although children do seem to act differently in situations depending on whether or not they have experienced them before in ways more consistent with implicit than explicit memory (Myers, Clifton, &

Clarkson, 1987; Perris, Myers, & Clifton, 1990), studies on memories for preschool classmates have suggested that implicit memory declines over time, even if not to chance levels (Newcombe & Fox, 1994; Lie & Newcombe, 1999). Thus, there is a mixed picture. It is possible that implicit memory of infant experiences can survive to influence behavior, but the influence may not be as strong as is sometimes imagined. This conclusion is quite tentative, however, and again, a call for future research seems an understatement.

Kinds of Memory: Semantic and Episodic Memory

The focus of much attention in studying long-term memory has been on assessing to what extent infants show explicit memory at all. However, although we know that, at least by 6 months, there is some evidence of explicit memory, we know less than we should about a further issue, namely the extent to which these measures of explicit memory tap semantic or episodic memory. Semantic memory refers to knowledge that is general and not necessarily linked to any specific past episode. Episodic memory refers to memory that is specific in nature, that includes the where, when, how, and even why of experience. It can be autobiographical in nature when it involves personally relevant events. Tulving (1985) has called it autonoetic consciousness.[1]

It is possible that memory in infants and toddlers is primarily semantic. Such a developmental pattern would be quite adaptive, as it is clearly more important for young children to learn about the world in a general way than to know just when, where, from whom, and so on information was acquired, and it would fit well with Tulving's (2002) speculation that episodic memory grows out of semantic memory. Thinking this way is consistent with findings that semantic memory can be laid down even when episodic memories are not, due to early hippocampal damage (Vargha-Khadem et al., 1997). Further, this hypothesis would help make sense of the fact that children younger than 2 years of age can form explicit memories (as we have seen) and yet, later on, they will not retain memories for autobiographical episodes in their lives (Bruce, Dolan, & Phillips-Grant, 2000). Having autobiographical memories may depend on a variety of abilities that take some time to develop, including the strategic recognition that different kinds of semantic memory offer clues as to whether or not an event really occurred (Sluzenski, Newcombe, & Ottinger, 2004) and the appearance of processes that bind together the semantic components that make a particular memory distinctive and hence episodic (or if personal, autobiographical; Sluzenski, Newcombe, & Kovacs, 2006).

Semantic memory ability may strengthen during early infancy, as we see increasing generalization of memory across contexts. For example, in VPC, infants' representations become more flexible as they grow older. Rose, Jankowski, and Feldman (2002) found that 7-month-olds familiarized to a face in full frontal view were only able to recognize the face when in a frontal or three-quarter pose, whereas 12-month-olds were able to recognize not only the three-quarter poses but also other profiles and rotations of the familiar face. Similarly, but in an older age range, Robinson and Pascalis (2004) reported that 12-month-olds failed to treat a picture of an object as familiar in VPC when the backgrounds against which pictures were shown changed, but that 18-month-olds did show recognition independent of background context. Analogous changes from narrowly context-bound memory to more generalizable memory have been found using deferred imitation and mobile reinforcement techniques. The ages and parameters across which such generalization is found vary, but the overall picture is one in which infants become progressively more able to build semantic memories that showed appropriate scope to be serviceable.

Episodic memory involves a different adaptive challenge. Sometimes, while maintaining general knowledge, we also need or want to encode and retain specific contextual details. We want to be able to recognize a person we know from a variety of poses, in a variety of lighting situations, and wearing varied clothing (e.g., we can recognize our friend Olivia whether she is on the beach in bright sunlight or in an elegant dress at night). That's the job of semantic memory. But we also sometimes remember just what that person looked like at a specific point in time (e.g., "Olivia looked lovely in her purple silk dress the Saturday night in July when she and I and Edgar dined by candlelight at the Ritz"). That's what episodic memory does. What we want to know about memory development is when children can both remember that they saw an object before, even when it appears in a new context, and also remember that they saw it in a particular context at a particular time. The Robinson and Pascalis (2004) experiment, and others like it, evaluated only the first ability.

Unfortunately, we do not currently have a paradigm for use with infants and toddlers that is well suited to investigate the existence of early episodic memory. Hayne (chapter 9) reports initial exploration of what she calls the spoon paradigm, using a name taken from a folktale cited by Tulving, for investigating episodic memory early in life. In those studies, 3-year-old children can remember where an object was hidden, what room contained what hidden object, and what order the objects were hidden in. Similar data were actually gathered some time ago with even younger children (DeLoache, 1984). However, we are not sure that these findings indicate episodic memory. Certainly, the situation that the children faced was far simpler than that confronted by the birds caching wax worms and peanuts (Clayton, 2004). More work along these lines seems vital.

We speculate that the earliest roots of episodic memory will be found around the second birthday, at roughly the same time that long-lasting autobiographical memories begin to appear. We further speculate that these earliest episodic abilities will be fragile, and that the years between ages 2 and 6 will see very rapid development in episodic skills. There are several findings consistent with this idea: Source memory changes markedly in this age range (Drummey & Newcombe, 2002), as does the ability to determine if an event really occurred or was only imagined (Sluzenski, Newcombe, & Ottinger, 2004) and the ability to determine if an animal seen before was shown against a background seen before (e.g., not just "I saw a tiger" and "I saw a street scene," but "I did (or did not) see a tiger in the street scene"; Sluzenski et al., 2006). The last paradigm is very close to being the flip side of Robinson and Pascalis's (2004) study of the ability to recognize objects even when backgrounds change. Children may first acquire the ability to ignore a background in the service of learning about the world (semantic memory), as studied by Robinson and Pascalis, and then later learn to link aspects of that world with other aspects to form episodes. Our last speculation is that this rise in episodic memory is linked to changes in the prefrontal areas of the brain, an idea for which we have gathered some tentative support (Drummey & Newcombe, 2002; Sluzenski, Newcombe, & Ottinger, 2004).

What Does It Mean to Have an Ability?

We have talked a great deal about one of the three questions we raised at the beginning of this chapter, namely, what kinds of memory there are. It is time to turn our attention to another issue, namely what we mean when we say a child has an ability. Developmental psychologists are often fascinated with discovering the earliest evidence of an ability. For example, Barr et al. (1996) found that, under the right circumstances, babies as young as 6 months could show deferred imitation. As mentioned above, this important finding marks the earliest point to which we can currently date explicit memory without having to make assumptions that are (at least to some) controversial. However, we find it equally fascinating that Barr et al. and others have found regular, age-related progress in when deferred imitation will appear: Older children need less exposure to the target actions and seem to remember more about the event sequences. In fact, many age-related changes in deferred imitation are discussed in chapters 9 and 10, including length of delay before events are forgotten, speed of encoding, complexity of the events that can be encoded, and resistance to interference. For example, while 21-month-old infants shown a three-step puppet sequence modeled on a cow puppet remembered the sequence when tested with the cow puppet and a duck puppet, 18-month-olds only remembered the sequence with the same puppet from acquisition (Hayne, MacDonald, & Barr, 1998).

Similarly, although infants may succeed in VPC at very young ages, this fact does not imply that their recognition memory does not also develop. We have already seen that generalization changes, and there are other changes as well. For example, Diamond (1990) habituated 4-, 6-, and 9-month-old infants to objects and tested them after delays of 10 seconds, 15 seconds, 1 minute, and 10 minutes. Four-month-olds only recognized the objects at delays of 10 seconds; the 6-month-olds recognized the objects up to a 1-minute delay, and 9-month-olds recognized objects after intervals as long as 10 minutes.

Documenting the gradual growth as well as the earliest emergence of mnemonic capabilities is a task that requires painstaking and imaginative work, and we are grateful that so much has been done to give us a rich and nuanced view of developmental sequences. What the community of developmental psychologists needs to be careful to do is to maintain awareness of nuance as they make summary statements. Do 6-month-old babies "have" explicit memory? Well, yes, but it is very, very fragile. In the real world, it may be only minimally useful. Do 1-year-old children "have" explicit memory? Well, yes, and now they have it more robustly, and it is more clearly evident to the naked eye. After all, they are poised to begin word learning, one of the greatest memory feats of all. And yet, they may not be accomplished mnemonists—in fact, we know they will soon improve. Faced with facts such as these, Thelen and Smith (1994) abjured the notions of competence or representation altogether. We think that move is unnecessarily radical, but simultaneous awareness of having abilities and "having a ways to go" is vital to maintain in describing children.

Where Do Abilities Come From?

Developmental psychology is often described as the study of change over time. Yet it is common to hear controversy concerning whether we are simply describing change rather than tackling the harder task of explaining it. For example, Mark Johnson and Yuko Munakata (2005) wrote, "There is general agreement among contemporary researchers that developmental psychology needs to move away from static descriptions of the cognitive system at different ages, and instead strengthen its focus on the underlying mechanisms that generate change" (p. 152). For this volume, Lisa Oakes and Patricia Bauer asked contributors to address the question of mechanism directly, and a variety of answers emerged. The explanations in these chapters focus to various extents on explaining memory development in three kinds of ways: by appeals to changes in more basic processes, by citing relevant experiences that can precipitate change, and by considering biological change that might propel behavioral change.

Changes in More Basic Processes

One appealing way to explain developmental change is in terms of underlying advances in basic components of an ability of interest. For example, Rose et al. (chapter 7) discuss several mechanisms that might account for developmental change in VPC performance. First, they cite Kail's (1991) suggestion that developments in many cognitive tasks are due to improvements in processing speed. There is evidence to suggest that processing speed plays a central role in performance on VPC tasks. For instance, older infants need less familiarization to recognize targets than younger infants (e.g., Rose, 1980, 1983) and infants take longer to habituate to complex stimuli and show larger novelty preferences when the novel and familiar stimuli are more dissimilar looking (Caron & Caron, 1969). To examine the role of processing speed in the VPC task more directly, Rose and colleagues designed a procedure that involved a cross between habituation and VPC. Infants of 5, 7, and 12 months of age who took more trials to become familiarized showed significantly lower novelty preferences. These data suggest that age-related developments in processing speed play a direct role in infants' performance on the VPC task.

Second, Rose et al. suggest that changes in attention influence infants' VPC performance. Infants can be classified as either "short lookers" or "long lookers" depending on the way they divide their attention when examining displays in the VPC. Short lookers are characterized by short looks, high shift rates (or frequent shifts of gaze), and widely distributed looks. In contrast, long lookers are characterized by long looks, low shift rates, and more narrowly distributed looks. There are dramatic age-related developments in infants' attention during the VPC task with mean looks and peak looks decreasing with age and mean shift rates becoming faster (e.g., Axia, Bonichini, & Benini, 1999; Rose, Feldman, & Jankowski, 2001). In a very nice study, the causal link between attention and VPC was shown by pacing long lookers through a short-looker approach to familiarization, with concomitant change in memory (Jankowski, Rose, & Feldman, 2001).

Finding changes in basic processes is a helpful step in the search for mechanism and explanation. Rose et al. spend the longest time on this strategy of explanation, but Bauer et al. (chapter 10) also discuss changes in encoding, consolidation, and storage, locating developmental differences more in the last two processes than in the first. However, there is a regress here, because the next logical step is to examine why basic processes change. When processing speeds, attention, consolidation, or storage change, they must do so for a reason. Often, in the end, the appeal is to a maturing aspect of the nervous system that creates a change in a basic process, as Bauer et al. do in discussing how changes in consolidation and storage may relate to neural development. More rarely, there is an appeal to aspects of the environment that may create change in basic processes. The training study by Jankowski et al. (2001) is an interesting clue showing what experience can affect in the short term. It would be interesting to push their insights further, thinking about what environmental experiences in the real world might be relevant to aiding infants' encoding ability. What do caretakers do to guide attention, given that they do not carry small flashlights with them routinely?

Experiences That Can Lead to Change

Chapters 7 through 10 contain several interesting observations relevant to how experiences may change and enhance memory. One theme, emphasized by Snyder (chapter 8), is that accumulating semantic knowledge will change memory. A basic tenet of a constructivist approach to memory, which is now tacitly accepted by most of the memory community, is that encoding and retention are enhanced by a cognitive structure that makes sense of experience and allows for fitting experience into schemata or scripts rather than having to retain "raw" information. Another factor that may influence infants' memory performance is the onset of independent locomotion. Hayne and colleagues have shown that, when infants' chronological age is held constant, crawling status affects the degree to which infants can remember target actions in new contexts. For example, 9-month-old infant crawlers showed excellent memory in a deferred imitation task even when objects and context were changed. Noncrawlers, however, only showed memory for modeled actions when the objects and context remained unchanged (Gross & Hayne, 2004; Herbert, Gross, & Hayne, 2003). The fact that babies must deal with changing contexts as they crawl may well have created this effect—one's high chair is the same when viewed from one vantage point, against the backdrop of a window, and when viewed from a different vantage point, against the backdrop of the refrigerator. Yet right now we can only speculate as to how crawling exerts its effect and why crawling does not create mnemonic independence of all context—remember that Robinson and Pascalis (2004) found change in the ability to succeed at VPC with changing backgrounds much later than crawling appears, between 12 and 18 months.

Underlying Biological Change

Chapters 7 through 10 frequently discuss the hippocampus, one of the most important cortical substrates for explicit memory, and frequently assert that portions of the human hippocampus reach maturity in the first 6 months of life. This idea fits well with the favored hypothesis that explicit memory is present early (Nelson, 1995; Seress, 2001). However, also presented in these chapters are lines of evidence that there is developmental improvement in the robustness of explicit memory. There is reason to believe that the human hippocampus may well develop in various ways over a fairly long period. Seress (2001) distinguished four periods in development, with the last one occupying the third to the fifth year. He stated that "full maturation is not expected to occur before the 5th postnatal year in the human" (p. 56). In a review, Bachevalier and Vargha-Khadem (2005) stated, "The available evidence to date suggests that the primate hippocampus appears to mature progressively during the first few years of life in both monkeys and humans" (p. 171).

An important distinction in explicit memory differentiates semantic and episodic memory. There is some evidence that they have different bases in the medial-temporal system. "[T]he hippocampal circuit provides the necessary processing for the encoding and retrieval of context-rich episodes and events, whereas the perirhinal and entorhinal cortices subserve the formation of context-free cognitive memories" (Bachevalier & Vargha-Khadem, 2005, p. 172). This suggestion might lead to a promising line of research that would more closely evaluate linkages between various forms of explicit memory and neural development in different medial-temporal lobe structures.

We find it striking that there is evidence from research on the development of spatial memory which suggests that there is pronounced developmental change between 18 and 24 months on tasks that are known to be supported by the hippocampus, such as place learning (Newcombe, Huttenlocher, Drummey, & Wiley, 1998) and delayed and relational spatial tasks (Sluzenski, Newcombe, & Satlow, 2004). Such behavioral evidence may indicate developmental change in the area of the brain also known to support episodic memory. Is it a coincidence that the earliest autobiographical memories that will last until adulthood date back only to this time? Perhaps, but we would speculate—perhaps not.

Conclusion

It was a pleasure to read these chapters. Although we differ with some of their conclusions—and they differ from each other—the most important fact is that we have reached a stage of scientific maturity where we have enough facts that our theorizing and hypothesis testing can be focused, and our differences can be specific rather than doctrinal. For the record, here is what we see as the current state of play. Explicit memory begins early, although we are not sure if early means 6 months or even earlier than that. It also changes and develops in very marked and functionally important ways, with perhaps one crucial time being toward the end of the first year when we can speculate that it becomes robust enough to support word learning. However, early explicit memory may be primarily semantic in nature, a fact that may have adaptive value. The capacity for truly episodic memory, involving relations among elements of semantic memory and context sensitivity, may begin to emerge around the second birthday and support the first appearance of autobiographical memory. Development continues through the preschool years and involves changes in the relation of explicit and implicit memory, strategies for evaluating memory, binding elements in episodic memory, and many more dimensions too numerous to name (for a discussion of some of the social factors we have neglected, see Nelson & Fivush, 2004). By the age of 5 or 6 years, memory systems are functionally mature, although there are changes in the use of strategies such as rehearsal, organization, and self-testing (e.g., for recent work in this tradition, see Schneider, Kron, Hunnerkopf, & Krajewski, 2004). Another 15 years of research of the excellence embodied in this book should tell us how right (or wrong) we are in this thumbnail sketch.

Acknowledgment

We thank Marianne Lloyd, Kristin Ratliff, and the editors of this volume for their comments on earlier drafts.

Note

1. Bauer et al. (chapter 10) define explicit memory in a way we would prefer to reserve for episodic memory, as involving "what happened, where, when and even why."

References

Aggleton, J. P., & Brown, M. W. (1999). Episodic memory, amnesia, and the hippocampal-anterior thalamic axis. *Behavioral and Brain Sciences, 22*(3), 425–444.

Axia, G., Bonichini, S., & Benini, F. (1999). Attention and reaction to distress in infancy: A longitudinal study. *Developmental Psychology, 35,* 500–504.

Bachevalier, J., Brickson, M., & Hagger, C. (1993). Limbic-dependent recognition memory in monkeys develops early in infancy. *Neuroreport: An International Journal for the Rapid Communication of Research in Neuroscience, 4,* 77–80.

Bachevalier, J., & Vargha-Khadem, F. (2005). The primate hippocampus: Ontogeny, early insult and memory. *Current Opinion in Neurobiology, 15,* 168–174.

Barr, R., Dowden, A., & Hayne, H. (1996). Developmental changes in deferred imitation by 6- to 24-month-old infants. *Infant Behavior and Development, 19,* 159–170.

Bauer, P. J., & Dow, G. A. (1994). Episodic memory in 16- and 20-month-old children: Specifics are generalized but not forgotten. *Developmental Psychology, 30,* 403–417.

Bauer, P. J., & Hertsgaard, L. A. (1993). Increasing steps in recall of events: Factors facilitating immediate and long-term memory in13.5- and 16.5-month-old children. *Child Development, 64,* 1204–1223.

Bauer, P. J., Kroupina, M. G., Schwade, J. A., Dropik, P. L. & Wewerka, S. S. (1998). If memory serves, will language? Later verbal accessibility of early memories. *Development and Psychopathology, 10,* 655–679.

Bauer, P. J., & Mandler, J. M. (1989). One thing follows another: Effects of temporal structure on 1- to 2-year-olds' recall of events. *Developmental Psychology, 25,* 197–206.

Bauer, P. J., Wiebe, S. A., Carver, L. J., Waters, J. M. & Nelson, C. A. (2003). Developments in long-term explicit memory late in the first year of life: Behavioral and electrophysiological indices. *Psychological Science, 14,* 629–635.

Brody, L. R. (1981). Visual short-term cued memory in infancy. *Child Development, 52,* 242–250.

Bruce, D., Dolan, A., & Phillips-Grant, K. (2000). On the transition from childhood amnesia to the recall of personal memories. *Psychological Science, 11,* 360–364.

Caron, R. F., & Caron, A. J. (1969). Degree of stimulus complexity and habituation of visual fixation in infants. *Psychonomic Review, 14,* 78–79.

Carver, L. J., Bauer, P. J., & Nelson, C. A. (2000). Associations between infant brain activity and recall memory. *Developmental Science, 3,* 234–246.

Chamberlain, D. B. http://www.birthpsychology.com/birthscene/intelligent2.html.

Clayton, N. S. (2004, December). *Retrospective and prospective cognition in animals: A Western scrub jay's perspective.* Paper presented at the Memory Theme Symposium, University of Otago, Dunedin, New Zealand.

Curran, T. (2000). Brain potentials of recollection and familiarity. *Memory and Cognition, 28,* 923–938.

de Haan, M., & Nelson, C. A. (1999). Brain activity differentiates face and object processing in 6-month-old infants. *Developmental Psychology, 35,* 1113–1121.

DeLoache, J. S. (1984). Where do I go next? Intelligent searching by very young children. *Developmental Psychology, 20,* 37–44.

Desimone, R., & Duncan, J. (1995). Neural mechanisms of selective visual attention. *Annual Review of Neuroscience, 18,* 193–222.

Diamond, A. (1990). Rate of maturation of the hippocampus and the developmental progression of children's performance on the delayed nonmatching sample and visual paired comparison tasks. In A. Diamond (Ed.), *Developments and neural bases of higher cognitive functions: Vol. 608. Annals of the New York Academy of Sciences* (pp. 394–426). New York: Academic Press.

Diana, R. A., Reder, L. M., Arndt, J. A. & Park, H. (2006). Models of recognition: A review of arguments in favor of a dual-process account. *Psychonomic Bulletin and Review, 13,* 1–21.

Drummey, A. B., & Newcombe, N. (1995). Remembering versus knowing the past: Children's explicit and implicit memories for pictures. *Journal of Experimental Child Psychology, 59,* 549–565.

Drummey, A. B., & Newcombe, N. (2002). Developmental changes in source memory. *Developmental Science, 5,* 502–513.

Dunn, J. C. (2004). Remember-know: A matter of confidence. *Psychological Review, 111,* 524–542.

Fantz, R. (1958). Pattern vision in young infants. *Psychological Record, 8,* 43–47.

Gardiner, J. M., Gawlik, B., & Richardson-Klavehn, A. (1994). Maintenance rehearsal affects knowing, but not remembering; elaborative rehearsal affects remembering, not knowing. *Psychonomic Bulletin and Review, 1,* 107–110.

Goshen-Gottstein, Y., & Kempinsky, H. (2001). Probing memory with conceptual cues at multiple retention intervals: A comparison of forgetting rates on implicit and explicit tests. *Psychonomic Bulletin and Review, 8,* 139–146.

Greenbaum, J. L., & Graf, P. (1989). Preschool period development of implicit memory and explicit remembering. *Bulletin of the Psychonomic Society, 27,* 417–420.

Gross, J., & Hayne, H. (2004, June). *Is there a relation between motor development and cognitive development in human infants?* Paper presented at the International Society for Developmental Psychobiology, Aix-en-Provence, France.

Guttentag, R., & Dunn, J. (2003). Judgements of remembering: The revelation effect in children and adults. *Journal of Experimental Child Psychology, 86,* 153–167.

Hayne, H. (2004). Infant memory development: Implications for childhood amnesia. *Developmental Review, 24,* 33–73.

Hayne, H., MacDonald, S., & Barr, R. (1998). Developmental changes in the specificity of memory over the second year of life. *Infant Behavior and Development, 20,* 233–245.

Herbert, J., Gross, J., & Hayne, H. (2003, November). *The effect of age and experience on deferred imitation in human infants.* Paper presented at the International Society of Developmental Psychobiology, New Orleans, LA.

Hill, W. L., Borovsky, D., & Rovee-Collier, C. (1988). Continuities in infant memory development. *Developmental Psychobiology, 21,* 43–62.

Hintzman, D. L., & Caulton, D. A. (1997). Recognition memory and modality judgments: A comparison of retrieval dynamics. *Journal of Memory and Language, 37,* 1–23.

Jacoby, L. L., & Kelley, C. M. (1992). Unconscious influences of memory: Dissociations and automaticity. In E. A. D. Milner & E. M. D. Rugg (Eds.), *The neurospychology of consciousness* (pp. 201–233). San Diego, CA: Academic Press.

Jacoby, L. L., Lindsay, D. S., & Toth, J. P. (1992). Unconscious influences revealed: Attention, awareness and control. *American Psychologist, 47,* 802–809.

Jankowski, J. J., Rose, S. A., & Feldman, J. F. (2001). Modifying the distribution of attention in infants. *Child Development, 72,* 339–351.

Johnson, M. H., & Munakata, Y. (2005). Processes of change in brain and cognitive development. *Trends in Cognitive Sciences, 9,* 152–188.

Kail, R. (1991). Developmental changes in speed of processing during childhood and adolescence. *Psychological Bulletin, 109,* 490–501.

Lie, E., & Newcombe, N. (1999). Elementary school children's explicit and implicit memory for faces of preschool classmates. *Developmental Psychology, 35,* 102–112.

Manns, J. R., Stark, C. E., & Squire, L. R. (2000). The visual paired-comparison task as a measure of declarative memory. *Proceedings of the National Academy of Sciences, USA, 97,* 12375–12379.

McClelland, J. L., & Chappell, M. (1998). Familiarity breeds differentiation: A subjective-likelihood approach to the effects of experience in recognition memory. *Psychological Review, 105,* 734–760.

McDonough, L., Mandler, J. M., McKee, R. D., & Squire, L. R. (1995). The deferred imitation task used as a nonverbal measure of declarative memory. *Proceedings of the National Academy of Sciences, 92,* 7580–7584.

McKee, R. D., & Squire, L. R. (1993). On the development of declarative memory. *Journal of Experimental Psychology: Learning, Memory and Cognition, 19,* 397–404.

Meltzoff, A. N. (1988). Infant imitation and memory: Nine-month-olds in immediate and deferred tests. *Child Development, 59,* 217–225.

Meltzoff, A. N. (1995). What infant memory tells us about infantile amnesia: Long-term recall and deferred imitation. *Journal of Experimental Child Psychology, 59,* 497–515.

Meltzoff, A. N., & Moore, M. K. (1977). Imitation of facial and manual gestures by human neonates. *Science, 198,* 75–78.

Meltzoff, A. N., & Moore, M. K. (1983). Newborn infants imitate adult facial gestures. *Child Development, 54,* 702–709.

Myers, N. A., Clifton, R. K., & Clarkson, M. G. (1987). When they were very young: Almost-threes remember two years ago. *Infant Behavior and Development, 10,* 123–132.

Naito, M. (1990). Repetition priming in children and adults: Age-related dissociation between implicit and explicit memory. *Journal of Experimental Child Psychology, 50,* 462–484.

Nelson, C. A. (1995). The ontogeny of human memory: A cognitive neuroscience perspective. *Developmental Psychology, 31,* 723–738.

Nelson, K., & Fivush, R. (2004). The emergence of autobiographical memory: A social cultural developmental theory. *Psychological Review, 111,* 486–511.

Newcombe, N., & Fox, N. (1994). Infantile amnesia: Through a glass darkly. *Child Development, 65,* 31–40.

Newcombe, N., Huttenlocher, J., Drummey, A. B., & Wiley, J. G. (1998). The development of spatial location coding: Place learning and dead reckoning in the second and third years. *Cognitive Development, 13,* 185–200.

Pascalis, O., & Bachevalier, J. (1999). Neonatal aspiration lesions of the hippocampal formation impair visual recognition memory when assessed by paired-comparison task but not by delayed nonmatching-to-sample task. *Hippocampus, 9,* 609–616.

Perris, E. E., Myers, N. A., & Clifton, R. K. (1990). Long-term memory for a single infancy experience. *Child Development, 61,* 1796–1807.

Richardson-Klavehn, A., & Bjork, R. A. (1988). Measures of memory. *Annual Review of Psychology, 39,* 475–543.

Robinson, A. J., & Pascalis, O. (2004). Development of flexible visual recognition memory in human infants. *Developmental Science, 7,* 527–533.

Rose, S. A. (1980). Enhancing visual recognition memory in preterm infants. *Developmental Psychology, 16,* 85–92.

Rose, S. A. (1983). Differential rates of visual information processing in full-term and preterm infants. *Child Development, 54,* 1189–1198.

Rose, S. A., Feldman, J. F., & Jankowski, J. J. (2001). Attention and recognition memory in the first year of life: A longitudinal study of preterm and full-term infants. *Developmental Psychology, 37,* 135–151.

Rose, S. A., Jankowski, J. J., & Feldman, J. F. (2002). Speed of processing and face recognition at 7 and 12 months. *Infancy, 3,* 435–455.

Rotello, C. M., Macmillan, N. A., & Reeder, J. A. (2004). Sum-difference theory of remembering and knowing: A two-dimensional signal-detection model. *Psychological Review, 111,* 588–616.

Rovee-Collier, C. (1997). Dissociations in infant memory: Rethinking the development of implicit and explicit memory. *Psychological Review, 104,* 467–498.

Rugg, M. D., & Yonelinas, A. P. (2003). Human recognition memory: A cognitive neuroscience perspective. *Trends in Cognitive Sciences, 7,* 313–319.

Schacter, D. L. (1983). Amnesia observed: Remembering and forgetting in a natural environment. *Journal of Abnormal Psychology, 92,* 236–242.

Schacter, D. L., Wagner, A. D., & Buckner, R. L. (2000). Memory systems of 1999. In E. Tulving & F. I. M. Craik (Eds.), *The Oxford handbook of memory* (pp. 627–643). New York: Oxford University Press.

Schneider, W., Kron, V., Hunnerkopf, M., & Krajewski, K. (2004). The development of young children's memory strategies: First findings from the Wurzburg Longitudinal Memory Study. *Journal of Experimental Child Psychology, 88,* 193–209.

Seress, L. (2001). Morphological changes of the human hippocampal formation from mid-gestation to early childhood. In C. A. Nelson & M. Luciana (Eds.), *Handbook of developmental cognitive neuroscience* (pp. 45–58). Cambridge, MA: MIT Press.

Shiffrin, R. M., & Steyvers, M. (1997). A model for recognition memory: REM—retrieving effectively from memory. *Psychonomic Bulletin and Review, 4,* 145–166.

Slotnick, S. D., & Dodson, C. S. (2005). Support for a continuous (single-process) model of recognition memory and source memory. *Memory and Cognition, 33,* 151–170.

Sluzenski, J., Newcombe, N., & Kovacs, S. L. (2006). Binding, relational memory, and recall of naturalistic events: A developmental perspective. *Journal of Experimental Psychology: Learning, Memory, and Cognition, 32,* 89–100.

Sluzenski, J., Newcombe, N., & Ottinger, W. (2004). Changes in reality monitoring and episodic memory in early childhood. *Developmental Science, 7,* 225–245.

Sluzenski, J., Newcombe, N., & Satlow, E. (2004). Knowing where things are in the second year of life: Implications for hippocampal development. *Journal of Cognitive Neuroscience, 16,* 1443–1451.

Snyder, K. A., Stolarova, M., & Nelson, C. A. (2006). *Neural correlates of novelty preferences.* Unpublished manuscript.

Squire, L. R. (2004). Memory systems of the brain: A brief history and current perspective. *Neurobiology of Learning and Memory, 82,* 171–177.

Thelen, E., & Smith, L. B. (1994). *A dynamic systems approach to the development of cognition and action.* Cambridge, MA: MIT Press.

Tulving, E. (1983). *Elements of episodic memory.* New York: Oxford University Press.

Tulving, E. (1985). Memory and consciousness. *Canadian Psychology, 26,* 1–12.

Tulving, E. (2002). Episodic memory: From mind to brain. *Annual Review of Psychology, 53,* 1–25.

Vargha-Khadem, F., Gadian, D. G., Watkins, K. E., Connelly, A., Van Paesschen, W., & Mishkin, M. (1997). Differential effects of early hippocampal pathology on episodic memory and semantic memory. *Science, 277,* 376–380.

Willingham, D. B., & Dumas, J. A. (1997). Long-term retention of a motor skill: Implicit sequence knowledge is not retained after a one-year delay. *Psychological Research/Psychologische Forschung, 60,* 113–119.

Wixted, J. T., & Stretch, V. (2004). In defense of the signal detection interpretation of remember/know judgments. *Psychonomic Bulletin and Review, 11,* 616–641.

Yonelinas, A. P. (2002). The nature of recollection and familiarity: A review of 30 years of research. *Journal of Memory and Language, 46,* 441–517.

Zola, S. M., Squire, L. R., Teng, E., Stefanacci, L., Buffalo, E. A., & Clark, R. E. (2000). Impaired recognition memory in memory after damage limited to the hippocampal region. *Journal of Neuroscience, 20,* 451–463.

Author Index

Adams, A., 17
Adams, S. E., 28, 32, 33, 34, 35, 38, 42
Adlam, A.-L. R., 244
Aggleton, J. P., 276, 297
Ahmed, A., 34
Ainsfeld, M., 8
Allemand, F., 16, 43
Allen, R., 140
Alp, E., 8
Alvarado, M. C., 169, 185
Alvarez, G. A., 55, 70, 113, 114, 118, 119
Amabile, T. A., 223
Ambridge, B., 29, 46, 135
Ames, E., 159, 216
Ames, E. W., 8, 159
Anand, K. J. S., 211
Andersen, R. A., 91
Anderson, C. M., 92
Anderson, J. R., 4
Andrade, J., 17
Andrews, R. V., 78
Arndt, J. A., 297
Arterberry, M. E., 79

Asaad, W. F., 91
Aslin, R. N., 17
Atkinson, J., 75, 86, 92
Atkinson, R. C., 4
Awh, E., 90
Axia, G., 167, 305

Bachevalier, J., xiv, 155, 156, 169, 182, 184, 185, 186, 224, 250, 280, 287, 295, 298, 306, 307
Bachevalier, J. M., 186
Baddeley, A., 17, 28, 127, 134, 135, 142
Baddeley, A. D., 4, 14, 16, 17, 28, 42, 77, 104, 105, 127, 128, 129, 132, 133, 134, 135, 140
Bahrick, L., 227
Bahrick, L. E., 160, 164
Baillargeon, R., 7, 34, 52, 76, 109, 114, 127
Baker, C. I., 112
Baldweg, T., 37
Baldwin, D. A., 244, 256
Bangston, S. K., 247
Barnat, S. B., 227, 244, 256

315

Barr, R., 214, 215, 216, 217, 219, 220, 221, 223, 227, 246, 247, 253, 256, 286, 298, 303
Barrett, L. F., 29
Barrouillet, P., 141
Bartsch, K., 32
Bastin, C., 276
Bates, E., 11, 17, 44, 67
Bates, E. A., 158, 163
Bates, J. C., 45
Bauer, P. J., 8, 94, 161, 162, 168, 210, 214, 216, 218, 224, 227, 240, 242, 243, 244, 245, 247, 248, 249, 250, 251, 252, 253, 254, 255, 256, 260, 262, 296, 298, 299
Baylis, G. C., 85, 91, 192
Begleiter, H., 187
Bell, M. A., 27, 28, 31, 32, 33, 34, 35, 36, 37, 38, 39, 40, 41, 42, 43, 44, 45, 93, 94, 110
Bell, S. M., 12
Belleville, S., 16
Benasich, A. A., 79
Benes, F. M., 250
Benini, F., 167, 305
Beninni, L., 11
Benson, J. B., 43
Berger, T. W., 260
Berlyne, D. E., 212
Bernardin, S., 141
Beschin, N., 131
Best, C. T., 126
Bhana, K., 158
Bhatt, R. S., 216, 219, 221, 227
Bird, C., 281, 287
Bjork, R. A., 154, 299
Black, J. E., 85, 93, 223
Blaser, E., 119
Blaxton, T. A., 281
Bleckley, M. K., 134
Bloom, P., 116, 120
Bodner, G. E., 283
Bogartz, R. S., 179
Boland, L. D., 231
Bolton, E., 16
Bomb, P., 130
Bomba, P. C., 276
Bonchini, S., 167, 305

Boniface, J., 215, 216, 217, 220, 221, 227, 253, 256
Bornstein, M. H., 79, 171, 198
Borovsky, D., 216, 217, 220, 227, 255, 291
Bourgeois, J.-P., 250
Bower, G. H., 4
Bower, T. G. R., 112
Brainerd, C. J., 251
Braver, T. S., 15, 90
Breinlinger, K., 114
Bretherton, I., 11, 17
Brezsnyak, M. E., 200
Brickson, M., 155, 184, 185, 186, 295
Bridger, W. H., 76, 159, 166, 216, 227
Broadbent, D. E., 103, 129
Brody, L. R., 294
Brown, A. L., 6
Brown, E., 76, 79, 88, 95
Brown, G. D. A., 130, 142
Brown, J., 4, 129
Brown, M. W., 187, 188, 297
Bruce, C. J., 6
Bruce, D., 301
Bruce, J., 45
Bruner, J. S., 11
Brunner, R. P., 137, 138
Buchanan, M., 127, 129, 132
Buchel, C., 111
Buckner, R. L., x, 181, 188, 194, 241, 258, 294
Buffalo, E. A., 156, 157, 185, 295
Buffalo, E. J., 155, 156
Bunting, M. F., 128, 136
Bures, J., 250
Burnham, D., 76, 79, 88, 95
Burock, M., 194
Busby, J., 230
Bush, G., 44, 45
Bushnell, E. W., 79, 88
Bushnell, I. W. R., 211
Butler, J., 220, 227

Callender, G., 27, 44
Camaioni, L., 11
Camos, V., 141
Campos, J. J., 33

Canfield, R. L., 200
Caravale, B., 16, 43
Carey, S., 55, 57, 58, 59, 60, 61, 62, 64, 66, 67, 68, 69, 71, 86, 92, 93, 109, 113, 119, 120, 121
Carlesimo, G. A., 16, 43
Caron, A. J., 198, 305
Caron, R. F., 198, 305
Carpenter, P. A., 17
Carriger, M. S., 153, 170
Carter, A., 11
Carver, L. J., 94, 161, 162, 242, 246, 247, 251, 252, 253, 255, 296
Casadei, A. M., 16
Casaer, P., 222
Casey, B. J., 37
Catherwood, D., 79, 88, 95
Caulton, D. A., 297
Cavanagh, P., 70, 113, 114, 118, 119
Cave, C. B., 276
Caza, N., 16
Cezayirli, E., 276, 278
Challis, B. H., 181
Chappell, M., 297
Charnallet, A., 276
Chase, W., 127
Chase, W. G., 63
Cheatham, C. L., 243, 252
Chelazzi, L., 188
Chen, M. L., 120, 121
Chen, Z., 132
Cheng, P. C.-H., 127
Cheries, E. W., 67
Chiang, W., 116, 120
Chiu, Y.-C., 140
Choi, S., 279
Chugani, H. T., 15, 27, 85, 87, 249
Chun, M. M., 118, 119, 139
Cipolotti, L., 281, 287
Clark, J. J., 78, 82
Clark, R. E., 156, 185, 263, 295
Clarkson, M., 286, 287
Clarkson, M. G., 301
Clayton, N. S., 229, 230, 302
Clearfield, M. W., 67
Clermont, T., 75
Clifton, R., 286, 287
Clifton, R. K., 191, 300, 301

Codren, J. T., 227
Cohen, J. D., 15, 90
Cohen, L. B., 79, 165, 190, 198, 199, 226
Cohen, M. X., 285
Cohen, N. J., 169, 248, 257, 258, 262
Cohen, P., 171
Colby, C. L., 183
Coldren, J. T., 163, 167
Collie, R., 215, 246, 286
Collins, P. F., 162
Colombo, J., 163, 166, 167, 168, 216
Colombo, M., 153, 155, 210, 213, 227
Conde, F., 86
Connelly, A., 301
Conrad, R., 142
Constable, R. T., 91
Conway, A. R. A., 5, 17, 128, 134, 135, 141
Corballis, M. C., 228
Corley, R., 14
Cornell, E. H., 80, 164, 169
Cornish, K. M., 16
Cornoldi, C., 16
Corsi, P. M., 8
Courage, M. L., ix, 78, 160, 164, 167, 227, 251
Courchesne, E., 161
Courtney, S. M., 90, 91, 104
Cowan, N., 11, 14, 53, 54, 55, 71, 78, 85, 113, 114, 126, 128, 129, 130, 131, 132, 133, 134, 135, 136, 137, 138, 139, 140, 141, 142, 143, 144, 145
Crane, J., 111
Crawley, R. A., 231
Croker, S., 127
Cross, D., 32
Crowder, R. G., 130
Csibra, G., 86, 91, 92, 112, 200
Culham, J., 14
Curran, T., 262, 263, 297
Czéh, B., 250
Czurkó, A., 250

Dabholkar, A. S., 15, 250
Dahl, R. E., 220
Dale, P. S., 67

Dallas, M., 275, 281
Dasadei, A. M., 43
Davis, E. P., 27, 45
Davis, J., 216, 217
Davis, P. L., 27
Davis Goldman, B., 35, 40
Day, R. H., 163
DeBoer, T., 260
DeCasper, A. J., 211
DeCoste, C., 67
de Haan, M., 37, 161, 162, 164, 192,
    243, 244, 253
Dehaene, S., 57, 62, 71, 283
Dehaene-Lambertz, G., 283
DeLeon, R., 16
Della Sala, S., 131
DeLoach, J. S., 6, 165, 226, 302
Denby, C., 276
De Renzi, E., 90
Deruelle, C., 211
De Saint Victor, C., 9
de Schonen, S., 164, 211
Desimone, R., 90, 94, 111, 187, 188,
    192, 296
Desmond, J. E., 194
D'Esposito, M., 285
de Ungria, M., 260
Devan, B. D., 210
DeVos, J., 7
Deyo, R. A., 258, 259
Diamond, A., 6, 12, 13, 27, 28, 31,
    32, 33, 34, 35, 36, 39, 43, 44, 46,
    53, 78, 93, 111, 114, 164, 303
Diana, R. A., 297
Dickinson, A., 229
Disterhoft, J. F., 258, 259
Dix, S., 276
Doar, B., 6, 12
Dobbing, J., 222
Dobkins, K. R., 92
Dobson, V., 86, 91
Dodds, C., 158, 165
Dodson, C. S., 297
Dolan, A., 301
Donahoe, A., 35, 40
Dow, G. A., 244, 255, 256, 299
Dowden, A., 215, 216, 217, 227,
    246, 247, 286, 298, 303
Driver, J., 85, 91

Dropik, P. L., 218, 227, 243, 244,
    247, 251, 253, 254, 299
Druin, D. P., 27, 44
Drummey, A. B., 298, 300,
    303, 307
Dufault, D., 223
Duhamel, J., 183
Dumas, J. A., 300
Duncan, J., 28, 187, 296
Duncan, M., 130
Dunn, J., 298
Dunn, J. C., 297
Dyb, C. J., 285

Eacott, M. J., 231
Earle, D., 76
Earley, L., 216, 217
Earley, L. A., 218, 223
Ebbinghaus, H., 254
Eckenhoff, M., 249
Eckerman, C. O., 259
Eich, E., 128
Eichenbaum, H., 169, 248, 257, 258,
    262
Eimas, P. D., 276, 284
Elliot, E. M., 11, 85, 130, 135, 136,
    137, 138, 139, 141, 143
Ellis, A. E., 35
Ellis, N. C., 17
Elman, J. L., 158, 163
Emslie, H., 42
Engle, R. W., 5, 17, 28, 29, 30, 31,
    33, 34, 44, 45, 128, 134, 135, 141
Erickson, C. A., 90, 94
Ericsson, K. A., 20, 63
Espy, K. A., 46
Ewing-Cobbs, L., 16

Fabre-Grenet, M., 211
Fagan, J. F., 76, 78, 157, 164, 165,
    166, 216, 281
Fagen, J. W., 223, 227
Fahy, F. L., 187, 188
Faloon, S., 63
Fanselow, M. S., 252
Fantie, B., 222
Fantz, R., 8, 216
Fantz, R. L., 80, 212
Fehnel, S. E., 16

Feigenson, L., 57, 58, 59, 60, 61, 62, 64, 65, 66, 67, 68, 69, 71, 119, 120
Feldman, H. D., 137
Feldman, J. F., 9, 153, 157, 163, 165, 166, 167, 168, 170, 171, 216, 227, 301, 305
Felt, B., 260
Fenson, L., 17, 67
Ferrera, V. P., 92
Fifer, W. P., 211
Fivush, R., ix, 244, 256, 307
Forshaw, M. J., 16
Fox, N., 300, 301
Fox, N. A., 27, 31, 32, 33, 35, 36, 37, 39, 40, 43, 44, 110
Frackowiak, R., 94
Franconeri, S. L., 55
Freeseman, L. J., 163, 167
French, R., 163
Frick, J. E., 161, 163
Friedman, A., 277
Friedman-Hill, S., 88, 93, 95
Fristoe, N. M., 137, 138
Fry, A. F., 170
Frye, D., 11
Funahashi, S., 6
Futterweit, L. R., 166, 167

Gabrieli, J. D. E., 194
Gadian, D. G., 301
Galanter, E., 4, 127
Gallistel, C. R., 121
Galluccio, L., 255
Ganz, L., 161
Gardiner, J. M., 297
Gathercole, S., 17
Gathercole, S. E., 11, 14, 17, 29, 30, 42, 46, 135
Gavin, W. J., 27
Gawlik, B., 297
Gekoski, M. J., 223
Gelade, G., 140
Gelber, E. R., 190, 198, 199
Gelman, R., 121
Georgieff, M., 260
Georgieff, M. K., 161
Gerardi-Caulton, G., 45
Gerhardstein, P. C., 216, 219, 221, 227

Gerstadt, C. L., 27
Gibbs, B., 71
Gibbs, B. J., 116, 140
Gilmore, R. O., 6, 31, 93, 95
Glanville, B. B., 126
Glascher, J., 111
Glenberg, A. M., 130
Glisky, M. L., 46
Glover, G. H., 194
Gobet, F., 127
Gochin, P. M., 187, 188
Goddard, S., 62, 68
Gold, P. E., 210
Goldberg, M. E., 183
Goldman, B. D., 12, 31, 40
Goldman-Rakic, P., 91
Goldman-Rakic, P. S., 6, 11, 15, 28, 43, 91, 94, 111, 250
Good, T., 281, 287
Goodale, M. A., 13, 14, 86
Goodell, N. A., 260
Goodman, J., 194
Gore, J. C., 88, 91, 93
Goshen-Gottstein, Y., 300
Gottfried, A. W., 76, 159, 166, 216, 227
Graber, M., 7, 34
Grabowecky, M., 88, 93, 95
Graf, P., 180, 275, 276, 281, 300
Grant, V. V., 231
Greco, C., 216, 217, 218, 223
Green, V., 79, 88, 95
Greenbaum, J. L., 300
Greenough, W. T., 85, 93, 223
Griesler, P., 216, 217
Griesler, P. C., 218, 223
Gross, C. G., 187, 188
Gross, J., 196, 224, 279, 281, 306
Gruetter, R., 260
Grunau, R. E., 211
Gulya, M., 255
Gunnar, M. R., 45
Guttentag, R., 298

Haaf, R. A., 227
Haden, P., 275
Hagger, C., 155, 184, 185, 186, 295
Haight, J. C., 251
Haiken-Vasen, J. H., 157

Haith, M. M., 43, 108, 200
Halberda, J., 54, 59, 64, 65, 66, 67,
    68, 120, 121
Hale, S., 170
Hall, D. G., 106, 118
Hall, L. K., 5
Hanna, E., 244, 256
Hartman, M., 16
Hartshorn, K., 213, 216, 218, 219,
    221, 227
Hasher, L., 16
Hauser, M., 57, 58, 61, 62, 67, 68,
    71, 119
Haxby, J. V., 90, 91, 104
Hayes, R. A., 79
Hayne, H., 153, 155, 196, 210, 213,
    214, 215, 216, 217, 218, 219, 220,
    221, 224, 226, 227, 231, 242, 243,
    246, 247, 253, 255, 256, 279, 281,
    286, 298, 299, 303, 306
Henderson, J. M., 75, 78
Henson, R., 281
Herbert, J., 196, 214, 215, 216, 220,
    223, 224, 227, 243, 256, 279, 281,
    306
Herbert, J. S., 259
Hernandez-Reif, M., 160, 164
Herschkowitz, N., 15
Hertsgaard, L. A., 227, 243, 299
Hespos, S. J., 57, 71, 116
Heth, C., 80
Hilden, K., ix
Hildreth, K., 222
Hill, W. H., 216, 217
Hill, W. L., 291
Hintzman, D. L., 297
Hismjatullina, A., 85, 130, 135, 136,
    138, 139, 141
Hitch, G. J., 4, 14, 17, 28, 77, 104,
    127, 140, 142
Hockey, R., 136
Hofstadter, M., 13, 32, 34, 35
Holdstock, J. S., 182, 183, 225, 276,
    278, 279, 287
Holley, F. B., 200
Hollingworth, A., 75, 78
Holt, C., 79, 88, 95
Hong, N. S., 210
Hong, Y. J., 27

Hood, B., 52
Horowitz, F. D., 158, 166, 167
Howe, M. L., ix, 78, 160, 164, 167,
    227, 251
Humphrey, G. K., 14
Hunkin, N. M., 182, 183, 225, 276,
    278, 279, 287
Hunnerkopf, M., 307
Hunt, J. M., 159
Hunter, M., 216
Hunter, M. A., 8, 159
Hunter, W. S., 6
Huntley-Fenner, G., 57, 71
Huttenlocher, J., 6, 7, 79, 307
Huttenlocher, P. R., 15, 27, 222, 250
Hutton, U. M. Z., 141

Ikejiri, T., 79, 88
Irwin, D. E., 75, 78
Isaac, C. L., 182, 183, 225, 276, 278,
    279, 287
Ivkovich, D., 260

Jacobson, K., 114
Jacoby, L. L., 275, 281, 297
James, T. W., 14
James, W., 54, 77, 211
James, W. J., 3, 4
Jankowski, J. J., 9, 165, 166, 167,
    168, 170, 183, 216, 227, 301, 305
Jarrold, C., 16
Jaspers-Fayer, F., 122
Jellema, T., 112
Jessell, T. M., 248
Johnson, I. B., 136
Johnson, M. H., 6, 31, 43, 79, 86,
    88, 91, 92, 93, 95, 109, 112, 158,
    163, 200, 304
Johnsrude, I., 111
Jones, G., 127
Jonides, J., 90, 94
Jorgenson, L. A., 260
Josephs, O., 94
Julesz, B., 115
Just, M. A., 17

Kagan, J., 8, 9, 14, 15, 253
Kahneman, D., 71, 114, 116, 140
Kail, R., 5, 217, 304

Kalakanis, L., 162
Káldy, Z., xi, 57, 70, 71, 79, 88, 90, 95,
    105, 106, 109, 111, 113, 116, 119
Kandel, E. R., 248
Kane, M. J., 28, 29, 30, 31, 33, 34,
    44, 45, 134
Karmiloff-Smith, A., 158, 163
Karrer, R., 200
Kaufman, J., 112
Kaufmann, P. M., 46
Kavŝek, M., 145
Kawahara, S., 252
Keeble, S., 108
Keele, S. W., 263
Keil, K., 90, 91
Keller, T. A., 17
Kelley, C. M., 297
Kellman, P. J., 79
Kempinsky, H., 300
Kennedy, C. B., 158, 165
Kermoian, R., 33
Keysers, C., 112
Kilb, A., 140
Kim, J. J., 252
Kinstch, W., 20
Kirino, Y., 252
Klatt, L., 57, 71
Klein, L., 196
Klein, P., 216, 219, 221
Klein, P. J., 227, 244, 256
Knaff, P. R., 136
Knowlton, B., 241, 259
Knox, H. A., 7
Koechlin, E., 57, 71, 283
Koeppe, R. A., 90
Köhler, S., 242
Kolb, B., 222
Koopman, R., 159
Kouider, S., 121
Koutstaal, W., 194
Kovacs, S. L., 301, 303
Krajewski, K., 307
Kramer, L., 16
Krinsky, S. J., 79
Krøjgaard, P., 118
Kron, V., 307
Kroupina, M. G., 243, 299
Krupa, D. J., 258
Krystal, J. H., 91

Landauer, T. K., 127
Landry, S. H., 16
Lane, P. C. R., 127
Lanfranchi, S., 16
Lange, E., 141
Langlois, J. H., 162
Laughlin, J. E., 5, 128, 134, 135, 141
Lazar, M. A., 199
Learmonth, A., 7, 79
Lechuga, M. T., 244, 256
Le Clec'h, G., 283
Leslie, A. M., 55, 57, 70, 71, 79, 86,
    88, 90, 93, 95, 105, 106, 108, 109,
    111, 113, 114, 116, 117, 118, 119,
    120, 121
Levenson, R., 126
Levin, D. T., 78
Levy, R., 28
Lewandowsky, S., 130
Lewis, D. A., 86
Li, L., 187, 188, 192
Lia, B., 92
Lie, E., 301
Lindsay, D. S., 297
Lipton, J. S., 62
Liston, C., 253
Loboschefski, T., 9
Logan, G. D., 144
Logie, R. H., 9, 29, 77, 128, 134
Lozoff, B., 260
Luciana, M., 27, 28, 31, 46, 260
Luck, S. J., xiv, 10, 54, 56, 59, 61,
    70, 71, 77, 78, 80, 81, 83, 84, 85,
    87, 88, 89, 90, 91, 113, 119, 131,
    132, 138, 139
Lueschow, A., 188
Lukowski, A. F., 251
Lund, J. S., 86
Lundy, B. L., 227
Lustig, C., 16
Luu, P., 44, 45

MacDonald, S., 216, 220, 231, 256,
    303
MacFarlane, A. J., 211
Machizawa, M. G., 85, 136, 138,
    139
Mack, A., 277
Macmanuse, D., 281, 287

Macmillan, N. A., 297
Macomber, J., 114
Malkova, L., 156
Mandler, G., 274, 275, 276, 277, 281
Mandler, J. M., xiv, 214, 225, 242,
    244, 246, 256, 257, 275, 277, 279,
    282, 283, 284, 287, 298, 299
Manns, J. R., 157, 186, 263, 287, 295
Maratsos, M., 263
Marcel, A. J., 283
Marconi, F., 16
Marcos-Ruiz, R., 244, 256
Marcus, G. F., 17
Mareschal, D., 79, 86, 88, 91, 92,
    109, 163
Markman, E. M., 244, 256
Markowitsch, H. J., 248
Marois, R., 85, 86, 88, 91, 93, 136
Martin, A. J., 17
Mash, C., 86, 91
Massaro, D. W., 126
Masson, M. E. J., 283
Matthews, A., 35
Mattock, A., 76, 79, 88, 95
Mattox, S., 85, 135, 136, 138, 139,
    141
Maunsell, J. H. R., 92
May, C. P., 16
Mayes, A. R., 182, 183, 225, 276,
    278, 279, 287
Mazziotta, J. C., 87
McCall, R. B., 9, 153, 158,
    165, 170
McCarthy, G., 91
McClelland, J. L., 163, 297
McCollough, A. W., 136, 138, 139
McCrink, K., 62
McDiamid, M. D., 46
McDonald, R. J., 210
McDonough, L., 225, 244, 246, 256,
    257, 279, 284, 287, 299
McDonough, L. M., xiv
McKee, R. D., xiv, 157, 182, 183,
    186, 225, 244, 257, 278, 279, 295,
    299
McKenzie, B. E., 163
McLin, D., 36
Mehler, J., 57, 71
Melartin, R. L., 244, 256

Melloy-Carminar, P., 76, 159, 166,
    216, 227
Meltzoff, A., 227
Meltzoff, A. N., 7, 8, 215, 244, 246,
    256, 298
Menard, E., 16
Meyer, D. E., 283
Miezin, F. M., 187, 188
Mikhail, A. A., 259
Miller, E. K., 90, 91, 94, 111, 187,
    188, 192
Miller, G. A., 4, 54, 62, 103, 127,
    132, 133, 141
Milner, A. D., 13, 14
Milner, B., 111, 154
Milner, D. A., 86
Minoshima, S., 90
Mintun, M. A., 90
Mishkin, M., 14, 86, 156, 244, 301
Mitchell, D. W., 166, 167, 216
Mitra, P. P., 91
Mitroff, S. R., 57
Mix, K. S., 67
Miyake, A., xi, 128
Monk, C. S., 15
Montaldi, D., 276
Moore, J. W., 260
Moore, M. K., 7, 8, 215, 298
Moray, N., 128
Morey, C. C., 85, 131, 132, 135,
    136, 138, 139, 141, 142
Morgan, K., 213, 216, 217, 219, 227
Morison, V., 76
Morrongiello, B. A., 223
Morrow, J., 35, 40
Morrow, J. D., 12, 31
Morse, P. A., 126, 134, 142
Morton, J., 211
Morton, J. A., 283
Moscovitch, M., 182, 224, 242
Mosier, C. E., 11
Mottron, L., 16
Moyer, J. R., Jr., 258, 259
Mueller, M., 283
Mullen, M. K., 231
Mullin, J. T., 211
Munakata, Y., 33, 52, 304
Munir, F., 16
Murray, E. A., 156

Murrell, G. A., 283
Musen, G., 241, 259
Myers, N., 286, 287
Myers, N. A., 300, 301

Nacccache, L., 283
Nadel, L., 7, 79, 250
Nairne, J. S., 11, 13, 130
Naito, M., 300
Nakamura, Y., 275
Narter, D. B., 86, 91
Naus, M. J., 141
Naveh-Benjamin, M., 140
Nealy, T. A., 92
Neath, I., 130
Neisser, U., 231
Nelson, C., 192
Nelson, C. A., ix, 15, 18, 27, 28, 31,
    35, 46, 93, 94, 153, 154, 155, 161,
    162, 164, 181, 182, 191, 192, 193,
    200, 210, 224, 242, 247, 249, 250,
    252, 253, 256, 260, 296, 306
Nelson, K., 240, 307
Nelson, M. N., 191
Nemanic, S., 185
Newcombe, N., 6, 7, 79, 298, 300,
    301, 303, 307
Newport, E. L., 17
Nichelli, P., 90
Nold, J., 260
Noles, N., 57
Noll, D. C., 90
Norcia, A. M., 161
Nugent, L. D., 130, 143
Nystrom, L. E., 90

Oakes, L. M., xiv, 10, 56, 59, 61, 70,
    71, 81, 83, 84, 85, 87, 88, 89, 90,
    119, 138, 139
Oberaurer, K., 141
Ohr, P., 227
Ojemann, J. G., 187, 188
Oliver, I., 127
Orban, G. A., 188
O'Regan, J., 78, 82
O'Reilly, R. C., 15, 276, 278
Orlian, E. K., 166
Ornstein, P. A., 141
O'Scalaidhe, S. P., 91

Ottinger, W., 301, 303
Owen, A. M., 28

Paden, L., 158
Papagno, C., 17
Parisi, D., 158, 163
Park, H., 297
Pascalis, O., 155, 156, 164, 182,
    183, 184, 211, 213, 216, 220, 221,
    225, 227, 278, 279, 280, 287, 295,
    302, 303, 306
Passingham, R. E., 94
Patterson, M. M., 259
Pearl, R. A., 226
Pearl, R. D., 165
Pearson, D. G., 10
Pelphrey, K. A., 6, 12, 13, 14, 18,
    35, 40
Penney, C. G., 142
Perlstein, W. M., 90
Perner, J., 228, 231
Perrett, D. I., 112
Perris, E. E., 301
Pesaran, B., 91
Petersen, S. E., 144, 187, 188
Peterson, C., 231
Peterson, L. R., 4, 129
Peterson, M. J., 4, 129
Peterson, S. E., 140
Pethick, S. J., 67
Petit, L., 104
Pezaris, J. S., 91
Phelps, M. E., 87
Phillips, C., 16
Phillips, L. H., 16
Phillips, W. A., 77
Phillips-Grant, K., 301
Piaget, J., 7, 76, 114, 145, 209, 215,
    240
Pickens, J., 227
Pickens, J. N., 160, 164
Pickering, S. J., 11, 14, 29, 46, 135
Pillemer, D. B., 240
Plunkett, K., 158, 163
Pollack, I., 136
Pomplun, M., 75
Porjesz, B., 187
Port, R. L., 259
Porter, F. L., 211

Posner, M. I., 44, 45, 140, 144, 145
Prasad, M. R., 16
Pressley, M., ix, xi
Preuss, L., 181
Prevor, M. B., 27, 44
Pribram, K. H., 4, 127
Puce, A., 91
Pylyshyn, Z., 55, 115, 117, 122
Pylyshyn, Z. W., xviii, 55, 93, 115, 117, 122

Quinn, P. C., 79, 86, 91, 163, 276, 284
Quint, N., 113

Rafal, R. D., 85, 91
Raffone, A., 91, 92
Raichle, M. E., 187, 188
Rainer, G., 91
Rakic, P. S., 249
Ramus, S. J., 156, 185
Ranganath, C., 285
Rao, R., 260
Rao, S. B., 17
Reber, P. J., 157
Reder, L. M., 297
Reed, J. M., 257
Reeder, J. A., 297
Reingold, E. M., 75
Rensink, R. A., 78, 82
Reynolds, G. D., 162, 169
Reznick, J. S., xiii, 6, 11, 12, 13, 14, 16, 17, 31, 32, 34, 35, 40, 67
Richards, J. E., 159, 161, 162, 166, 169, 170, 200
Richards, R. S., 186
Richardson-Klavehn, A., 154, 297, 299
Riches, I. P., 187, 188
Richmond, J., 213, 227
Rickheit, G., 75
Ritter, H., 75
Roberts, N., 276, 278
Robertson, L., 88, 93, 95
Robinson, A. J., 213, 216, 220, 221, 227, 302, 303, 306
Robinson, J., 14
Rochat, P., 57, 71, 116
Rock, I., 277

Roder, B. J., 79, 88
Roediger, H. L., 181, 189
Roediger, H. L. I., 281
Rogoff, B., 11
Rolls, E. T., 192
Romano, A. G., 259
Rose, D., 76
Rose, M., 111
Rose, S. A., 9, 12, 76, 78, 153, 157, 159, 162, 163, 164, 165, 166, 167, 168, 170, 171, 216, 217, 227, 301, 305
Rosenkrantz, S. L., 284
Ross, G., 240
Ross, H. S., 159
Rosser, R., 7, 79
Ross-Sheehy, S., xiv, 10, 12, 56, 59, 61, 70, 71, 81, 83, 84, 85, 87, 88, 89, 90, 119, 138, 139
Rotello, C. M., 297
Rothbart, M. K., 44, 45, 145
Rotte, M., 194
Rouder, J. N., 132
Rouleau, N., 16
Rovee, C. K., 213
Rovee, D. T., 213
Rovee-Collier, C., 153, 155, 196, 210, 213, 216, 217, 218, 219, 220, 221, 222, 223, 226, 227, 242, 255, 256, 291, 299
Rowe, J. B., 94
Rubenstein, A. J., 162
Rudge, P., 281, 287
Rueda, M. R., 145
Ruff, H. A., 44, 45, 167
Ruffman, T., 34, 228, 231
Rugg, M. D., 278, 285, 297
Russell, J., 33

Saffran, J. R., 17
Sagi, D., 115
Sahani, M., 91
Sai, F., 211
Sakovits, L. J., 159
Salinas, J. A., 260
Salthouse, T. A., 16
Sandberg, E., 6
Sands, J., 222
Sary, G., 188

Sasson, N., 35, 40
Satlow, E., 307
Saults, J. S., 11, 85, 130, 135, 136, 137, 138, 139, 140, 141, 142, 143
Saunders, R. C., 186
Schacter, D. L., x, 154, 180, 181, 182, 194, 224, 241, 258, 281, 283, 294, 300
Schmidt, A. T., 260
Schneider, W., xi, 307
Scholl, B. J., 55, 57, 71, 86, 93, 109, 114, 117, 118, 122, xviii
Schrock, G., 78
Schrock, J. C., 29, 30, 44
Schröger, E., 130
Schvaneveldt, R. W., 283
Schwade, J. A., 243, 299
Schwartz, B. B., 6, 13
Schwartz, J. H., 248
Scoville, W. B., 154
Segalowitz, S. J., 27
Self, P., 158
Senior, G. J., 163
Seress, L., 169, 224, 249, 250, 306
Service, E., 17
Seth, N., 122
Shafritz, K. M., 88, 93
Shah, P., x, 128
Shallice, T., 281, 287
Shanks, D. R., 163
Shankweiler, D., 126
Shen, J., 75
Sherman, T., 162
Shiffrin, R. M., 4, 297
Shimojo, S., 79, 88
Shinskey, J. L., 52, 179
Shore, C. M., 244
Sichelschmidt, L., 75
Sigafoos, A. D., 211
Sigala, N., 106, 111
Simon, H. A., 63, 127
Simon, T., 57, 71
Simon, T. J., 71, 114, 116
Simons, D., 54, 59
Simons, D. J., 77, 78
Sinclair, S. G., 17
Siqueland, E. R., 276
Sires, S. F., 59
Skoien, P., 79, 88, 95

Skouteris, H., 163
Slater, A., 76, 79, 88, 95
Slater, A. M., 79
Slobin, D. I., 171
Slotnick, S. D., 297
Sluzenski, J., 301, 303, 307
Smith, E. E., 15, 90, 94
Smith, E. G., 200
Smith, L. B., 36, 304
Smith, P. H., 9
Snow, K. L., 200
Snyder, J., 12, 17, 31, 40, 192
Snyder, K. A., 186, 187, 193, 195, 197, 296
Soeda, A., 79, 88
Sokolov, E. N., 145, 158
Sokolov, Y. N., 189
Solomon, P. R., 258, 260
Sommer, T., 111
Sophian, C., 190
Sowell, E. R., 27
Sowerby, P., 196, 213, 227, 279, 281
Speaker, C. J., 179
Spear, L. P., 222
Spelke, E., 68, 69, 120
Spelke, E. S., 52, 62, 68, 76, 114
Spence, M. J., 211
Sperling, G., 54
Squire, L. R., xiv, 43, 154, 155, 156, 157, 181, 182, 183, 185, 186, 187, 188, 210, 224, 225, 241, 244, 248, 257, 258, 259, 263, 273, 276, 278, 279, 282, 285, 287, 294, 295, 299
Stadler, M. A., 128
Stanton, M. E., 258, 259, 260
Stark, C. E., 157, 295
Stark, C. E. L., 154, 186, 287
Stark, H., 281
Stefanacci, L., 155, 156, 185, 295
Steinmetz, J. E., 259
Sternberg, S., 8
Steyvers, M., 297
Stolarova, M., 193, 296
Storm, R., 122
Storm, R. W., 55
Strand Cary, M., 243, 252
Stretch, V., 297
Studdert-Kennedy, M., 126
Suddendorf, T., 228, 230

Sullivan, D., 260
Suomi, K., 126, 142
Surprenant, A., 130
Suzuki, W. A., 111
Swanson, N. C., 130

Tachibana, T., 79, 88
Taga, G., 79, 88
Takehara, K., 252
Takeuchi, K., 79, 88
Tamis-Lemonda, C. S., 165, 171
Taylor, M. J., 37
Teng, E., 155, 156, 185, 295
Tessner, K. D., 27
Thal, D., 67
Thelen, E., 36, 304
Thomas, K. M., 256
Thompson, J. K., 258
Thompson, P. M., 27
Thompson, R. F., 258, 259
Thomson, D. M., 218
Thomson, N., 127, 129, 132
Titzer, R., 36
Tkac, I., 260
Todd, J. J., 85, 86, 91, 93, 136
Toga, A. W., 27
Tomb, S. M., 285
Toni, I., 94
Toth, J. P., 297
Townsend, E. L., 260
Towse, J. N., 141
Travis, L., 243
Treisman, A., 71, 88, 93, 95, 114,
    116, 140
Treisman, A. M., 88, 140
Tremoulet, P. D., 86, 106, 114, 117,
    118
Trick, L., 55
Trick, L. M., 122
Tucker, L. A., 200
Tugade, M. M., 29
Tuholski, S. W., 5, 128, 134,
    135, 141
Tulholski, S. W., 29, 44
Tulving, E., 154, 181, 211, 218,
    226, 228, 229, 231, 281, 283,
    299, 301
Tustin, K., 231

Uesiliana, K., 231
Uller, C., 57, 71
Ungerleider, L. G., 14, 86, 90, 91,
    104, 188, 276
Unsworth, N., 29, 30, 44
Usher, J. N., 231

Van Abbema, D. L., 243, 252, 253
Vander Linde, E., 227
Van der Linden, M., 276
Vander Schaaf, E. R., 258
Vann, S. D., 276
Van Paesschen, W., 301
Van Rossem, R., 170
van Zandt, B. J., 275
Vargha-Khadem, F., 244, 298, 301,
    306, 307
Vecchi, T., 16
Vecera, S. P., 91
Vianello, R., 16
Vicari, S., 16, 43
Videen, T. O., 187, 188
Vijayan, S., 17
Vishton, P. M., 17
Vogel, E. K., 10, 54, 56, 59, 77, 78,
    80, 84, 85, 88, 91, 113, 131, 132,
    136, 138, 139
Vogels, R., 188
Volterra, V., 11

Wagner, A. D., x, 181, 194, 241,
    258, 294
Wagner, K., 75
Wagner, S. H., 159
Waldow, K. J., 260
Wallace, C. S., 85, 93, 223
Wallace, I. F., 171
Wang, W., 187
Warrington, E., 154
Warrington, E. K., 276
Wasserman, S., 52, 114
Waters, J. M., 162, 247, 251, 252,
    253, 296
Watkins, K. E., 301
Wearing, H., 29, 46, 135
Webb, S. J., 192, 193
Weiskrantz, L., 154, 276
Weisz, D. J., 259

Weldon, M. S., 181
Wellman, H. M., 32
Wenner, J. A., 218, 227, 246, 247, 251, 253, 254
Wentworth, N., 200
Wetherhold, J., 54, 59
Wewerka, S., 260
Wewerka, S. S., 218, 227, 243, 246, 247, 251, 253, 254, 299
Wheeler, M. E., 88
White, S. H., 240
Wicker, B., 112
Wiebe, S. A., 162, 247, 251, 252, 253, 296
Wilcox, T., 7, 76, 79, 109
Wilding, J., 16
Wiley, J. G., 307
Wilk, A., 255
Wilk, A. E., 196
Willats, P., 11, 52
Willingham, D. B., 181, 300
Willis, C., 17
Willis, C. S., 42
Willner, J., 250
Wilson, F. A. W., 91, 187
Winkler, I., 130
Witherspoon, D., 275
Wixted, J. T., 297

Wobken, J. D., 260
Wolbers, T., 111
Wolfe, C. D., 27, 42, 44, 45
Wolters, G., 91, 92
Wondoloski, T. L., 216, 219, 221
Wood, J., 121
Wood, N. L., 128
Woodman, G. F., 77, 78
Wright, F., 231
Wu, P., 260
Wynn, K., 57, 62, 67, 71, 116, 120

Xu, F., 62, 68, 86, 92, 93, 109, 113, 114, 117, 118
Xu, Y., 78, 118, 119, 139

Yang, C.-T., 140
Yeh, Y.-Y., 140
Yonelinas, A. P., 278, 285, 297
Young, A., 76, 79, 88, 95

Zbrodoff, N. J., 144
Zelazo, P. D., 11, 145
Zilles, K., 15
Zola, S. M., 154, 155, 156, 185, 248, 258, 295
Zola-Morgan, S., 43

Subject Index

A page number followed by the letter *t* or *f* indicates a table or figure, respectively, on that page.

abilities, 303–307
adults
  amnesia-impaired performance
      on visual paired-comparison,
      156–157
  chess and, 63
  chunking, 62–64
  memory model, 210–211, 210*f*
  preferential looking, 197
  short-term memory capacity,
      53–55
  working memory, 127–133
    attention to store information,
      131–132
    capacity limit, 132–133
    definition and model, 128, 129*f*
    history of research, 127–128
    representations, 128–130
age
  age-related changes in retention,
      219*f*
  age-related changes on infant
      memory retrieval, 221*f*
  changes in long-term declarative
      memory, 245–247, 246*t*, 247*t*

phenotypic changes, 12–15
  1–3 years, 14–15
  onset, 12, 13*f*
  6–12 months, 12–14
  visual recognition memory
      changes and, 162–165
  voluntary eye movements and,
      200
amnesia, 279
  impaired performance on visual
      paired-comparison task,
      156–157
  test, 244, 244*t*
A-not-B reaching task, 27, 31, 33,
      46, 111, 137. *See also* Piaget,
      Jean
  performance, 41*f*
  toys and, 31
attentional capacity, 29–30,
      131–132, 136
  changes in, 167–168
  neural mechanisms and, 179–208
  scope-of-attention tasks, 136
  sustained, 161
  termination, 161

autism, 16, 19
autobiographical memory, ix, 231,
    273

behavior, evidence of visual
    paired-comparison, 186–187
brain
    effects of repetition on infant
        brain activity, 191–193, 193*f*
    mechanisms and working memory,
        110–112
    relation between infant brain
        activity during encoding and
        preferential looking at test,
        193–195, 194*f*, 195*f*
    substrates in development, 169

capacity
    definitions, 14
    limit, 132–133
categorization, 19
change preference score, 83–84,
    84*f*
chess, 63
children. *See also* infants
    abilities, 303–307
    age-related phenotypic changes,
        12–15
        onset, 12, 13*f*
        1–3 years, 14–15
    biological changes, 306–307
    longitudinal investigations across
        infancy and childhood,
        45–46
choices, of infants, 57–58, 58*f*
chunking, 132
    in adults, 62–64
    computations of discrete and
        continuous quantity, 67–68
    in infants, 64–66, 65*f*
    initiating, 66–67
    memory storage, 62–66
    object files and, 119–120
cognition
    in infants, 52
    visual recognition memory in
        infancy and, 170–171
Cognitive Development Society, x–xi
cognitive skills, 27

colors, 79, 86, 89*f*, 95
color stimulus, 8, 10
conditioning, in infants, 213
    conditioned stimulus, 258–259,
        259*f*
consciousness, working memory
    and, 17–18
content, 244*t*

declarative memory, 240–270, 273*f*.
    See also long-term memory
    age-related changes in, 246–247,
        246*t*, 247–254, 247*t*, 248*f*
    changes in, 245–247, 246*t*, 247*t*
    development of neural network,
        249–251
    measurement in infancy and
        early childhood, 243–245,
        244*t*
    neural substrate and its
        development, 248–249, 248*f*
    temporal extent of, 245–246, 246*t*
delay activity, 90–91
delayed-nonmatch-to-sample
    (DNMS) test, 280
delayed response tasks, 40–41
development
    continuity of format and
        computation, 51–74
    typical versus atypical, 19
DNMS. *See* delayed-nonmatch-to-
    sample test
dopamine levels in the prefrontal
    cortex, 43–44
double dissociation, 68, 69*f*
Down syndrome, 16

EEG. *See* electroencephalogram
electroencephalogram (EEG)
    baseline, 36–37
    task-related, 37–38
emotions, reactivity, 44–45
Engle's model of working memory,
    29–30, 44, 135
episodic memory, 227–229,
    230–233, 301–303
ERPs. *See* event-related potentials
event-related potentials (ERPs), 92,
    111, 245

in memory measurement, 161
eye movements, development of
    voluntary control of,
    199–200

facial expressions, effect on
    measurement results, 38
familiarize-recognize procedures,
    8–10
FINST theory, 93, 115, 117
fMRI. *See* functional magnetic
    resonance imaging
forgetting, 130, 291–292
Fragile X syndrome, 16, 19
functional magnetic resonance
    imaging (fMRI), 90, 111,
    136–137, 285

habituation paradigm, 158
hide-find procedures, 6–7
hippocampus, 155
    input and output pathways of
        hippocampal formation, 248*f*
    involvement in tasks, 259–260
    in memory networks, 258–259,
        259*f*
    role in recollective processes,
        285–286

imitation, 19
    deferred, 298–299
    tasks, 214–215
        as measures of explicit memory,
            244*t*
inattentional blindness, 277–278
infants. *See also* children; working
    memory
    ability to discriminate objects,
        61*f*
    age-related phenotypic changes,
        12–15, 13*f*
        onset, 12, 13*f*
        6–12 months, 12–14
    assessment of memory, 10
    binding and, 139–141
    capacity development, 84–86,
        85*f*, 138–139
    changes in attention, 167–168

changes in temporal extension of
    recall memory over the first
    two years, 246*t*
changes of working memory with
    development, 109–110
choices, 57–58, 58*f*
chunking, 64–66, 65*f*
cognition, 52
development, 19
    of working memory, 27–50
discrimination of mother's breast
    milk, 211
effects of repetition on brain
    activity, 191–193, 193*f*
electrophysical studies of
    preferential looking, 191, 192*f*
individual differences in
    development of working
    memory, 27–50
longitudinal investigations across
    infancy and childhood,
    45–46
low birth weight, 16, 43
measurement
    of declarative memory,
        243–245, 244*t*
    of short-term memory, 55–56
    of visual short-term memory,
        80–83, 81*f*
mechanisms of developmental
    change, xv–xvi
memory development, 209–239
    changes over course of
        development, 215–220, 216*t*
        in older infants, 215–220, 219*f*
    kinds of memory, 224–233, 227*t*
        episodic, 227–229, 230–233
        spoon test in studies with
            nonhuman animals, 229–
            230
    measurement, 21–215
        imitation tasks, 214–215
        mobile conjugate reinforce-
            ment paradigm, 213–214
        operant conditioning
            procedures, 213
        train paradigm, 214–215
        visual paired comparison
            task, 212–213

infants (*cont.*)
    mechanisms of changes, 220–224
        experience, 222–224
        maturation, 220–222
    memory formation, 160
    methods to study working
        memory, 108–109
        ecological validity, 109
    mother and, 32
    motivation of infants and
        top-down effect, 112–113
    object location development,
        86–88, 87*f*
    object representation development,
        88–90, 89*f*
    percentage showing evidence of
        ordered recall after various
        delays, 247*t*
    preferences, 83–84, 84*f*, 85*f*
    premature, 43
    reasoning, 53
    relation between infant brain
        activity during encoding and
        preferential looking at test,
        193–195, 194*f*, 195*f*
    representing objects, 83–84,
        84*f*
    research, 127–128, 141–142
    response modality, 13–14
    studies on infant memory, 293,
        293*f*
    studying working memory in,
        103–125
    visual recognition memory,
        153–178
    working memory, 133–137
        versus adult working memory,
            137–138
        during first postnatal year,
            39–42, 41*f*
information processing system, 128,
    129*f*
intelligence, 19
IQ, 170, 171

language, 170
    working memory and, 17
learning, sensorimotor, 284–285
long-term memory (LTM)
    age-related changes in declarative
        memory, 245–247, 246*t*,
        247–254, 247*t*, 248*f*
        changes in reliability, 246–247,
            247*t*
        changes in temporal extent of
            declarative memory,
            245–246, 246*t*
        neural substrate of declarative
            event and its development,
            248–249, 248*f*
    development of a particular
        memory system, 29*f*,
        254–261, 291–313
    development of neural network for
        declarative memory, 249–251
    in infants, 211
    measuring declarative memory in
        infancy and early childhood,
        243–245, 244*t*
        imitation-based tasks, 244*t*
    retrieval, 253–254
    theoretical models, 210–211, 210*f*
    visual short-term memory and, 76
low birth weight infants, 16, 43
LTM. *See* long-term memory

means-ends analysis, 19
measurement, xiv–xv
    challenges and limitations, 18
    of individual differences in devel-
        opment during infancy, 30–36
        classic tasks, 31–34
        contemporary tasks, 34–36
        differences in working memory,
            36
medial temporal lobe
    development of system, 200–201
    in performance of visual paired-
        comparison task, 155–156
memory. *See also* long-term memory;
        short-term memory; visual
        short-term memory; working
        memory
    age-related phenotypic changes,
        12–15
        1–3 years, 14–15
        onset, 12, 13*f*
        6–12 months, 12–14

autobiographical, ix
capacity, 14
children's autobiographical, ix
comparisons among types of
    memory and other cognitive
    abilities, 19
declarative, 240–270
definition, 5–6
delayed tasks, 31
development, xv, 15–16
  in infants, 209–239
  neural substrate, 15–16
  social context, 16
distinctions between, 240–242
    semantic and episodic, 301–303
elementary, 3–4
episodic, 227–229, 230–233
explicit versus implicit, 153–154,
    294–301, 300–301
familiarize-recognize procedures,
    8–10
forgetting, 130, 291–292
formation, 160
forms of memory/memory systems,
    180–181
functional significance of infant
    working memory, 16–18
hide-find procedures, 6–7
hypothesis of novelty
    preferences, 181–182
inattentional blindness, 277–278
measurement, xiv–xv
  challenges and limitations, 18
mechanisms of developmental
    change, xv–xvi
memory-span tasks, 30–31
model, 210–211, 210f
multiple memory systems,
    240–270
neural mechanisms and, 179–208
nondeclarative versus implicit,
    241
null preferences and memory
    loss, 195–197, 196f
observe-perform procedures, 7–8
resistance to interference, 165
retention, 164–165
sample studies, 227t
systems, 254–261, 272

temporal dimensions, xi–xiii
types, xiii–xiv, 3–5
typical versus atypical
    development, 19
vulnerability, 252–253
mnemonic processes, 251, 262
mobile conjugate reinforcement
    paradigm, 213–214, 299–300
mothers, infants and, 32
  discrimination of breast milk,
    211
  recognition, 211

neural mechanisms, 179–208
  delay activity, 90
  of developmental changes, 90–94
  for development of declarative
    memory, 249–251
  explicit memory hypothesis of
    novelty preferences, 181–182
  forms of memory/memory
    systems, 180–181
  visual recognition memory and,
    155
neural substrate
  declarative event and its
    development, 248–249, 248f
  development, 15–16
neuroscience
  findings on working memory,
    110–112
  maintenance, 104
  manipulation, 104
  neuropsychological evidence of
    visual-paired comparison,
    182–184

object arrays, 52–62
  bound objects development,
    95–96
  capacity in adults, 53–55
  color, 78
  computations of discrete and
    continuous quantity, 67–68
  identity and location, 94–95
  measuring short-term memory in
    infancy, 55–56
  memory storage via chunking,
    62–66

object arrays (*cont.*)
  naturalistic, 56–62, 58*f*, 60*f*, 61*f*
  orientation, 78
  working memory and, 113–115
object files, 117
  chunking and, 119–120
object index, 117–118
observe-perform procedures, 7–8
one-trial learning, 244*t*
orienting, 161

perirhinal cortex, 156
PET studies, 90
phenylaline, 43–44
phenylketonuria (PKU), 43–44
Piaget, Jean, 43, 209. *See also*
    A-not-B reaching task
  relation between imitation and
    memory, 215
PKU. *See* phenylketonuria
preferential looking, 18–190
  in adults, 197
  challenges and limitations,
    190–191
  definition, 179
  effects of repetition on infant
    brain activity, 191–193, 193*f*
  electrophysical studies with in-
    fants, 191, 192*f*
  mechanisms of change in infants'
    task performance, 198–202
  development
    of the medial-temporal lobe
      system, 200–201
    of voluntary control over eye
      movements, 199–200
    effects of experience, 201–202
    visual processing and cortical
      development, 198–199
  null preferences and memory
    loss, 195–197, 196*f*
  procedures, 190–197
  relation between infant brain
    activity during encoding and
    preferential looking at test,
    193–195, 194*f*, 195*f*
prefrontal cortex
  cognitive skills, 27
  development and maturation, 43

dopamine levels, 43–44
maturation, 43
premature infants, 43
problem-solving, in infants, 11

reasoning, in infants, 53
recognition memory, 165–168,
    272–273
  changes in attention, 167–168
  changes in processing speed,
    165–167
  developmental trajectory,
    168–169
  dual processes, 296–298
  familiarity, 277
  joint effect of changes in process-
    ing speed and attention, 168
  primitive, 275
repetition suppression, 187–188
response modality, in infants,
    13–14

scope-of-attention tasks, 136
selective attention, 19
semantic memory, 301–303
sensorimotor learning, 284–285
Serial Reaction Time, 256
short-term memory (STM). *See also*
    memory; visual short-term
    memory
  continuity of format and compu-
    tation in development, 51–74
  definition, 51–52
  for object arrays, 52–62
    capacity in adults, 53–55
    development, 68–71, 69*f*
    dissociation, 68–71, 69*f*
    measuring short-term memory
      in infancy, 55–56
    memory storage via chunking,
      62–66
      in adults, 62–64
      computations of discrete
        and continuous quantity,
        67–68
      in infants, 64–66, 65*f*
      initiating, 66–67
    naturalistic, 56–62, 58*f*, 60*f*, 61*f*
    trials, 60*f*

versus working memory, 5
  working memory and, 141
slave systems, 77
social development, in infants, 16
sticky index, 117
STM. *See* short-term memory

temperament, self-regulation, 44–45
temporal dimensions, xi–xiii
testing. *See also* visual
      paired-comparison
  amnesia, 244, 244*t*
  delayed-nonmatch-to-sample, 280
  looking at, 193–195, 194*f*, 195*f*
  parameter tests, 280
  spoon test, 229–230
tetanus, 257–258
toys, 31, 38, 75. *See also* A-not-B
      reaching task
traces, 244*t*
train paradigm, 214–215
traumatic brain injury, 16
Turner's syndrome, 16
tyrosine, 43–44

visual paired-comparison (VPC),
      155
  amnesia-impaired performance in
      adults, 156–157
  behavioral evidence, 186–187
  index of explicit memory,
      294–296
  lesion studies in nonhuman
      primates, 184–186
  measurement, 212–213, 274–282
  neural mechanisms and, 179–182
    explicit memory hypothesis of
      novelty preferences, 181–182
    forms of memory/memory
      systems, 180–181
  neuropsychological evidence,
      182–184
  preferential looking, 188–190
    challenges and limitations,
      190–191
    effects of repetition on infant
      brain activity, 191–193, 193*f*
    electrophysical studies with
      infants, 191, 192*f*

mechanisms of change in
      infants' task performance,
      198–202
  development of the medial-
      temporal lobe system,
      200–201
  development of voluntary
      control over eye
      movements, 199–200
  effects of experience,
      201–202
  visual processing and cortical
      development, 198–199
null preferences and memory
      loss, 195–197, 196*f*
procedures, 190–197
relation between infant brain
      activity during encoding and
      preferential looking at test,
      193–195, 194*f*, 195*f*
repetition suppression in the
      occipitotemporal visual
      processing pathway, 187–188
visual recognition memory, in
      infancy, 153–178
  brain substrates in development,
      169
  changes with age, 162–165
    representations, 162–164
    retention, 164–165
  developmental trajectory of
      delayed recognition, 168–169
  explicit versus implicit memory,
      153–154
  factors influencing recognition
      memory, 165–168
    changes in attention, 167–168
    changes in processing speed,
      165–167
    joint effect of changes in proces-
      sing speed and attention, 168
  later cognition and, 170–171
  measuring visual recognition
      memory, 157–162
    habituation paradigm, 158
    interpretation, 158–161
    recent advances, 161–162
    visual paired-comparison task,
      157–158

visual recognition memory,
in infancy (*cont.*)
medial temporal lobe in performance of visual paired-
comparison task, 155–156
neuroanatomical evidence, 155
visual short-term memory (VSTM),
75–102. *See also* short-term
memory
characterization, 83–90
capacity development in
infancy, 84–86, 85*f*
infants representing objects,
83–84, 84*f*
maturation of object representation in infants, 88–90, 89*f*
of object location development
in infants, 86–88, 87*f*
delay activity, 90–91
description, 77–80, 77*f*
future directions, 94–96
ability to represent bound
objects development, 95–96
developmental trajectories of
capacity for object identity
and location, 94–95
identification of objects, 76
measuring in infancy, 80–83, 81*f*
neural mechanisms of developmental changes, 90–94
origins, 78
visuospatial sketchpad, 77
VPC. *See* visual paired-comparison
VSTM. *See* visual short-term memory

WM. *See* working memory
working memory (WM), xiii–xiv,
3–26, 103–125. *See also*
infants; memory
in adults, 127–133
attention to store information,
131–132
capacity limit, 132–133
definition and model, 128, 129*f*
history of research, 127–128
representations, 128–130
attentional capacity, 29–30
binding and infants, 139–141

brain mechanisms and, 110–112
capacity and infants, 29–30,
138–139
changes with development,
109–110
consciousness and, 17–18
construct, 29
convergence versus divergence,
115–121
definition, 28–29, 128
delayed response tasks, 39–40
deterioration, 16–17
development, 126–150
ecological validity, 109
functional significance of
infant's, 16–18
individual differences in development during infancy, 27–50
A-not-B reaching task, 46
baseline EEG, 36–37
definition, 28–29
Engle's model, 29–30
during the first postnatal year,
39–42, 41*f*
longitudinal investigations
across infancy and
childhood, 45–46
measurement, 30–36
classic tasks, 31–34
contemporary tasks, 34–36
differences in working
memory, 36
mechanisms underlying
development, 42–45
dopamine levels in the
prefrontal cortex, 43–44
maturation of the
prefrontal cortex, 43
temperament and self-
regulation, 44–45
task-related EEG, 37–38
in infancy, 133–137
in infants versus adults, 11–12,
137–138
language and, 17
limits, 115, 127–128
methods to study infants,
108–109

model, 128
motivation and top-down effects,
    112–113
nature of representations in
    infants, 107–108
neuroscientific findings, 110–
    112

objects and, 103–125, 113–115
performance increases, 39, 41*f*
research, 127–128
    in infants, 141–142
versus short-term memory, 5
short-term memory and, 141
structure and variation, 134–137